Please renew/return this item by the last date shown.

So that your telephone call is charged at local rate, please call the numbers as set out below:

	From Area codes 01923 or 0208:	From the rest of Herts:
Renewals:	01923 471373	01438 737373
Enquiries:	01923 471333	01438 737333
Minicom:	01923 471599	01438 737599

L32b

THE FILM OF MEMORY

SHANE LESLIE

★

The Film of Memory

MICHAEL JOSEPH LTD.
26, *Bloomsbury Street, London, W.C.*1

FIRST PUBLISHED OCTOBER 1938
SECOND IMPRESSION DECEMBER 1938

" The power of evoking the past is as
strange a gift and better than the
power of reading the future."

ANATOLE FRANCE : *Livre de Pierre.*

*Set and printed in Great Britain by William Brendon & Son,
Ltd., at the Mayflower Press, Plymouth, in Old Style type,
eleven point, leaded, on a toned antique-wove paper made by
John Dickinson, and bound by James Burn.*

Contents

*

5

CONTENTS

Foreword

*

O N MARCH 26, 1937, I HAD THE MISFORTUNE TO INCUR
what probably will occur to most folk sooner or
later : some form of accident by, with or in a motor. I
was walking across Park Lane one drizzly night and that
is all I can remember. . . .

I sighted the passing bus I intended to board, but a
passing car saw me not and I was swept into unconscious-
ness. The laws of Belisha and the great Newton are not
to be disregarded and whether I was between the beacons
or not I was wiped out as a thoughtful entity. My only
consolation has been that I might have perished under
the statues of Shakespeare and Milton with Dante himself
standing ready to guide me into the next world.

The police with their usual promptitude in the removal
of nuisances, retrieved me from the jetsam of the streets
and despatched me to St George's Hospital.

I lay for a fortnight without moving from the accident
ward. I can never ask for better or more ungrudging
treatment than is given in that ward. I have a strong
suspicion that folk without means get as good a deal in
a public hospital ward as the wealthy in a private nursing
home : in fact, I am convinced, slightly better.

I endured a mentally uncomfortable time before I
could feel sure of myself. Fractures and concussions
mean little compared to the nightmare uncertainty in
the mind. Identity is liable to lapse. How can one
describe the loosening of the ties between ethereal self
and the bag of bones ? One feels like a goldfish nosing the
glass walls of a tank. One is set free but within confined

7

and cabined limits. The return to sensible mind and sensitive body is not too pleasant. How would a moth feel to be forced back into his cocoon ?

By the time I returned to my senses I had been ably stitched and patched. I pulled myself up to investigate my chart and learned that I was suffering from " slight irrationality." This seemed humorous to visiting friends, who insisted that, if it were so, my reason had been rather improved by the accident than otherwise.

I attributed my speedy cure to the sister in charge of the accident ward, who must know more about fractures than even the superintendent of a doll's hospital. And what praise can I offer the nurses and probationers who toiled in twelve hour shifts ? The spirits of the fractured floated entirely on their buoyancy. When they woke and washed us between sheets in the early hours every morning they made me think of Angels preparing a morgue for the Resurrection.

Thinking is the chief occupation in hospital, and I discovered that if the brain is allowed to lie still it will begin to run down hill while the past floats past like a disconnected film. Psychologists explain this process of the memory, once it is started, after the manner of Mr Pelman, whose memorising system I once arduously acquired in view of examinations.

My accident produced a curious effect on the memory. The previous ten years of life seemed dulled. The more recent the more forgotten. On the other hand, days in the remoter past, days lived in the past century, forty years ago, revived pleasantly and in patches vividly. After revisioning a number of scenes and persons I began taking notes of whatever came into my mind.

It called for no intentional effort and became a little uncanny when I found myself recalling dreams I had forgotten for forty years. I came to the conclusion that nothing is wholly forgotten. Everything lies latent in the memory, even the trivial and the absurd.

Mr Gladstone once foretold that our conversatiors

would one day be peeled off the walls within which they had been uttered years before. Something like this must have begun to take place under my own brain cap.

The greater the memory the less interesting are the things remembered. What a subtle difference there lies amid the *memorabilia* and the *memoranda* of life, between what can be remembered and what is worth remembering !

I had always intended to write certain notes and anecdotes : odds and ends, connected with places, phases and persons—for publication on my hundreth birthday, which is drawing near as fast as time will allow.

This interesting event will take place on September 24, 1985, and I hope I shall remember to say, when asked how I am feeling, that I am feeling only fifty-fifty ! More could not be expected.

Some of the notes and memories in this book will then appear curious and even interesting. Trivialities will have assumed the patina of the antique. Whatever a centenarian says is noteworthy, and the antiquarians catch the crumbs that fall from his mumbling chops. For that reason this publication is a little previous. Whether the wheel comes full circle in fifty or in a hundred years there is an excellent Irish proverb which applies to either segment of historical time : it will all be the same in a hundred of years !

Glaslough

LIFE FOR ME HAS ALWAYS BEEN LIVED IN A LIBRARY. Books have been equally my approach and my escape in dealing with the Universe. But in childhood I knew only the world of persons and a number of personages, amusing, puzzling, friendly, dominant accompanied my infantile pilgrimage. I was born within a step of what is now Selfridge's shop. I was brought to Ireland as an infant and there baptised in the old church at Glaslough by old Canon John Hudson. My god-parents, Clara Frewen and Randolph Churchill, were absent, but the venerable Lady Caledon survives as a witness of the scene. For the first time I caused the appearance of print, for an extremely rare tract recording the event shows that Hymns 371 and 374 were sung into my unheeding ears (November 8, 1885).

With the months I gradually took sense of my beautiful surroundings. I looked out of nursery windows into the tops of enormous trees which surrounded the family mansion, known locally as the Castle, on every side. They were lime trees made musical in summer with myriads of bees and raucous in winter evenings by passing rooks. My first memory is of thousands of rooks streaming across the lake apparently compelled to keep the same bed-hour as myself. Beyond a half-mile of green water was the biggest crows' roost in Ireland. Between ten and twenty thousand rooks slept in our woods every night. One of the first facts I established in Natural History was that rooks talk in their sleep.

The lake after which our home was called means in

Gaelic the Green Lake and, like many Irish lakes, seemed to stretch away for ever into the little mounded hills which compose County Monaghan. In the far distance were wooded islands and to one, delectably named Picnic Island, I was brought as soon as I could enjoy country life. Here stood a famous birch tree on which the Leslies and their friends had cut their names for fifty years. The sculptor, Henry Taylor, was staying in the house to do some work for my grandfather. He climbed as high as he could and cut my initials above all the others. The tree has since fallen, which must be the end of all trees sylvan or stemmatic.

As soon as I grew beyond the toddling age I was spoiled by maids and housekeepers. There was what was called a still-room maid who spent her whole life making light refreshments. It was a house of plenty and bounty. Endless beggars came to the door to collect a silver dole and there was an unceasing barrel of beer to refresh every retainer or servant who called in the course of his duties.

My favourites were the gamekeeper, Jimmy Vogan, and the coachman, Bob Weir. The gamekeeper lived in a house in the woods like something in Grimm's fairy tales. He had a biscuit-box on his chimney shelf painted with a St Bernard dog. I was regularly held up to ask the dog for a biscuit, which was always forthcoming, and my sagacity applauded. The keeper carried a bag which was always full of dead birds and animals and made an exciting subject to investigate. On Sundays we always visited the stables and the coachman used to place me on the backs of horses and ponies where my astonishing horsemanship could be admired unless his supporting arm was removed, when I instantly fell off.

Motors were undreamed of and even passing trains were considered dangerous. Horses were reined in partly from precaution and partly to enable me to sit up and enjoy the " puff-puff." Horses, ponies, donkeys were the half of life then. We used to be driven in such obsolete

wagons as Denmarks, Broughams and Sociables. More
rapidly and adventurously we rode on an Irish jaunting
car. We used to be driven slowly and rhythmically to
distant houses for parties and Christmas trees. We used
to return after dark with the oil-lamps casting a weird
light on the great tree-trunks which thronged an Irish
demesne. They exerted a mysterious, almost mystical
effect on me ; and I used to believe in the personal life of
each tree. Very early the gardeners taught me which
trees were tenanted by fairies : invariably thorn trees
alone in the fields.

An earliest memory is slumbering in a closed Brougham
after dark and hearing Weir's cry of " Ga-a-a-te ! "
when we came to a lodge entrance. It was the old cry
of the turnpikes. as I have found recorded in old books
about coaching.

I had a fixed sensation (in which I was probably right
from Einstein's point of view) that there was no Time :
that everybody remained precisely as old or young as
we had always been. The passing of days made no
difference to me. I had not the slightest intention of
growing up. The only hour which affected me as a
distinct hour in the clock's face was the bed-hour. I
was an early believer in daylight saving, or at least in
remaining out of bed while the sun lasted. Otherwise I
would have wished no change and was willing to continue
life amid the same grown-ups, the same servants, the
same trees and the same rooks. All these symbols of
my past life have gone or changed except the rooks.
Trees have fallen, servants have gone, leaving me with
an aching desire to thank them for all the kindnesses they
poured upon me. Servants were still Victorian : willing
and respectful, ill-accommodated and poorly paid, but
they were more than the friends of the family. They
were *us* as much as ours, and this is a relation which the
present age has destroyed. I think they were happy.
They gave so much, and in our absurd feudal manner
we loved them. I ask what man could love his valet

to-day or what woman love her chauffeur ? It is only in my heart that I can think of certain gamekeepers, coachmen and housemaids and of the old white-haired butler.

All has changed at Glaslough in fifty years save the rooks. They still pass identically above the home of my infancy in the same flights and formations and in the same numbers. Their cawing is music to my soul.

The time-sense only dawns on a child when it is made to do lessons. The first ardent wish comes for a certain hour to cease and for a less arduous chunk of time to begin. Space I never realised until a day wherein I studied a tall derelict poplar and felt the background of sky withdrawing into the remote distances. I found I was gently shuddering at the abyss—and for many years I could not bear to look at an isolated tree-top against the waste of air. The unknown seemed immeasurably focused beyond.

Everything was believed literally. Santa Claus was as real as the maid who pulled the blinds, only he used the chimney instead of the door. The existence and majestic superintendence of God was humbly accepted. The Supreme Being was settled in the Infinity which had so much alarmed me in the sky. Heaven was the background of all Irish life. The poor believed it was theirs because they were poor. The rich believed it was coming to them because they were so good to the poor ! I remember my first idea of Heaven as a place where there were fireworks every night. There was always the tempering regret that all servants would enjoy higher positions, while their employers took a lower pew. This saddened me for many a day. Much as I loved the servants, I was not prepared for them to enjoy celestial compensations. It was my first thought in the realms of Theology. My second was a regret I could not collect postage stamps in the Kingdom of Heaven. Otherwise I had every reason to believe I was a happy child.

Visitors approached me early on the subject of a profession. It was suggested that I should become a soldier like my father. But I unkindly insisted that I intended to be one of the enemies who shoot Papas !

I was frequently photographed in Monaghan or Armagh, and as often deceived by members of the photographic profession, who promised that little birds would fly out of the cameras if I kept my eyes fixed on the dial. To this very general form of deception I attribute the disappointed looks on thousands of infant faces stored in family albums.

On the other hand there was a cuckoo-clock on the nursery landing at Glaslough which afforded me more pleasure and interest than any bird in a cage. I felt towards it the same affection that inanimate things inspire in children reading Hans Christian Andersen. For me the chiming cuckoo lived and therefore it was as good as alive. To hear a real cuckoo has a magical effect on me which I shall never outlive. With closed eyes I strain my ears and almost see a little boy in sailor trousers holding the bannisters and peering at the melodious little wooden bird : cuckoo, cuckoo, cuckoo ! A world without cuckoos would be a sad one for me indeed.

Early there swam into observation a venerable pair of grandparents who had made Glaslough their home. I learnt to call one Daddi-Pa and the other Granny Boo. They lived one in a Daddi-Parlour and the other in a Granny Boudoir. They had enjoyed the whole Victorian period together, and on Sundays they dressed as though they were going to one of Queen Victoria's garden parties. They were in full sail for their golden wedding which they achieved in 1906. As far as we could observe, there had never been the faintest dispute between them. This was due, as in most successful marriages, to one hand, not two, being laid on the reins. Early in married days he took his bride for a ride in Rotten Row. They cantered pleasantly round ; but when he reached the other end the saddle beside him was empty. The indignant occupant had been left unnoticed after a fall. Henceforth she took the matrimonial reins.

Naturally I never saw her in the beauty which had appealed to Watts, but her wit and vivacity survived into the twentieth century. They both reached the period of the Great War. Rather than see the finish my grandfather sacrificed any hope of living a century. His own generation had been killed in the Crimea. He had grown up amongst the veterans of Waterloo, including his father-in-law, George Dawson Damer, who had two horses shot under him on that interesting occasion.

What a lifetime ! Born in 1822, he had only missed George III by two years, but he had lived through the reigns of George IV, William IV, Queen Victoria, Edward VII and died in the fifth year of George V. He died in 1916, and she survived till 1925.

She was a great pet amongst elderly wits and surviving raconteurs. Her own sayings flew from mouth to mouth, and women a little feared her. It is difficult to say where her vivacity sprang from, for she was the reverse of her rather ponderous Damer sisters. Her mother was a Seymour, the adopted daughter of Mrs Fitzherbert. She was the youngest and an afterthought, almost Latin in her spirit and outlook, irresistibly amusing and deliciously unscrupulous in small matters. She was more royal than the Queen, and at moments could be more religious than an archbishop. When she set off for a Royal Garden Party in a purple dress, she looked like an excommunicated Abbess. She had entertained both Dickens and Thackeray. Three generations had known her as Boo. Once she was cleverly portrayed on the Stage by Lady Tree, but perhaps on the unkindly side, for she was no respecter of persons.

I can see her sweeping through the church at Glaslough in a picturesque bonnet and enveloping cloak. Before she reached the front pew, all the tenants and dependants had straightened in their pews while the organ harmonium (played by a venerable Miss Sophy Smith) burst into a joyful jig.

Every face and profile in the choir returns to me after two score years, mostly of long lean maidens who only opened their mouths to be abashed by their own sound or by the hearty bellowing of one Andrew Whitsitt, the clerk of the estate, whose ready repertoire covered the whole hymn book. My grandmother always talked in Church. She would address the Rector or speak to members of her family with a freedom which I attributed to divine dispensation. My early impression of public worship was that she was allowed to talk whereas governesses only dared whisper, and children might not utter a sound. Another grown-up privilege was my father's. He was allowed to sketch in church and I remember watching with fascinated eyes during a dry and turbid sermon while he skilfully transferred the swollen features of the Reverend John Hudson to the flyleaf of one of the big Prayer Books stamped with the family arms.

The old parish church of St Saviour was in the nature of a family chapel. It seemed to grow tower, chancel and cemetery out of our gardens, or as they were locally called "the Pleasure Grounds." It had been built by the old "fighting Bishop" John Leslie of the Isles, Raphoe and Clogher under the wing of the old castle he had modernised in 1660. His huge sepulchral stone proclaimed that he died in his hundredth year, the oldest bishop in Christendom. His devotion to the House of Stuart was such that at the Restoration he rode from Chester to London (180 miles) in twenty-four hours in order to salute King Charles the Second. This feat sounds credible when I record that he married after seventy and proved the powerful father of many children. He was made of stiff stuff.

His son Charles continued his devotion to the Cause and refused the oath to William of Orange, became a Non-Juror and a Jacobite, following the Old Pretender (Heaven forgive me for so styling the rightful King James III) to

B

St. Germain. He devoted himself to keeping the exiled
king in Anglican grace. For political rather than religious
reasons he was allowed to perform the Anglican liturgy
under the Royal roof. No doubt if he could have weaned
him from Rome, there would have been a second
Restoration.

The church built by the Bishop had no chancel until
my grandfather (who was the Non-Juror's grandson's
grandson) enlarged the east-end over a new vault into
which all available ancestors were translated. The Non-
Juror was missing and I spent the second centenary of
his death trying to locate his bones. But Irish graveyards are terrible heaps of confusion. I could not find
the Non-Juror, but at the time I happened to be seen
carrying the bones of an extinct Irish elk which had
been found in Donagh Bog. It was immediately remarked that I had been successful in finding the remains
of my ancestor : " but weren't them auld Leslies thick in
the hip ? "

In Irish graveyards the families are buried in each
other's arms so that each can present the thickest rank
on the Day of Judgment. The old sexton assured
me that he often cut grandparents in half to admit
their grand-children and had thrown up the skulls of
people he had known in his childhood. The grave-
digging scene in *Hamlet* could be often matched in
Ireland.

The Life of Charles Leslie the Non-Juror is one of the
books I have purposed writing during a lifetime. The
material is immense as he and his son became secret
agents of the Stuarts abroad. At home he issued pamphlets with reasoned scorn against Whigs, Socinians,
Quakers and Deists. Together with Swift and Defoe he
helped to found English political journalism. If Charles
Leslie like them had condescended to write one good book
of adventure he would not need a biographer to drag him
from oblivion. One of his unread masterpieces was called

"a Short and Easy Method with the Deists." I had a pious great-aunt who always referred to it as an Easy Way with the Dentist ! Doctor Johnson insisted that Leslie was a reasoner not to be reasoned against.

For an Irish church Glaslough was quite cheerful. We sat above the congregation in a huge gallery divided into twain by a wooden partition. My grandfather sat in a corner while we children leaned over the edge watching for the least diversion to break the monotony. The servants under Mr Samuel Adams, the fine old family butler, were marshalled on the other side of the partition. The plate was taken round generally by volunteers from the Royal Irish Constabulary. A newly-joined member of the Force once attempted to reach us by climbing the partition. One enormous boot was over before Adams could collar and lead him round to the private door. We writhed and rolled with delight. Few Sunday scenes remain clearer in my memory : the immense strapping yahoo in his dark green uniform : the puzzled look with which he stood looking over the fence and then the desperate attempt to scramble over !

The history of humour demands a volume on the comic things that are done or said in church.

Our Irish services were very Low Church. As an English visitor once complained : the Church of Ireland was so Low that the east-end often faced west ! We watched anxiously for the end of service. My favourite text that I had marked in my Prayer Book consisted of the simple words : " Here endeth the Litany." The only attempt at ritual came with the twelfth of July when all the Orangemen appeared in their coloured sashes, and the old church tower became gorgeous with banners of orange and blue, which curiously enough were always hoisted by the old Catholic stonemason, Bob Kearney. Kearney had married a Protestant wife and remained neutral. Once I expounded Ireland's greatness in the past to him, but he had one shattering phrase with which he

closed down History : " Och, the Irish Army's bate."
It was an echo of the famous defeatist ballad :

> " Oh John O'Dwyer a Glanna
> We're worsted in the game ! "

My grandfather brought some religious statuary from
Italy and there was much discussion where it should be
placed. Kearney was set putting it up with iron bars
and cement in the outside loggia of the house. There
was a Madonna ; and I remember the anxious Curate
telling my grandmother that the people would prefer a
replica of the devil in the church ! My grandmother was
enraptured by Kearney's devout handling of these pieces
and approached to overhear his appreciation. Unfortunately one of the statues slipped or gave him trouble
and she only collected some language no Protestant would
have dared release. But when his work was finished he
was forgiven after summing it up as only an Irish mason
would : " Sir John has placed a beautiful crown upon
Glaslough."

My grandmother, who was English to the fingertips
as regards the Irish, often returned overcome by the
phrases of the people. When she went to condole with a
tailor and his wife over the death of their only son, the
bereaved mother met her with a shining countenance,
uttering only the words : " A thousand welcomes to the
Will of God ! " If I were God, the Irish would be my
pets.

My grandparents did all that an Orange Vestry would
allow them to do to the church. Stained glass was
finally permitted in the chancel, but they were kept to
what were called Protestant subjects : Abraham's
sacrifice, Job comforted by his friends, with the Good
Samaritan. I believe there is a tendency to beards in
Church of Ireland windows ever since a Vestry were asked
to approve a cartoon of Aaron in his priestly robes. This
they would only accept on condition a beard was added to

his smooth features. Otherwise he might too easily be
mistaken for the Virgin Mary !

Certain buildings on this planet impressed at impressionable ages remain like landmarks in the mind. One
collects certain buildings like friends to love all one's life.
They wear even better than friends, and in their sound
and shadow the soul finds peace. For me three buildings
survive in memory's anchorage : Upper Chapel at Eton,
King's College Chapel at Cambridge and the old Church at
Glaslough. I have only to stand in their portals to see
and even hear a troop of ghosts. It is true that inefficient
preachers have bored me for hours in all three. But
within their walls I have felt all the emotions which
belong to childhood, boyhood and the dawn to manhood.
Under their echoing roofs I received the first strange
inspirations which cannot be altogether one's own
thoughts : thoughts that flow from the dead, from tradition, from higher and inscrutable influences. The mind of
youth is as pliant as the imagination itself. Youth is
reverence tempered by a suspicion of the ridiculous. It
was under the sacred roofs to the sound of droning
voices or lazy music that one first began thinking. Hence
followed first hopes, delights, bewilderments . . . nostalgia of the soul.

The Sunday service at Glaslough was very slow. I
memorised every cranny and every window including a
curious little peephole high in the roof, but so unapproachable from within or without that I gravely concluded that
it was reserved for God to look down upon the congregation. No doubt the Almighty counted them, apart from
the calculations made after every service by a Crimean
veteran balanced on his stump. What Mr Hamilton
Woods had suffered in the Crimea was enough to raise
the hair and lower the temperature. We became great
friends, and he left me his Crimean medals which my
grandmother restored to his family. I listened to his tales
while we searched the pews for bats which had fallen out of

the roof. During weekdays the church presented many attractions to a naturalist. There were owls snoring in the tower and jackdaws' eggs to be plucked amid rotten planks and perilous ladders. What sounded like a cannonised kettle-drum swung in the top loft. On the supporting timbers of the bell we carved our names more lastingly than on Picnic Island.

The church tower was sixty feet high and there was a tradition that early in the century one of the workmen placing the pinacles fell to the ground but by grasping a plank successfully broke his fall. During Evening Service in 1896 one of the pinnacles was hit by lightning and crashed in front of the entrance incidentally smashing the tomb of a worthy tradesman. The terrified congregation said they saw a ball of fire descending through the chancel but no one was hurt. The Constabulary had the presence of mind to prevent people escaping from the church. The Insurance paid up ninety pounds to repair the damages caused by an Act of God, and fortunately nobody sought to draw theological conclusions one way or another.

The structure had endured the fostering hand of my grandmother who had English ideas of the beauty deserved by God's House. She invoked funds out of which a magnificent beamed roof was erected. The south windows were glazed to commemorate my father's safe return from the Egyptian War of 1882. In deference to Protestant susceptibilities they were kept very tame : slightly tinted blanks with texts at the foot of each. She also added a new pulpit in Carpenter's Gothic which charmed everyone except my grandfather, who recalled that its tub-shaped predecessor had traditionally been used by Swift on one of his northern visits. Swift's tub was relegated to a desolate church up-country, called Shanco, where it received my veneration and that of all passing Swiftians.

In the old days we possessed a manuscript poem Swift had written to the sons of the Non-Juror, but by devious ways it passed into the Forster Collection and is now in the South Kensington Museum.

The clergymen at Glaslough were our family Chaplains and lunched with us every Sunday. They were the Rectors of Donagh. Mr —— was a coarse and boisterous creature, exactly like one of the caricatures of " Phiz " that illustrate our local novel *Valentine McClutchy*. William Carleton, the lost Walter Scott of Ireland, was educated in a Hedge School in our parts. It is no use lamenting the loss of his genius. He could under happier circumstances have been Ireland's national novelist and romancer. He had the genius but not the geniality for the position. He turned bitter and attacked for hire. He was our greatest literary might-have-been.

The Rev. Mr —— had an amusing, but I think innocent, admiration of the fair sex. He admired the classical grace of my Aunt Dosia who was represented in the family caricature book as fleecing him at Whist. Later he admired May Yohé, who had entered the County as the wife of our neighbour at Castleblayney, Lord Francis Hope. The Hope Diamond cannot have brought much luck, for Castleblayney demesne is now derelict, and May Yohé long fled to the protection of an American gentleman called Strong. She cabled back to her friends that she had lost hope but was feeling strong ! Poor Mr ——'s devotion must have been too Platonic. He was a good trencherman and we children used to egg him on at Sunday lunch to see how many helpings of roast goose he could be persuaded to consume. His formula before embarking on a second or a seventh help was always the same : " I'll try a little goose." And so he did.

His laughter was magnificent : something between an earthquake and a prolonged hissing, as though all the geese he had devoured were rising in his stomach. He afforded us endless stories, ridicules and mimicries. The most famous series of caricatures in the family collection were drawn by my father representing his fall into the fountain on his way to church, an occasion when he had to be rescued, dried and sent to preach in the butler's trousers. The slightly libellous caricatures represented him as a Saint Anthony removing his hat to a beautiful nymph dancing on the waters into which he splashed. The pictures were entitled the " Temptation, Fall and Repentance of Saint ——," and offered the first studies in the nude which we saw as children. To spare our infant eyes our grandmother had mercilessly cut a splendid collection of Rowlandson's drawings. We could only imagine from what remained the wickedness of what had been removed.

Education depends immensely on imagination. Hence the perennial failure of most of the Public School system. What is crammed and forcibly fed is of very little value. No knowledge is usefully acquired which is not pleasantly acquired. There is no more exquisite instrument than the young imagination.

Lessons had no effect on me unless they struck the gleam of wonder or spark of curiosity. My early and truest education was based on bound volumes of *Punch* and the *Illustrated London News*. But there were two volumes to which I owed an enormous debt. There was an illustrated Bible composed of huge German prints in dull coloured lithographs : all pictures and no text, which was unravelled on Sundays and inspired some exciting games of Biblical Characters.

The other volume was one of family caricatures, mostly from the pencils of my father and grandfather. These enthralling pages were full of sketches of our neighbours and dependants, ourselves and whoever appealed to some wild humour of the moment. I wonder if other families keep such depositories.

They included three famous sketches of the three most famous gamekeepers in Ulster :

Lord Rossmore's Hughey
Lord Caledon's Francey
Sir John Leslie's Menzies.

All three were fantastic characters and memorable in the families which they served. What memories their names would evoke amongst sportsmen of old time ! The variety in this precious volume was very great. There was a picture of the Primate of Armagh taking a mustard footbath in the Porch room, and of my mother bursting in to have her stays unloosed. She had mistaken the room believing it to be occupied by her sister-in-law. Another showed Pope Leo XIII dining at Glaslough. This followed a vivid dream of my father who came down one morning and said he had distinctly heard the butler, old Sammy, saying : " Port wine, your 'Oliness ! "

I perused whole volumes of *Punch*, absorbing the pictures and skipping the text. I realised the whole world of politics and society as Du Maurier and Tenniel viewed them. It was not for many years that I perceived any were intended to be funny.

I obtained an intense close-up of Europe in the Fifties and Sixties from the *Illustrated London News*. I learnt to read through my desire to decipher the meaning of those beautiful woodcuts chiefly of the Crimean War and the Great Exhibition. The foreign world I still see through Victorian spectacles in consequence. Reading became a real occupation and I learnt to attribute almost mystic properties to any old tattered volume. Ten years of subsequent education under the best auspices could not add to this acquirement which I made for myself.

Hours of contented bliss were passed under sofas and tables engrossed in " the War in the East " or the progresses of Queen Victoria or later in a House of Commons visualised and pencilised by Harry Furniss. Fantastic beings swam out of the *Punch* of the Eighties and Seventies : Dizzy and the Grand Old Man—the Irish members and their English contestants. They became mixed in my mind with Grimm's Fairy Tales, but I understood from many an anxious undertone that Gladstone still lived to do ill—a kind of monstrous Jabberwock swathed in enormous starched collars and

swaying an axe. Later I understood that one of these
figures of fancy was actually a living uncle of mine and
that as my godfather he had presented me with a beautiful
cup. This was Uncle Randolph, whom my father had
gone to meet at Larne when he arrived to bid Ulster
revolt against Home Rule.

Meantime a German governess, Fräulein Clara Woelke,
had arrived to teach me and my brother Norman. Norman was only a year younger, and we played in a couple,
divided everything, fought for everything and rioted out
of the nursery into the schoolroom. We regarded the
village children as our prey and descended upon them,
carried off the boys to play with us and harried the
girls (I should say from motions of dislike rather than
love). The Rector once reported that he had seen all the
mothers rushing for their children and hurrying them
indoors at our approach. Nevertheless some of the
children grown to mature years remembered our incursions
amongst their happiest days especially when we gave tea
parties at the gamekeeper's, at which no grown-ups were
present.

The poor Fräulein was led a grievous dance, but she
persevered with a devotion which was eventually rewarded. The poor Frolldery Doll! She had previously
instructed the sons of Sir Felix Semon, a distinguished
German throat-doctor. Naturally we were brought up to
believe that all Semons were paragons of virtue and
obedience. Perhaps they were and I believe when
Fräulein afterwards entered the family of the Speaker
Fitzroy that his children added the virtues of the Leslies
to their youthful illusions. I have often wished to collect
the Semons and Fitzroys to discuss our alleged sanctities.

Meanwhile we drove Fräulein from woe to woe. We
must have exceeded the wickedness of other boys for her
woes were a subject amongst other governesses. When
we were not revolting from her guidance in deadly alliance,
we were locked in deadlier fisticuffs. Yet she seemed to

love us, for her patience was unending and slowly we ascended the barbarous ladder of German letters.

A third brother appeared about this time and Norman's request to see his " weedy brother " caused much amusement. Seymour was produced and set amongst us. His cherubic face swathed in brown curls was seized by my grandfather as a model for some church paintings. His elder brothers were fond of setting him up and felling him with well-directed cushions. He fell and fell, rising cheerfully under the blows which shook his balance. It is a clear-cut memory and probably forgotten by the present venerable Appeal Secretary of Queen Charlotte's Maternity Hospital. Should he ever reach the Peerage, he has deserved two storks as his supporters with " Good Lord, deliver us " as a suitable motto.

We continued learning and writing tedious information in German lettering. But our afternoons were spent with the gamekeeper, a magnificent personage with a flaming red beard out of Celtic Saga. Here was one of Nature's gentlemen and a great sportsman. He proved more potent than governesses or tutors. James Vogan had that honesty, devotion, fidelity, and absolute content with his lot which alone made the feudal system a part of Christian civilisation. I think he would have given his life for any member of the family without hesitation. A world has grown up where such servitors and retainers are unknown. So much the worse for the world !

We had no wish to learn German until Fräulein hit on the expedient of making us translate Grimm's Fairy Tales into English. We were encouraged to believe that our translations would one day be published. It was a real disappointment to discover later that Grimm had already reached an English version. But for the time lessons were not wearisome. There was an attracting object as there should be in all education.

Poor Fräulein entered into Irish life and I can see her tobogganing with my Aunt Olive in old-fashioned tin hip-baths down the hill to the lake. They wore my father's old riding breeches and had to take hasty refuge in the boathouse every time my grandmother passed. Another sport devised by Olive was sailing the row-boat down the lake in a gale with the aid of a huge carriage umbrella. It was the only form of yachting I ever enjoyed.

Poor Fräulein was not outside romance and felt bitterly when the Curate Robert Byrne was snatched from her by one of those Jenny Wrens who help themselves to tall, good-looking men. The Curate was a total contrast to the Rector of whose coarse talk he often showed himself ashamed. He was well built with black curly hair, a fine swimmer with an eager, mystic face and a power of preaching deep sermons. He would have made an artist's model for St John, to whom my grandmother likened him. Happy the Church of Ireland when it was served by such! For a while he was Rector and was succeeded by a less spiritual but delightfully companionable friend to us all. Sam Cunningham was a clerical Bohemian and he filled his Rectory with amusing roysterers from Trinity, Dublin. He had played first-class Rugby football and made an ideal tutor for us all. He prepared us for Confirmation in a very practical cheerful way and warned us quaintly against Mrs Langtry, whose signed photograph hung in our London house.

Previously to Sam's arrival we had felt very inimical to the Church. When all threats failed, our revered father could always reduce us to tears by threatening to make us Bishops when we grew up. This seemed a prospect too awful to be borne. But with Sam all anti-clericalism faded away. He was simple, straight as a die and overflowing with fun. We ran wild in his gloomy old Rectory which could only be reached by a haunted road. Beside Fort Johnston was a tree against which a nurse in the Johnston family had been killed in a carriage accident. Her brother carved a cross in the tree and at night horses often refused to pass the spot. Again and again Byrne had been compelled to turn his horse's head and return to Glaslough for the night.

Sam Cunningham brought us into the life of the Parish which received our uproarious visitations. We went the rounds with him and were received with feudal delight. For five miles round there was no house or cottage into which we could not enter and be a hundred times welcome. At first I am sorry to say we rather disapproved of paupers and I heard my father complain that we could not be sent on charitable errands as we spat at the poor! The unexpected humours of the Irish poor soon taught us the perennial amusement of visiting them. Looking back I think they were a privilege and a blessing to their friends and supporters. The old-fashioned Irish poor have disappeared. I remember the happy-go-lucky creatures who went barefoot, slept in sacking and lived on their potatoes. Many were cheerfully bedridden and only indignant at the idea they could ever get better. Their patience and their good spirits were an honour to their Creator.

Once a year there was a distribution of blankets to scores of poor old crones. We boys presented them out of the shop door while Sam read the names to a gurgle of Irish blessings. When proceedings seemed slow, we used to roll the blankets in a ball and make the old ladies run the gauntlet. As each passed, she received her blanket with a thump. They shrieked with laughter as they staggered past and poured benedictions on the young gentlemen so-called! Included were a few old men, one of whom protested when he received a brown blanket instead of white. He swore with hurt pride he would use it to cover his ass. " He means himself," chuckled a voice.

Poor old Jackson lived in a rabbit hutch under an open roof. He used to run out and entreat the young gentlemen to help themselves to his damsels! He possessed a fine orchard of damsons for which the County was famous.

A Boys' Church Brigade was gathered and officered by us although we were under the proper age. This meant drilling in the schoolhouse once a week but it was regarded as excitedly as a School Treat. Children who have never seen toys, and boys without organised games are easy to amuse. The annual School Treat was unforgettable. Once the date was fixed children began walking in from other parishes. We believed they started overnight ! Such were the attractions of an orange and a bun in the Nineties. It was difficult to believe so much human pleasure could proceed from a few swings and races. The children who had walked in for miles were too exhausted to compete. They could only enjoy themselves. The village children had spent the morning in church being excitedly examined, I recall one question and answer :

" What was the food of St John the Baptist ? "

" Was it midges he was ating ? "

From the church emerged a procession headed by a banner on which were broidered the touching words " GOD BLESS THE LESLIES." The winning scholar was always a girl and received a " Rizpah " brooch. It all sounds pathetic compared to what is done for children to-day, but those were happier days than the world has since dreamed of.

On select occasions the 'keeper gave tea parties in the woods and we invited our friends. A wild form of hide and seek (called for some reason " high windies ") was played in the woods. Bill Madden the underkeeper and Wee Davy, the dog-boy, were adepts in making hides and I can see the latter, a gnome-like hunchback, tearing along like something in a Rackham illustration until he could be tripped and somersaulted amid outrageous mirth.

Wee Davy was one of the survivors of the ancient Irish race of dog-boys. They lived with the old wolfhounds and in modern times with the foxhounds. We had a grim story of a pack of new hounds sent north under charge of a dog-boy who brought them by road and lodged them in their new kennel. A year later he was passing and being benighted thought he would crawl in and sleep as he used to in old days amongst his friends. But alas they had forgotten his smell and in the morning the huntsman found a well-picked skeleton. Henceforth they were called the Man-eaters !

We were not much troubled by sects in Northern Ireland. Everyone believed in William of Orange or the Pope. Anybody else was probably an atheist and not likely to come to any good. An atheist was always mentioned as "bloody." The sanguinary expletive still retains a certain dignity in Ireland. In England it has become a mere enclytic, but in Ireland it was reserved as the special epithet for the atheist, the welsher and the late Lord Balfour.

New sects were hardly needed. In my time came the Salvation Army and the Dippers. Sam Cunningham was much disturbed but he dealt with them, as is the Irish fashion, by retailing humorous anecdotes.

The Dippers were chiefly occupied in washing away the sins of innocent girls by public immersion. Sam attended one of these and reported a most amusing scene he had witnessed from the bank. Some servant-girl was taken into mid-stream and the waters doused over her. At this moment a small boy in the crowd shouted out : " That will take the clucking off yer." The metaphor was perfect, for the normal method of cooling an amorous hen is by immersion in cold water.

As the girl struggled back to the bank she slipped and fell backward. The same relentless voice continued : " Now's your chance, Meenister, baptise her wicked end as well ! "

The idea of being baptised in sections goes back to the heroic age in Ireland when warriors refused to allow their sword-arms to be christened for fear of delivering weaker blows.

Sam had the laugh turned against him once. He made a protest at Monaghan station. He said he had seen an officer of the Salvation Army in uniform travelling in a special saloon carriage. Sam exploded with indignation until it was explained that the officer he had seen was the Duke of Connaught wearing the new Army cap !

Before the Disestablishment the clergy were almost entirely drawn from the gentry and nobility and full of quaint characters. In our county we had an old gentleman who, when transferred to a new parish, dug up and transported his dead wives with him ! In Glaslough itself it was difficult to believe all that my grandfather remembered about a parson called Pratt who boasted the splendid nickname of " Skip-the-Litany Pratt ! "

Pratt wore gaiters under naval uniform with gilt buttons which was as good a uniform for an Established Church as any. According to my grandfather Pratt always began service by an argument with the Clerk as to the day of the month, which generally had to be settled by Mrs Johnston of Fort Johnston from the front pew. The Clerk was deaf and if he began the Litany Pratt would stop him by saying in an audible whisper : " Damn you, didn't I tell you to skip the Litany ? " Hence his very popular nickname.

The feature of his services was that he made every blunder possible and when corrected used strong language. The stories were unbelievable. He was once reading the burial service in the old churchyard when he noticed a terrier hunting a rat among the gravestones and kept his eyes on the hunt. The mourners were suddenly startled to hear Pratt ejaculate : " The Devil if he hasn't got him at last ! "

From Pratt sprang a droll story which has been attributed in many quarters since. A man living opposite the Glebe kept a pig which used to trespass on Pratt's lawn to his great annoyance. On one occasion Pratt descended in wrath and told the man to take that pig to Hell out of that ! Returning to the Rectory he found the

man solemnly driving the pig after him. He asked the
man what he was doing and the man replied : " Sure your
Reverence, I always heard that the best way to find the
road to Hell was to follow the Devil " !

I always felt such clergymen as Pratt and Hudson
fulfilled their Divine Mission by the great amusement
which they caused to others. It is better to make children
laugh than angels weep.

Religion was instilled pleasantly in the schoolroom.
Only the church services were a terrible drag. Learning
the Sunday Collect by heart was like acquiring so much
gibberish, for what child ever understood what a Collect
means ? My earliest impression of hymns was that they
were pure nonsense purposely chosen to go with the
tunes. But Mrs Alexander's " Hymns for Little Children "
came as a revelation.

The gracious poetess visited Glaslough and heard
Norman and myself recite " There is a Green Hill far
away." I can remember the anxious rehearsals conducted
by aunts in the nursery. She then inscribed our much-
thumbed copy which remains the first autographed
book in my collection. And around her name, my grandmother wrote in red ink :

" Granny Boo gives these Hymns to her dear little
grandsons Jackie and Norman Oct 30, 1890 when
Mrs Alexander came here and wrote her name in the
book for them."

Nearly fifty years have passed but I can see myself
practising and practising the words behind a curtain.
No actress worked harder over her first part.

The volume was a sixty-sixth edition (so popular had it
been) and it carried the imprimatur of John Keble
whom she surpassed as a hymn writer both in simplicity
and beauty. These hymns gave me a first insight into
poetry. Glaslough seemed enshrined in the hymn
C

beginning "All things bright and beautiful," especially in the stanza :

> " The tall trees in the greenwood
> The meadows where we play :
> The rushes by the water
> We gather every day."

In our later days there was a fuss over the lines about :

> " The rich man in his Castle
> The poor man at his Gate,"

and they were removed to suit modern tastes, but they exactly described the old countryside, when both rich and poor were happy, which neither are to-day. I then suggested as a substitution :

> " The Labour Peer inside his Castle
> The newly Poor is at his gate :
> The Premier made them high or lowly
> And Taxes settle their Estate."

No picture came to me more vividly than the hymn about the sickly child and the Holy Ghost :

> " There used to come a little dove
> Before his window small :
> And sing to him with her sweet voice
> Out of the fir tree tall."

I never caught sight of a wood pigeon darting from a spruce tree without a feeling of religious awe—might it be——?

I was greatly thrilled on hearing that Charlie Duke, the footman, had seen an angel standing on the agency steps. It was the first supernatural fact to pass my way and I had no doubt of its truth. Charlie Duke was a fat and sporting servant much loved by my grandmother. He was the son of the huntsman at Curraghmore and considered himself one of the Beresfords and always journeyed to attend family funerals at Curraghmore.

For a long time I believed everything I was told. Till my twelfth year I believed that if you made a grimace

in the glass while the clock was striking your grin
remained fixed. Also that if you said the Lord's Prayer
backwards at midnight there was a fair chance of seeing
the Evil One! I never dared try either experiment.
Even to-day I have the feeling that when the conversation
dies down simultaneously, an angel is passing. Why
not ?

I remember sometimes as a child hearing the grown-ups
discuss the Catholic religion. So great is the gulf in Ireland
that voices are lowered and eyes are cast round in case
one of the offending creed is within hearing. English
people might suppose for fear of giving the least offence.
" Och no, for fear some wee Pope is spying on you ! "

Our seminary was dedicated to Saint Macartan who had
played Saint Christopher to Saint Patrick by carrying
him on his back over streams. Saint Patrick blessed him
as his strong man (*Trean-fhir*). Hence the clan name of
Treanor in our neighbourhood. The Catholic-Celtic
legend is a delightful growth, primitive and exotic ; but
save for a few holy wells and stones and local traditions
I heard nothing. The Church of Rome seemed to hang
sinisterly over the Protestant community. The fault was
mutual. Both Churches had obscured their gospel by
plunging head over heels into politics. Canon John
Hudson used to raise the Orange Lodges and the Priests
sat in the polling booths at election time in Monaghan.

The lies which Catholic and Protestant told about each
other in Ireland were fantastic. Having been on both sides
of the fence I can only tell them how much they have
misunderstood each other.

How well I remember the drive past Saint Macartan's
and hearing a grown-up state that it was conducted by
blind old priests, who caught all the small boys in the
neighbourhood and made them as blind as themselves. I
had no idea that this referred to theological blindness and,
henceforth, I never passed the building without a shudder
of fear.

A casual remark by old Sophy Smith always remained

in my mind. The Catholics were always ruining themselves in order to build beautiful churches ! A singular sect it seemed to me and why build churches which to me were temples of boredom ? If churches are empty in London to-day it is the penalty for boring children. I hardly know where we were bored most, in London or Irish churches. Oh the dreary Berkeley Chapel ! oh the dreary Quebec Chapel ! oh the dreary Grosvenor Chapel !

I had never seen the old House at Glaslough which had been pulled down and rebuilt by my grandfather in 1878. I have grieved all my life that I never saw old " Castle Lesley " with its haunted stairway. A ghost came up the stairs every time there was a death. The Castle had belonged to the McKennas and I supposed it was a hint from the dispossessed clan that another Leslie's time was up. It came up the stairs for my great-uncle Charles, who died on his return from India in 1871. He died as Burke and Debrett tactfully say *sine prole legitima*, leaving my grandfather to inherit Glaslough.

The old House was said to have been rickety and rat-ridden, but the inner walls would only yield to dynamite. The people had prophesied that treasure would be found in the foundations but nothing was found save a fine fireplace walled up and (a hint to those whose houses are damp) a course of peat-turf acting like a sponge in the outer walls. It is true that the lovely view down the lake of the great wood, which Arthur Young admired in his book of Irish travels, was only visible from the kitchen window. The sanitary offices were situated half-way down the slope to the lake. Four magnificent lime trees mark the spot to-day.

The new " Glaslough House " as it was called was the last word in Irish country places. It was lit with gasolene, which was thought wonderful, and it possessed the first bathroom built in Ulster. People washed in tin trays and rusty hip-baths. Neighbours used to be shewn the bath working. On the top story, it soon became relegated to the use of dogs and children. It was supplied with water pumped out of the lake and had the exciting property of becoming an aquarium when the animalculae of the lake were pumped in alive.

Boyhood was a dream at Glaslough. There are days which float back in vision, especially warm early springs when the sound of the scythe was abroad in the land. I could hear the gardeners slowly mowing the Pleasure Grounds by hand and pausing to whet their blades on their hones. It was a sweet steady harmony compared to the horrible screech of the lawn-mower. As they mowed through the grass they revealed white ducks sitting on nests full of greeny eggs. White ducks, black rooks and the orangy-brown corncrakes were the first birds to pass into my notice. Quantities of corncrakes lay low in the rushes and could be traced by their cry. There was a corncrake in every corner in those days, and their craking filled the lower airs.

As though the county were not sufficiently furnished with water from lake and bog and stream we were furrowed with the Ulster Canal on the southern border. On the north between Glaslough and Lord Caledon's demesne flowed the Blackwater. The Blackwater was historical. It divided two parishes, two baronies, two counties, two dioceses, two deaneries, two kingdoms and it was the boundary of the O'Neills. To-day it divides the Free State from the Northern customs.

The Canal had been cut, thanks to cheap labour, shortly before the coming of railways. It was bought by the new Companies and allowed to lie in waste full of lush weeds and mares' tails. The rotting gates swing idly out of the cut-stone locks. There is nothing more melancholy than an abandoned canal, to which nature will only play step-mother, reserving all her real beauties for the rivers and streams which are the daughters of her womb.

Fifty years ago there was still water enough in the canal and once I saw a boat slowly sailing between the fields. It was as strange as a ship out of faery. I always see it in memory when I pass the spot from which I glimpsed it as a child. I once made the passage between Caledon and Middletown by canal in a steam launch belonging to the late Earl of Caledon. It made a prodigious wash and sounded a small syren though there could have been nothing in its way for years and years. It was manipulated by real sailors while the owner stood at the wheel. The passengers were chiefly delighted children. We were four boys at Glaslough and there were four boys at Caledon.

We believed that when Home Rule came Lord Caledon would sound a bell and gather a great army. He had his own drum and fife band in white uniforms. They used to come over and serenade Glaslough sometimes. He was a romantic figure. Silent and unassuming he had once fought a mill with a pugilist using his bare fists to show that a gentleman could take punishment. He and his brother had lived amongst the Blackfoot Indians. He had bought back Wapiti and crossed them with the red-deer in the Park. There was a bear-pit at Caledon Hill to which I used to be taken with baskets of apples to feed the hairy exiles from the Big Horn Mountains. No poacher ever dared scale the Caledon walls as it was believed the bears were let loose at night. Lord Caledon died young, leaving a brood of boys in green Caledon tweeds. One became a Harrow cricketer and the youngest General in the Army. The eldest became the best of neighbours and we proceeded to Eton and Cambridge together.

The happiness of being bred in the Irish atmosphere is that you believe everything. The Irish of all creeds are born with a double dose of credulity. I was always waiting to hear Lord Caledon ring a great bell and to join his army.

Glaslough had a fairy atmosphere. There were old people who had distinct memories of the fairy folk. The great Bog of Donagh alone was a concomitant that no English life could know. Apart from its flora and turf, it had yielded the skeleton of an Irish elk, a buried Celtic Cross and a mummied woman with golden hair !

Everything that grown-ups said was true. Once I was warned that if I ran bareheaded in the sun I should die of sunstroke. One night I awoke and remembered I had dispensed with my sailor hat during a hot summer's evening and immediately prepared myself for death in a great agony of contrition.

Later I believed that whatever I saw printed must be literally true. For instance the sign " Umbrellas recovered in 20 minutes " which I saw in Oxford Street meant that a bureau of detectives would immediately set to work and restore any lost umbrella in that time. Later still I mistook " Turf Commission Agent " for some kind of lawn-gardener.

I believed that atlases were infallible and that Geography was an exact science. I used to draw non-existent mountains and rivers secretly into atlases and then suffer remorse at the thought of the explorers who would be led astray—provided, of course, some expedition to the Sahara or Tibet borrowed our schoolroom copy !

An early hobby was Astronomy. At first it was only an excuse for sitting up late. Astronomy is a fascinating aside from the littlenesses of earth. There is no more majestic means for quelling the hates and envies and follies of this life than peeping beyond our poor planetary existence. The Middle Ages taught that Man was less than the dust. Astronomy shows that the Earth itself is less.

My first thrill was given me by a visiting member of the Parsons family who came to Glaslough and drew pictures of Lord Rosse's great telescope at Birr. He drew a pattern of the stars above and the spiders in the earth below which seemed a very convincing correspondence. On paper stars and long-legged spiders look very much alike.

In January, 1894, I acquired a shilling Primer by Sir

Norman Lockyer on Astronomy. It recommended proving the earth was round by the difficult experiment of inducing flies to walk round an orange. I first saw pictures of Comets and began to count the years for the return of Halley's.

In the following month I was one of the few human beings who beheld a sign of surpassing beauty in the heavens. On February 8, 1894, I was walking at midday in full sunshine on the terrace of Glaslough when I saw an immense and brilliant pear emerge from the sky and descend noiselessly and rapidly, as I thought, into a lake beyond the woods. Bewildered and enchanted I told and re-told my story. It could not be believed. On the next day a letter appeared in the *Irish Times* from Arthur Rambaut the Astronomer Royal at Dublin. He had been helping his little son to fly a kite and he had seen the same meteor :

" I was looking towards the East when it suddenly burst into view with an intense brilliance and shone out against the cloudless blue sky with a green metallic lustre, or as my little son described it, of a brightish, flaming, yellowish-greenish colour. In shape it resembled a very elongated pear like most fireballs of the sort. It emitted no visible sparks and disappeared quite noiselessly. The time of its occurrence was 12h. 3m. mean Dublin time."

So swiftly it passed that I never batted an eyelid. But the incredible beauty of it ! It was like a white-hot pearl slipping through the blue-silk sky—out and then in again, or as I believed into one of our lakes. To my dying day I shall be able to refashion the most purely beautiful thing I have ever seen : and I have also seen a white swallow and at another time a lunar rainbow over a black peat bog.

Life is too short to allow a sight of all the possible comets and eclipses. I lived to see Halley's Comet in 1910 and to stand in Yorkshire under the shadow of the

sun's total eclipse in 1928. The comet I saw in Dun-
gannon in January, 1910 : a silver streak in a corner of
the sky. It remained in the heavens until after the death
of King Edward VII fulfilling a famous line of Shakespeare
" The Heavens themselves blaze forth the death of Princes."

My grandfather was called " the old Sir John." He had
a very good memory for all that had happened long before
the Crimean War, such as the newsboys crying the death
of George the Fourth. His grandfather had been in the old
Irish Parliament and had refused to vote for the Union
with England. His name figures in the Red List as
compared to the Black List published by Sir Jonah
Barrington. He told his fellow-members that if they
went to London they would only be laughed at. His two
distinctions were that he had thereby avoided a Peerage
and that his portrait was painted by Gilbert Stuart.

His son died leaving a large family by his second wife,
who were brought up by their formidable mother, a
Fosbery from Limerick. She decided the boys would be
spoilt by the adulation of the tenants and transferred
them to London and Harrow in its roughest days. Meantime she managed the Irish estates in times of stress and
famine. Her portrait by Grant, a forgotten President
of the Royal Academy, hangs over the dining-room fire-
place. I have sought and touched her coffin in the snug
family vault which has also proved a safe deposit for guns
and silver. The Irish, however much inflamed against
the living, will never rob the dead.

During a minority of many years she administered
the estate. Her deeds have never been recorded. She
built the Protestant church at Pettigo, in Donegal, and
schools for Catholics and Protestants alike. Her husband had
been a strong Tory and opposed to Catholic Emancipation.
The old Priest at Pettigo foretold that the Catholic
Schools she built would bring the Faith to her descendants.

Oddly enough old Colonel Leslie's daughter by his
first wife bred Catholics (Cliffes and Gurdons). This

branch of the family was not much alluded to. There
was a suspicion as though of cheating at cards or something
socially unfortunate.

Old Mrs Leslie may have softened towards Catholics
but she never forgave their champions the Whig Rossmores, who dominated Monaghan. At election times
the Rossmore and Leslie mobs clashed fiercely. There
was even a battle remembered as " Stony Saturday," so
much ammunition was brought to bear by Glaslough
Tories on the Whig windowpanes in Monaghan. For a
century no Westenra or Leslie spoke to each other. Old
Mrs Leslie retained the feud, for she had seen her
husband's carriage shot to pieces in Monaghan by the
opposing faction. She lived to see her eldest son, Charles,
fall in love with a beautiful Lady Rossmore. (There have
been three beautiful Lady Rossmores in succession.) On
hearing that Charles wished to propose marriage, old
Mrs Leslie retired to bed and died. The marriage with
the beautiful widow never took place, for she became a
Catholic and the County Monaghan knew her no more.

Charles Leslie was constantly thwarted in love He
paid court to the famous old German Duchess of Manchester, but when her husband died she preferred to
marry another Duke and rule over Devonshire House.
Meeting me as a small boy she remembered how much
she had been admired by my great-uncle and decided I
was worthy of a gold sovereign. She was very fat and
closely dressed and I spent ten minutes searching her
multitudinous pockets before I could rescue her purse.

Charles then turned his hopes toward Christine Nielson,
the Swedish prima donna. She would have accepted him
but she could not bear his sisters who were as disagreeable
to her as Victorian Christianity taught the respectable
to behave to artists of the Stage. In the end Charles
kept house with a lady whom he would not marry as she
was a Catholic. She bore him a son whom I was pleased
to meet in his old age. He could not succeed to his father's
estates but he inherited his mother's Faith. He was
prevented by his birth from becoming a priest in the

London Oratory, but he spent a large sum decorating the
Chapel of the Magdalen, which I have always treated as
our family pew in consequence.

And so Glaslough passed to his brother John, my
beloved grandfather.

Charles' devotion to Christine Nielson had led to many
pathetic scenes at the Opera. On one occasion he was so
heart-strung while sitting in a box that he wished he
could make ravishing love to her on the stage. " Oh no,"
observed the witty Alfred Montgomery, " that would
never do. The audience would call for an encore ! "

The Donegal estate, including the holy Lough Derg
and the Pilgrimage of Saint Patrick's Purgatory, had
belonged to John as the younger son. He had left
Dr Longley's Harrow for Newman's Oxford and later
joined the Life Guards. He hunted at Melton in the
great days of Lord Wilton and Mr Gilmour. With the
Irish famine of '47 he had to sell his hunters and had
the courage to return to Ireland. He remembered seeing
the living skeletons who came in from the mountains to feed
at the soup-kitchens which were organised by his mother.
He found himself penniless and had to sell his Commission. He travelled abroad and studied in the art
schools. He won the Grand Military Steeplechase on his
own horse and lived a life amongst sportsmen and painters.
Millais and Landseer were among his friends and at the
same time he was a patron of cricket. An original
member of the Zingari, he lived to become the doyen of
the M.C.C. Unharassed by ambition or family troubles
his had been a happy life such as is now inconceivable.
Late in life he unexpectedly came to Glaslough, succeeded
to a seat in Parliament and entered Irish politics.

It was not a difficult estate to run. Charles Leslie had
improved Monaghan farming out of recognition between
1850 and 1870. He had sent his best tenants to learn
new methods in Scotland and the value of farms had
changed. In 1893 old Patton, our best tenant, won a

Challenge Prize for the best farm in Ulster. A dinner in his honour was the first public function I ever attended and heard all classes and creeds honour the Toast of

" The Best Landlord, the Best Tenant and the Best Land Agent in Ireland."

The old Sir John lived happily among his tenants and retainers. He lived in a previous century, and though his rents were shrinking he always gave alms to the poor, who visited him daily. It was part of the butler's duties to keep a supply of silver on hand. Sammy Adams used to iron *The Times* newspaper every morning before he brought it in. Through Sammy we were socially related to the Duke of Grafton, whose footman he had once been.

I remember driving into Monaghan with my grandfather in a swaying Sociable and a footman with a clasp-knife with which he jumped down to pick out the stones which wedged into the horses' hoofs. He made comments on every field of corn, and finally pointed out where his father's carriage had been fired to pieces during election time.

He had always used muzzle-loaders requiring ramrod and powder-flask, and long after his friends turned to breechloaders ; but he was often complimented on bringing down birds which were out of shot for them. He used to say that the finest shot he had ever seen was not Lord Walsingham but Lord Huntingfield.

He used to talk of incidents when the new House was built. It was said to have cost three lives. One workman fell off the scaffolding, and his mother died within a week of a broken heart. A plumber engaged on the work went down to bathe in the lake. He left a boy to watch his clothes. My grandfather found the boy at his post and muttering : " He's in the lake an hour and I'm waiting for him yet." He had taken a header and stuck in the mud, but the simple boy believed that he was walking about at the bottom and might return at any moment !

Those were the days before simpletons were popped

into asylums. Charles Leslie kept a Fool called Owny McCrudden to amuse servants and visitors from England. Owny sat barefooted in the kitchen and lived a life of his own. For some reason he would never take white money, only copper, and it was always a joke to watch him prefer a penny to a shilling. He collected so many coppers in this way that he was probably not such a fool. He set an example of religious tolerance, for he ran on Sundays from Church to Chapel and heard all the sermons in turn, sitting under each pulpit with open mouth and staring eyes. Once the Presbyterian Minister gave him an old wig, which he brought to the Priest to be baptised ! He was found lying dead in a ditch on his way home from a wake : a joyous death under the stars.

Crime was excessively rare. As a child I was thrilled by the story of a pig-stealer who came to grief on the railway. Every week a truck of dead pigs was run from Monaghan to Belfast and every week one carcase was missing. There was no telling how until one morning a dead man was found lying on a bend of the railway beside a dead pig. He had leaped on the pig's back once too often.

When my father was Sheriff there was a strange murder at Clones and I saw the good-looking young murderer, Fee, handcuffed in the station. He was a butcher who murdered a friend for a few notes and gave out that the murdered man had gone to America. The body he buried under a dunghill but absent-mindedly ordered the manure to be removed a few months later. The pitchfork brought up a human foot and Fee was arrested. The local jury disagreed and he had to be found guilty elsewhere. The Coroner told me that what condemned him was that he had cut his victim's throat as only a butcher knows how : down and not across.

Glaslough village was divided into two parts. The poor lived in one and the respectable in the other. The lodge gates were occupied by the Sexton and the Head Gardener. There was a Constabulary and an Orange Hall,

a general store and some shops. Irish shops are always
amusing if not very productive. The shopkeepers are
more interested in good gossip than in disposing their
goods. It seemed almost a rule that if you asked for one
thing you were offered another !

Whatever gibes may be thrown at the Irish no one
would call them " a nation of shopkeepers." I remember
an Irish shopkeeper who devoted his afternoons to
conversation with his friends. One year he stocked a
popular style of tennis shoe which he sold out. The next
year customers were surprised to be told he was no longer
selling the article. He had found that the increase of
business interfered with the time he devoted to his
friends, and he declined to be bothered with the extra
trade which destroyed his tranquillity !

The Glaslough shops were always sources of fun. All
were open to us except one which was boycotted by my
grandmother's orders because the draper had boasted
he had voted against Sir John. In time the draper died
and was buried at the church door ; but divine wrath
as well as human indignation was waiting him. Fire
descended from Heaven and struck a pinnacle from the
tower, smashing his gravestone to smithereens. A new
one had to be furnished by his widow and fragments of
the old were used to mend the cow-byre of the very Sir
John against whom he had voted so impiously at the
elections !

In the midst of so much that was Irish my grandmother
remained more English than the English. The highest
praise she awarded Patton's farm was that it reminded
her of England with its close-cut hedges and tidy fields.
Like every real personage in life she never ceased being
herself. She always lived up to her own characteristics like
a person in a Victorian novel. This was a peculiarity of the
Victorians, whether they acted from character or wilfulness
or mere pride. She was wilful and she was witty.

Her wit was always ready to spring. When a lady had

a child by a Mr Luke White who was better-looking than her husband, somebody asked what did she say to her husband ? " A white lie," said my grandmother.

Asked to name a racehorse born of Semolina she suggested " Sa-go " ! with a little hiatus in the middle of the word.

When she was asked whether she was saved, she answered the Salvationist with quiet dignity : " I had a very good mother." And there was nothing more to be said.

When Sunderland House was built to the disfigurement of Curzon Street, there was some query as to the naming of the town palace of the Churchills. " Marlborough House " was already taken. A second Blenheim Palace, was impossible. My grandmother suggested " Malplaquet ! "

She kept on remarkably good terms with the Almighty. When distressed by a letter, like Hezekiah, she always showed it to the Lord. In her eyes Queen Victoria and " dear John " could do no wrong. She had a happy belief that when she bowed from her carriage the movement resembled Queen Victoria's. They must be protected : Queen Victoria from Mr Gladstone and her " dear John " from Mr Parnell, but also from his Leslie sisters, for whom she had no tolerance.

Her third great aversion was lockjaw. She had a curious horror of the working of tetanus and could not see a child using a fruit knife without an anguished cry that the child's jaws would shortly lock. Even the sharpening of a pencil seemed a flirtation with death. She would never open an umbrella or wind a watch, for which she gave no reasons.

It was easier to understand her horror of funerals ; and as the graveyard lay immediately in front of the House, it was her lifelong ambition to have it closed. The Sexton was forbidden to toll the bell and a new cemetery was opened under the railway. Then commenced a long struggle between her wishes and the Irish who bury

obstinately with their ancestors. In vain she visited and
counselled the dying to use new and uncontaminated
ground. In vain the relatives of the dead were offered a
free hearse if they would abandon the old yard. In vain
were her appeals to the Health authority. The old yard
was neither contaminating to the lake nor to the wells. The
old people clung to their thickly populated graves.

The new cemetery remained virgin until the fortunate
accident which deprived Doctor Stewart of his leg. He
consented to send it to the new cemetery and as he was
bound to follow his leg in time, the villagers followed one
by one. Each time that a funeral started for the new
cemetery, my grandmother hurriedly cleared the House
of flowers and rushed with a bouquet to the grave.

Mr Parnell was another aversion and was never mentioned save as a " very wicked man." He was a relation
through the Damers, but this blot on the escutcheon
was never mentioned. Parnell had sent his scurrilous
secretary, Tim Healy, and wrested away the family seat
in Parliament from my grandfather. Parnell was making
his first inroad into Ulster, and what Mr Healy said about
the Leslie family is best forgotten. A generation later
he apologized in the charming formula which I commend
to all who engage in Irish faction : " No Irishman can
possibly mean what he says about other Irishmen at
election time."

Mr Parnell called a Nationalist meeting in County
Monaghan whereat the Orangemen countered forces
under Lord Rossmore. Hence the famous incident still
known as " the Battle of Roslea." The Orange meeting
was proclaimed by Dublin Castle. Still the Orangemen
marched until there was only a hedge between the advance
guards. Revolvers were spitting and drums rolling
but there were no casualties. My grandfather demolished
a Hibernian arch with his umbrella. He was afterwards
trying to ward off the rain when an Orangeman
approached him with : " Hell to your soul ! Will yer not
be keeping yer umbrella over the big drum ? "

The Resident Magistrate arrived and ordered Lord Rossmore to retire, which he refused to do. Both sides eventually retreated and both naturally claimed the victory. Lord Rossmore was deprived of his Justiceship of the Peace. My grandfather grandiloquently offered to resign his. All Orangery rose in addresses of indignation from Glasgow to Australia. Had Rossmore possessed any eloquence he could have seized the leadership of Ulster in that fervid moment. Such was the " Battle of Roslea " sung in ballads and spoken of with bated breath for many a long day.

Derry Rossmore was a lively and unforgettable character, one of the darlings of Ulster, and as popular with one side as the other. He had stepped straight out of a novel by Charles Lever. He had lived the life as it could only be lived by a gilded Buckeen in the Ireland that is past. He had an infectious laugh which could be heard through the County. He was one of the crack shots, especially after a glass of Port. He told endless good stories with a verve that was all his own. I never knew the meaning of " good stories " until I heard him hold the table for an hour after dinner. One followed another and as a collection I have never heard them equalled. He could draw on a fund of Irish Bulls, sayings and situations that never failed. It was he who popularised the story of a noble earl with a double title who was seen staggering in an Irish railway station. " And who may that gentleman be ? " asked a stranger. " The Earl of —— and ——," replied a porter, " and both of them drunk ! "

Perhaps it was the drollery with which he told his story that carried it off. I remember the uproarious mirth with which he described a visit to the Catholic Bishop. In his later days Derry was converted by an American evangelist, Mr Mott, whom he heard in London. To the great loss of his friends he gave up telling stories of a Rabelaisian or Bacchanalian nature. He took up Temperance and paid the Catholic Bishop a visit to suggest a Crusade in that direction. The hospitable

D

Bishop produced a bottle of very good champagne, the Secretaries joined in and they conversed freely on every subject for an hour. Not until they had finished the bottle did the Bishop ask the reason of his visit ? " Temperance and Total Abstinence for all classes," said Derry, and realising the comicality of the situation burst into peals of laughter in which the good Bishop joined.

Some of Derry's stories were terrific. I can always recall one of them. Years after Derry was dead I was landed at a very dull dinner table where the stories were inexcusably vulgar without being funny : of the type which has made the Stock Exchange such an arsenal of Wit. When I could stand it no longer I slowly recited one of Derry's most fearsome stories. It took a little telling but my blood was up and it dropped like a thunder-bolt. Half the men roared till they shook. The other half were shocked. They had never heard such a story before. And serve them right !

The rights and wrongs of telling bawdy stories have never been settled. It is the English rule that once ladies have left the room gentlemen may tell whatever they like. I remember a foolish man entering a room with a " good story " and cheerfully asking " are there any ladies here ? "

" No but there are some gentlemen," said an old-fashioned Major fixing him with his glass. And the " good story " never came.

Bawdy is inseparable from life. There is no class or profession which does not lightly indulge. Schoolmasters, clerics, wiseacres and women will all unbend after their manner to what is well told, but it should only be of the best vintage. Cheap bawdy is like cheap champagne. It makes one sick without the benefit of the sparkle. Bawdy should never be told in the presence of youth. *Maxima debetur pueris reverentia*, as Juvenal remarked.

There are various means of squelching the inferior brand. The late Lord Lovat overhearing a young aristo-crat regale an audience thus, which included some

débutante girls, merely emptied the lobster salad over his
head without a word !

While he lived, Derry was the life and glory of sport
in Monaghan. He enjoyed that feudal kingship which
English Peers never know. The English may love a
lord but the Irish have the power of making one feel that
he is loved, provided that he ever shows the least humour
or courage or delight in that strange country. Derry was
one of those who felt that his order could have led the
country had they tried. Under George Wyndham's
influence he turned later towards Devolution, but it was
too late. Belfast spewed out half-measures and the
Nationalists were obstinately setting sail for the rocks.

Derry had succeeded to the estates owing to the death
of his elder brother who was killed steeplechasing on the
old course at Windsor in front of the Queen's carriage.
She drove away and never returned to the Windsor
Races. A monument was erected to his memory in the
Monaghan Diamond, and the opening was celebrated by
a county ball. Fifty years later a curious coincidence
occurred when the present Lord Rossmore took a house
in Windsor without knowledge of its history. A stranger
passing one day observed that he remembered a Lord
Rossmore carried into that same house after his accident.

The Rossmores have an authentic Banshee, which is
strange as their family name Westenra is Dutch not
Celtic. Sir Jonah Barrington gives a thrilling account
in his *Memoirs* of the Banshee coming to a country house
in Wicklow and summoning the first of the title.

Derry collected boon companions and daring riders
about him. The most daring was Willie Woodwright of
Gola, whose riding deserves memory even in a land of
wild riders. There was no fence in Monaghan against
which Willie would not ride. Although he took some
memorable and fantastic leaps he never injured himself
seriously. To this day some appalling places are pointed
out where he leaped. Derry once showed me a double-

hedged sunken road on a hill-slope which Willie Woodwright had cleared. On another occasion he found the
railway cutting at Ballinode in his way and charged
the annoying thing! His horses were not very good but
they soon acquired a taste for risking their owner's
neck. His most famous feat was driving his tandem over
the ice at Glaslough during one of the rare Irish freezes.
He was with difficulty dissuaded from crossing the lake
while my grandmother wailed from the bank: " remember
you are an only son "!

He seemed doomed to die in the saddle, but fate
ordained otherwise. Derry and Peter Westenra went to
Kimberley in early days taking Willie with them. They
lived in a mud house on the diamond diggings. Willie
caught fever and died soon after his return to Ireland.
The venture was abandoned but the next owner found
diamonds plastered in the very walls of their mud house.
South Africa has found connection with Monaghan since,
for Abe Bailey was fortunate enough to marry Lord
Rossmore's only daughter.

The feud between Westenras and Leslies had long ceased
and they were united at last in my grandfather's efforts to
hold the seat against the Nationalists. The Land Acts
and Land War threw all the Landlords together for
protection. Our differences had arisen at the time of the
Union in 1800 when the Westenras voted for that measure
while the county members (Leslie and Dawson) voted
against. Tradition says that Dawson's uncle, Lord
Cremorne, was playing cards at Windsor with the Royal
Family when news arrived of the nephew's vote against
the Government. Very loyally Lord Cremorne rose from
the table and fainted at the old Queen Charlotte's feet.

County families were few in Monaghan. There were
the Maddens of Hilton Park, descended from " Premium "
Madden who wrote the suppressed *Memoirs of the Twentieth Century* with a prophecy of " King George VI." At
Carrickmacross were seated the Shirleys of whom came
the historian of the county, the great antiquary and book-

collector Evelyn Philip Shirley. It was a tradition that he had once proposed to a maiden Miss Leslie in his delight at finding her reading a book of Heraldry! And oldest of all were the Anketells of Anketell Grove who have since become extinct like the Blayneys of Castleblayney. It was over a Mr Anketell that my grandfather made his chief speech in Parliament. Mr Anketell had been chivied by a dog while riding. He dismounted and cut the dog's throat. There was a question in the House, and my grandfather, whose sympathies were all with the dog, had to defend an important voter. The only possible excuse was that either the dog or Mr Anketell was mad.

In those days rabies had not been stamped out. Word was often brought by excited gatekeepers that there was a mad dog on one of the roads and we were kept within the Pleasure Grounds while keepers watched over the walls with guns. At a sign of froth from the mouth a dog was shot.

A small boy was bitten by a mad dog and my grandmother sent him over to Pasteur in Paris on the impulse of the moment. She telegraphed to Mr Leo de Rothschild, who with generous alacrity met the boy in London and sent him over in charge of his valet. Pasteur was successful and the boy returned cured. Every Christmas for years a card brought his mother's gratitude and a Miss Pinchun, whose articles had been bitterest at election time, wrote floods of passionate repentance. In Ireland charity is always the last word.

My grandmother was a perfect Lady Bountiful and seemed able to bring some of the grandeur of London life into the land of bogs. She did her best to introduce English customs into church such as kneeling instead of sprawling in the pews. To give the example she used to sit and kneel in the sanctuary opposite the Parson and even bow at the Sacred Name, but idolatry is never popular in the Church of Ireland. Her neighbours found her formidable but a valuable auxiliary in trouble. When some local friends were threatened by bailiffs she drove over in her Sociable and returned with their best silver hidden under the carriage rug.

There was nothing Irish about her except her wit. Once she was mistaken by a gushing lady for a certain Mrs Lowther who was very plain. She answered : " You have made a mistake, but I have prayed all my life that God would make me humble and to-day He has answered my prayer."

The background of our lives was set against the most amusing and unexpected people in the world. In spite of contrariness and sudden reversions of sentiment they were the easiest to deal with, the friendliest and the most faithful. Rarely they showed odd streaks of behaviour inherited from a chequered past.

Retainers, gardeners and all who "wrought in the demesne," partook in our sports and escapades. They abetted us through thick and thin. They had a most useful idea of what was due to the family. My grandfather, who was indulgent to tenant or employee, was venerated like a patriarch. He would never consent to dismissals or evictions. Only wilful wickedness led to an old servant's going. The most accomplished of gamekeepers, after being found guilty of selling hampers of game, was only dismissed when a starved dog was added to his misdeeds ; and he ended miserably as a gravedigger in New York.

There was an office for taking rent, but the part of the owing tenant was always pleaded by the under-agent, Andy Whitsitt, against the sterner Mr McCullagh, who in the end pressed no man. Weather and crops were always taken into consideration and at the time of the Purchase there were £14,000 of arrears forgiven. Tenants, henceforth, became debtors to the Government and paid annuities instead of rent. Many have regretted the old days when payment could be deferred by raising a smile or a sigh. There was a story that a famous step-dancer, Jemmy Smith of Toneygarvey, was forgiven three years

rent by my great-uncle when he whistled and danced the
" Royal Charlie." There was an artistic gesture ! I
doubt if the Dublin officials would remit a shilling for the
loveliest ballad-tune or the most picturesque of steps.

There was always an amusing gulf between English and
Irish minds. The Irish simply said things which would
never occur to the Saxon. Their speech bubbled out of
something primitive and archaic, sometimes with a tinge
of passion or modulation of irony which would be lost on
the other side of the Channel.

Scores of sayings and quaintnesses remained in family
memory. When my father introduced golf on the lawn
and was seen for the first time putting, old Matty, the
faithful washerwoman, happened to approach the House
with her bundle of washing, which she cast to the ground
crying : " That I should live to see the Colonel himself
playing ball like an innocent child " ! A good primitive
observation to make at first sight of the ubiquitous game !

Old Matty of the hundred wrinkles remains a picture,
wearing a tattered poke-bonnet and an old jet-black
cape that my mother has cast upon her. All her life she
slaved at a hand laundry, never took a holiday and saved
all her money to be spent by friends at her own wake. I
sometimes wonder if God has a place good enough for
people like old Matty ?

My favourite phrase garnered from an Irish pulpit
referred to Enoch the man " who walked with God."
The Curate began his sermon " My dear brethren, I would
like to mention this most eminent pedestrian " ! and
really what else could be deduced of his habits ?

It has been said that the Irish have a way of confusing
their English, but of clarifying the truth. No doubt
the fervency of the Passionists merits them the name of
the " Passionate Fathers " and who will not think " the
indignant sick " a better description for the Charity
devoted to the Indigent Sick ?

To be reared in Ireland is to be deficient in the sense of
time. Philosophically this is a great advantage. It

used to be a serious failing on Irish railways but even so it told sometimes in favour of the traveller. How often one missed a train and discovered that the train had missed itself by a greater margin ! I shall never forget the faces of some English visitors being driven to the station at Glaslough in time to see the train pass out across the level crossing whereat Bob Weir waved his whip to the engine-driver and the train stopped and slowly moved back ! Surely there was no hurry for anyone.

My father once returned by train and was found asleep by the porters who politely took out his bags and golf-sticks but left him to sleep till the next junction. When he returned and was indignant, it was only said : " Surely no one here would put a hand on you in your sleep ! "

But they are not always so kind to those whom they find exacting or patronising. An Englishman who had taken the Rossmore shooting came to Glaslough to shoot, attended by Rossmore's old keeper, Hughey, who was by this time disgusted with him. At our best pheasant drive the visitor missed twenty-five birds in succession. Furiously he ordered a cartridge opened and it was discovered that the wicked Hughey was loading him snipe-shot ! There was a frightful outburst which Hughey met with the contemptuous words : " Sure I'm no scholard." How should he be able to read the number of the shot ? Even more contemptuous was an Irish keeper's remark to a visitor who was over proud of having dropped a high pheasant : " Surely the fall alone would have killed him " !

Annually the Monaghan Militia went into camp at Cornacassa, a small demesne near the town. The Leslies believed they were hereditary or honorary Colonels since their appearance at the battle of Ballinamuck when some French flags were taken in Ninety-eight. Great-uncle Charles had come to inspect them and died the actual day of the inspection. He gallantly crossed from England with a bad throat on a Thursday and died on Monday because no one knew how to operate for tracheotomy : an

operation which was explained to a retainer who replied :
" Would ye save a man's life by cutting his throat ? "

My father, having served at Tel-el-Kebir, made an
efficient Colonel : the last before the disbandment of
all Irish Militias. The Regiment had its incidents and
accidents. Sir Timothy O'Brien, Ireland's greatest
cricketer, was serving as a captain and once obtained
leave to attend a grandmother's funeral. It was really to
play for Middlesex at Lord's under an assumed name.
Unfortunately the Press gave him away.

On one occasion Major Tom Richardson was left man-
fully presenting arms while the whole regiment
manœuvred away from him, much to the amusement of
the visiting General.

For a month the yeomen and yahoos of the county
were drilled with the local gentry as officers. An annual
event was the baiting of the great-hearted but fiery-
tempered Major Madden, whose colossal figure could be
seen in pursuit of the diminutive Captain Richardson
running like mad between the ropes.

The troops were raw, but proved wonderful fighters
whenever they strayed into Regiments of the Line.
After the inspection there were glorious sports in which
we were allowed to course against the drummer boys.
There was one athletic competition which I have never
seen elsewhere. Large sodden buns were suspended on
cords dripping with treacle while competitors endeavoured to chew them with huge uplifted mouths. We
were not allowed to compete for fear our white sailor
suits might get sticky !

The days of the Militia are over. The flags of the Regiment hang at Glaslough and the snuff-box of the Mess
remains as an heirloom on the dining-table. The Barracks
were devoted to Belgian Refugees, and now afford an
amiable suburb called Belgian Park. *Sic Transit* as the
humorous Latinist described a rough journey on the
Irish Channel.

The squireens and buckeens have disappeared and

" stout farmers " have taken their place. They raced
horses and fought cocks on a handful of rack-rents.
The Land Acts wiped them out. One of our last
attended the Dundalk Races and told an English
officer he had made money over him. The Englishman
was delighted at the compliment and unwisely inquired
further. " Well, I had a bet you would be the first to fall
off ! " They are gone with their brag and buckaneering.
They lie embalmed in Lever's novels just as the peasantry
whom they racked and rioted with are presented in the
pages of Carleton.

The physique of the Irish peasant was still remarkable.
The labourers were stronger and wrought harder. Across
the years they seem to have been hardier and happier.
The race, which sustained so many years of famine, had
developed a wonderful power of endurance. I remember
many stories current of their feats in our neighbourhood.

The original " bog-trotters " were the runners who
carried messages or mails down to the coaching days. We
had a much loved groom, Frank Treanor, whose father was
the last in our parts to wear the traditional swallow-tail
coat. Treanor's grandfather used to run the sixteen miles
to Castleblayney and back to meet the coach with the
letters. Once he was taken by my great-grandfather into
Dublin in the course of a lawsuit. It was then found
that some important papers remained at Glaslough.
Treanor ran back from Dublin that night (60 miles) to
fetch them and caught the midday coach from Castleblayney the following day. Before he started on his run
he called for three raw eggs. He dropped one into each
shoe and swallowed the third and thus accomplished
the feat. Henceforth he was known as " Paddy of the
three eggs."

Another traditional feat followed the judgment given
by the same old Colonel Leslie when the local stone Cross
was found in Donagh Bog where it had been buried
since troublous times. The Colonel had to decide betwixt
the clans who claimed it for a headpiece to the family

grave. Donagh old graveyard was on top of a hill and he awarded it to any family who could carry it up between them. The cross weighed half a ton but a man called O'Callaghan and his sons shouldered it to the top and sank it in their grave, whence I excavated and erected it a century later.

Many memories came down from old times which the present generation have clean forgotten. There was shown a wonderful leap called " Carleton's lep " supposed to have been leaped by the celebrated novelist : a good twenty foot over rough ground.

There was Connelly, the strong man, who had thrown another man out of the bog sitting on his shovel.

And there was Kate Korny who married for a third time when she was a hundred and three years old. Old people remembered seeing her dancing in spite of her hundred years.

And there was Bartley MacAleer, whose son and grandson became Sextons of the old graveyard. At the Monaghan election of the Twenties he drew Colonel Leslie's carriage single-handed from the Court House to Gibson's Yard under fire from Lord Rossmore's rascals the whole way. The horses were too valuable to be risked and had been unharnessed and hidden.

Another story was told of Hugh McKenna who was working at the Home Farm when he heard that the price of meal was advancing. Though only ten stone himself he lifted a ten stone bag of meal from Middleton to Glenarichey, I don't know how many miles. The tradition was that not a button was left on his waistcoat —or elsewhere I should imagine.

I remember the old fiddler who though stone blind, —couldn't see a stim as they say—and over seventy, insisted on taking his left foot with his right hand and jumping through with the other !

I remember old Heatley who with his father had been rat-catchers on the estate. A penny used to be given for every tail, and I believe tails were collected from as far

as Sligo and Armagh ! Heatley had once run into Armagh
and back (22 miles) so quickly for Uncle Charles that he
was given a bottle of whisky. He used to describe the
supreme night he had spent consuming it in the Churchyard " rowling and rowling through the gravestones all
night." He used to tell us tales of his father, a retired
veteran of the Peninsular with a hooked arm. His chief
memory of that campaign was receiving thirty lashes
for stealing and eating an onion as he marched through a
field. The Iron Duke had given orders there was to be no
looting !

There was George Hearst the old carpenter, a stickler
for Holy Scriptures. Year by year I watched him going
to and from his work. When he died I wrote a memory :

THE OLD CARPENTER

Our Carpenter passed not to-day.
" Of wood the Ark was built forby man's guilt."
From Holy Book came half his say.
The children coming home from school
Will miss his wisdom on the way :
" Yon wood was good whereby the Temple stood,
For man and plank need iron rule."
Laid sick, he sent for every tool,
For saw and hammer, nails and plane :
" Though far I fare, maybe I'll need them there,"
Said he, and never passed again."

These were what O'Connell called " the finest peasantry
in the world." And so they were until consumption and
tea-poisoning took toll of their physique. They are the
only people whose food has changed sadly for the worse
in modern times. Potatoes, buttermilk and home-made
bread reared a splendid race which has been lowered by
shop bread, tinned foods and standing black tea.

The Barony of Truagh was largely inhabited by Mc-
Kennas. Kipling makes a mistake in his " Daughter of
the Regiment " by bringing McKenna from Portarlington
instead of Monaghan. McKennas have scattered over the
world : generals in South America and Chancellors in
England. I met one on the Supreme Bench of the United
States.

There was a lovely ballad called " McKenna's dream " which used to be sung in the cottages. In my quest for folk-lore I used to cultivate ballad singers and story-tellers. Those who could neither write nor read were always the best source as they relied on unspoilt memories. The old people were a simpler and wiser race. They spoke in proverbs. Even the simpletons on the road were worth talking to. John Hagley amongst them was so honest that he trudged a long walk to return a single turf he had found on the road.

The countryside was populated by characters, bad and good, but all amusing. When we shot in the deserted woods of Anketell Grove we were always joined by a voluntary beater who in professional life was a postman. He had committed every crime possible to that profession and we frequently had to vouch for him to the Post-master-General. He drank. He absconded. He opened and read letters before distribution. This was put down to the " onwee " of rural life. He had a wooden leg and drove himself about in a battered mailcart to meets and shooting parties. He had a passion for fishing and would act as a beater if there was no poaching to be done. On one occasion there was an ominous crack as he came through a wood. His wooden leg had snapped and while he sat vociferating in a ditch, his friends cut him a new leg out of the hedge, and thus accommodated with a spliced stump he continued his day. He was a poacher, a fisher-man, a anecdotist and a gossip (this depending largely on what he had last gleaned from opening letters). He was anything but a regular postman. Like several other characters in my memory he will be recorded in two books only : in my own insufficient memoirs and in the more accurate pages which fortunately cannot be published until the Last Day.

We lived more and more with the gamekeeper. Not content with every weekday, we rushed on Sundays over the hill and through the woods. We were never tired of his company during the years and we always had something to say or do together. He saw us off to school from the platform and was expected to meet us at the next station with the dogs when we returned. It was the great absorbing friendship of our youth. He retired and outlived one of us. Troubled times came again and he was found lying dead in his bed with his gun beside him. He lies in the old cemetery that hangs over the lake, not far from the House he served so well. His stone is simple :

JAMES VOGAN, LOYAL AND TRUE

Anthologists have borrowed the lines which I intended to belong to his memory only

THE DEAD GAMEKEEPER

Earth now holds him in her rooty snare
Beneath the rat-run sycamore :
Far is fur and feather from his care.
Another watcher lifts the door.
Now vermilion-fanged the vermin dare
Creep out from fosse and fen and cave :
And the wild hawks on the flowing air
Poise and pass above his grave.

Near the 'keeper's house was a hollow ash filled with hundredweights of honey. There was a gaping hole which revealed the clean comb. This postern gate was guarded by a flying squad of apian prickers. We used to run down the hill and as we passed the tree jab the comb with a long stick. At the bottom of the hill we licked the sticks dry and returned for a second course. It was a tiring but most exciting way of eating honey. It was a question of seconds whether one was stung or not.

When unengaged in digging rats, trapping hawks or devitalising rabbits in various ways, we went out with 'keepers over bog and marsh in pursuit of the elusive snipe. Jimmy was an authority on their habits and made strange calculations about full moons and red bogs which were generally right. He would sometimes lead me to a bush in a distant bog and whisper that there would be a snipe behind it. Twice he had shot two snipe at a shot and it was my ambition to do the same. But I never could bring it off until quite accidentally twenty years later at Lord Acton's in Shropshire. Having achieved this fluke I never shot snipe again.

One of the greatest of snipe-shooters often came to Glaslough to practise the art : the renowned and redoubtable Professor Mahaffy, or as he became, Sir John Pentland Mahaffy, Provost of Trinity, Dublin. He claimed to come from County Monaghan and had, though a friend of Kings and Emperors, deigned to play Sheriff amid our local grandees. How indignant he was when Lord Rossmore as Lieutenant of the County and *custos rotulorum* (whatever there may be behind that phrase) failed to meet him with javelin men at the station. His fame in scholarship needs no record. All the tales told of Doctor Whewell of Trinity, Cambridge (" the inferior College of that name ") were applied to Mahaffy. Omniscience was a bye-hobby of his genius. He was unforgiving in conversation and unforgiving in controversy.

He frequently invited himself to Glaslough for the snipe-shooting. And what marvellous company he was in the field and after the Port. He always ordered the best (" I think I remember some excellent Port here : there should still be a bottle left "— and invariably there was). He had a slight Germanised brogue. When not regaling us with his fluent conversation, he poured forth his erudition on Irish ethnology (he insisted that the mountainy people in our parts were the original Firbolgs) or on Greek literature (Sir Richard Jebb was " a vain impostor who gave what time he did not waste on his studies to the adornment of his person ") or on the German Kaiser (" my favourite Emperor ").

Of his talents he left no doubt in the mind of his hearers. He was a linguist and a musician (he was an authority on the Irish harp), a beautiful shot (he shot for Ireland with a rifle at Bisley) and he claimed to be a first-class cricketer. He bowled in matches in the Phœnix Park

and after a good but unsuccessful ball was fond of saying
loudly : " Morally bowled." When, as was sometimes
the case, he was hit to the boundary he would take time
to recover from his amazement and slowly approach the
batsman to offer his congratulations on such a boast-
worthy achievement. But snipe-shooting was the accomplishment he carried furthest into life. It was said
that the sons of Ulster gentry with a little snipe-shooting
at their disposal were never ploughed at Trinity examinations, at least not at the *viva voce* when Mahaffy could
interpolate the query : " Are the snipe in yet ? "

Once we boys were sent out sniping with the Professor,
who seldom missed more than one out of three. I saw
him fire a famous shot at a very distant bird and kill it
with the central pickle of shot. His theory was that if
you saw the white glint under the breast it was possible.
The bird dropped ahead and we paced the distance
from the spot where he fired. It was ninety paces. The
fame of this shot remained in the annals of Irish sport ; and
forty years later it was mentioned as a legend in the
Daily Express. I was able to send chapter and verse.

Another day on a small bog toward Lough Emy an
incident occurred unforgettable till death. We emerged
through some rushes and a big briar hedge. There were
partridges, a very rare bird with us, in the rushes and I
never knew that what I had shot was my first partridge.
Excitedly we pressed through the hedge and my brother's
gun went off. The Professor's clerical hat floated away
but he was uninjured. In a deathly sweat we stood
awaiting judgment. He was very typical of himself.
He never blenched but he said solemnly : " If that shot
had been half a foot lower, it would have blown half
the Greek out of Ireland ! " And he never mentioned the
subject again.

Every sportsman has fired dangerously once or twice
in a lifetime. I fired once at a duck which must have been
very close to Lord Rossmore, for I could hear old Hughey
wailing : " Watch his Lordship now ! " and when I

remarked that I had just missed the duck Hughey grimly added that I had just missed his Lordship! I then had the curious feeling that the cockles of my heart were being seasick.

It was duck-shooting that brought me nearest to shooting our beloved Jimmy Vogan. When I realised how near a thing it had been, I threw down my gun in a torrent of fury and tears. Nothing can be better for a young shooter than such an experience. I made up my mind I would never fire at a bird again unless I could see sky behind. It was a grand lesson. On the other hand Lord Wolseley, when commanding in Ireland, was actually boastful of his dangerous shooting. He always justified himself for firing down the line as he believed that the sooner young officers learnt to be under fire, the better!

If a young man made a mistake out shooting in the old days he was spoken to by some older and wiser hand. The present generation seems to have been brought up without fathers or uncles to drop upon them with the signal severity which is only needed once. This accounts for all the shooting accidents which have been hushed up since the War. England is oblivious of the escape of scandal into the Press; but dangerous shooting is kept more secret than leprosy.

The first funeral I saw was following a shooting accident. Sophy Smith's nephew blew in the back of old Hudson's coachman going through a hedge. When the funeral passed, all the morbid maids rushed out. The agent had sternly decreed that the unhappy perpetrator should follow the corpse as chief mourner. He said the countryside demanded it, but it seemed a piece of needless cruelty. Whenever we visited the Old House, where his aunt lived, the poor fellow was sitting before the fire with his head in his hands—and there he would sit for hours and hours.

Woodcock make Irish covert shooting exciting, and any man is forgiven if he takes a chance against that wilful bird. A low pheasant can always be left for the next beat. Pheasants fly over in three different ways: to

E

right, to left or straight over. The only variation lies in the height at which they fly. But I never remember shooting two woodcock in the same spot or the same way. Their flight is of an infinite variety. After thirty years I remember how individual birds came to me. I have seen them flutter like an owl or skim like a swallow. I have seen and missed one drifting like a leaf in a high wind over the top of beech trees and I have shot one slipping upward almost off my nose as straight as a geyser. Woodcock seem to have a natural instinct of humour. To watch one pass in and out of line of dumbfounded guns and finally escape with ten shots under the tail always amuses me as much as I hope it amuses the bird.

I am one of those dubious sportsmen who always enjoy watching a bird get away provided it is not wounded. An hour is not too much to devote to the search for a wounded bird. Nor could we bear to fail picking up the dead. We used to swim into the wintry Blackwater to prevent the flood carrying away a floating duck, while anxious keepers followed on the bank with our clothes. I wish I could repeat the amusing remarks which passed between Jimmy Vogan and an old Irish woman who once surprised me swimming in the vesture of Eden with a snipe between my teeth.

To return to Professor Mahaffy, who made so distinct a figure in our youth. Mahaffy was in Holy Orders but he always insisted he was not a clergyman in any obnoxious sense of the word.

He had been an inspiring tutor to the few he had picked, like Oscar Wilde or Jack Bury. When he took Wilde for a jaunt in Greece, the Aesthetic Movement was born. Mahaffy was fond, during his hostile visits to Cambridge, of threatening the startled company that he had a boy in Dublin who would one day make hares of them all! Bury eventually succeeded Lord Acton in Cambridge.

Nobody could be more entertaining when he was in

form. The American Minister Lowell expressed the great
delight he had felt in listening to him. Mahaffy's comment was : " Poor man, has he never listened to the
conversation of an Irish gentleman before ? "

The classical story of his conversational powers is also
told of Whewell, but I have traced it to Antony Malone
and the eighteenth century in that rarest of suppressed
gossip-books *The Grand Juries of West Meath*. Like
Mahaffy, Malone always held the table to the exclusion
of his Juniors who planned in desperation to introduce
a topic on which he could have no special knowledge.
They studied the subject of horse-breeding and mastered
the pedigrees from the Godolphin Arabian. To their
amazement Malone interrupted and corrected them on
points. He had had two hours notice of the trap and in
extreme haste had also mastered a new subject.

The same story used to be told of Mahaffy except that
the subject was the Ming Dynasty learnt up from a rare
anonymous pamphlet, which Mahaffy was supposed
to claim as one of his earlier writings, informing
his bewildered audience that he had changed the views
they had so studiously acquired !

I believe it was from Mahaffy that I heard the definition
of an Irish Atheist as a man who went about wishing to
God he could believe in God ! He had a very sound idea
of what a Viceroy should be in Ireland : " We have no
use for a man who does not waste both his time and his
money."

He could do anything but ride, and he knew something
about every literature except Celtic. Under the guidance
of Professor Atkinson he made the celebrated statement
that old Irish literature was " silly or obscene." This
produced a cry of wailing fury and answers from the
appropriate scholars of the time. Oddly enough it was
George Moore, who knew no more Irish than Mahaffy,
who jumped into the lists and insulted the Professor past
reconciliation.

Mahaffy used to pour mockery on the two savants

who mistook a two-year-old donkey-shed made of heaped stones in the Aran Islands for remains of grey antiquity. Nevertheless it should be recorded that Mahaffy was one of those Trinity men who approved the forgotten proposal to bring Zeuss, the greatest of Celtic Scholars, from Germany to Dublin.

He used to say there was no luck in the Gaelic and that whenever a rising scholar came to lift the language out of the dust he died young. He used to instance a young Trinity man whose name was I think Lecky. But there were others, too many who perished as soon as they were doing good work in Celtic. Perhaps this was even more so in England where we lost men like Strachan and Quiggin. Mahaffy used to say that the Irish were always fated to be forced to learn a language they did not understand. First it was Norman French. Then it was English and with the whirligig of time it became Irish again.

I was very grateful to Mahaffy for showing me the Book of Kells preserved in the Trinity Library. As a Senior Fellow he could turn the sacred pages. Angelic pens were believed to have illuminated that volume which the old Irish knew as " The Gospel of Columcille." As he turned over one page ; " observe the wealth of Qs, but the scribe was obviously tiring of his own richness." When he turned the blank page on which Queen Victoria and some minor German Royalty had been invited to write their names he observed : " Behold the quintessence of snobbery ! "

In later years Queen Victoria visited Dublin and Mahaffy was not content with passing her in the Levée but halted in the line and amiably said : " Madam, I met your grandson lately." The old dame sat stolidly stock-still looking rather like her statue in Dublin. A few minutes later the great Professor was heard to murmur in the next room : " What a disagreeable old lady ! "

It was a great shame that the other Fellows would not allow Mahaffy to succeed Dr Salmon as Provost : but they had heard him too often. Dr Traill was appointed by the

Crown to Mahaffy's intense disappointment and to the great surprise of Europe. Mahaffy told Bury he could never speak to the other Fellows again. Traill was a Cromwellian colonel devoid of grace or culture. He could not even handle a rifle as well as Mahaffy. According to Professor Tyrrell he was either a buffalo turned man or a man degenerating into buffalo, but he could never be certain which. Once the Fellows had shown themselves inimical, the Government chose Traill as a price for the Ulster vote on some difficult questions at the time. It was rather like giving the part of Hamlet to the " chucker-out " although there was an Irving available, however unpopular with his company.

Mahaffy made no bones of his opinion of the new Provost. It was even uttered aloud to Mr Birrell when seated actually beside the Provost. " Our Provost is a beast ! " he remarked, and he quickly added, seeing Birrell's embarrassment " but he is a deaf beast " !

Fortunately for the fame of Trinity Mahaffy succeeded Traill, and the University was crowned by a name that was international in learning and perfectly unique in individuality. It would have been a cruel wrong to Ireland as well as Trinity if Mahaffy had not become Provost in the end.

He was the first great conversationalist I ever heard. He could not lecture nor orate, but he could hold the cultured and the feeble-minded by the zest and fertility of his anecdotes. He had a singular power of making himself the centre of every story that he told. Out of scores I remember hearing him tell the story of the Phœnix Park murders with the curious idea added that the tragedy might have been greater, had Mahaffy himself been included ! He described the beauty of that evening in May and how he had accompanied Mr Burke and Lord Frederick Cavendish for a part of their last walk. While they walked on to their doom he had returned and left by the park gates. No one could be a better guide to Dublin than Mahaffy ; and no doubt he engaged the distinguished and newly arrived Secretary in conversation. He might so easily have continued walking with them. Perhaps Lord Frederick did not press him. Possibly poor Burke showed himself a little bored. And so Fate bade Mahaffy live to the exasperation of a few but to the delight of most. That he has no biography is a big blank in the history of Dublin.

The guest book at Glaslough made interesting reading. The great houses in Ireland practically took the place of hotels in the old days. Duchesses even had been entertained at Glaslough but always with disastrous results. One Duchess had insomnia and changed her room three times, thereupon the housekeeper made the ducal behaviour an excuse for taking to drink! Another visiting Duchess woke in the morning to find a litter of baby mice in her hair. They had been born in the night and this she said was the most curious thing to have happened to her even in Ireland!

The Eighties and Nineties were clouded in Ireland by the ever-besetting threat that Home Rule was coming. Outside the paradise of the demesne the controversy was unceasing. An early memory is of " Fighting Saunderson " passing Glaslough station on his way to open Ulster's campaign. The keen, humorous-faced Colonel and his son were met by every Unionist in the village led by my grandmother who presented him with a lovely blue and orange sprig of *Strelitzia Regina*, a gorgeous tropical plant which sometimes bloomed at Glaslough at appropriate political moments. It was admirable as a wreath upon the coffins of Protestant Archbishops or Grand Masters of the Orange Order.

Saunderson was the only country gentleman who could stand up to Gladstone, whom he heartily believed to be a Jesuit in disguise as well as a secret enemy of the Queen. He was a match for the wit of the Irish members in Parliament. Asked to give a single reason against Home Rule he quickly said " eighty " and pointed to the whole Irish Party. He said of one Irish member that he was not fit to carry guts to a bear ! Whatever this cryptic information might mean, the Speaker decided it was un-Parliamentary, so Saunderson instantly revised his meaning and said that the Honourable Member *was* fit to carry offal to a bear !

Great defenders of the Union came to Glaslough, like Michael Hicks-Beach and Stafford Northcote. Hicks Beach was Irish Secretary when he visited us. We sent him late to catch a non-existent train at some distant junction, which he recorded in humorous verses in the visitor's book. Light verse was not often recorded from " Black Michael." Poor Northcote was too gentlemanly for politics. Having served as Gladstone's secretary he could not stand up to the Terrible Old Man. This gave sting to Randolph Churchill's comparison of Northcote to the cringing Publican, while the role of Pharisee was played by Gladstone.

On one great occasion Randolph came to Belfast crying havoc and loosening the slogans of war. His famous " Ulster will fight and Ulster will be right," which some people believe altered Irish history, does not appear in his Belfast address. But he uttered the words on landing at Larne and for forty years they raged on the lips of the Ulstermen.

Home Rule split like a fissure through English and Irish life. Tories and Liberals could not meet in country houses. No Home Ruler ever crossed the threshold at Glaslough. Even the Viceroy, Lord Spencer, was not allowed to repeat his visit after he had seceded from righteousness. When he invited my grandfather to dine without informing him of the presence of Mr Gladstone, Sir John Leslie walked out and forfeited his dinner rather than sit at table with one who bore all the marks of " self-deceiving leprosy." As for Lord Spencer, when he became a Home Ruler himself, he could continue hunting the Pytchley in England : but as for coming to the North of Ireland he could go and singe his red beard in hell !

These were common sentiments in Ulster. Home Rule

became the ceaseless sickening talk. Gladstone and Salisbury were fighting their last General Election over the corpse of the Union. Schoolroom lessons could always be varied by the loyal necessity of burning the effigy of Mr Gladstone cut from the *Daily Graphic*, then the only illustrated morning paper. The rivals were pictured every day climbing the ladders of the constituencies. The very shapes of their heads and backs are glued on my memory : the wicked old serpent's head on the one side and the honest old ram butting upward on the other. Salisbury won and a lull descended upon Ireland as when snow and fog obscure the nature of a volcano.

I only once heard my grandfather make a political speech : in the course of a dreary meeting in the Monaghan Court House. I can see him standing there amid a hush of respect as the defeated champion of law and order, perfectly dressed and repeating irreproachable sentiments in a dignified and hesitating manner. Any sound of heckling or applause was instantly subdued by my grandmother with fierce looks. In the evening we adjourned to the Westenra Arms where Mary had prepared some light relief. Old Greacen brought in a large pie which opened to allow a small pig to escape and run squealing round the floor. The success of this form of social entertainment was crowned by uproarious laughter.
Practical joking played a considerable part in our lives. I grew up believing it was one of the principal occupations of the grown-up.

Life in Ireland was varied by longer periods in England. Memories remain of London, Brighton, Eastbourne, Berkhampstead in the Nineties. We used to winter sometimes in Lady Sarah Spencer's house at Berkhampstead looking over the railway and the Castle. The Castle remains and now resembles the neatly cleaned specimens in an American Museum. It was then a jungle of disorder and ivy. Outside the station there used to be a roughly

planked shed under which Lord Brownlow's carriage and
horses used to await the trains. My grandfather mourn-
fully pointed it out as one of the last privileges of the
aristocracy.

Berkhampstead was fixed in my mind by a domestic
tragedy. Frank Treanor, the favourite Irish groom, fell
from an open stairway and dashed his brains against the
cobbles. We always called him " Punch " because of his
excitement in London at the sound or sign of a Punch and
Judy show. Any ride had to be diverted to witness a
street performance. My grandfather's grief was great.
The country was scoured for a Catholic priest, who could
only be found with the greatest difficulty and naturally
could do no more than bless the corpse. Bob Weir came
over to fetch him for burial and the widow was transferred
into a lodge gate for the rest of her life. Treanor's
lodge had been called Gamble's in my infancy. Gamble
was an old man with a long white beard like Methuselah
whose duty was to ring a bell high up in a lime tree in
front of the House every day at six, at twelve and again
at six as a signal to gardeners and workmen and the
pathetic pensioners who collected the leaves that seemed
to fall for their benefit all the autumn months.

I can see the old man studying his watch to the second
—not unlike Father Time himself—his hooked nose
and bent shoulders with long wispy locks made him also
the double of General Booth. His sense of punctuality
was developed in his son who became a distinguished
station-master.

Once old Gamble halted the nursery procession and
contemplated me at great length. Then he murmured :
" One day he will be Sir John." Nurses seemed awestruck at this prophecy and wheeled me away. Gradually
it dawned upon me that everything would slowly change
and that I would grow older and that there would be a
bitter day when old Sir John would no longer be at
Glaslough.

The Beresfords

*

THERE WAS A MARRIAGE LINK BETWEEN THE LESLIES AND
the Beresfords and the result was the exciting occasional
presence of the three Beresford brothers on the horizons
of childhood : Bill, Charles and Marcus.

My great-aunt Christina Leslie had been thrown to a
wild Irish Rector, the Reverend Lord John Beresford of
Mullybrack in the County of Armagh. He was a savage
kind of Christian, but she loved him dearly in her letters.
He knocked Christina about and his brothers-in-law would
have interfered had it not been for his sudden accession
to the Marquisate of Waterford. It was felt that a
coronet covered all possible knocks. When her son Bill
in later years was banqueted after winning a V.C. he
declared that he would rather meet an army of Zulus
than his reverend father in a bad temper.

It is only fair to say that all Christina's letters reveal
her grief when separated from Lord John, for whom she
prayed and hoped a Bishopric. His uncle was reigning
Primate of Ireland. No doubt the Primate was intended
to see a letter she wrote describing service at Glaslough
in the Forties :

" Pratt performed all the duty here yesterday. He
announced the First Chapter of Proverbs for the Second
Lesson and read it through composedly. He does not
know to this moment what he did. His conduct at the
Sacrament was disgraceful. He was drawing out the cork
while the money was collecting and when it was nearly
done he shouted out the first sentence without looking at
his book, pouring out the wine all the time."

74

It is the only written record which remains to prove there was such a character as " skip-the-Litany Pratt." Otherwise I would not publish it. There was a type of Parson eccentric apparently to irreverence in those days, but they contented their people and there was no absence from Church. My father had a fantastic story of a Protestant rector who lost his flock in the old days and borrowed a congregation from a boon-companion for the occasion of the Bishop's visit. The Established Church of Ireland was very strange, but the body, which gave Swift, Berkeley and Jeremy Taylor to Ireland, was not unjustified. It also produced a succession of Beresford Bishops and Archbishops.

When the third Lord Waterford was killed hunting in 1849, Christina became a Marchioness and took her five boys to live at glorious Curraghmore. The third Lord was famous for his wild jokes and freaks of conduct which left even Jack Mytton in the shade. They sometimes alarmed the Primate, but endeared him to the Irish public. He had begun life by challenging draymen and butchers. At Eton he once ate a raw chop before fighting another boy. When the Captain of the Boats refused to allow him to man a boat exclusively with Irishmen, he resigned and proceeded to defeat Westminster with his own crew of Hibernians. He was the first to steal the Swishing Block, which has remained an heirloom at Curraghmore for over a century.

Many tales have been attributed to him but he never behaved like a cad or a coward. Certainly he often went too far ; as when he aniseeded the hoofs of a Parson's horse and hunted him with bloodhounds. It was nothing to paint the toll-bar red at Melton. He put a donkey into a stranger's bed and smashed a French clock at Crockford's with a blow of his fist. This must have been on the theory that glass hit hard enough will not cut the hand. In a leased house he shot out the eyes of the family portraits with a revolver. At Curraghmore the mouths of portraits were slit and cigars inserted. Once he fought a Dublin Jarvey, dressing himself in the Primate's gown and trencher cap, and shouting between blows : " What the Hell do you mean by overcharging my nephew ? " It was this same Primate who found the Eton Block secreted under his table and mistook it for a new kind of footstool.

Such was the riotous legend, but there was another side. To women he was all chivalry. There was the perfect knight who galloped at the Eglinton Tournament in full armour. There was the organiser against Famine, who took command and ordered the last pheasant and the last deer to be boiled into soup to save the hungry. He was an implacable hunter of " old Crafty " and while pitting his hounds against a famous grey old fox he broke his neck. A Celtic cross marks the lonely spot where he fell. He was my grandfather's great friend and he, like many others, remembered him as the grandest man they had ever known to draw breath or a fox. But how else could such a bold horseman occupy himself in the lull between Waterloo and the Charge of Balaclava ?

His death in the saddle was attributed to a curse which was due to run through six generations : and this has finished in our own time. May all good luck attend the young and eighth Marquess !

But it was remarkable that Christina's son, the fifth, shot himself following a severe hunting accident, that her grandson the sixth was accidentally drowned and that her great-grandson the seventh was also killed by accident. It is true that Beresfords seldom die in their boots, but they always had a double dose of courage.

Christina had not married into a hunting family in vain. She was provided with jewelry made entirely out of fox-teeth. Her husband being in Holy Orders was presumably immune from the curse. When he died, Christina's sons made Curraghmore their happy and adventurous home.

The new Lord Waterford saddened his life by eloping with Mrs Vivyan, the wife of a rising politician. The story can be told more charitably than in books devoted to Mayfair scandals. Christina and Charles Leslie, who was Waterford's Trustee, extracted a promise from him not to marry the lady, but the Right Honourable Mr Vivyan (and he deserved the words) sent Waterford word that he would shoot him if he did not. Waterford did what was honourable and in nine months a still-born child accompanied its mother into another world. Christina's comment was simple : " What a happy delivery ! "

Florence Lady Waterford certainly died for her love's sake. It was written of those who have loved much that they shall be forgiven ; and in her last hour came spiritual solace. She had to give up hopes of the Catholic Church in order to marry Waterford, but finding the end near she begged for a priest. Waterford fetched no less than Cardinal Manning. She died while the Cardinal and her husband were kneeling at her bedside. *Quia multum amavit.*

We used to spend Christmastimes at the Deepdene, Dorking. Here I remember Christina, a venerable old lady, chaffed to death by her adoring sons. After the death of their father they taught her to hunt by strapping her to a hunter. To improve her nerve they made her mount on the bedroom passage and ride downstairs. A photograph survives of her with all five sons equipped for the hunt.

At Deepdene the three, Bill, Charlie and Marcus, exchanged stories of the old times. They used to accuse Christina of having smacked them so often with her hair-brush that her coronet and her initials C.W. reversed had marked them for life.

Marcus was at Harrow and once visited Bill, who was at Eton, in a hired gig. After treating him very freely he drove off leaving him prostrate in the garden of a public-house to find his way back to his Tutor's. Bill was convinced that Dr Warre had once had him unjustly flogged. Bill never forgot, and in later years when he was riding through Eton with his Lancers, he remembered. The cavalry was halted while Bill rode off to give the majestic Warre his opinion of him.

Bill won a sporting V.C. in the Ulundi campaign by rescuing a wounded trooper under the approaching Zulus. The trooper refused to endanger Bill's life by mounting his horse behind him until Bill threatened to punch his head. By that time the assegais were singing in the air and a sergeant rode back to cover Bill's retreat. It was typical of Bill that he refused the V.C. unless the sergeant received the same.

In later life Bill married wealth and beauty in Lily, Duchess of Marlborough. This dear lady had married once for money, once for a title and once for love. With the Hammersley millions she repaired the roof of Blenheim and paid Bill's racing debts. The sum was the same in each case : forty thousand pounds.

Bill helped to introduce Tod Sloan, the American Jockey, to the English Turf. In the old days Jockeys rode upright on the horse's back. The idea of taking the streamline from the animal's shoulders was very novel. Whatever Bill won by ownership he lost again to gambling ; and there was an unlucky Oaks when Tod was left at the post and Bill failed to recover his losses.

Meantime they gave splendid parties for Christmas in famous " glades and galleries of Deepdene ", the palatial pile raised by Anastasius Hope, the merchant of Amsterdam, who had entertained Disraeli. Here was *Coningsby* writ, and in an underground passage cut in the hillside were housed the Hope statues. These were colossal nudities and the Duchess was properly shocked. We induced a gardener to let us into this forbidden cavern. The statues were damp and heavily draped, resembling giants drying themselves in a Turkish Bath.

For children the Deepdene afforded the wildest excitement, for the Beresfords encouraged every revolt against discipline. They once put up my brother and myself to fight each other until our noses ran blood. My brother was given a gold sovereign for winning and I was awarded another for taking it well.

The roads were still devoted to horses in the Nineties. Bill used to drive the Dorking Coach from London, and on one occasion met with an accident in a ponycart. He returned for dinner with his head stitched and bandaged. In order not to frighten his mother, she was told that he was coming down to dinner in an Indian Turban for some reason. This he wore over his bandages to the wild amusement of those who knew, but Christina never found out what was wrong. During those days the ladies were kept in laughing hysterics by the Beresford brothers. We began to suspect that life for grown-ups was one long uproarious party carried on from house to house and visit to visit. There was pheasant-shooting for the men and hockey for women and children, but always with some practical joke waiting in the background.

The women were slight and wasp-waisted, but too heavily skirted and veiled for outdoor sports. Only one of them was always taciturn and to children disagreeable, Lady Marcus Beresford. It was whispered of her that she had three living husbands. This was so rare and terrible in Victorian Society that Deepdene was the only country house left open to her. The Beresford trio married chivalrously but left no sons, though Bill's Duchess unexpectedly produced a boy in Jubilee year, 1897. We were much impressed on hearing that it was washed in a silver tub and spoon-fed with brandy.

The jests of the Beresfords could not all be recorded by the staid historian. Memoirs and the Press repeat monotonously some of Charlie's feats and wagers. Every publishing season tells how he won a bet to drive a carriage down Rotten Row. It is well known that he bribed the driver of the official watercart to lend him his place on the box. A more difficult feat was riding a pig down Park

Lane. There was an honest downright simplicity about
Victorian humour. A pig is a most difficult but violent
mount. Even more astonishing was the wager he won to
walk from Hyde Park Corner to White's without a
stitch on his person. This he achieved by slowly, but
nakedly, walking inside a four-wheeler with the floor
knocked out and the windows pasted over.

Charlie performed public service by driving off with a
toll-bar near Portsmouth and solemnly burning it on a
warship. His quaintest achievement was a famous
tattoo dating from Malta days. He had the Waterford
Hounds tattoed in full cry down his back with the brush
of the fox disappearing where it should disappear.

No family funeral could be dull with the Beresfords
present. Uncle Tom Leslie had married the heiress of
Scriven, in Yorkshire, and taken the name of Slingsby.
When she died, the Beresfords and Leslies, whom she had
always excluded from a visit, arrived at Knaresborough
and the driver of the hearse was made tipsy. As a
result he drove with his top-hat the wrong way round and
a long crape weeper floating over his face. Apparently
he mistook it for an insect and kept snatching it. Finally
the Beresfords took the reins and the horses learnt what
it was to be tooled by first-class drivers.

The end for Deepdene festivities came in 1900. The
annual Saturnalia were suddenly postponed and to our
endless grief Bill died during Christmas Week.

It was thirty-five years later that chance took me to
Deepdene, since converted into a country hotel. I know
no passage in literature describing the curious ghost-like
feeling which exudes from an old and Stately Home of
England after it has gone down in the world. I wandered
through the corridors and gardens which I could people
out of the past. A bye-road had been cut through the
hillside. There was nothing left save the famous Tulip
tree, the corner in which the Duchess sank her silver bath
and a copy of the picture of the Assumption which had
been in the Hope Collection. A weird subconscious

thrill comes on revisiting a home unseen for so many years. For a moment there is a feeling of rejuvenescence like a little flame which falls back into ashes. If a quarter of a century can pass so quickly, why not a half-century—and all be the same in a hundred years ? To be a survivor of all the gay crowds who filled those walls ! Who remembers now the Beresfords and all their wild humours ? Who ever spent such Christmases as we did ? I began to feel the painless agonies of a ghost : the recapture of hours when the soul had no pangs and the young body no pains.

What are the ethics of practical joking ? It has certainly become a discountenanced pastime. It is no longer thought amusing to call out a Fire Brigade on a false call or to send a man batting in a cricket match a message purporting that his mother-in-law is dead.

Yet there were many which were worth doing and they have made legend. A good practical joke should be perfectly original, harmless to everyone concerned, making only those who deserve it look ridiculous, and of course it should be unrepeatable. No more delightful moment than the excitement which Claude Lowther staged at a Covent Garden ball. He was suddenly seen by the auditorium engaged in fisticuffs with a dummy made to resemble Sir Augustus Harris, which to everyone's horror he finally knocked out of the box !

Country houses were devoted to practical jokes verging almost to Bedlam. There was a noble pile in the South of Ireland, long since dismantled, where simple English guests were bewildered by a succession of booby-traps and synthetic jokes which took the place of cards or conversation. The guests once included the pompous but well-behaved Prince Christian. There were practical jokes all day, but to save the Royal countenance the whole party were drawn up once every evening and made to give him elaborate bows and curtseys.

Practical joking flourished at Glaslough in old days.

F

On one occasion the party had set trimmers for pike in the lake. Charlie Beresford took the trouble to row out during the night and fasten sardine boxes and kettles full of stones to every line.

Marcus' jokes were more subtle. Once he disguised himself as the Duke of Portland and invited a tipsy bounder at some races to stay with him at Welbeck for Doncaster Week. Marcus was the wit of the family. Frenchmen of the ancient days might have been proud of some of his flashes, especially as they came without premeditation. At Highcliffe Castle he was once shown a very short camp-bed which was supposed to have contained Marshal Ney. His comment was simply : " It must have been a *nez retroussé.*"

He delighted King Edward VII, whose horses he used to train and whose early motoring perils he used to share. Sometimes his sallies exceeded the mark, or shall we say himself ? When the King was anxious to show someone a special sign of disfavour Marcus suggested : " Give him the Victorian Order." On a bounder who had been raised to the Peerage he suggested : " Why not fire him on the Coronet ? " Another unwanted individual complained that he had been offered £500 to take his name off the Turf Club. What was he to do ? Marcus advised him to sit tight as they were sure to make it a thousand !

The reckless Beresfords sometimes came into conflict with the sedater Leslies. Once they took off half the knockers in Berkeley Square before they were arrested by the police. Bill promptly gave his name as " Mr John Leslie, M.P., of Stratford House, Stratford Place." As a result my poor grandfather had to write to *The Times* to explain that he was not the culprit. My grandmother was too indignant ever to forgive Bill.

The Beresfords much disapproved of the meanness of one of their aunts, Penelope Leslie, who married George Cavendish Bentinck. They made this felt when they attended Sunday lunch where there was a bare sufficiency provided for guests. Charlie was fond of bringing a favourite bulldog and throwing it the joint before anyone could be helped. Another day, because Aunt Penelope would not pay her share of the cab, they carried off in a hilarious mood the marble bust of their pompous and parsimonious host to Pratt's Club where they left it with moustaches painted on the cheeks.

At a family ball they were deputed to remain outside and help the guests. Aunt Penelope came along with her sweet daughter, but stood so long dawdling on the steps that the boys lost patience, picked them both up, hurled them into their carriage, and after throwing in the link-boy with his torch alight, slammed the door and ordered the carriage off ! Aunt Penelope's dress was fired and she sent in a bill for damages. All the celebrated stories of meanness were attributed to Aunt Penelope at the time, including one that she furnished her dinner table with flowers which she had snatched while attending a funeral earlier in the day ! But I think this was impossible.

Her brother, " old Sir John," was the incarnation of generosity ; but the two streaks descend side by side in the family. I have often surprised myself in acts and intentions of unconscious meanness. I believe it is a hereditary disease like gout.

Charlie Beresford being in the Navy was not much seen until his latter years in Parliament. Jimmy the game-keeper remembered his days of leave at Glaslough. On one occasion he was taken out snipe-shooting on McQuade's Bog. He sank to his armpits trying to cross that celebrated quagmire. Charlie's newly acquired naval language was such that the 'keepers stood convulsed with laughter and shaking like the bog itself before they rescued him.

In my childhood he returned as a sea captain with Lady Charles. She was an extraordinary old girl supposed to be a relative of the King of Würtemberg. In later days Mary Crawshay called them " The Red Admiral and the Painted Lady." She was very picturesque, and Charlie spoke of her as his little pinnace with a new coat of paint on !

After luncheon we were brought down to receive those oddments of desert such as broken biscuits, ginger and sugar lumps dissolving in the dregs of coffee, which for some reason were thought suitable to childish digestion. My brother and I were rewarded by my grandfather for solemnly saying : " I am a fine child, but a stupid child." We did not know what this meant, but it always amused the guests.

I made a sad social mistake the first time I saw Mina Beresford's fantastic face hover over me. I perceived what I thought a butterfly fluttering in the draught and with chubby fingers I grasped and dislodged an eyebrow. I was led from the room.

Charlie returned once to visit his father's old rectory in Armagh. He remembered that whenever he fell off his pony, his father thrashed him with orders not to remount until he had learnt to ride !

There was a sheaf of stories told about Charlie. In those days personality did not tell against a career in the Navy. He carried his high spirits into the gunroom. There was one story which immediately sealed him as a hero in our eyes. In some remote West Indian cathedral hung a tattered English ensign captured from Nelson in his youth. This trophy was stolen by Charlie and his friends, but returned thereafter by the authorities. At the bombardment of Alexandria he saw his opportunity to push his gunboat under the elevation of the guns in the fort. The flagship signalled the famous compliment : " Well done, *Condor !* "

He had been one of the three most popular men in England. At one General Election no less than twenty Conservative seats were offered him. With all the advantages he enjoyed in the Navy, in the House and in Society he never came to greatness. The Great War found him too old to command a fleet. His nearest chance to make history came in 1905 when he cleared his decks for action and prepared to intercept the Russian Fleet after it had fired on the Hull fishing boats.

In Society he was a lion sought everywhere until the Prince of Wales (Edward VII) ordained that he should be cut. Wild rumours passed that they had met in the boudoir of a lady they both admired and that Charlie had refused to withdraw and even knocked his rival down. The truth was that he had pushed the Prince, who dropped into a sofa murmuring : " Really, Lord Charles, you forget yourself." That was Charlie's version. The courtiers, of course, told another. They became friends again and their relations must have been very good ; for Charlie permitted himself to send the Prince one of the few truthful refusals ever sent, the celebrated telegram : " Regret cannot come. Lie follows by Post."

As King, Charlie received his full confidence. Indeed if the King had had his way Charlie would have become a Prime Minister. After Salisbury's death and Balfour's weaknesses there was a moment when Charlie saw his destiny coming. He left Malta and said good-bye to the Fleet under the conviction that he would be called upon to form a Cabinet. But the incident remains obscure.

The Beresfords must always be a puzzle to students of heredity. A mixture of roisterers and heroes on one side with a fine ecclesiastical streak on the other. The two best Primates of the nineteenth century were both Beresfords and reigned magnificently in Armagh. Old people still remember the old Primate, Lord John, going up to the Temple of God on the heights of Armagh in a coach and four horses.

He deserves his sleep in a marble tomb in the Cathedral for he bought back the Book of Armagh for Armagh and encased the old Cathedral in solid stone.

Primate Lord Marcus died in the year of my birth, but he used to come over to Glaslough and was very interested in the stuffed Great Northern Diver which had been shot on the lake. His quaint accent was a tradition—" Howtcher do ? "

He wrote a stirring Orange ballad which has never
been published.   He suffered disestablishment in his day
and avenged himself with an epigram recorded in the
Glaslough Scrap Book :

> " Gladstone, ambitious of his own renown,
> A Temple raises and a Church pulls down :
> The Church was Christ's, the other 'tis not known
> What God or Demon claims him for his own."

The reference was to his colleague, Archbishop Temple,
whom Gladstone had made a bishop in spite of his heresy.

Lord Marcus was a great old dear and did not deserve
the stings of fate, such as being turned out of the House
of Lords in his old days.   On a grim day my aunts went
to lunch at the Palace in Armagh.   During the meal the
chandelier began to wag above the table, which puzzled
the Primate very much.   Mary suggested the nursemaid
was dancing a jig upstairs.   Alas—the Primate's daughter
had hung herself and the vibration was caused by the
efforts of the servants to cut her down.

Stratford House

*

By ITS NAME STRATFORD HOUSE MIGHT SEEM ONE OF
the destroyed mansions of London which the twentieth
century has thrown to the house-breaker. As a matter of
fact it is one of the half-dozen survivors. It has been
camouflaged as Derby House, but Stratford House it was
when my grandfather inhabited its unhygienic splendours.

I have to presume that my family have been going
down in the London world. My great grandmother
old Mrs Leslie lived in Berkeley Square. To her great
credit (according to Ralph Nevill) she once saved the
immense plane-trees which with the fountain nymph
will soon be all that remains of that fine eighteenth-century
Square. What matter! The domestic treasures of that
enlightened and artistic century can supply the demand
made by lighter pleasures and heavier taxes.

My grandfather passed across Oxford Street (for long
the Social Rubicon) down Stratford Place and lodged
himself in that *cul-de-sac* which contains one of the lesser
glories of London architecture.

My parents held out later for a generation in Great
Cumberland Place. My own generation has retreated
to a flat in St John's Wood, a quarter which has become
respectable in the memory of man. It used to be a haunt
of well-kept Cyprians, to use the Victorian verbiage. As
it was also the home of cricket it could be neatly summed
as the indigenous quarter for " Lords " and " Ladies "
in the restricted senses of the words.

To return to Stratford Place days, the house was fantastic. It was all Adams within and Greek classical

without from Flaxman's designs. It was built by the
Lord Aldborough who built Aldborough House in Dublin
and gave Amiens Street its name from happy connections
with that cathedral city and not from the Peace of that
name.

The peerage is extinct, but the two great mansions
remain. One is a store-house in Dublin and the other
invites demolition to allow a pass out of Oxford Street.

Oddly enough the " New River " once passed under the
house before proceeding underground to Conduit Street.
The owner of Stratford House still owns the centre road
going down Stratford Place for that reason. My grandfather remembered when the water came to the surface
in Lower Brook Street and was crossed by splashing
carriages in front of the Guard's Club. The site of the
house had been the Lord Mayor's fishing cottage, and
the Corporation were the landlords. Archæologists must
investigate where the aldermen threw fly and worm into
the current.

The house was incredible and, as such houses will soon
be forgotten in the past, it deserves description.

It was originally built on wooden piles in the manner of
a Venetian Palace. Two successive owners have had to
restore the entire foundations.

The front of the house was built upon columns which
supported the only pediment known on a private London
dwelling. I never could decipher the mythology of the
statuary, but believe it contained the Aldboro Supporters.
The stonework was veneer rather than solid. On either
side stretched a colonade behind which were kitchens
and stables. Round the top of the house was a stone
balcony and there were heavy stone stairs but insufficient
to keep the foundations quiet in the river bed.

No one has, unfortunately, written the history of the
great London Houses. Whole streets are perishing in
which every house had its memories, romances, tragedies,
follies, names, ghosts. Flats will yield no more history
than the hotels in railway stations. Stratford House

was inhabited in man's memory by the blind Lady Anne
Beckett, who left her hand-railing round the back garden.
She was Lord Randolph Churchill's godmother ; and when
she died one of the last hatchments seen in London was
hung over the portals. Hatchments are the lozenge-
shaped coats of arms which are found hanging in churches
with " Resurgam " instead of the owner's motto. Each
is the relic of a Victorian funeral. Stratford House was
left to George Bentinck, but my grandfather telegraphed
and bought the lease. The horses and the young Miss
Leslies were brought over from Ireland for the season.
My aunts could ride their ponies through the colonnade
and over the pavement into the street.

It was absurdly magnificent and uncomfortable within.
There was a big hall with a huge stuffed chair in which
generations of porters had slumbered. I remember
a full-sized plaster statue of the Venus de Milo blackened
by many fogs and a perfect advertisement for Mr Pears to
exhibit as the state of ladies before the invention of his
famous soap. From the open front-door one looked into
a horse-scented and horse-trafficking Oxford Street. On
either side of the entry into Stratford Place were brick
sentry-boxes surmounted by Adams' best lions. Lilley
and Skinner have since displaced one of the lions by making
an extension which has left Stratford Place lopsided and
it will be a mercy if the other lion is added to the destroyed
landmarks of London. In due time the Capital will be
architecturally worthy of a nation of shopkeepers !

Within the house a great Y-shaped staircase branched
to either side of the balconied landings which led into
drawing rooms. The whole house was sacrificed to these
enormous vistas. It was of them that Disraeli said to
please my grandmother : " What perspective ! What
perspective ! "

She had stood once on the top of the stairs to receive
Disraeli at a Conservative reception. In his honour she
sent to Paris for a red velvet dress which immediately

caught his eye. Fixing her through his famous eye-glass
he approached her slowly and after stroking her dress :
" From Damascus I presume ? " he observed : " this
must be *cramoisi*. All my life I have wished to see
cramoisi." And uttered no more.

The ceilings in drawing- and dining-rooms were by
Angelica Kauffmann and the chimney pieces were such as
only Adams could conceive or construct for the English
aristocracy. But within and apart from the stains of
gas and fog it was filth and corruption like the whited
sepulchres which gave Our Lord so memorable a metaphor.
The " New River " had been used to fill an open cesspool
which fumed the house and strange to say never caused
the least malady.

My grandfather rejoiced in the old sanitation and was
offended when Murray Guthrie (who subsequently bought
the house) asked permission to cover the cesspool at his
own expense for fear his prospective bride should die of
typhoid !

It will interest the votaries of modern plumbing to know
that so considerable a house contained only two *garde-
robes :* one for gentlemen, windowless, under the stairs.
and one for ladies which let into the servants' bedrooms.
The footmen slept in the servants' hall.

The kitchens were out of doors and contained the only
hot-water tap on the establishment. A stream of housemaids supplied with unending cans every hot bath taken
by the family. Upstairs there was a single sink from
which proceeded a chilly bilge. Owing to the lack of a
decent bedroom two of my brothers had to be born in the
drawing-room !

At the back was a grimy garden with half a dozen lilac
bushes and fig-trees which, however much they strove to
fig, could never deliver their wooden wombs of a single
fruit. Herein the blind Lady Anne had tottered around
of an evening.

The stables were pervaded by a comparatively healthy
odour. They accommodated chickens as well as horses

since my grandmother liked her eggs fresh. Once my mother went driving and discovered that a hen had laid in the Sociable. Such was London life in the Eighties!

But let me transcribe Augustus Hare's picture from his diaries :

" Called on Mrs Leslie in her glorious old house in Stratford Place which is beautiful because all the colour is subdued, no new gilding or smartness. She herself sat in the window embroidering with the bright sunlight just glinting on her rippled hair and sweet face at once a picture and a poem."

It sounds like a Pre-Raphaelite picture.

Behind the Lady Bountiful she had a very good heart. She introduced a system (noted in the Press) for supplying coachmen and footmen with hot tea at night while their employers danced or listened to Joachim and Rubinstein in Stratford House. She lived in the atmosphere of Dizzy's novel *Endymion*, most of whose charaters she had known.

Unlike most London streets all the neighbours in Stratford Place knew each other, watched each other and gathered each other's gossip. This is inevitable in a cul-de-sac. Stratford Place must once have been well worth living in. There had been Edward Lear the Nonsense writer for one, when he was staying in England. In one house the Chevalier Delanges was always painting, but his failure at the Academy was attributed by my grandfather to his use of gas light. He was succeeded by the Sirdar Lord Grenfell with a museum of Egyptian treasures which we were taken to visit as children. Here I first heard the legend of General Gordon.

The Place was also inhabited by the beautiful Lady Alresford whom the Prince of Wales came to visit most afternoons in his private hansom cab. Later she caused chivalrous dispute between the Prince and the Churchill family. Further down lived Lord Rosslyn with his surprising collection of daughters and step-daughters

all in the first rank of beauties. There was also Lord
Bective, who could never manage to take the sharp turn
into Oxford Street with his four-in-hand. To my grandfather's derision he used to start with two horses harnessed
to the coach while grooms rode the leaders to Marble
Arch where they were hitched to the wheelers.

One priest only was ever admitted to Stratford House,
Father James Healy the Irish wit. Once he called and my
grandmother did not like to explain that her husband
was away in Ireland presiding over an Orange meeting.
Father Healy remembered the date, July 12, and suddenly
said : " Oh I can be colour-blind where my friends are
concerned ! "

My grandfather naturally was very proud of living in
a house with a real pediment. I can see him standing by
the window admiring the Philippo Lippis he had bought
in Italy. He wore pearl-grey clothes with a white top-hat
and a bright-red carnation. His strictness in dress was
a memory of d'Orsay whom he had known as a young
man. He had even shared a " tiger " or diminutive groom
with him.

He was a very lovable old man, with a mop of silvery
hair. I was fond of sitting with him after lunch or dinner
while he broke up big water-biscuits and discovered human
faced in the clipped edges. He believed that much of the
Book of Revelation had been fulfilled in his own time,
especially in 1870 when the Pope lost his temporal power.
His memory was brighter on the other side of the Crimean
War. After the port we used to try him with names we
had read about.

When we first heard Harriet Wilson mentioned, we
asked him who she was. His old eyes flickered and he
raised his shoulders. We laughed immoderately when
he said : " Do you mean a lady of ill-fame ? " If he
had not known her, he had known the generation which
had. It was astonishing the number of famous people
whom he had seen in the past : Wordsworth, Talleyrand,
Rossini, O'Connell, Louis Napoleon and Sir Walter Scott.

Louis Napoleon he remembered as a vagrant when he haunted St James's Street. He described him as far too gloomy for a Frenchman even though he was very down in his market. To keep on good terms with his English hosts he was always ready to talk sport which he detested. His political schemes were always in the background and he sometimes flashed through the gloom with a prophetic threat to reach the Tuileries yet. My grandfather attended the great review he gave as Emperor in 1867 in the presence of the Emperor Francis Joseph.

My grandfather had been in Paris during the Revolution of 1848 and witnessed the sack of the Tuileries, which I can hear him vividly describing. Furniture and brocades were being hurled out of the windows. When he returned to England he met Louis Philippe strutting through Hyde Park very like a fat *maître d'hôtel* out of his job. He would have done better as a Minister in a republic than as *le roi des Français*, which was apparently more democratic than being *roi de France*.

He remembered all the three adventurers in the Forties : Louis Napoleon, d'Orsay and Disraeli when they were glad of a little hospitality and had not yet thrown dice with the goddess whose iron feet dance the Wheel of Life. He himself was a good spectator in a good seat through the whole Victorian interlude. The social trouble with Dizzy and Louis Napoleon was that London would not take them for gentlemen. But d'Orsay, who had fought a duel solely for the honour of the Blessed Virgin, belonged to the Age of Chivalry.

What a wonderful " Imaginary Conversation " Landor could have built up by imagining these three playboys of Europe in the London of the Forties discussing their hopes and futures. At one time d'Orsay must have seemed the most hopeful of the three. Little could my grandfather have dreamed that the seedy bright-eyed Semite, who took the Parliamentary oath " on the honour of a Christian," would one day make him a baronet in the name of the Conservative Party.

In the game of writing truthful epitaphs for the great I once scribbled one for Dizzy.

" He made Queen Victoria an empress and Abercorn a duke. He also conferred a baronetcy upon the House of Leslie of Glaslough ! "

I need not enlarge on the grievances of the Order of Baronets. A duke has been pleased to describe baronets as the middle classes ! Contrary to the initial promises of King James baronets are continually denied supporters to their arms. This leaves them in a dubious position between peers and plebs. Neither the College of Heralds nor the League of Nations in its very varied activities seems interested in our plight. I am afraid our precedence at Court is not as it should be. As the eldest son of a baronet I found I was officially placed between Masters in Lunacy and the Fifth Class of the Victorian Order ! According to Burke's Peerage my " relative rank " is number 84,752. This is really disappointing and I prefer to abstain from Court.

Yet Judge Ashton in his book of memoirs says truly that there are only two real distinctions in England : Firstly : Single colours registered for Racing. Secondly : a Nova Scotia baronetcy.

I believe entry into the Order is now purchasable, but my grandfather only paid the fees. He was very surprised at his elevation, which he modestly attributed to his deceased brother's political and agricultural successes. He was distrustful of all changes, even of himself into a baronet. He lived to see some sad changes in the rights of Irish property, in the conduct of the House of Commons and in the game of cricket. He lived to be the senior member of the M.C.C. but he left the ground with indignation the first time he saw a batsman credited with a boundary hit for four without having to run it out. To his sporting mind a run was a run. He himself had played cricket at Oxford in a top-hat. There was a legend often

printed that he was the original of " Colonel Newcome."
The dates would not fit so pleasing an attribution, but I
think it was due to Thackeray's once remarking how
much Mr John Leslie resembled that creation of his
pen.

Some people collect postage stamps, others autographs,
and I believe I have read of a collection of echoes. I have
always noted down what are called links with the past.
They originated in the mind of Horace Walpole who liked
to recall that he had seen a mistress of James II and
attended the funeral of Marlborough. They give a pro-
found idea how a few lives can bridge the centuries. My
grandfather was such a link incarnate.

When he was a schoolboy he had crossed tracks with
Sir Francis Macnaghten of Bushmills, whose father as a
boy of ten had passed through the siege of Derry. Another
stretch with the past I derived from Dr Alexander who
had been Bishop of Derry. He told me that his father
had seen the body of the last wolf killed in Ireland
brought in from the Barnesmore mountains in Donegal.

As a débutante my grandmother danced with the
ninth Lord Huntly, when over ninety, because he could
boast of having danced with Marie Antoinette before the
French Revolution.

My Uncle Moreton's father, old Mr Frewen of Brickwall
Northiam who died in 1870, remembered his elderly
father who had seen the old housekeeper at Woollaton
Hall when she was well into her hundreds. She remem-
bered as a small girl seeing Cromwell come in after the
Battle of Naseby and kneel to say his prayers.

The most remarkable series of links with the past could
be recorded of the fourth Lord Lansdowne if he had really
heard old Sir Edward Bayntoun speak of his friend Sir
Stephen Fox, who had been officer on guard at the
execution of King Charles. Sir Stephen Fox was
acquainted with old Lady Dacre who had been a friend
of the ancient Countess of Desmond, who had danced a
corambo with King Richard III.

Of this Lord Lansdowne Thackeray drew (according to my grandmother) a wicked caricature in *Vanity Fair*. It was unmistakably Lord Lansdowne but it was labelled the " Marquis of Steyne " who was Thackeray's replica of the wicked Lord Hertford. As Hertford was dead when the novel was published, the plate was probably suppressed in deference to Lord Lansdowne. This is the solution of the bibliographical puzzle.

My father having attained eighty in 1937 has also some links to his memory. He recalled his nurse's grief for the death of the Prince Consort in 1861, and the wedding procession of Edward VII and Queen Alexandra in 1863 (In 1893 I watched the wedding troop of George V and Queen Mary from a balcony in Piccadilly.) My father remembers the spikes for traitors' heads on Temple Bar, and seeing Napoleon's last veterans from the Invalides decorating the Vendôme Column in 1870 for the last time before the fall of the dynasty.

Links with the past give the restless mind a halting place. Can a generation pass so quickly ? Has one only to live to eighty or even fifty to become a mark by which others can measure the passage of historical time ?

I often used to sound my grandfather and see how far I could plumb the past. His earliest memories were of fires. While his mother lived in Upper Harley Street he witnessed across the street the conflagration which took the life of the third Lord Walsingham while his wife only survived him by a few hours (April 26, 1831). This he described to me after eighty years, a seventh Lord Walsingham having since succeeded to the title. A few years later in 1834 he witnessed the famous fire which destroyed the old Houses of Parliament. The red glow he saw from the top of Dr Longley's at Harrow.

Longley, who afterwards became Archbishop of Canterbury, was succeeded by a son of the poet Wordsworth. This gave my grandfather the chance of meeting and conversing with the Laureate on a visit to Harrow. Other distinguished Harrovians he remembered, such as Drury

(Byron's tutor) Faber and Manning, later " ornaments of the Roman persuasion."

He was preceded at Harrow by his cousin and namesake, John Leslie, who became Head of the school and captain of cricket. He was obviously too good for this world and became an " Archangel " while yet on earth in the Irvingite Church.

My grandfather's fag-master was Sir William Gregory, and his fag the eccentric Sir Tatton Sykes, to whom he presented his first toothbrush. Sir Tatton later married his niece, Jessica Bentinck.

He kept a very clear memory of the abominable cruelties at English public schools at that time. Anthony Trollope and Augustus Hare bore the same testimony of their Harrow days. Fags were roasted at fires till they fainted. My grandfather was sent to Harrow from Ireland, coaching on both sides of the Channel. He sat on top of the coach and in spite of the winter's season he was not provided with an overcoat. There was no Tubular Bridge over the Menai Straits across which he had to ferry ! Certainly he developed an iron constitution.

But he remembered some happy days as the day he ran away to see the Derby of 1839 and saw " Bloomsbury " win from between the legs of the crowd. This was the year when Fuller Craven unsuccessfully objected to the winner with " Deception." The happiest days were the last of term when the boys used to race hired chaises down the Harrow Road to the Marble Arch. The boy who hired a postilion called Newman, from the King's Head, generally won this forgotten contest.

He once attended the swishing of another boy wearing wicket-keeper gloves out of bravado. He was turned down himself ! He remembered a master called Drury who was a wit. When a boy called Long crawled unseen under Drury's desk, the master noticing which boy was missing, delivered a kick under the desk with the words : " Man needs but little nor wants that little long ! "

He never forgot his Harrow sufferings, and sent his

G

own boy to Eton. A curious incident happened. When he lodged my father at Miss Gulliver's he took him in search of his tutor, Mr Leslie Cameron. When they had been introduced Mr Cameron remarked : " I think I have met you before as you were tutored privately by my father. In fact I am your godson."

He used to show us the white scar on his hand, the result of grasping a poker which was offered to him after the redness, but not the heat, had died down. He lived to become the oldest Harrovian by seniority, although not by years : a senile honour which went to the seventh Duke of Grafton who managed to outlive him and even survived the Great War by a few days.

At Oxford he remembered being warned by his tutor against listening to Newman and was sent down, for sharing in a rag, by Dean Gaisford. It was for something as simple as throwing all the lamps of the Quad at Christ Church into " Mercury." At Oxford he rode hard and appreciated the Fancy. He never missed a good prize fight and with the late Field Marshal Lord Grenfell was the last to remember the greatest of fights : the encounter between Sayers, the Game Chicken, and Heenan, the American Champion. He saw the ropes being cut to save Sayers' life when his blinded adversary had caught him in Chancery and was slowly breaking him up. The fight caused bitterer feeling than all the yacht races between England and America since.

After the Irish Famine his estate in Donegal failed him and he retired from the Life Guards, of which he lived to be the doyen or oldest surviving officer. He studied painting in the Black Forest in Germany under the Düsseldorf School. He painted a picture of some German children which was exhibited at the Royal Academy and drew the attention of the Prince Consort, who wrote him a complimentary letter. It was also noticed by a Waterloo veteran, a Colonel George Dawson-Damer, who pointed it out to his daughter, the future wife of the artist.

In the same year he won the Military Grand Steeple-chase on his own horse at Leamington.   He combined his love for the horse with a love for the palette.   The brush of the fox was not his only pursuit.   At Newport Lodge, Melton, he painted a famous fresco of the Belvoir Hunt in the early fifties with the famous riders of the day in full cry : Mr Little Gilmore, Lord Forester, the Duke of Rutland, the second and the fourth earls of Wilton, Lord Bradford and Sir Richard Sutton.   In years to come Moreton Frewen contemplated this ancient hunt and wrote in his own clinking style :

" Of the twelve apostles in that Belvoir apocalypse only their delineator survives to look out upon his work. The other eleven, how inexorably their stumps are scattered by that fine bowler Time ! Still protect your wicket, gallant Sir John, albeit the bowling is ever more accurate and the bowler's pace more terrific still.   Just one good hit to the boundary for six and up goes your century on a really fine innings."

He failed to realise himself amongst the centurions, but his linkage with the past was secure.   He reached the centenary of Waterloo and remembered his father who had been born in 1769, the same year as Napoleon and Wellington.

He carried his love of Art into friendship with many artists.   He was Landseer's closest friend and saw him through all the public disputes which followed the appearance of Landseer's lions in Trafalgar Square.   An amusing incident occurred in the regiment owing to his close knowledge of Landseer's technique. A fellow-officer, Graham, owned and prized a stag drawn by Landseer. For this artistic feeling he was much chaffed by other officers who stole the original and persuaded my grand-father to replace it by a copy.   Unfortunately the copy was good enough to deceive the owner, who refused to

exchange it even when the joke had been explained to
him. As a result the original still hangs at Glaslough.

His later artistic friends included Millais and Watts.
When Watts decided to marry Ellen Terry he wrote my
grandmother a charming letter in 1862 :

" Knowing how much you are interested in the Miss
Terrys I am going to tell you a thing that will perhaps
surprise you. I have determined to remove the
youngest from the temptations and abominations of
the Stage, give her an education and if she continues
to have the affection she now feels for me, marry her.
There is a great difference between her age and mine
and I shall not think of putting any pressure upon her
inclinations, but I think whatever the future brings, I
can hardly regret taking the poor child out of her present
life and fitting her for a better. I hope in what I have
undertaken to do, I shall have the countenance of my
friends, for it is no light matter from any point of view.
Even the expense will be considerable, as I shall have
to compensate her family for loss of her services. If
you and any others, whose opinion may be valued,
think well of my object, I would be very glad if you
would tell Mrs Prinsep and her family, for you know
the prejudice that is against the Stage. (I have it
myself). Miss Terry is very young and I do not see the
future at all distinctly but giving her a chance of
qualifying herself for a good position in true Society I
do not think I ought to be thought ill of.

" Yours most sincerely Signor.

" To make the poor child what I wish her to be will
take a long time and most likely cost a great deal of
trouble ; and I shall want the sympathy of all my
friends, so I hope none will look coldly on my
endeavours."

The marriage never lasted, indeed was never consum-
mated and later an official Mrs Watts arrived to take

her place. Never was so ludicrous an effort of Victorian prudery to remove a great artist from the stage. In later years, half a century later, Ellen Terry was going to America and was not feeling sure she would return, so she wrote to my grandmother bidding her carry her devotion to the dear " Signor " and to tell him what a beautiful influence he had been in her life.

More interesting than the painters whom Boo entertained when she first lived in London were the writers. First editions of Dickens and Thackeray with autograph invitations and inscribed envelopes figured in her collection. Thackeray was to have dined with her the last night of his life and his exquisite letter of refusal was the last effort of his pen. Busy novelists had little time to dispose to eager young hostesses and her real friendships were made with their daughters. Through their acquaintance she purveyed rather beautiful versions of their fathers' love-affairs. Apparently " Dickens brought home a beautiful girl to live with his daughters. He told them he had saved her from ruin (which was probably the case) after a while he found he had fallen in love with her and had to place her elsewhere, which he did."

Thackeray's love affair with Mrs Brookfield was more platonic and was translated into the most beautiful love-letters in the language—but how many living have ever read them ? It was one of those soul-marriages which may have commenced on earth but can only be concluded in Heaven.

I learnt that Dickens had no fixed beliefs, although he practically restored Christmas to England.

He did not care for Church but he could not abide what was blasphemous. I once heard one of his daughters make the quaintest criticism. She said that the great qualification to be a Dickensian was a lack of humour. This struck me as a proper reason for his enormous appeal to the English.

I have only met two real Dickensians in my life : Dr

James, the late Provost of Eton, and the late Sir Mark
Sykes. Both could pass an immediate examination
giving chapter and verse for any character or scene
or for any characteristic quotation in the novels. To
hear them examining each other on remote points in
Dickens was like hearing Peter borrowing from Paul or
Athanasius catechizing Jerome !

The friendship with Ellen Terry was lifelong and I
never felt shyer than as a schoolboy hearing my
grandmother sustain Ellen Terry through a rehearsal by
chirruping her delight from the stalls.

All her Victorian memories were not so golden. There
was a very black blot for the Countess of Cardigan, who
had once invited " dear John " to stay with her alone at
Deane. His fond wife was absent at the time but she had
an intuition and her letter forbidding him to go reached
him by the same post as the invitation ! A clear case of
conjugal second-sight.

Naturally she never forgave Lady Cardigan for her
famous or infamous book of memoirs. She could not
pardon the attacks on Lady Aylesbury and Lady Bradford ;
and she recorded the reasons in an annotated copy : that
Lady Cardigan herself, as a Miss de Horsey, had been
seduced in youth by Lady Bradford's brother. Lady
Cardigan had been tenderly and charitably cared for by
Lady Aylesbury and could never forgive her benefactress.

Boo once dreamt a Derby winner and sent out her
footman to lay twenty pounds on ' Persimmon ' which won
the classic for the Prince of Wales. She endowed a bed
in some charity with the proceeds. It was the occasion
when the Stock Exchange sang " God save the Prince of
Wales " with streaming eyes upturned to Heaven : one
of the rare moments of great British emotion.

When Stratford House was sold, old Sir John retired to
a corner of Manchester Square. He was comforted there
by the presence of the Wallace Collection which should,
of course, have been named after the Lord Hertford

who collected it. My grandmother being half a
Seymour regarded Lord Hertford as the head of the family.
She and her husband were entertained at Sudbourne by
the rather puzzling Sir Richard Wallace who she did not
consider was Hertford's illegitimate son. Had he had
any Seymour blood, the Marquis would not have left
him anything ! He had been warped by his own relations
in youth : but that is another story.

The other æsthetic pleasure of Manchester Square was
a tree my grandfather considered the finest plane in
London. Every evening he would stroll out to watch
the tracery of its boughs against the sunset.

I came to know him better and better in these days
and never failed to glean something new after the ritual
passing of the port. He would then help himself to a little
snuff out of an old family snuff-box with a white greyhound carved on the lid. I might say that he and Cardinal
Logue were the last of the old snuff-takers I ever saw.
Snuffers like T. P. O'Connor made a terrible dribble over
their coats but the genteel manner was to throw back the
head and lift the pinch on the edge of the thumb to the
nostril. No smoking was allowed until the last red drop
of port had trickled away. I do not think my grandfather
was ever offered a modern cocktail but I have no doubt
he would have used it to clean a gun or pickle a corpse !

I remember he laid down strict rules for ringing bells :

> Once for maid or footman.
> Twice for the housekeeper.
> Three times for a death.
> Four times for fire !

I heard the instruction on these points with the greatest
awe and to this day I fear to ring even an electric bell too
often.

Under his gentle appearance and my grandmother's
presumption that he must be watched and coddled there
was a grain of iron surviving from the days of the Regency

when men were bucks. She took wonderful care of him
but she could not bear seeing him clean his false teeth
in a fingerbowl so she invented a table decoration which
she called a *cache-mari*. He hated being fussed or treated
like a child. Sometimes he revealed to us some of the
amusements of his youth.

At Oxford he paid a shilling to see a gypsy woman
draw a badger out of a tub with her bare shoulder. He
had also seen a man kill live rats by catching them in his
teeth and banging them to death. The only one of his
experiences we envied was that of an Execution breakfast.
This sounded thrilling. When there was a public hanging
at Newgate, he and his fellow-bucks used to saunter down
Oxford Street arm in arm to watch the drop or slow
strangulation which took place outside a window. This
pleasant sight witnessed, they returned and breakfasted
heartily. At least these were the amusements of a gilded
and not of the gelded youth of to-day.

He kept certain family traditions. He was proud that
his grandfather had sat in the old Irish Parliament,
had married a sister of Wellington's mother and had
interposed in the young Wellesley's behalf when there
was a question of removing him from school for economy.
The great duke was never forgetful and always showed
himself ready to give away a Miss Leslie at a wedding.

There was a Church tradition. The family held the
bishopric of Kilmore twice. One member becoming bishop
shortly before Disestablishment felt the disaster so
considerably that he died a few weeks after consecration.

During all those years I never remember but one
improper story being attributed to him. He could
imitate the Scotch minister who after passionately
imploring his hearers not to imperil their souls in Eternity,
remarked : " And for a pleasure which I am creditably
informed canna last mair than twenty minutes ! "

The abiding interest of his life was painting. As a
water-colourist he could not have asked for a talent more
adroit. He quarrelled violently with Ruskin over Lady

Waterford's water-colours. She had a depth of colour which made her palette famous ; but when the professional Ruskin tried to improve her drawing it was a mistake. Her art was spontaneous and natural. If the duel had been still available my grandfather would have ordered pistols for two and coffee for one. Ruskin proved an " insolent capon " and did his best to spoil Lady Waterford's talent.

My grandfather like many good amateurs involved himself with oils. He could paint a small sketch admirably but lost himself on the big canvas. He was a good judge. At Althorp once he discovered Poussin's " Marriage of Thetis " in the butler's bedroom. It had displeased for reasons of prudery and was later sent to Christie's where he had the courage to buy what the dealers guessed wrongly had been thrown out as a poor picture. It is now one of the finest pictures in the Dublin Gallery bought by the unerring Sir Hugh Lane.

He remembered the Ansidei Madonna before it was sold out of Blenheim and insisted that it had been spoilt on its way to the National Gallery. He said that Raphael's ivory tints had been cleaned till they resembled chalk. He was angry enough to make a scene when the picture was first shown publicly ; but probably he was right.

In 1875 he purchased Carlo Dolci's large canvas of the Aldobrandini family entertaining Our Lord, with the head of the family posing as the Pharisee and the fair daughter as the Magdalen.

This picture I had grown familiar with all my life and been shown as a child the artist's delightful signature : a tiny face of himself painted over the Saviour's hand. As it came from the Aldobrandini Chapel in Genoa (where the empty space yet yawns) I presumed it was as unique as genuine. Imagine my surprise on finding an identical canvas in Lord Methuen's collection at Corsham purchased in Italy two centuries ago. It was dark with age and I could only ask if it was signed. I indicated the spot where ours was signed and lo and behold with a little search and rubbing the tiny head became apparent. It had never been noticed.

But which is the original ? Did the artist make a perfect replica of his work or did the Aldobrandinis copy and then sell their picture to Ambassador Sir Paul Methuen ? This is one of the puzzles and to me romances in picture-collecting. Puzzles which only a selling dealer can ever answer decisively.

I always think that pictures belong to those who can enjoy them and not to those who are clever enough to sell or rich enough to buy them.

Italy, Florence and Rome were my grandfather's artistic home. His first visit took place during a grand tour in 1848 when he rode through Spain and drove down Italy. He found himself in a Roman street amid a sudden hush and a kneeling crowd. He wisely did as Rome did and was rewarded by seeing Pio Nono walking in his own city. When he returned in later years it was thought advisable not to glimpse or visit Leo XIII, as his Irish election depended on Protestant votes. In old age he returned to weep over modern improvements but he was consoled by some of the new bronzes found in excavation. I remember asking him if St Peter's was bigger than the church at Glaslough. He saw the Pope carried in procession at St Peter's. He described and imitated the Pope gracefully waving his arm in benediction but skilfully bringing back his hand so as to catch the drop which insisted on forming on the tip of his aquiline nose.

To avoid death duties and make the future possible for his successors he withdrew from Glaslough and the house he had built. After his final visit to the retainers, some of them asserted that they wept for a week. He had no financial acumen and was the nicer for it. Like most people, who had been born before the Reform Bill of 1832, he believed rather pathetically in fixity of incomes. He used to regard making money in the City as rather dishonest and certainly fit for no gentleman.

He became a well-known figure in Manchester Square. In his last years he was guided through the traffic by an angel-faced page-boy whom my grandmother had discovered for him. The couple made a picture which a Victorian sentimentalist would have gladly painted under the title of Innocence protecting Old Age. No one could have dreamed that the little page-boy would become celebrated as the murderer Sidney Fox and add a volume to the *Famous Trials Series*.

I am sorry to say Fox stole the Family Bible and used the signatures for his own purposes. In time he fell under the power of the law for stealing from shops. My grandmother insisted that his good services should be remembered and I spent an uncomfortable hour appearing as his friend in court. I arranged with the humane governor of Wandsworth Gaol for him to learn the carpentering trade.

It was all in vain. The late Mr Hambrook of the Yard revealed to me a career squalid and terrifying. Long before he had suffocated his mother in a Margate hotel for the insurance, he had lived a life with men of wealth who should have known better. He showed me his photograph in female dress with his beautiful eyes upturned to Heaven. It was indeed the corruption of the lily.

When he was condemned to death he showed himself obdurate in Maidstone gaol to any spiritual call. My Aunt Dosia Bagot went down to plead with him and successfully. He made his peace with his Creator and wrote her a letter of full contrition. His last words to her before his execution were of a charming naïveté: " I shall soon see Sir John ! "

Dosia was the most beautiful of my Leslie aunts. Her mother used to say she looked like a Venus de Milo and slouched like a gamekeeper. As a girl she was once missing in church after a hurried count of the Miss Leslies. The bell pounded on and even extra time, but no Dosia.

After the last peal she ran in, breathless. She had prevailed on the sexton to let her pull the rope.

She had a touch of Florence Nightingale, and served as a nurse in South Africa with her sister Olive, when hospitals were bungled and men died like flies. She wrote her experiences in *Shadows of the War*. They were both splendid with the soldiers and deserved their medals. We were most impressed as boys on hearing that Olive had succoured a young wounded officer who was full of gratitude and murmured : " I suppose you don't know who I am ? " She was afraid she didn't. " I am Jackson." Still she didn't know. It was Jackson the cricketer, the idol of every schoolboy in the Nineties. How well I remember the crowd chaffing his exquisite swagger at Lords.

Dosia's face reappears in all Sir Frank Dicksee's pictures. He was utterly devoted to her beauty, and when he was dying she was awakened and saw a light in her room. She came the nearest to second sight in the family. She married Josceline Bagot and saw the famous ghost at Levens Hall, but that is another story.

English Excursions

*

IRELAND WAS THE BACKGROUND BUT ENGLAND AFFORDED many early impressions to my young years.

The first vision of the sea is memorable. The cry of Xenophon's retreating army when they caught sight of the inviolable brine has an echo in every human life: Thalatta! Thalatta! Lodgings at Brighton and later a hired house at Eastbourne were our first saline associations. How quiet and modest was Eastbourne in the early Nineties before it had been developed. There were discreet visits to an old-fashioned house called Compton Place and visions of an old saturnine gentleman with a beard who never spoke but was said to own Eastbourne. What different characters those watering places of Sussex possessed! Hastings like an antique dame bolstered by pride and pedigree: Brighton a swelling *nouveau-riche*, but Eastbourne was their Cinderella. I can remember going on the chain pier at Brighton which was swept away in the gale of December, 1894. It was the mother of all modern piers.

At Eastbourne we first saw a corpse. A dead body was washed up near Beachy Head. It was surrounded by a few passers-by while the police were fetched. We watched awestruck with our grandfather. After the body had been searched he turned round to us and said in funereal tones: "There were no visiting cards found on him." No visiting cards! and in that pathetic information we walked silently home. A new importance dawned on my mind attributable to those little social pasteboards especially in case of shipwreck.

From Eastbourne to Worthing and back I enjoyed my first trip on a paddle-steamer, sitting in the filth of the engine-room watching the unerring paddles churning and re-churning the foam in their leaking boxes. The party of grown-ups was led by Monty Guest, a great *bon viveur*, raconteur and sportsman, a type of the younger son who practised leisure and other social arts. His disgust at my appearance was very marked, for then gentlemen dressed as gentlemen, and the common crowd circled round him admiring his clothes. He was an uncle of Lord Wimborne and died during a house party at Windsor Castle. What more can be added to his epitaph !

At the seaside new cousins came into our lives : Clare Frewen and her brothers, Hugh and Oswald. We were photographed in a family group. No photographs that survive are to my credit. In one I was caught scratching a bare leg and in another I held my hand over my eyes, whether in grief at my dingy surroundings or in disappointment at the failure of the photographer to produce a promised cuckoo. I still retained the fascination caused by the cuckoo clock at Glaslough, whose performances were so gratifying to the ear and numerically so regular.

My faith in man's word was somewhat restored by my first sight of electric light. We lived in a tall red-brick house in London (53 Seymour Street) which I can still locate, as it was opposite a pastrycook's called Tait, a landmark in our childish epicureanism. One day workmen arrived in the nursery and fumbled with wires. When all was complete they whispered to our nurse, who announced : " Watch and you will see a new sun." This sounded incredible but, when blinds had been drawn and the light switched on in a foggy atmosphere, the reality amounted to the expectation. We stood in the new electrical age. Hitherto all going to bed was associated with guttering candles and corridors with gloomy blue gas-jets.

Little is to be remembered of all those years in Seymour Street before we emigrated to Great Cumberland Place.

Our greatest treat at night was to sit up and watch the
mice which entered from the empty house next door in
search of food. We were taken to Quebec Chapel on
Sundays, a most dismal performance. The West End
was then peppered with chapels, some of which have been
pulled down : Grosvenor Chapel, Berkeley Chapel. I
remember a sarcastic tirade in the latter because the
clergyman had found a farthing in the plate. Our
Fräulein's agitation proved that she was the delinquent.
We never returned to Berkeley Chapel. Suppose he had
found the widow's mites in the treasury of the Temple ?

From Seymour Street we first learnt that there was
something to be said for little girls. We learnt a certain
bashfulness partly at the dancing classes conducted at
the Portman Rooms by a large lady in a swishing Court
dress and carrying a big bouquet. Boys were not then
expected to learn dancing, which even young men pro-
foundly despised. A fringe of boys in sailor suits hung
to the edge of the class and were alluded to as " the
young Masters Elephant " for their pains. Another
civilising tendency came from playing hide-and-seek at
Consuelo Manchester's house down the street in Portman
Square. The Manchester twins were the two most
beautiful and delicate girls imaginable. They both died
before the world of men or worry could add a line of
sorrow to their angel faces. Who remembers them
to-day ? I have a faded photograph of them signed in
childish scrawl : Mary—Alice.

It was in Seymour Street that we heard of the sinking
of the *Victoria* and I remember concluding from the
agonised talk of our elders that something terrible had
happened. And at Sunday parade we met the Harry
Bourkes weekly and their brother was the captain of the
Victoria. There were grim pictures in the papers of the
ship sinking and the men being caught in the revolving
screws. It was never discovered why the Admiral, Sir
George Tryon, gave the impossible order. What stirred

me most was hearing it whispered that the Admiral's ghost appeared at a party at Malta that night. It was thrilling to meet Ward, one of the midshipmen who had swum away through a sea of sharks and oil. Has it ever been observed that the names of English Queens have proved unlucky for battleships ?

Uncle Randolph was the first celebrated man I had ever seen. This was at Connaught Place whence he had issued on his fatal day of resignation. He could be as kind as summer to a friend but as acrid as winter to a bore. When the Wenlocks entertained him in Madras, a fine old Anglo-Indian talker was produced at dinner. " Our best raconteur," suggested Lady Wenlock. " And most interminable," added Randolph. Even his own supporters forsook him one by one.

People did not realise how sick and agonised he was in those days. Yet his tastes were most English. He once confessed that the great thrills of his life had been : (1) Big Game Hunting, (2) Bringing off a racing coup, (3) Above all : political intrigue.

One spring we stayed at a country house called Banstead, near Newmarket. Here Frewens and Churchills mingled. It was a hired home where Uncle Randolph sought consolation for his political miseries in racing. His story has often been told. With Parnell and Oscar Wilde he seems the most perennial memory from the Eighties. They were all outlaws in their way and died outside the barriers and conventions of Victorian grace. Hence their attraction for the modern reader.

To a child Randolph was then a grizzled and bearded hunter returned from South Africa. I associated him only with the skins of lions and horns of hartebeeste. I ventured once to offer him the fruits of my own hunting in the local bush : an empty bird's nest. He stared at me long and sadly, perhaps madly, without uttering a word. It looked a harassed and haunted face and when he came into the room everyone started whispering as in church.

Winston was the leading spirit among the cousins and

we all toddled or marched wherever he led us. He and his brother Jack had manufactured a fortress called the Den. It was two-chambered or, as they say, bi-cameral and it was abundantly carpeted with straw and surrounded by real water in the rainy season. A real drawbridge could be let down over the puddles which formed in the moat. As we walked to church Jack pointed out to me a surly youth whom Winston was alleged to have hided. Sitting on wet straw in the Den was a privilege that yielded utter joy. I remember some early ablutions at the hands of old Mrs Everest, the Churchills' nurse. She was a devoted soul who practically brought them up while their parents were over-occupied and troubled elsewhere.

Winston made a great impression on us all. I remember his indignant return from the Tower of London, furious because he had not been shown the instruments of torture. His governess " Lulu " was an old family friend ; but when she once ventured to call him a raggamuffin he absolutely declined to receive apology. His sense for phrase and epigram developed early and two of his Harrow sentiments passed into my memory :

" Punctuality is the Thief of Time "
" Poetry is the gilt on the gingerbread of Life "

These appeared to me as words of immense wisdom.

Winston had been literally born in the Primrose, for his mother had been enrolled as the first of all Primrose Dames. He had been prematurely born at a party at Blenheim. He had not been intended to see light there ; but it may have been on omen.

Through Jennie Churchill there was an early visit to Paris. This I scarcely remember, but I understand my parents took in their hurry the apartments of a deserted *cocotte* in the Rue Marbœuf. Over the family bed was an enormous snake with the pretty legend :

J'enlace et jamais j'en lasse.

This was half a century ago in 1888, and the gay Prince

H

of Wales accompanied by Stanley Clarke sometimes
visited English acquaintances when he wished to make up
up a theatre party. To this is due my only presentation
to a king. At the age of three I was taken out of bed,
drenched by a loyal nurse with eau-de-cologne and
exhibited to the future Edward VII. He is probably the
first person I can remember outside the family. All my
life there has been some Prince of Wales or other whose
amours and movements have been the excitement of a
whole society. It seems dull without one.

The London of the Nineties smelt very much of horses.
A feature of Oxford Street were the active boys who darted
in and out of the traffic collecting what horses left. At
one time it looked to me an exciting profession of its
kind. The distant roar of the traffic was not unpleasant
compared to the modern stridency. It sounded like a
distant rumbling sea and instead of motor hooting we
heard the fairy-like sound of the bells on the hansom cabs.
How different it was from the modern rather doubtful
adaption of New York to Mayfair and the banks of the
Thames.

Clothes made the great distinction between classes.
People were visibly rich or poor. The rest were tradesmen
and cads and did not count in life. You had only to walk
in Hyde Park on Sundays to realise that dress divided
the " two nations " whom Disraeli had once described.
Sunday after Sunday a shining top hat was necessary
for a man whether as a medium for prayer or a contribu-
tion to the smartness of society. The women were always
as well dressed as for Ascot.

Four-in-hands gracefully circled the Park and sometimes Queen Victoria was seen driving past the Serpentine.
I remember being rushed by nurses to catch a royal
glimpse from the railings. There were real footmen to be
seen (exactly as in Thackeray's novels) with plush and
powder. Certain town types have entirely disappeared :
flunkeys with overcoats sweeping to their feet and

boyish grooms sitting behind in white breeches and cockaded hats. In Rotten Row men rode in top hats and frock-coats and the women invariably glued to side-saddles and as well-mannered as their horses. The Prince rode daily at one time, accompanied by Mrs Langtry mounted on a horse provided by Uncle Moreton which looked splendid but was warranted safe. His name was " Redskin " and he looked it, but he was suited to a very nervous rider. I am afraid one of our interests was seeing women occasionally bolted with and pursued by chivalrous Lotharios galloping with top hats floating behind on strings. There was a very clear difference between boys and girls then. Nine girls out of ten whom we met wished themselves boys. Modern girls having added the pursuits of boys to their own privileges as girls seem content to remain as nature made them.

The circus preceded the theatre in our life, and I have a recollection of very rough and ready performances almost entirely of clowns and ladies jumping through hoops on horseback. The first circus we attended remains as clear as daylight. The whole performance is still a vivid reality ; for a lady rider fell from her horse. We both rose in our seats shouting : " She's killed ! " Fortunately this was not so, but when the attendants began to rake over the ground we rose again and caused the greatest embarrassment by shouting : " Now they are going to bury her." At this everyone roared with laughter but we were great laughter-makers in public.

When we attended the theatre with our friends and governesses we were always seated half an hour ahead of matinée time and kept up the highest spirits. I remember watching a very ordinary play, but we were in such convulsive hysterics of enjoyment after our long wait that we hailed the most ordinary conversation with peals of laughter much to the surprise of the actors. There is no rule in theatres against laughing when no joke is intended or applauding dull situations. We had decided we had come to see a comic play and by the time it was finished it had become a comic play ; for we soon had all the stalls laughing with us.

The first shows I saw at Olympia had to do with the Chitral campaign. Dummies were blown into the air and I had no idea the casualties were not real. I harboured the rather cold-blooded thought that it must be very expensive to hire fresh men to be killed every day.

But of all pageants and shows the most resplendent was Buffalo Bill's Wild West Exhibition as Earl's Court in the early Nineties. Buffalo Bill had been a scout on Uncle Moreton's ranch in Wyoming and had mounted thence to universal fame. The whole scene of hanging a horse thief (his face actually turned green in the process) was taken from an afternoon's work on the Powder River Ranch. To our huge excitement our elders were invited by Buffalo Bill himself to take a drive in the battered old Deadwood Coach. It was an inspiring sight to see Uncle Moreton, Charlie and Bill Beresford and our fond father setting off in that famous vehicle, each wearing top hat and frock-coat but holding a rifle. Cowboys drove them and a sharpshooter lay on the roof. The coach was duly scented and pursued by mounted Indians who received a heavy fire from the well-dressed occupants. The combination of whirling horses and Indian feathers with fashionable gentlemen firing for their lives made one of the most wonderful of afternoons in memory. We were too excited to cheer while our eyes drank in the fantastic sight of the actual persons, who had been sitting in the same box as ourselves, now firing rifles while six horses dragged them round and round the arena. It was really a disappointment to see them return without a scratch while Buffalo Bill shook their hands and begged them to come again. To join such a show seemed a worthy prospect in life. But unfortunately Buffalo Bill was taking no candidates, no cadets. . . .

A quarter of a century later I met him in America. He was white-bearded and his features were finely drawn. He is the only man who looked like the traditional Uncle

Sam. He had become the best-known American in the world. Why he was never made President of the United States we boys could never understand.

So much for shows. The theatre was the Christmas Pantomime and little else. The first play I saw was a Dreyfus play acted with great spirit by William Terriss, who was murdered in Maiden Lane the next year as he came out of his theatre. His acting reduced us to tears and agonies of apprehension. I was still in the happy stage when everything acted seemed real and everything in real life part of a phantasma.

But the pantomime was Dan Leno ; and the impression he made was greater than all our pastors and masters and governesses. His merry art reached a joyous climax when as the Widow Twankey he imitated the unsuccessful gate-crasher at the Palace. Again and again the Widow struggled to thrust her way through the line of supercilious footmen. She began by being pompous. Then she beamed conciliation—but to no purpose. A large silent footman always barred entry. She walked in unconcernedly. She returned in a scurry. She attached herself to other parties but she was always separated in the end. We laughed and shouted and we rolled on the floor of a box with cracking ribs. Pantomime followed pantomime and when Dan Leno died I never went to another. I believe there is evidence that his ghost has been seen in the dressing-rooms back of Drury Lane. His ghost certainly walks in my memory.

The only other humorist who could crackle my ribs was Arthur Roberts playing the drunken admiral coming aboard. The universal delight which an intoxicated sailor can cause the Empire shows what an appeal can be made by the theme of drunkenness at sea. Even the sea-sick curate has not touched British taste more poignantly. Arthur Roberts was attended by a row of chorus-girls in sailor suits and part of the fun was watching them collapse with merriment one by one and withdraw from the stage.

These were scenes I shall be happy to remember on my death-bed, when the rest of earth's civilised pageant has withdrawn from my eyes. Uproarious, stifling, pealing laughter is one of the gifts of the gods ; but occasions and inspirations thereto seem to have scarcened since the War.

The new generation will never understand what London was in the Nineties. Unless one has experienced life in the two very different societies one cannot realise the gulf. It was not only on the big counts. Life was lived more for class than for the state. Citizenship was rigid, though patriotism had not been invented. Patriotism was bred by Kipling out of Jubilee with the *Daily Mail* as trainer.

I remember the coming of the *Daily Mail*, which at first cost only a halfpenny. There used to be a *Standard* daily which was even more Conservative than the regretted *Morning Post*, whose excellence will only be a dream to our children. There were no children's pages and we took in the *Daily Graphic* for the lovely illustrations, apart from the Lady of the weather on the front page. Photographic processes were unknown.

I was not old enough to judge the morals of that time. I am told by those who should know that the men were more romantic even to derring-do while the women took more risks. They were rewarded by the secrecy which they obtained. Liaisons were often so long and regularly conducted that they lingered into respectability.

Even streets and hotels have changed names. The Berkeley was the St James and the Connaught was the Coburg. And the Ritz, the Caravanserai of Cosmopolis, was not yet invented.

Opposite the Ritz was the sequestered Devonshire House beyond gardens and brick walls. Only the magnificent gates betrayed the dwelling of a duke. To have passed behind those portals is already a cherished memory: a lingering lapse into that eighteenth century which made London beautiful as well as great.

I am happy to have trodden the floors of Dorchester House, Lansdowne House and Grosvenor House, while they were in their retired splendour. It would have seemed inconceivable that such mansions could ever be brought low. Their memory is ever before me when I pass through the Mayfair, whose streets have become motor-corridors and whose spacious squares are being reduced to herbaged courts. Lansdowne House with its lodge gate and concierge in a top hat, and its hall filled with immense classical statues discoloured by a century of fogs. Grosvenor House with Gainsborough's 'Blue Boy' and Sir Joshua's glory of 'Mrs Siddons as the Tragic Muse,' both hanging, uncleaned, unappointed, unannealed! Dorchester House with a carriage drive always laid down with ground red-brick, the immense stairway and the glass cases full of Shakespearean folios, and during the tenancy of the American Ambassador with a white marble eagle over the entrance.

Well they are all gone and even Stafford House, which Queen Victoria envied as a superior neighbour to Buckingham Palace, is become the shell of a Museum and its glories a scene in a cavalcade.

I console myself with what Horace Walpole wrote in 1787 : " For me who have seen Houghton plundered. Claremont has just now been sold in parcels and bought on speculation. Cannons was demolished a few years ago. Such is sublunary grandeur : my morality is that if everything is transient, misfortune must be so." With different houses and estates this sentiment could be rewritten every year.

A very early memory is my first garden party at Holland House, home of the Hollands, the Fox family and the Whig Society. While everybody was moving elegantly on the lawns we boys found a boat on a pond and cleared the bullrushes which we showed in triumph to our host. By his expression it was clear that he had planted them very carefully, but we mistook them for wild specimens.

My grandmother had some very interesting gossip
about a Miss Marie Fox supposedly the illegitimate but
adopted daughter of Lord Holland. When time came
for her to marry, her spouse, Prince Lichtenstein, demanded her quarterings. These could not be furnished
but Queen Victoria gave him the necessary assurance
that it was all right. Whoever Marie was, she was not
a Fox.

Cowes was still the splendid aftermath of the London
season. My first visit there we all stayed at Egypt House,
at the end of the Parade. In the train we travelled down
with old Sir Clare Ford, who had been ambassador to
Spain and was son of the Ford who wrote Murray's
inimitable guide to that country.

I remember old Admiral Sir Harry Keppel grieving
because he had found his Memoirs in the Royal Yacht
Squadron uncut. He was a great link with the past, for
his father had once placed him in the same chair at the
Admiralty in which he had been sitting when he started
Nelson on his career !

There was a splendid Cowes week in Jubilee year, 1897.
I remember seeing the Empress Eugenie pass swathed in
many veils. The splendid Goelet yacht was lying in the
Roads. Mr Goelet had died on board and when we visited
the *Mayflower* there was no one left except a solitary girl
who showed me the wonderful engines behind a plate
glass window. This must have been May Goelet who died
in 1937 as Duchess of Roxburghe.

Cowes was made glorious by great yachts such as the
world will never see again unless the dictators take to
super-dinghys. One year an American cousin, Kitty Mott,
came with her husband, her husband's friend and her
husband's friend's yacht, the *Utowana*. As a small boy
I found life very exciting aboard and made friends with
a Peruvian cook, which still seems unusual. The *Utowana*
possessed towering full-rigged masts and a complete
ocean crew.

But the greatest yacht came from France not America, the *Valhalla*, in which the Comte and Comtesse Boni de Castellane challenged the society of two countries. We were invited aboard. It was like stepping on to a pirate ship. Hundreds of villainous-looking sailors in red and blue caps and jerseys were gambling in every corner of the decks while the dapper little Comte strutted his little polished feet on the bridge. His wife, Anna Gould, had paid for it all. Unlike most American heiresses she was getting her money's worth in grandiose fêtes and social sensations. He was an amusing mixture of *grand seigneur*, dandy and *nouveau riche*. When he wished the Pope in later years to nullify the marriage, Archbishop Ireland, whom I met later, took a special journey to persuade the Vatican that however legally just Anna's annulment would scandalise the Catholics of the United States. As a Protestant, of course, she did not mind, but the Comte could never marry again.

Even if he was only a fop he lived splendidly up to his wife's income. But even a fop could be a character in those days. It is curious what a different brand of social leaders, dandies, stars, idols have come into existence. In the perspective of history it will perhaps be possible to decide what is the very distinct yet subtle difference between the shining lights and their opposite numbers in the next generation. What is it that distinguishes :

A Beresford from a Jellicoe at sea,
a Wellesley from a Haig in war,
a Tennyson from a Bridges in verse,
an Archbishop Benson from an Archbishop Lang in
    the Primacy,
an Edward VII from an Edward VIII in the role of
    Prince of Wales,
a Lillie Langtry from a Gladys Cooper in beauty,
a Jabez Balfour from a Clarence Hatry in the City,
a Salisbury from a Baldwin in Conservatism,
a Millais from an Orpen in portraiture,

a Boehm from an Epstein in sculpture,
a W. G. Grace from a Bradman in cricket,
a Stanley from a Sheppard in Deans,
a Whiteley from a Selfridge in stores.
Is it the indescribable difference between an orange and
a tangerine ?

This age has submerged the minor characters. Unless
a star-woman or an idol-man is almost the sum of all
rivals and substitutes, there can be no clangorous fame.
In the old days many were appreciated from among their
fellows for quaintness' sake alone. The turf, the clubs,
the universities and the school were full of picturesque
characters. And this was the case down to the humblest
grades of society.

We shall never see another Davy selling papers on
Kingstown Pier, nor an " Old Kate " giving tips to the
nobility at Epsom : nor watch a Cunninghame Graham
spur a broncho in South American costume down the
Row, nor hear an " Earl Poulett " playing a barrel-organ
in the streets, nor admire Lord Lonsdale smoking his giant
cigars in the middle of the Christmas Circus, nor look to a
William Gillett as the *arbiter elegantiarum*. He, who
founded the Bachelors' Club, is now vaguely supposed to
have given his honoured name to a razor. Yet he must
be reckoned amongst founders of clubs with the original
White, the primitive Brooks and the prehistoric Boodle.
The last time I saw poor Gillett totter like a paralysed
harlequin through Claridge's there arose a memory of all
the hostesses who had used his exclusive list of who was
to be invited.

London brought us into touch with certain great-aunts
and great-uncles. Julia and Emily lived in complacent
spinsterhood in Bourdon House, the Manor of the
Grosvenor Estate. How they came to occupy that
green-umbraged omphalos of Mayfair, Heaven knows.

Both had been disappointed or disappointing. Emily should have married the Lord Longford of the day and Julia had a long flirtation with Sir Edwin Landseer, whose love-letters remain in the family archives.

Older and older maids they became and Bourdon House was consecrated to virginity. Although they lived in the same house, the sisters seldom met. Their tastes and friendships were different. Julia affected the artistic and Emily the clerical. Through Emily I met the good Lord Halifax. She became very High Church and used to help Father Black make his public protests when divorced people were remarried in London churches.

When the sisters gave simultaneous parties, their guests passed each other on the stairs without speaking and were received in different rooms.

Julia died and Emily was left. My brother and I were sent Sunday after Sunday to tea in Bourdon House, with testamentary hopes, I think, on the part of our elders. We were bored and passed the time by calling for more and more food until the last cake was eaten and, as it was Sunday, no more could be bought. This form of table-outrage has a particular name. It was known as " broziering your dame " at Eton and was the opposite of a strike. Eton dames met it by larger supplies of salt meat.

In her last years Emily was allowed to return to Glaslough. My grandmother had boycotted all Leslie relatives with dire results when wills came to be read. But Emily's testament was the only one I ever knew to come home. She was a good old soul and was only amused when we boys drove her in a donkey-cart into the floods and abandoned her sitting helplessly behind a bogged donkey.

Her brother, Tom Leslie, (who became Slingsby) preceded her, but his money went to his nephew, Lord Delaval, the youngest of the Beresfords. Delaval ranched in America and lost his life in a railway accident in North Dakota. His money was claimed by a semi-negress who had to be disposed of by law.

Tom with his brothers had planted the great yew hedge at Glaslough before he started for the Crimea. The Alma casualty list was preserved at Glaslough as it was headed by the names of Tom Leslie and his brother-in-law, Frank Haygarth. He was on Lord Raglan's staff and Raglan sent his mother the bullet which was extracted from Tom. He was sent as far as Constantinople with the Inkerman Despatches.

After his return he became a hero and the protector of the Laura Bell who became Mrs Thistlethwaite. During the Indian Mutiny she had persuaded an Indian potentate to swing his state to the British interest with immense results. She received no more reward for her valuable work than Emma Hamilton received from the British Government for hers. Tom later married Miss Slingsby, the heiress of Scriven in Yorkshire, and took her name. His wife made a condition that no Leslies should be ever invited to Scriven, which would have interested me as it had a ghost and an old Catholic tradition. Tom had no issue and on his death it passed to cousins and became subject to a famous lawsuit when the unknown laws of heredity were invoked to prove a blood descent.

In 1900 Tom Slingsby came to Glaslough and gave a circumstantial account of the charge of Balaclava. Colonel Nolan, who gave the order all wrong, had snatched the honour of giving it from him, but of course he had never lived to explain. Thirty years later I listened in Duart Castle to old Sir Fitzroy Maclean describing the battle of the Alma.

Crimean memories and veterans swarmed in my childhood. Old Sir George Wombwell of Newburgh took me for a drive once in order that I could say I had driven with a survivor of the Balaclava charge. Names of places have their interest and Balaclava must be Celtic, for it is the same as Dublin's new Gaelic name B'lacliath.

There was a Crimean soldier who swept the crossing at the Orchard Street corner of Portman Square on two stumps. We boys opened a collection for him, and I only hope that half the shillings collected ever reached his cap. Whenever we passed, he used to salute us with his broom-handle.

Uncle Tom Haygarth had been left for dead at the Alma. He tried to save the life of Lord Chewton, who was lying beside him, from a Russian soldier who then turned and re-bayonetted him. As a result he was lamed for life and ended as a churchwarden. He was much perturbed when he heard that the Scots Guards were not taking their Colours to the South African War. They used to be carried by young ensigns who were invariably killed in the episodes known as " the Fight for the Flag."

He married one of my grandmother's sisters, Blanche, who told me she had been present in Mrs Fitzherbert's death-chamber, and showed me her rosary. Another sister married Frank Sutton, whose brother Sir Richard made the most sporting of efforts to win back the America's Cup. The Suttons owned a slice of Piccadilly which was a useful inheritance and enabled them to keep the hounds at Melton. In his old age Frank went blind, but he remained contented with life and in his good simplicity like a character out of Dickens. He could be pleased with anything or anybody. " I am glad I don't see," he used to say, "I should be so sorry at many of the things I should see."

His happiest memories had been reading the healthy, humorous hunting works of Surtees. Once he was being led past Swan and Edgar's shop. He was informed of the name and shouted with joy : " Why this is where Mr Jorrocks bought a bonnet for Mrs Jorrocks ! " It was a red-letter day in his life. He was one of those who showed how happy a place the world can be for those who are pleased by little things. He was undeservedly hen-pecked. He was fond of buying pieces of silver but Aunt Evie returned it all to the shops. When she died he ordered champagne.

The most startling and brilliant relative was Jessica Sykes, a daughter of Penelope Cavendish Bentinck, *née* Leslie, who had married her to Sir Tatton Sykes, much to

the surprise of Yorkshire. He devoted his fortune to his
famous stud and to building neo-Gothic churches. There
was no predilection on the daughter's part and no subter-
fuge by the mother. The guileless baronet was invited
to accompany an innocent girl in a railway carriage from
York to London, where Penelope met them and instantly
announced the match. Jessica was not consulted and the
baronet made a last-hour appeal to his brother Christopher
to disentangle him, but in vain. Penelope's web held.
He became a little restive during his engagement, but on
his wedding day Penelope fetched him in a brougham to
Westminster Abbey. Here the "amazing marriage"
was solemnized amid ambitious Cavendish Bentincks,
amused Beresfords, unprotesting Sykes, and wondering
Leslies.

The marriage was justified by the birth of the unique
and talented Mark, who was educated by means of
excursions round the whole of the habitable world.
Sir Tatton was vague but no fool. When the family
jewels were missing, it was found that he had sent them
to town enclosed in a cabbage for safety. He devised
one of the best means ever attempted for meeting the
English climate. He wore several pairs of trousers and
several overcoats at the same time. By judiciously shedding them he could always meet a rise in the temperature.

Jessica was brilliant, a linguist and a conversationalist
attractive to such great monologuers as Gladstone and
Lord Randolph. She kept open house at Sledmere during
Doncaster Week and entertained the most distinguished
gamblers in society while Sir Tatton pondered over
church designs upstairs. At one time he proposed (or
she proposed for him) reproducing the Cathedral of
Milan on the present site of Westminster Cathedral.

The late Sir Mark Sykes was their son and brilliantly
he acquitted his birth. While he was at Cambridge he
became an explorer of Turkestan, coming home to make
peace between his parents and settle their complicated
lawsuit. Sir Tatton had refused to pay a bill for £60,000,

insisting that it was not his signature. As a matter of fact he never could be induced to sign cheques, which his wife did for him. The matter came into court and was settled by Mark magnanimously shouldering the debt on his own prospects. The judge had been a frequent guest at Sledmere for Doncaster, and there was a dramatic moment when the stubs of Jessica's cheque books were sent for. By the time they reached court the trial had taken another turn, but counsel realised with a gasp that one of the first cheques for a considerable sum had been paid to the judge himself for baccarat !

Jessica wrote amusing Society novels, but they are exceedingly scarce. *The Macdonnells* was believed to be an inner survey of the Leslies, and *Mark Alston* was an exposure of the Bentincks and Lowthers ! The hero was John Ruskin, who was apparently an admirer of Jessica. The families concerned preferred to ignore or destroy all available copies.

No question is more difficult to answer than an inquiry whether the great difference between one generation and another lies in the character of people or in the change of circumstance.

The great difference always lies in circumstances. The change was as great for my grandfather to contemplate in 1900 as it has been for me in 1938. He talked about coaching days when travel consisted of bowling through an English countryside more beautiful than our dreams. He looked back to a time without railways, without wire in the air or the field, without postage stamps ; an age in which politics were a spirited game arranged between the pick of the London clubs and the county magnates. The game was played without professionals. Battleships were made of wood, newspapers were rightly taxed and there was no greater speed attainable than by a galloping horse. It took him as long to get to Rome as it took Cæsar to reach Britain.

He had seen an England before the Reform Bill, when

the rottenest boroughs returned the best members. He had seen the accession of William IV, used Mulready envelopes before stamps were scissored by postmasters, seen the great bruisers like Tom Cribb and " Gentleman " Jackson, passed O'Connell in the street, watched Newman as an Oxford tutor in Oriel Lane, heard Faraday lecture, seen Fuller Pilch batting, to say nothing of meeting Cavour, Mendelssohn, Chopin and George Sand. He even played cards with Mr Gladstone before he went Liberal. . . .

It was difficult to imagine the world of which he spoke, but who of the present generation can realise the Nineties when there were no motors nor aeroplanes, when there was little electric light and the telephone was a toy, when buses were horse-drawn and roads alternately dust or mud, when servants were paid half as much and were twice as content, when a divorced woman could neither be seen nor heard, when Society went to church, when the cricket over contained five balls, when Queen Victoria was on her throne, the dew on the thorn, God in His Heaven and all seemed right with the world ?

Ludgrove Preparatory School

*

I ASSOCIATE MY FIRST GLIMPSE OF THE WORLD OF SCHOOL, which is so important in English life, with a hot summer's day. My brother and I in white sailor suits were taken for a visit to Ludgrove School, then in its infancy. How many hundreds of boys have found their way there since 1894. The school has since emigrated to Wixenford, beyond Ascot, but the buildings are still visible from the old Great Northern Railway between New Barnet and Hadley Woods. The little country village of Cockfosters has become a Tube terminus and the landscape seethes with brick villas and the futile garden life which gives many people the illusion they are living in the country.

But in the Nineties it was still country. Arthur Dunn had pitched his tent on the hillside and was much amused by the two boys who arrived from London and treated his grounds as a bear-garden in Paradise. While parents mapped out our future education we hunted butterflies like mad. We were sorry to have to return to Stratford Place and I remember our solemn pride in believing we were already schoolboys.

A winter passed before we entered this delectable life and we returned meanwhile to Glaslough to find a frozen lake. This was the famous freeze of 1894-5 when England enjoyed two months of skating. Glaslough was as white and resilient as a Christmas card. We lunched and picnicked on the ice and skated after the pike imprisoned in the shallows. An aunt fell through the ice early in the season and was rescued by Jimmy, whom we boys insisted on decorating with a medal.

With the New Year we were back in London and the shadow of death was upon our elders. One morning my mother came into the schoolroom swathed with black. Uncle Randolph had died. It was the first death I had ever heard announced. I was swung off my hinges. I did not believe grown-ups could die. This was a fate I believed reserved for the heathen, for pirates and enemies of the Queen.

Living in Ireland I grew up aware that there were "enemies of the Queen." When I first inquired the reason of sentries at Buckingham Palace I was told to avert "the enemies of the Queen." I was always watching for them, and once seeing some eager tourists lolling against the Palace I was certain they were the long-sought enemies. I wished to stop and call the attention of sentries to shoot them where they stood.

In time I knew the Queen would get rid of all her enemies, including Mr Gladstone, but I was not prepared for a servant of the Crown meeting his death. I wept for Uncle Randolph as I only had wept before over the corpse of a wild bird and with a grief I never knew again until——

I was due to go to school for the first time, but I was kept for the funeral in Westminster Abbey. It was immensely solemn and the great roof stretched over us in icy space. It was like a cathedral of the Arctics. I heard the lugubrious choir and the voice of Dean Farrar and then the Dead March in Saul crept into our shivering souls. When it was over, I caught sight of Parliamentary heroes only known through the caricatures in *Punch*. Down the aisle passed Arthur Balfour and the grizzly "Black Michael" Hicks-Beach. Both had been Irish Secretaries and there was a certain queer look which distinguished English statesmen who had ever held that office. Sir William Harcourt, looking like Jumbo, and Lord Rosebery followed. There was a flag half-mast on St Margaret's, and in Parliament Square we were told to rise and bow from the carriage to a grey-bearded gentleman of prophetic appearance, who returned our bow solemnly. It was Lord Salisbury, who no doubt mistook us for Randolph's brood. It was well known he was one of those who could not tell a heron from a handsaw. The haggard Sir Henry Irving also passed down the aisle. In youth Randolph was said to have asked Irving in Dublin how the play of *Hamlet* finished ! Randolph was finishing like Hamlet himself. There were four Captains to bear him to his grave. " For he was likely, had he lived, to have proved most royal." The funeral procession passed to Paddington followed by Waldron, the faithful valet, and thence under the shadow of Blenheim into the endless Nirvana which swallows the short and agitated lives of statesmen, if they could only realise it.

It was my first funeral and, as godson to the deceased, I thought myself bound to observe the strictest mourning. I became susceptible to the grief of my elders. In hushed whispers they mentioned Randolph's last miseries and madnesses and I recorded the event in my first diary (Jan 24, 1895).

" Uncle Randolph became a saint in Heaven."

It was my solution and when found and read I saw my elders smile and received the widow's sweetest expression of thanks. She lay in bed at 50 Grosvenor Square : the most beautiful vision of woman I have ever seen : raven-black hair caught with diamonds over her face whiter than death, and eyes that shone like wet ebony.

There seemed to me several reasons for Uncle Randolph's passing to high reward. He had shot lions. He was therefore brave. He had defended the Queen against Mr Gladstone. He was therefore good. He was one of our relatives and I could not conceive a relative not reaching the same precedence in the next world as in this, in spite of the theological suspicion that servants and the poor were bound to have a better time than their masters.

A few days later Fräulein took me to Ludgrove. I recall the icy blast which met us on the footbridge over the line at New Barnet as the spark-gushing engine passed underfoot. A slow horse-dragged fly took us into the depths of country. Trees, hedges and woodland surrounded us! The oil lamps gleamed upon piles of snow. It was a scene similar to scenes I have known in Russia. Oh the silence and the quiet, and we were only twelve miles from Trafalgar Square.

At Ludgrove we were welcomed by Arthur and Helen Dunn. They were young and good-looking. Their school was in its third year. I was shown Theo Pelly who was actually the first boy in the school. Though he has since become a retired general-officer I still regard him as " Ludgrovian : Number One." I was the thirty-sixth and I have always regarded thirty-six as my lucky number ever since, whether on the door in an hotel or in a Casino.

The only drawback was a sudden fit of homesickness which can be as mysterious and irresistible as sickness by sea. The climax came while sitting with thirty strange boys at tea. Mr H. P. Hansell, a tall dark-haired master, was exchanging chaff and merriment with the boys around him when he observed the distress of a lonely Irish boy. To cheer me up he sent a message down the table asking what it was that Irishmen used to hit each other on the head ? Here was my chance to make myself agreeable in this new company, and I pulled myself together. The proper answer to the question, as every well-trained English child must know, is " Please sir, a shillelagh." But of shillelaghs I had never heard, and only remembering stories of the " Battle of Roslea " I answered : " A bloody blackthorn, sir ! "

It must have been the first time that the sanguinary expletive was heard at Ludgrove, and probably the last for I never came across it again except as a rowing term at Eton. The incredulous start on Hansell's face warned me that I had made a blunder of the first magnitude. Most solemnly he warned me never to say that word again. He seemed too startled to say why. The boys were bewildered and looked at me in grinning silence. It was a little comic. The weeping new boy had shocked the whole school by his first utterance. The truth was that in Victorian times to say " bloody " was socially worse than expectorating in the soup.

Arthur Dunn soothed my homesickness by giving me picture books of Oxford and Cambridge ; and I was engrossed in views as fabulous as drawings by Gustave Doré. I was placed bottom of the school, or rather, left to contest that inconspicuous position with a boy called Luther, who had held it against all opposition and was jubilant on hearing that I knew no Latin. It was his chance of a rise, but by prodigious efforts I surpassed him. Hansell's report survives :

" Just lately he has done some excellent work for me in Divinity. I decided to drop German, as his mind was in such a state of confusion."

On German it still is. But Latin was a new acquisition ; and before long I was declining *mensa*, a table, with that apparently senseless vocative case ; for as Winston has asked in his academical memoirs why and when should we ever become familiar enough with a deal table to wish to say : *Mensa* O table !

I must confess that it never occurred to me to question the validity or use of such a case. Ten years later as a matter of fact when I was dabbling with the occult at Cambridge, I had a chance to use the neglected case. With some other searchers for truth we were table-turning and trying to get messages from an Ouija-board which our leader constantly addressed personally and finally, said : " Come along, old table, answer our raps." In a second the hard-learnt evocation floated into my mind and for the first time I muttered " *Mensa* O table !" I forget if the table responded beyond rising on one leg and executing a whirl. This was attributed by a young Don present to our stores of natural electricity. In any case it was the only time I had occasion to address a table, but it had occurred !

Meantime six weeks' skating on the pond at Ludgrove.

Every evening it was flooded and refrozen until there was a yard of ice over a few inches of water. The whole school were fair skaters by Easter, but who has enjoyed such a winter since ?

I never enjoyed outdoor games as I did at Ludgrove when we were deprived of football. Snow and sunshine and thirty-six boys made merry hours in an enclosed yard. We played a game called " Widdy " which gave me more pleasure than any game I have ever played since. Two boys started hand in hand to catch the others one by one and add each capture to their chain, which the survivors could always break by furious charges. The few rules, the element of pursuit, the chance of escape, the breakneck speed, all made " Widdy " my favourite of games. I have never met it since.

Football was the serious game at Ludgrove ; for Arthur Dunn had captained England and was one of the most accomplished full-backs the Association game has ever known. It was typical of his sporting modesty that he slipped away one morning without telling his wife he was going to captain England against Scotland.

No words can describe his deliberate speed and swerving power on the field. He went through life in perfect training. That winter he skimmed the ice like a human swallow.

Sometimes we went to skate at Trent Park, where we were hospitably entertained by the Bevans. Old Mr Bevan looked the fine old English patriarch with banking and the Bible in his blood. The Bevans were a source of amusement to the school, especially when the younger members were late for church. We became familiar with a sandy-haired hopeful who fell in later years from financial grace. We understood he was clever at mathematics. I had assimilated my early and precocious knowledge of divinity from a work by a Miss Bevan of Trent Park, called *Line upon Line.*

At Ludgrove I proceeded to Dr Maclear's handbook to the Old Testament, which I knew almost by heart. This

admirable summary omitted much that was tedious and
all that was unfit for virginal minds. It was a short cut
to Arthur Dunn's favour to know the Scriptures. There
were few examinations in divinity in which I did show
the knowledge of a rabbi. But the classics entailed a
severe grind under the auspices of Dr Gunion Rutherford
and Dr Benjamin Hall Kennedy. May they be ploughed
in Greek and Latin respectively in another world!

Arthur Dunn was enthusiasm itself. In some ways he
was a perfect type of Englishman, doing whatever he had
to do with all his heart and soul. He was a Sir Galahad in
flannels. Rectitude, keenness, chivalry were in his flashing
eyes. Most of us felt towards him as Dr Arnold's pupils
felt towards Arnold. Arthur Dunn did as much service
for the Preparatory School. He achieved more than
making his own fashionable. He made it pleasant for boys
and a satisfying career for his staff.

Most of the boys were sons of Norfolk squires, and with
them came Mr Hansell, the giant Norfolk goalkeeper,
later tutor to the Prince of Wales. He looked like Gulliver
in Lilliput when the boys swarmed round him. He had a
great show of running cups and confessed himself a " pot-
hunter." He was a man of varied temper and vagarious
parts. He used to dine with the Liveried Companies in
London and bring us back boxes of " paralysed plums."
He taught French, sometimes in a stormy mood and sometimes in a spirit of mockery and mimicry. His classroom
rang to mirth or wrath, both of which are better than
stagnation. He was fond of setting impossible *poenas*
such as " five hundred lines of Greek with the accents,"
which of course were never done. He could tell us of life
in a German university and of travels in France. He was
that very rare form of politician : a supporter of the late
General Boulanger, whom he could never forgive for not
having brought off his *coup d'état* in Paris. A boy called
Baker arrived and Hansell insisted on treating him as
le brave général, and railing at him for not having marched
on the Élysée when France was waiting. " Ah, Monsieur

Boulanger, why did you not march ? There was nothing between you and the dictatorship of France." And poor Hansell would lie back in his chair as though it had been a personal disaster.

I was so impressed that I became, and after forty years remain, General Boulanger's last supporter in the world. Whenever I find myself in a French political riot or procession I always counter-cry " *Vive Boulanger !* " for one cry is as good as another.

Mr Hansell was not a scholar and was fond of sleeping in class, but he was a splendid goalkeeper, prancing with his six feet four into the air between the posts, and he was a connoisseur of old china. Boys wishing to curry his favour used to steal their parents' best Chelsea and Worcester " because Mr Hansell likes old crockery " ! On the whole he was an exciting master and to him I owe my first impulses in English literature. He read us Wells' story about the Stolen Bacillus and he recited with wild success the Bab Ballads and the Jabberwock. " Oh I am the Mate of the *Nancy* brig " was his masterpiece in delivery.

A school notice-board is dull enough but Mr Hansell used to cut out amusing odds and ends, pictures from advertisements which he pasted on the board with school allusions cleverly interwoven. On these occasions the corridor rang with laughter. It was an education in humour.

Mr Hansell had a lucky star in the sky one evening when two boys, Roger Coke and Evelyn Barclay, absconded to London. They had no grievances, but proposed to make a living by the purchase of a cage of white rats. By chance they took lodgings in a house run by an old servant of the Leicesters and Roger Coke was safely reported to his family. Meantime Mr Hansell had been sent to London wearing an impeccable frock-coat and top hat to allay Lady Leicester's fears. His fame was spread after the interview, and the ideal tutor was bruited through Mayfair. To shorten the tale, Mr

Hansell entered various royal families, ending as bear-ward to the Prince of Wales. . . . He was very broken when I last met him hobbling along the Hastings front. He recalled old days and still attributed the turn in his life to the two boys who ran away from Ludgrove. He died shortly before the debacle of his most famous pupil. He was lucky even in that.

In the year following Roger Coke's flight I foolishly ran away myself without a thought of the worry it would cause. I bought and smoked my first cigarette outside King's Cross and then walked to Maple's Furniture Shop in search of work. I believed that a slight knowledge of Euclid opened a considerable career as a floor walker, but I was disappointed. Both Maple's and myself missed a great opportunity. I proceeded to Hyde Park where I was recognised by a house-maid and for the first and last time left that dangerous area in company with one of the fair sex. I was brought home to 10 Great Cumberland Place and wrote a letter of apology to Arthur Dunn. My guardian angel must have held my pen for after he read it aloud to the school there were wet eyes amongst the hearers and I was taken back on condition that I started working hard for Eton.

The effect was instantaneous ; for I gave up interest in games and became a bookworm. Such was Arthur Dunn's influence. In the next year I took Remove at Eton. My brother followed suit and our names with Michael Palairet's headed the long list of Ludgrovians who have entered Eton by that pleasant form of " flying start."

The three clever boys at Ludgrove were Michael Palairet, who was the last British Minister to Vienna, Norman Chamberlain, a cousin of the Prime Minister, who was killed in the War, and Timmy Jekyll who took the top Eton Scholarship in 1895. Arthur Dunn was so delighted that he took the whole school to the Zoo where we revelled for an afternoon amongst the elephants and

camels. Jekyll was one of those prodigies who warm a
schoolmaster's heart. I remember the masters laughing
over an entry they had found in his diary : " Rebuked
for porcine behaviour ! " Arthur Dunn had told him not
to eat like a pig. He won the Newcastle at Eton in 1900
and made his mark later in music. Years later I used to
see him in the British Museum. In that mausoleum of
dead and living brains we passed each other like ships in
the night.

It is a chance whether one meets old school fellows
again. David Copperfield's experiences with Traddles
and Steerforth seem to have been unique. The majority
disappear into the multitude. After forty years the most
tender of friendships, the most bitter of rivalries have
been forgotten.

Seldom comes a meeting after forty years. Sometimes
a rumour, an obituary, a newspaper paragraph or a flash
of fame recall some boyish character or features. Of
Ludgrove friends a dozen, alas, were killed in the War.
One of the Barclays fell to a lion. One became president of
the Cambridge crew. Another became Indian Viceroy.
The present Lord Linlithgow arrived—a pleasant boy and
plump—under the name of " Hope " and Arthur Dunn
had to explain why his name was carved on the board
without initials. He was a Lord, the first to come to
Ludgrove. It seemed to us as strange as though his
sole name were " Faith " or " Charity." Twice I have
seen him leave Victoria for India, once by accident and
once by design. And now he sits in the chair of the
Great Mogul !

Sportsmen we had like Eric Crankshaw, Philip Williams
and Charles Hatfield who all played for Eton against
Harrow. A very good-looking sportsman was the late
Niko Wood who won the Metropolitan Stakes with
Windbloom. He was very dashing and admired Miss
Pauline Chase, the original Peter Pan. Later he assisted
Miss Gaby Delys to escape from Portugal. When the
Revolution obscured the Monarchy, Niko was waiting

for her with a car. He was generous and passed through his big fortune. He was too ready to accommodate loans to wrong 'uns and died a poor man at Brighton. He was decoratively dressed to the end and presented the perfect type of what is mysteriously called " a man about town."

The Bowes-Lyon boys were sent to Ludgrove (Pat, Jock, the Minimus and Fergus). I was in a dormitory which Arthur Dunn called ' Caledonia ' owing to the Celtic element. It included George Baxter from Dundee, who became a great runner at Eton. We were all Jacobites and believed that " Prince Charlie " was our rightful King. The Lyons' sister, our present gracious Queen, had not yet been born. There was one argument in Caledonia which could never be settled : whether Ireland conquered Scotland or Scotland Ireland. Perhaps neither did when it comes to history. We used to tell ghost stories in bed, but in deference to the Lyons there was never any reference to Glamis.

In 1896 I believe the Lyons brothers wrote home an astonishing letter concerning the Leslie brothers which caused some amusement at the time. In October Dr Benson, Archbishop of Canterbury, paid a visit to Glaslough and was snapshotted on the terrace. He was the first English primate to visit Armagh and was brought over by Dr Alexander. His mystical signature " Edw : Cantuar " remains in our visitors' book to show that he had not feared to visit a County where legend stated that some of the murderers of his predecessor Becket had taken refuge and root, changing their name of Fitz Urse to Macmahon, which also means " Son of the Bear."

A few days afterwards Archbishop Benson visited Mr Gladstone and fell dead in Hawarden church. I am sorry to say that we boys expressed regret that this had not happened in Glaslough church. Our words were reported to the parents of the Lyons in a Sunday letter to the effect that " wasn't it awful bad luck on the Leslies as they missed seeing the Archbishop die in church and would have got out without a sermon ! "

Then there were the Hall brothers : Percy and Julian,
full of the highest spirits. I remember wild scenes in a
dormitory and Julian leaping in a sheet from bed to bed.
Percy was killed in the War ; but Julian ? I found to my
amazement a chapter devoted to him in the Biography of
Marshall Hall, who defended the actress who killed Julian
in a fit of jealousy. It was a great pity as Julian was one
of the earliest and most intrepid of air pioneers and
was killed before the War would have given him his
opportunity.

Life at school was lived in that intensity of freshness
which we shared with the skipping lamb and the opening
bud. We enjoyed collecting whatever could be collected :
stamps, moths, butterflies, postmarks, chestnuts and even
buttons. I often wonder what became of the friends
who shared or rivalled in those hoards which meant so
much to our souls. I remember the agony of thinking
that I would not be able to take my stamp collection
into the next world. What fun could there be in Heaven
unless, O rapturous thought, there were daily issues of
celestial stamps !

Ludgrove friendships were closer for me than any I made
at Eton. There were so many whom I knew so closely and
whom I never saw again except perhaps in the Eton
distances. Harry and Gervase Birkbeck—— ? who in
our opinion had model parents or sisters as they used to
receive a letter from home every day of term. And John
Titus Salt with whom I collected moths ? He and Henry
Hurt were Ludgrove's contributions to the Navy. Hurt's
name passing into the old abolished *Britannia* headed
the honours board. Salt also went to sea and we thought
that he had chosen the proper profession to suit his name.

Other good fellows were Gerald Valerian Wellesley,
who afterwards took a big hand in boys' clubs, Basil
Blackett (Eton Eleven) and the Lacons of Fakenham
(the minor took an Association Blue at Oxford) and
Humphrey Pelly with whom I helped to make many a

desperate defence for Ludgrove on the football field in my last year. My great friend was Jack Howey. At that time we were both set on becoming engine-drivers, which still seems to me a noble profession. Howey certainly achieved our ambition for he owns the famous light railway he built at Littlestone. We made a curious connection in later years when we shared the same Nannie for our children.

There were some delightful Barrington-Kennetts, all killed and so were Francis Hudson and George Ross. A few like Tom Vesey and Dick Wyndham Quin I have seen in the distances since. William Baker I met to my surprise as a priest in the Oratory. Eric Crankshaw I have seen playing cricket gallantly with one arm.

Arthur Dunn's infectious training made us a merry band of comrades and we worked like a team. It was Ludgrove against all others and I composed a short school anthem reviling our rivals at Cheam and Northaw and Elstree.

We once staged charades in a dormitory, chiefly at the expense of the Bevan family. Mr Hansell was apparently listening at the keyhole and was much amused. He gave us a severe warning privately, and being a gentleman never reported us. Arthur Dunn got wind and begged me privately to tell him if any improper things had been recited. With scarlet embarrassment I said I couldn't think of anything worse than rhymes about :

> " The animals went in two and two
> They all grew thin but the Bevans grew !
> The animals went out by four and four
> But old Mr. Bevan stuck in the door ! "

Arthur laughed and laughed. He threw his arm round me and shook with delight. " But there's nothing wrong in that," and he lay back and laughed till he rocked. I think it was due to his relief at discovering how very innocent the atmosphere was in his school.

Towards the end of my time he used to hint mysteriously about Eton life. He had kept us so innocent we could not

pierce the mystery. We only realised that " the greatest
sin there is " was awaiting us. But he was too modest to
come to the point and we were left a little bewildered.
What could the greatest sin possibly be ? We could find
no such description in the Catechism we laboriously learnt
for the Bishop of St Albans. " Putting poison in the
tea " was suggested. My solution was " shooting the
Queen " and there the difficult question was left.

During my whole time at Ludgrove (1895–1898) I
never heard a single oath or expression conveying the
mildest indecency. I still believed that human beings,
though born in original sin and remaining bad as boys,
became better as they grew up, in fact better and better.
It was a long time before I knew the truth. Parallel with
that belief was my financial fancy that everybody on
coming of age was given the same amount of money by
the Banks. Later they might lose or improve their fortunes but they started even. Of course the poor were not
included, only the educated classes. Without knowing it
I had stumbled on the whole modern theory of Social
Credits.

We were not cut off from the outside world which we
knew by public disasters or jubilees. There was a fierce
fire in the neighbourhood my first term when the old
Royal Hunting Lodge at Cockfosters was burnt. All
water was frozen and every pipe had long been cracked.
In fact we really did find ice in our pitchers of a morning.
In consequence the staff, who were roused in the middle of
the night, could do nothing. An old Mrs Gladstone, aged
eighty, was carried out alive, but the house, a thing of
beauty, became an ash for ever.

Next morning we visited the gritty remains, but the
fire which remains in my mind was the burning of the Hyde
Park Hotel. This I saw alight from Great Cumberland
Place. We rushed into the Park and saw a splendid sight.
In those days fire-engines were drawn by horses and I
never saw a more thrilling show than forty engines
galloping at full speed through the Park with all traffic

held up. The chariot race in *Ben Hur* could have been nothing in comparison.

We reached the Albert Gate and were jammed in a huge crowd for two hours watching the spectacle of climbing firemen and spurting hoses. Every now and again a coping stone crashed into the street. An old gentleman was rescued wearing his pyjamas and a top hat. But no lives were lost and everybody seemed to have enjoyed it including the glorious horses.

A real disaster was signalled by the sinking of the *Drummond Castle* off Ushant. There was great loss of life and one Sunday we stood in Cockfosters church while the " Dead March in Saul " was played. For days and nights I only thought of the *Drummond Castle* and imagined her slow descent into deep waters. Thirty years later I read an account given by some divers of finding her hull. Her red and green signs were still discernible. In a moment returned to me the abysmal horror of the years and I relived that mood of boyhood. I seemed in an instant to be standing in the old unregenerated church at Cockfosters wondering why Arthur's face looked so grave. For me the " Dead March in Saul " is the eternal requiem for the *Drummond Castle*.

Previously the *Stella*, a Channel excursion boat, sank with loss of life and a stewardess showed great heroism. In my sketch-book I drew the scene after the wreck. I still have this picture of a feminine body drifting ashore with long floating hair, but it is as disappointing a work of art as my first Christmas Card, drawn for my parents. In a corner of the sky there was an angry and distorted face blowing winds and snow over the landscape. It might have passed for the north wind, but unfortunately I labelled it God.

The greatest event in the Nineties was the Queen's Diamond Jubilee. I watched the procession from a window in Madame von André's house at the corner of Piccadilly and Bolton Street. The house had been scaffolded against the all-night crowd and rows of human hands, weary but still clinging, could be seen between the railings and the planks, their owners invisible. Over the way was the house of the venerable Baroness Burdett Coutts, who had been actually present at Queen Victoria's Coronation. In her central window hung the famous china parrot. People in the street could never decide whether it was real or not. It was said that a mob of the unemployed once halted to discuss the question. Here forty-six years previously she had by an access of grief drawn all her window blinds for the Duke of Wellington's funeral.

The old Baroness was very popular with the crowd and synonymised Victorian charity. She was one of the few great characters I ever met. All our Victorian elder sons had proposed to her at some time or another in duty bound except Lord Houghton. Eventually she married her young American secretary who properly took her name. I made a great hit with him once by mistaking him for Marcus Beresford. His chief marital duty was cataloguing the Baroness' lace.

She was a great link with the past. Dickens had dedicated *Chuzzlewit* to her and she had been mentioned in the *Ingoldsby Legends*. It was interesting to think that she had watched Archbishop Howley in his wig crown the Queen sixty years before. I was once deputed at a family wedding to hand her to her carriage and had the pleasure of being cheered in the London street. The only other time I was cheered was many years later leaving Euston station when I was mistaken for a member of Jardine's successful team then returning from Australia. In each case it was very gratifying.

To return to the Jubilee procession. One remembers all the details. Captain Oswald Ames, the tallest officer in the British Army, rode in the front. There was a dead stop of about a quarter of an hour in Piccadilly and there were sighs of dismay : " how dreadful—just in front of all the foreigners watching from Devonshire House ! But the slower it went, the more gorgeous it seemed. I remember a carriage of papal delegates bowing delightedly to a Protestant crowd who mistook them for Abyssinians ! The Queen herself might have been playing her own part in a film of the future. She looked exactly as expected, carrying the little sunshade presented by Mr Villiers, the Father of the House. And we heard later of the two casualties of the day : Lord Howe and the Lord Mayor, who toppled off their horses.

Powerful searchlights were set around St Paul's Cathedral with the result that the dome was floodlit thirty years before the time. Otherwise the illuminations were not the equal of an ordinary night of modern advertisements. At best they were gas-stars or strings of night lights in little coloured lamps. But those who saw the Jubilee of 1897 looked on the climax of a world which had lasted roughly since Queen Anne and is now dead no less.

Four full years passed for me at Ludgrove. Rewards were more plentiful than punishments. Tickets marked V.G. were distributed for good work and a sufficient number of V.G.s entitled the possessor to a hilarious tea-party in the private part of the house followed by parlour games. Offences were expiated by extra drills carried out in the school yard by Sergeant Everett. I was present at the first extra drill ever performed and not as a mere spectator.

School drill was once honoured by inspection by Lord Falmouth. Mr Hansell supervised and brought us up to scratch. He warned us I remember against showing our tongues. He related a story of Rossall, where he had been a master, on inspection day. A distinguished general had reviewed the school corps and selected a leading boy to point out as a fine specimen of British manhood. This was too much for British modesty and the blushing youth allowed his tongue to drop out of his mouth as far as it could go !

K

We all kept our tongues in our cheeks but there was a
curious story which Arthur Dunn used to tell in support
of heredity. A visitor was watching the football at Ludgrove and for some reason I was playing with my tongue
hanging out of my mouth. The visitor casually observed :
" How curious ! the only boy I ever saw playing football
with his tongue out was a boy at Eton called Leslie."
This turned out to be my father. It was at least a coincidence if not a startling advance in the science of heredity.

Sunday at Ludgrove was wisely made a happy day.
There was the long lie abed and for breakfast there was
" squish." Parties were made up for church and each boy
could choose how far he wished to walk, whether to Cockfosters or New Barnet or Oakleigh Park. Cockfosters was
a drab and dreary church, since beautified by Bevan
benevolence. A whiskered Mr Warren declaimed through
the Liturgy accompanied by an organ and a moustachioed
curate. I remember one incident of humour in church.
One of the Barclays (surnamed the Goat) intended to drop
a penny in the plate as the usual schoolboy offering, but
by mistake extended a florin. As quickly he withdrew it
only to catch sight of the impatient Arthur holding the
plate. Two and three times he held it over the plate,
tried to withdraw it and finally dropped it with a groan.
The struggle between his conflicting emotions reduced
us all to suppressed hysterics. We chaffed him all the
way back from church. Such tragedies will always occur
at collection time until it becomes customary to demand
change.

By Eton jackets and collars white we observed the
Sabbath day. Profane books such as Scott and Henty
were returned to the library and a special Sunday shelf
opened such improving literature as *Ben Hur* and *Pilgrim's
Progress* to our minds. Best of all Mrs Dunn read aloud
from the best of school novels *The Fifth Form at St
St Dominic's*. I have always classed *St Dominic's*
first in that literary growth of school stories which is

peculiar to this country. First with *Tom Brown* a good second and *Eric, or Little by Little* a bad third. In sheer fiction our generation was fed on Rider Haggard, with his *King Solomon's Mines*, Max Pemberton with his *Iron Pirate* and with Henty, who never wrote a good book nor a bad one among his fifty books for boys. The summers were then immensely hot and we lay in the garden on rugs knowing all literary delight. I could not ask to be happier.

School-matches made us aware of rival establishments. For our size we played pluckily but Cheam and Elstree could never be defeated at football nor Northaw (coached by Mr Poland) at cricket. Northaw produced the Carlisle brothers, one of whom made 160 against us although Phil Hamond (D.S.O.) struck his wicket in his first over without dropping a bail. One of the Northaw bowlers, Master William Jowitt, has since become Attorney-General and is the only one of our many opponents I have met again. I may say that then as now he was conspicuous for his *length* and good looks. I feel sure that his forensic length is as good as his bowling length.

Since the War Cheam and Northaw have moved south. Elstree remains to dispute her name with the film studios which little as the public know it are situated in the neighbouring Boreham Wood. It was impossible not to become athletic at Ludgrove but we were trained and not driven. Our masters behaved with forbearance during matches. Not so one of our rivals, where masters stood at every corner of the ground and hurled ejaculations at their nervous charges. It was at Cheam that I kicked my first goal in inter-collegiate football. Unfortunately it went through our own goal in spite of Norman Chamberlain, our goalkeeper. For years I used to eye that ground with shame from the railway. It has now been built over and the bricks have blurred the poignancy of memory. From our Cheam opponents I only recall Sheepshanks, now an Eton master : outside-left and very fast for his small size, but that was forty years ago.

We sometimes played cricket against ladies, who generally won. They wore long swishing skirts with which they could cleverly, but unfairly, impede the travelling ball. In those prudish days a lady's ankle could only be seen unswathed at the pantomime, There was a masculine horror of a female assuming the dress of the male. I remember an early lady bicyclist wearing bloomers and a trilby hat in Bond Street. She was pursued by the extinct race of shawl-wearing milkmaids shouting : " Tommy ! Tommy ! " I saw safety bicycles for the first time at Ludgrove. Arthur had learnt on an enormous wheel called the " penny-farthing " owing to the diminutive wheel behind. One of the curates at Glaslough rode one with immense agility. My mother was one of the first women to ride in Ireland, and the old steward sent in his resignation unless her practice was confined to the pleasure grounds. He could not suffer the shame she was bringing on the family to be witnessed by the farmhands.

We used to play against the choir of King's College, Cambridge, and on a red-letter day I saw what was to become in after years my spiritual home. We started in a saloon carriage playing whist all the way. Need I say that the game of bridge had not been introduced ? Arthur had been a lucky or brilliant card player at the Varsity. He had stopped when he found he was taking too much from his friends : not because he was losing.

First sight of Cambridge (Oct 22, 1898) was like a dream. A pack of diminutive schoolboys, we wandered through colossal buildings and mighty courts like mites in a Gothic wedding-cake. In spite of unfair attempts to fill us with indigestible pudding we won our match. We then heard the most beautiful service in England : Evensong sung at King's. Our muddy rivals meanwhile had transformed themselves into surpliced cherubs. Old

Swain, the chaplain, entertained us with musical glasses and sands which danced into patterns. It was one of those days that cheat the sorrow of the years.

Football was almost a religion with Arthur. His appearance transfigured any game in which he joined. When there was a crowd watching, his name passed like magic from lip to lip. All eyes were fixed on him rather than on the ball. This must be the test of a star player. There was always a hushed expectancy that something would happen as soon as the ball came his way.

Most of the Ludgrove staff were internationals. " Joe " Smith and W. J. Oakley came to Ludgrove in my day. " Joe " looked a frail, wire-woven youth with a large head and a glittering eye. He was the finest centre-forward in history. He was also the hero of the Oxford and Cambridge cricket in 1897. Cambridge had triumphed and even prevented Oxford's follow-on by bowling wides to the boundary. When Oxford finally came in " Joe " made 132. In those days the crowd was top-hatted and " Joe's " reception from the pavilion was believed to be the greatest ever given to an individual at Lords. Such an occasion, such an audience and such a reversal of fortune as even cricket seldom shows !

W. J. Oakley was an all-round athlete : a tower of strength at full-back for Oxford or England. He became head-master and was killed in a motor accident shortly after his retirement.

It was something to have played in the field with three such players as England will not see again.

At Ludgrove I first realised the importance of writing correct Latin verses as a passport to Eton and the Varsity.

The top division was under T. C. Weatherhead who had the tricks of Latin versification at his fingers' ends. To turn the Bab Ballads into Ovidian shape seems as exquisite an accomplishment as *petit-point* embroidery or timing the cricket ball. The " Feather " as we called him had a pretty temper and a pretty wit. He was full of sarcasm and asthma. His division had the benefit of his jokes

which sometimes found their way to *Punch*. The famous
witticism about " pointing maxims " at Lobengula was his.
I remember another he made in class by way of impressing
us with the power of Greek tragedy. He told us that the
spectators were always sitting in tiers (tears !) His profile
made a very distinct memory with a sandy-peaked beard,
contemptuous little eyes and the quickest of tempers !
During a master's match he once refused to kick a goal
though he had the ball at his feet. Years and years later
I was looking at El Greco's portraits in Toledo when I
recognised the " Feather."

The staff were unlike ordinary usherdom and contained
at least one genius : Cecil Sharp, who taught us music,
ringing, catches and chanteys, glees and madrigals.
When Cecil Sharp was about, everybody had to sing.
The school was divided into two classes and there was a
master's Quartette. I can see him with his large hooked
nose, wispy light hair and merry brown eyes which glowed
with the devotion of a fanatic as he waved his arms,
chanted, chirruped and instilled harmony into unmelodious
boys. None of us realised what a privilege it was to be
taught by him. To us it was a perpetual joke that C
Sharp was a musical note.

He had returned penniless from Australia and gave
his life to salving the ballads and folk-song of his country.
With the delectable Charles Marson he collected the
folk-song of Somerset. What he could not recover in
England he afterwards discovered amongst the " poor
whites " in America. How he saved the lost minstrelsy
of Merry England by tramping the Appalachian Mountains is one of the romances of our time. He had the same
rare feeling for a ballad as Walter Scott. I chanced to
meet him again in Washington after his return from living
amongst the wild men and moonshine-makers of Tennessee.
I presided at a lecture during which he revealed some of
his finds. He saved something which will outlive all
that passes for popular music in England to-day. Had he
done the same for Ireland or Wales he would be remem-

bered as a national hero, for in both these countries the ballads are more important than the laws.

I saw Ludgrove boomed into success during my time. A converted country villa assumed the requirements of the modern school. Stables were turned into a changing room and the Bevans' carriage house became a racquet court. The hall with inscribed boards was added in my first term. An Eton Fives Court was built : like a symbol of Arthur's lifelong devotion to the best of schools. We were taught to play Eton Fives : a virtue as useful as the fabrication of Eton Latin verses. The mysteries of the Pepperpot and Dead Man's Hole were made known to us. Finally the hill-side was levelled and a fine ground prepared for football matches. But it was stony ground and regularly masters and boys stoned the field, kneeling between baskets. Splendid matches were played against Oxford and Cambridge whereat Arthur still showed some of his dazzling form. He played with the energy of twenty until he was forty. He took no warning from his gallant heart. Often he had to lie down during a game in progress, appearing exhausted to death. But he never stopped playing, and he would never allow others to surpass him in the field. After playing to the end he died in the night of February 22, 1902.

At Ludgrove I won my only athletic trophy : a challenge cup for sports. Jack Howey and myself qualified with twelve points apiece. Basil Blackett had eleven. Howey and I had to go through the whole programme again, he winning the jumps and I the races. In the deciding 220 yards I won by a yard after a downright struggle. Thirty-five years later Lord Carson showed me proudly a cup won by his boy at Ludgrove. I had the curious feeling that I had seen it before and found my name amongst many others on the shields.

But athletics knew me no more. Under Arthur's suasions I had joined the despised company of " saps " and parted from the important world which is called sporting.

I was really sad at leaving Ludgrove. It had so completely been my world for four years. The last Prize Supper and Concert came, the last prize-books were added to my shelf, first friendships were scattered, and for the last time we sang the wonderful school songs of Harrow. In an establishment devoted to Eton this was the only concession permitted to the Hill. Harrow school songs are so good that the School might have been founded to fit the songs. The Eton *Carmen* requires an organ and full harmony to bring it out, and I discovered was scarcely ever sung at Eton. As for the Eton boating-song it proved saccharine mixed with Thames water. But the Harrow songs that we sang under Cecil Sharp were worth all the school chanteys that were ever written. There must be some reason for boys going to Harrow.

Eton College

*

THE CHRISTMAS HOLIDAYS OF 1898 WERE SPENT
preparing for the Eton Entrance, which then took place
at the beginning of each half. Mr F. L. Crabtree, one
of the Ludgrove masters, came to Glaslough and every
morning we struggled up the *gradus ad Parnassum*. By
that time I had a feeling that even entry into the Kingdom
of Heaven might depend on correct Latin verses.

In January 1899 Mr Crabtree brought me to Eton
with high hopes and my mind well stuffed with tags and
endings, warranted to help out a budding pentameter or
pregnant hexameter at any stage of eruption.

In a slow horse-drawn cab I drove through Windsor
into the Eton of the nineteenth century. We were
preceded by another cab in which sat a boy whose intelligent countenance impressed my memory, but I was
unable to meet him until Cambridge days. He was a
King's Scholar, and in those days there was a gulf between
the Tugs and the Oppidans or townboys who quite wrongly
considered themselves the true Etonians. He turned out
to be Gordon Selwyn the present Dean of Winchester.
We were both looking around with wonderment, but he
had not the terror of the Entrance upon him. He was
already in fifth form by virtue of his scholarship.

Mr Crabtree showed me Upper Chapel; and unforgettable was the marble statue of the Holy Founder.
Thence into College itself (for Mr Crabtree had been a
colleger) where I saw his name cut in the stone as well as
those of all occupants of the room. Another room preserved
a list of Derby winners to posterity. I was left at my

dame's, a house opposite the old cemetery. Behind the
stucco frontage, which was dated 1844, there lay a three-
storied warren of ill-lit and ill-ventilated rooms. They would
have been condemned by any modern housing authority.
The passages were lit with gas and the boys used stumpy
candles. But this was an Eton before the era of School
Stores and before the Old Etonian tie had been invented.
I glanced at the school list. There were old masters who
had taught my father, names that had been memorable
since the Seventies and which I knew already by nickname : " Pecker " Rouse, " Arthur Jack " (James),
" Mike " (R. A. H. Mitchell), Walter Durnford (W.D.),
and most ancient was " Sammy " Evans, who dated his
drawing lessons from the Fifties. At the bottom of the
masters' list was the Rev. Cyril Argentine Alington, whose
first sermon I must have heard in Lower Chapel.

It was still an Eton of the old dominies, fantastic old
characters who were equally ragged and respected by the
boys. Provided they behaved like gentlemen, they were
never let down by their fond pupils. That is the first
and only rule for house masters.

Only Dickens could have described their types. There
was even a surviving " Eton dame " who ran her house
without male assistance, old Jane Evans. My own dame
was subsidiary to a house master, and a frightening old
lady I found her. With a very red face, a hooky nose, and
unwieldy figure she bullied servants and trades-people
and Lower Boys. But she had her good points. She was
believed to be an authority on medicine and the Bible,
and was consulted by boys on both. She was a good
Churchwoman, and once you were in her good books, you
could " stay out " of Early School as often as you asked.
Early School was that mediæval custom which has
impaired Eton tempers and digestions for generations.
It took the place of the early Mass once said before dawn
in old Catholic days.

Meantime I was put through the Entrance Exam in
Upper School. Some seventy boys scribbled with beauti-

ful quill-pens on battered old desks which might have come out of curiosity shops. Around us the panelled walls were carved with thousands of names. Busts of great Etonians frowned from the walls. I felt much alarmed until I glanced at the Greek translation paper which I had fortunately seen before. While others chewed their quills I wrote with a blissful and beating heart. I took Remove !

A fellow Ludgrovian rushed to tell me my good luck, and Arthur's congratulations were overwhelming. I rushed round the rails in front of Ingalton Drake's and absorbed every letter in Doctor Warre's purple ink and noble penmanship.

At the head of the list were the few names placed in Remove :

Lord Balgonie	Holland
Mr Coventry	Leslie
Hely Hutchinson	Mr Somerset

No less than three were connected with the Peerage.

I have never met any since of that six. " Mr Somerset " which is Etonian parlance for " Honourable " became Lord Raglan and amuses me with his iconoclastic writings. Balgonie died after a hunting accident in 1913 (we were both Leslies). Tom Coventry became a statesman in British Columbia. Hely Hutchinson had the most divine boy's voice in the school.

Amongst the Ushers who watched us in Upper School from their high pews was my future tutor (now Master of Magdalene, Cambridge) to whom I owe my first glimmerings of the rhythmic or beautiful in literature. He was the most exquisite Latin versifier in England and his script would have been a credit to the Renaissance. To him I read my first chapter of Greek Testament on my first Eton Sunday. It was a surprise to discover that the Gospel had been written in Greek and a greater surprise to be told that my Greek was good. It wasn't, but I

knew the English version by heart. Up to that moment
I had believed that Our Lord talked good English. It
was only Pilate's linguistic swank that led him to write the
superscription in three dead tongues !

I was placed in Division 25, a class of thirty boys under
Hugh Macnaghten, a Fellow of Trinity, and the most inspiring of teachers, living or dead. The form was crammed
into a low, high-tiered room under Upper School called
Black Hole. It has since become a cavernous school
office. The wooden seats rose almost to the ceiling and
a thin sunlight leaked through the latticed windows which
did so much architectural credit to Sir Christopher Wren.
But the London County Council would have condemned
it off-hand as well as the hole in which I lived and slept at
my dame's. We sat in an airless room amid piles of books
and top hats while a teacher, who was in the succession of
Socrates, revealed glimpses of that Greek and Latin
world which haunts all European education. " Muggins "
taught us with an earnest flame in his eyes. He introduced Byron's Hebrew Melodies into my first Sunday
Qs, that constant tax on the leisure of Eton Sundays. He
never missed a chance of making an interesting comment
and he made the classical dead live again. I soon learnt
that Cicero was a lovable bore and that Caligula was a
criminal lunatic. " Muggins " was wise and patient and
was compelled to suffer fools gladly. A handful of " saps,"
who had taken Remove, worked hard for him, but it was
before the days when boys of equal merit were herded in
divisions. There was no " select," and Division 25 was
full of laggards, Peers, and young gentlemen of the world
who were content to bask in idleness. " Saps " were
watched with contempt, but made to spout hard-learnt
construes like the gulls made to disgorge by bigger gulls.
It was extraordinary how little work could be done.
There was a system by which the tutor kept check on
work done by his pupils in classes under other masters.
Astley Minor, the most dashing and best looking boy in

my time, boasted that he had served up the same set of
verses to his tutor every week in one half with certain
alterations. His class master apparently saw none. The
tendency of masters was to leave the lazy alone and to
drive the willing. I found myself constantly overworked
all the time I was at Eton, and finally left the school
suffering from mild brain-fever.

But " Muggins " enticed boys to work hard. He was
a poet under the great grammarian. He released Catullus
and Virgil alive into class on the wings of Tennyson's
verse. One was " tenderest of Roman poets nineteen
hundred. years ago," and the other " wielder of the
stateliest measure ever moulded by the lips of man."
Could one ever forget such lines ?

I used to bring " Muggins " my work in the quaint old
tumbledown two-story house called " Drury's " which
looked very like the photographs of the slum dwellings
which are removed by reformers to-day. The pompous
portico of the school library stands there to-day. I
remember serving him with a charming scriptural essay,
in which I had unfortunately substituted the word
" prostitute " for proselyte throughout. It concluded
by saying that the Jews compassed the earth to make one
prostitute. " Muggins " observed sadly that they could
not be as bad as that ! " Drury's " was pulled down that
same year and was only remarkable for having a namesake
in the Harrow nomenclature and having inspired a line
of Mackworth Praed : " a happy boy at Drury's."

Here was a superb scholar, who once reread the whole
of Plato as some would reread Scott, taking endless pains
with boy's ingratitude. It was a mixed class. There was
Hussain Mir Ekhram, a relative of the Nawab of Hydera-
bad. He was near the bottom of class, but " Muggins "
typically gave him first prize " because he worked so
hard," whereas the top boy, Hely Hutchinson, was not
given the prize " because he should have done better ! "
Hussain was a follower of the Prophet and was excused
Sunday Qs. There was an embarrassing scene when

" Muggins " inadvertently asked him once for his Sunday
Qs and then apologised in the best taste.

The jester of the class was Portarlington (then known
as Lord Carlow). Like most Irish Peers he was not expected to work, and lest his indifference to letters should
spread to others he was segregated under an alcove
window, whence he made the most alarming signs to
passing tourists. When he was put on to construe, the
whole class settled down to a little fun. Like a born actor
he always tackled the passage with the greatest confidence
and energy, but always ended in ridiculous grief. He was
always good-tempered and amusing and " Muggins " was
never angry. Whenever I see him in night clubs or on the
Turf I recall the comic relief he supplied us in the Black
Hole in the days of good Queen Victoria.

As a new boy I recall him with gratitude. As a cousin
with two years seniority he could have been contemptuous,
but he introduced me into Layton's teashop up town
and produced an old waitress who had known my father
as " Chico " in the Seventies. At Carlow's command
I was provided with refreshments. This was called being
" socked." There was a whole Eton slang to be learnt
afresh for it differed from the school talk at Ludgrove.
The word " crib " was substituted for the fine old English
word " cog " for instance. The Glossary supplied all
Eton terms except the really useful and important ones,
which were omitted for reasons of prudery. By dire
experience one learnt them one by one and I shall not
reproduce them here.

" Sock," whether as verb or noun, denoted feeding and
food. I was also " socked " to the extent of a buttered bun
by " Mr Curzon," now Earl Howe, the most daring of
those who race their own cars. I recall his condescension
in taking me to a sock shop opposite Tangier Lane, where
our bedmakers and maids were believed to live in squalid
confusion.

Over the maids presided a superior boys' maid, who was
very little below the dame. Most boys' maids were called

"the Hag," and a very suitable denominator it was. Ours was an epitome of punctuality, good order, and ubiquity. She would have been valuable in the Customs. She could see such contraband as cribs, port wine, and cigarettes through the boards. Mrs Sowray, prompt, punctilious, and precise, only overslept herself once in history. I can see her dashing round on a winter's morning to light a candle in every bedroom in the house : reminding me of the Continental acolyte, who tries to light thirty or forty candles simultaneously. May indeed she be chosen to call us all on the Last Day !

My first year I lived down a sloping passage in a miserable little room looking out on Charlie Wise's yard. There was always a reek of foul straw in the air and large rats played on the stable roof below. We used to lay traps of bread for them and then ambush them with lumps of coal. So small were my quarters that at night, when my bed was let down, my unused bath had to go on the table. I was too busy filling and emptying my fagmaster's tubs to have time for my own. I made up in summer time by bathing three times a day in the river. In any case my bath had been appropriated by a bigger boy as a hide for his gramophone, a new and forbidden luxury. Later in the year my brother joined me and two bath tubs had to be piled at night. It was bitterly cold and the firing so wretched we used to hack bricks out of the chimney and heat them. At night I seldom undressed as a Lower Boy, and preferred sleeping in my clothes excepting only boots and top hat, not so much for warmth as for the pleasure of enjoying a half-hour extra in bed before Early School.

I shall never forget my infantile astonishment at the prevalent use of strong liquors and strong language at Eton. Beer seemed to me the beverage of Bill Sikes till I learnt the amenities of Tap. Port wine hidden in ottomans seemed very wicked.

The House was a rough and unforgettable experience. The life of a " sap " was rightly made unpleasant. The handful of Ludgrovians were swamped. We had to barricade ourselves in to finish our work. I used to read after lights-out with a candle flickering between my eyes and book. Evening seemed an equal struggle against Homer and the rowdier spirits in the house. It was too strong a combination. Supper was a melancholy mixture of beer and cheese best avoided at that hour. Prayers were a gabble. We were assembling for Prayers in my first days when I found myself sparring with Batchelor, another Lower Boy. We went at each other with swinging fists until a cross-cut " drew the claret " from my nose. I fled upstairs and bled a basinful, wondering what dreadful penalty I would incur. To my surprise nothing was ever said.

There was a pleasant consumption of coffee and bun before Early School, but not until morning Chapel did the organ wake up the blood and the day's rhythm begin. For a year I worshipped as a Lower Boy in Lower Chapel and hearkened to the lessons nasalised by " the Flea." Edward Austen Leigh was Lower Master and deserved his nickname for he was a hearty swisher and could draw blood with his birch. Lower Chapel lacked any sparkle of ritual or song. There has been a great improvement since, and a choir of boy choristers wear the scarlet of a Royal foundation. It was understood that His Late Majesty was asked to give them leave to wear the red cassocks. He returned word that they had his permission for red hassocks !

Lower Chapel was a crush of small boys in jackets. Only two towered above the others wearing Charity Tails : C. H. A. Paget (now Lord Anglesey) and " Brooky " who was the late Lord Warwick. " Brooky " actually won his house-colours as a Lower boy at Donaldson's. He never waited for Fifth Form, for as soon as the Boer War broke out we heard that he had pawned his uncle's overcoat and enlisted for service on the veldt.

The South African War filled my Eton days. As a Lower boy I picked up a newspaper in South Meadow bearing Kruger's Ultimatum and wondered at the

Latinity of the word. I was in Upper Fifth and my last Half when peace was declared. Winston came down to lecture in Windsor after his escape from Pretoria. We all drove in a cab from Eton together. As we passed the posters announcing his lecture, he took one glance and leaning back in the cab, shouted : " Fame ! Fame ! " How we all cheered and I dropped his lecture slides which luckily did not crack. " Look well at them," he said as he opened his lecture with a lantern-map of the two republics : " They are ours ! " and a shout shook the roof.

Eton was deeply affected. Major Myers the beloved adjutant of the Eton Corps had rushed into the trouble and been immediately killed. The Black Week of December, 1899, weighed like an iron curtain between the two Centuries. Until then England had seemed invincible by land and sea. It was the last year of the old Victorian splendours, but even the most mad and flame-eyed prophet would not have dared foresee the next twenty years.

Queen Victoria was still an Eton neighbour and drove almost daily past the playing fields. I can see her passing down the Slough Road while we played cricket in Agar's Plough, a recent acquisition to the school. My first Half I was once late going into school when I was all but run over by the Royal carriage. Hurrying past the " Burning Bush " with an elbowful of books I suddenly visioned the Queen within two yards of my face. I had the presence of mind to whip off my top hat but at the cost of dropping all my books under her chariot wheels. She appreciated my difficulty and turned round to bow. It was the Queen : and all that has been written since by biographers and cheap-jacks or thrown upon picture or stage will never reawaken the thrill it was to have seen her pass as close as that !

It was our belief at Eton that the Queen always bowed to Eton boys but never to tradesmen or officials.

My first summer Half she celebrated her eightieth birthday and the whole School marched up Windsor Hill to serenade her with such music as Dr Lloyd could extort

L

and extract from us with much beating of his baton. My experiences were contained in a letter to my brother : " Last Wednesday was the Queen's birthday and the whole school trooped up there and sang the Jubilee Hymn. Thirteen chaps fainted in about ten minutes. We got a whole holiday and the Queen will most likely give us an extra week's holidays."

Before two years we lined the last lap for her funeral, between the park gates and the Castle. Every minute of the scene returns. The school paraded in School Yard. We already wore the traditional hat-band of mourning for her grandfather, George III. Imagine having seen a little lady whose grandpa had actually owned all America ! We all felt the pressure of history when we marched out of the yard preceded by our own Volunteers, wearing their purple-grey uniforms with light-blue facings. We turned in by the South Western Station to the back of the Castle to escape the seething crowd which blocked every inch of Windsor. It was three o'clock before the bells began tolling and the one and eighty guns thundered salute to the dead. In time there appeared a very small coffin surmounted by sceptre and crown and slowly hauled by blue-jackets in their straw hats up the slope. A bunch of kings and emperors followed. Grim fates, exiles, dethronements and assassinations were awaiting them. How unimportant they all seemed, the kings of the earth, compared to the little packet of ashes they were honouring with bowed heads and shuffling tread. A cortège of diplomats passed like so many resplendent lacqueys behind a Sovereign who had been served by Palmerston and Stratford de Redcliffe. The colour scheme was only broken by Mr Choate of New York wearing his dull Republican mufti.

Lord Roberts passed in tears, looking tiny in his big boots and cocked hat. And the Kaiser was obviously suffering from nerves, for compared to the solemnity of the others, he was chatting and twisting round. He had rushed loyally to the funeral and whisper said he had offered to lift his grandmother into her coffin but that the Queen's surviving sons had interposed and lifted her reverently . . . it was incredible how light she was . . . as though some last ray of departing glory had stricken her to a handful of ash. . . .

Behind the corner of the Castle the little Prince Edward, son of the new Prince of Wales, was being discreetly driven. A few years later Mr Hansell used to collect a few Eton boys to play decorous cricket with his young charge. Of all whom I watched following Queen Victoria to the grave I only recognised one in the procession which followed King George V thirty-five years later : the young Duke of Albany, who had returned as the white-haired haggard Duke of Saxe-Coburg. In the summer Half of 1899 I was in the same division as he up to Mr Kindersley. Albany was a pleasant boy who was believed to add to his pocket-money by the sale of Royal autographs. The War caught him with an English heart in a German uniform, but he has since become a popular figure in Anglo-German relations.

On the following Sunday (Feb 3, 1901) the Queen still lay in state in St George's Chapel before interment at Frogmore. There the lonely Prince Consort awaited her and many good Victorians were glad that she would not be too near Henry VIII. My cousin, Hugh Frewen, and myself were fortunate enough to obtain entry to the Clarence Memorial Chapel, where the body lay in a space suffocated by a carnage of flowers. Four Lifeguardsmen stood ironically in the presence of death. The sweet and sickly air smelt like laughing gas and the soldiers toppled over from time to time under the fumes. We were allowed to move slowly round and on our return Hugh, who was the school poet, composed a poem for the *Eton Chronicle*, which was shown to the new King. He was kind enough to express a wish that Hugh would one day become his Poet Laureate.

We were at Glaslough at the moment of the Queen's

death. For some reason the rumour preceded the event by two days. My brother and I were drilling the Boys' Brigade in the school house and we seized the opportunity to sing " God save the King," the words which had not been heard since 1837. Dr Stewart the one-legged doctor interposed to say there was no official news that the Queen was dead. The Parson said he had been told so on the strength of a telegram sent to Lord Rossmore which everybody had read *en route*. The advantage of sending a telegram in Ireland is that the whole county knows the contents before the recipient. After a little discussion " God save the Queen " was sung as an after-thought. It was of minor historical importance, but " God save the King " was sung for the first time in the twentieth century in the Glaslough schoolhouse (Jan 20, 1901).

Two days later the real news arrived and the church bell was solemnly tolled while we sat gloomily in the gallery. The main interest was whether national mourning would be extended to the classroom. After some protests we were sent back to Eton. London was plunged in fog and crape. Every shop window was streaked by a mourning shutter. The women, old and young, were draped with veils and most touching was the mourning worn by the prostitutes, in whose existence the old Queen had always refused to believe. Even the crossing sweepers carried crape on their brooms. Old men were already boasting that they had lived in three reigns. My grandmother prepared to go into perpetual mourning. It seemed as though the keystone had fallen out of the arch of Heaven.

Once the Queen was dead, all restraint passed from people's tongues and long suppressed anecdotes came to the surface. The most famous word of the Queen " we are not amused " has become proverbial. I remember the unfortunate officer " Bully " Oliphant who provoked the famous rebuke. His name, otherwise forgotten, deserves at least the fame of association, though at the time he believed his career was finished. The story he told at the Queen's table was a light one, but presumed that a lady could become motherly during her husband's absence. When the Queen called on him to repeat what had apparently amused her guests, he had not the presence of mind to substitute a chaster yarn.

The only *bon-mot* being whispered was " Death where is thy sting ? " and the answer was : " in the pen of Alfred Austin "—the ridiculous Poet Laureate. The anecdotes which sprang to life would have filled a Suetonius but they all showed how strong and human a woman she was : how she had received Gladstone after the death of General Gordon much as Queen Elizabeth had received the French Ambassador after the Massacre of St Bartholomew : how, as her sons, one by one, fell in love with Mrs Langtry she had taken down the signed photographs from their bedsides with her own royal hands.

Two stories remained in my mind which could not have been invented. There was the story of the most faithful and long serving of her secretaries. Years and years had passed in the Royal service but one day a tiny cell broke in his head and as he left her room he murmured aloud " what a funny little old woman." The Queen was puzzled and rang the bell : " I do not think you are quite well," and the incident passed. Inadvertently he had said what doubtless he had been thinking for years.

Perhaps the most delightful was the story of the Queen passing down a corridor in the night and pausing to open a window. While she looked out into the scene she heard a lonely sentry murmur : " Good evening, Miss." On this occasion she really was amused.

The new King gave us a considerable shock by falling ill shortly before his Coronation. I was at Winchester watching the match between Eton and Winchester when the news was passed and the great event postponed till the King's appendix could be removed. All that year there was a loyal rush of courtiers and snobs to undergo the Royal operation. It is curious what divinity seems to hedge even the ailments of the great. I remember the Empress Eugenie exploding with ridicule when an American flatteress had gone too far. It was at Cowes and the Empress had been persuaded to visit a Trans-atlantic yacht. The hostess had a religious cult for Napoleon, and on the mention of cancer observed " Oh blessed disease, most blessed disease." The Empress queried this, and the other continued : " Since it was the disease the great Emperor died of " ! This was too much for Eugenie, who burst out : " *Ça c'est trop fort !* "

To return to Eton. Hugh Frewen's poem on the Queen marked Eton grief and then we became re-absorbed in the routine. Hugh was my closest friend though we were at different Houses. He was the only boy in the school to possess a typewriter. A third friend played an amusing joke on him by getting an improper note typed in London and sending it to a master who naturally concluded that Hugh must have been the typist. We became " wet bobs " and rowed on the river to escape the dreariness of cricket. One date I shall always remember (May 4, 1901) when we ran down a gig which we found to our consternation was being rowed by two sons of the Head and steered by the majestic Dr Warre himself : a couple of eaglets paddling the old eagle. We were convinced we would be swished, but we heard no more on the matter. Old Edmond Warre was the greatest head master Eton or England ever produced. Boys and masters were equally frightened of him. School clerks stood to atten-tion as though he were royalty. A tremor shot our ranks in chapel or in class when his immense and towering frame was seen. His decisions were slow and weighty ; and, like papal pronouncements, could be described as " of themselves irreformable." Once the whole school was collected for a wigging. There were cat-calls and murmurings. Warre only lifted his hand and all was still. Warre had taken over and reformed the ill-disciplined school of Hornby who had become Provost. For fifteen years Warre ruled by benevolent prestige and he had made Eton efficient when she was beginning to become effete. His position at Eton was that of Zeus on Mount Olympus. His words were law but sometimes they were received with Homeric laughter. He was getting old and he ruled by the greatness of his past. I heard him preach once or twice in tones of melancholy thunder. We all knew his favourite text : " Oh pray for the Peace of Jerusalem : they shall prosper that love thee." He meant, of course, Eton and those who loved Eton ways. He had a favourite hymn " O thou wrestler all unknown," but the school used to sing with greater gusto the hymn-lines : " When comes thy promised time when war shall be no more ? " But when Warre passed to the little Eton cemetery in later years, it was felt in the Empire like the passing of a king.

He addressed the school on certain great occasions in Upper School. When the keyholes were filled with plaster of Paris in the New Schools on a merry examination morning, Warre took away all leave, but later he summoned Fifth and Sixth Form and restored it. He understood that the culprits were no longer members of the school and he was only punishing the innocent. His heavy booming note was hardly intelligible, but the wildest souls were quelled when he spoke. His most emotional effort followed a famous row. A younger boy was expelled, but not wholly with the approval of the school. When he drove away, bouquets were lowered into his cab and a mob deluged him with rice and confetti. There was a scrimmage in Keate's Lane. The Head took it severely to heart as a challenge to his own authority. No one who heard his famous and terrible outburst could ever forget it.

Mathematics and French were much improved by Warre's habit of occasional inspection. It is true that our notebooks bore a threatening slip to say :

" This book will be inspected by the Head Master "

but we knew it for an empty threat. But at any moment
he might sweep majestically into a classroom. I was once
put on to construe a Greek passage in his presence. Even
the relief of knowing the words correctly did not compensate for the accompanying nerve attack. I was present
in a mathematical class which was found all unprepared
to meet him. He strode in and he strode out ignoring
the collapse of the boys and the pathetic excuses of the
unfortunate master. But all our leave was stopped.

Hornby was still Provost, but we only saw him in
Upper Chapel. He preached giving the effect of a cocka-
too in the pulpit, for his hair waved in a crest. He made
his points with his head thrown back like a cackling hen.
He was a mountaineer and a skater and the best after-
dinner speaker in England. Hornby had swished our
parents and we felt a kindly disposition towards him.
His swishing had been better than Warre's, who turned
his head away and only scraped and scratched the boy.
Warre whipped with a lady's wrist. The record swishing
was given by Lower Master Joynes. According to
tradition he had used three birches and been hissed
going into Chambers. In future he was reduced to six
strokes.

All swishing was innocuous compared to what could be
handed out by the big boys. There was bullying in
Houses where the discipline was bad. When louts became
fag-masters they were fond of beating for nothing, and ten
running strokes with a cane left a boy cooling on his bed
for an hour. It was looked on as part of the hardening
process of life. No London County Council would permit
the treatment which was rife in some Houses. My brother
and I escaped quickly into Fifth Form out of the Lower
boy purgatory. Some boys were picked out for regular
canings however they behaved. One, whom I met in later
years, when he was a retired officer of the Guards, told me
he had attempted suicide by crawling up the pipes in the
lavatory one night and chewing the green copperas
which he believed to be a deadly poison. After lying

down to die he was much annoyed to be called next morning for Early School, which cannot be the accompaniment of any celestial existence.

At the end of my time I had a fag myself and as he was stronger than myself I refrained from beating him. When I returned as an " old boy," he told me he had been having a hellish time and been caned till he had " a bottom of tin." I advised him to use it on the river and so laid the foundation of a great rowing career. He became Captain of the Boats and when we last met on the Cambridge towpath he was President of the Varsity boat, no less than the famous " Soccer " Williams.

The canings given in the House made swishings seem little less than " the impulse from a vernal wood." But once the terror was past, life was very free and happy. Our own House was very slack compared to the glorious *esprit de corps* of a House like Miss Evans. There was an amusing boy called Keppel at Evans who held a record of ten canings in a Half. My cousin, Oswald Frewen, was at Evans and showed me his canings marked religiously on his school calendar amid the Red Letter Saints. He grew weary of the treatment and withdrew into the Navy passing as a Lower boy into the old *Britannia*. In consequence he was the only Lower boy who ever secured a a leaving book from the Head. This distinction was reserved for boys leaving Fifth Form without expulsion. The book was always Gray's *Poems* which was regarded as a certificate of not being sacked. But no boy ever sacked from Eton was excommunicated from the loving and chivalrous freemasonry of Old Etonians.

Present Etonians seem to differ from their forbears in every generation, but Old Etonians become essentially the same. I think we were much closer to *Tom Brown's Schooldays* than the present generation. Is it still thought to be amusing to dive off Windsor Bridge in a top hat ? My brother did it after winning the Headers at Athens, the delectable bathing place for those who had passed in swimming. We collected stamps, moths and railway tickets. To catch the hawk-moths in the playing fields I used to anoint the great elms with my supply of jam. Half a dozen of the biggest trees fell in 1903 and to-day there is only a handful surviving from what I remember as a grove. The young elms and chestnuts in Agar's Plough date from my first Half in 1899. They are as old as the century.

Collecting railway tickets was an exciting sport which entailed lying under the seat, assuming illness, travelling with the luggage or escaping from a train before it stopped —in order to avoid the official collector.

Betting was conducted through the race of Jobies— a kind of hereditary touts who supplied tips, laid bets, loaned shot-guns or caught moths for us. Betting proved so expensive that some of us dispensed with bookies and stood each other's bets. When one of us won a surplus he purchased himself a so-called racing pot : a modest piece of chinaware.

The damps and fogs of winter were made up for by the brilliance of the summers. The same Father of Fogs became our sparkling playfellow for three months. No one has really tasted Eton life without sharing the River. Two miles of Thames with all her creeks and back-waters are part of the unique heritage. My happiest days were spent bathing at Cuckoo Weir or Athens. I developed a special lung power while diving for fossils on the river gravels. I looked to the river for cleanliness, relaxation and exercise. My idea of being a Wet Bob was purely literal.

Cuckoo Weir was not deep. There was always a swarm of small boys struggling like white maggots in the greenish shallows. Spong, the old waterman, was in charge of the Passing. I was passed by Stuart Donaldson : a quiet, grave-looking master wearing a Leander ribbon. There was a tragedy attached to his name as he was brother to the last Eton boy drowned in the river. Ever since this disaster no boy was allowed on the river without passing the test : header, breast-stroke, and treadwater. Spong, in straw hat and whiskers, looked exactly like one of Leech's bathing men in some remote number of *Punch*. There was a plank bridge laid across the shallows and I remember the late Lord Conyngham taking a header therefrom into twelve inches of water. He was lucky to do no more than skin his nose.

Hall, a lean, sun-tanned waterman, was in charge at Athens. I can see him slipping like an eel in and out of his punt, carrying towels and watching for delinquents. One most delightful pastime was forbidden but irresistible. We used to catch hold of the houseboats being towed to Henley and be dragged ourselves half-way to Boveney. It was a form of surf-riding, but passed chiefly under the surf.

However rough the house, one could always escape to the river. There were many hours of great buoyancy and boyish ecstasies. The house in 1900 emigrated down the Eton Wick Road where we were the first to occupy a now venerable building called "Westbury." As the first occupant of my room I thought it fit to cut my initials in the stonework. This was resented in the name of the Governing Body and payment was charged for restoring the stonework. Most boys on leaving Eton pay to have their names cut up. I must be the only one made to pay to have his obliterated.

Oswald Frewen was at Miss Evans', the very last of the Dames. I had the privilege to take Sunday tea with her in Keate's Lane. Her hall was baronial and set with antlers and military trophies. She was benignant, but she could be adamant and was credited with expelling the relative of a duke. It was a grand experience to sit beside the old lady who had terrified the Governing Body by the threat of an interview, and inspired Sargent to paint his finest study of a woman. All his butterfly beauties seemed garish compared to Jane's kind old face.

She talked of the past. She had known the fathers and grandfathers of the boys. She lived to see a boy from her house return as Head. I heard her once tell an un-

believeable story of a small boy arriving at Eton in petti-
coats. His parents had sent him there from India. She
noticed him stumbling on the stairs and carried him up
under her arm.

The history of her house shows that the houses of Eton
Dames should not have been abolished. These old
matriarchs could be martinets when required. At least
they knew how to keep order and the most unruly rallied
to them. Miss Edgar, Miss Gulliver, Miss van Rosen, and
above all Miss Evans. It seemed a pity to abolish one of
the few professions a lady could often fulfil better than
men. Their success was uniform compared to the many
masters' houses which were failures towards the end of
Warre's time.

My father was at Gulliver's, which had the wonderful
record of beating the rest of the school at football and
enjoyed the privilege of playing in the Field. All parents
made the same joke when they started their sons on their
" Gulliver's travels." Gulliver's was the little brick house
near Barnes Pool, and there were two Miss Gullivers, one
of whom kept the accounts and the other kept order with
the aid of an immense ear-trumpet with which she
detected the least noise ! But the boys were chivalrous and
the old ladies stood them wine !

The so-called dames of to-day are not the historical
article. They are super-matrons and very excellent in
their way. My own dame had good points and bad,
but she was no lady and was detested by most of the boys.
Those she disliked she mentioned to the captain for
caning. The day came when a tradesboy wrote his
opinion of the dame on the wall. There was a fearful
row and the whole house save the seniors were caned.
This did not improve her popularity. She rather amused
me, for I have never met her like outside Musical Comedy.

She was High Church and talked of the Seven Sacra-
ments and of strange beings called " Cowley Fathers,"
whom pious boys in the house wished to join. In her
fussy manner she did much good. She was interested in

the work of the Clewer Sisters and we suspected that reformed Magdalens assisted sometimes as menials in the house. I haste to add that we never parted with anything more precious than the sovereigns and half-sovereigns which disappeared from our rooms. In those far-off days schoolboys carried gold pieces jingling in their pockets. Gold currency was easily lost and more easily stolen. It was as well to get it spent before it was borrowed.

The Boer War became very serious in my Eton time. To-day I believe schoolboys sometimes ask whether England fought for or against the Boers. Europe, led by Germany and France, showed hysterical hatred. However the Old Etonian Association provided such generals as Methuen, Buller, and Roberts, and all was for the best. There were occasional scenes. The ailing Queen reviewed the Household Cavalry who entrained from Windsor. We rushed up from Windsor and joined the seething crowd which shouted for revenge for Majuba! It was a curious contrast to return to Ireland in holiday time where the Irish regiments were entraining and giving three cheers for Kruger, which was certainly done in a feeling of fairer play. Majuba was the British variant of Adowa to Italy and Sedan to France. Well, they are all avenged now and it is to be hoped the world feels better for it. The United States were bitterly pro-Boer, perhaps more opposed to England than the present generation can credit. President McKinley would not even give his name to the hospital ship *Maine*, which was organised by the American women in London. This was a bit of a blow for my aunts on the committee, but in those days America considered the Boers a small nation like Abyssinia unjustly attacked. The Irish attitude was easy to understand, but when the Irish troops returned with full honours they gave their cheers still to Kruger. In the field their prowess was such that the old Queen dragged herself over to Dublin. Ireland was always

feudally loyal to the Royal Family, but was lost to the
Empire by criminal stupidity in Westminster in the
subsequent reigns.

Mafeking Day was like a prelude to Armistice Day
eighteen years later. It was a day of days at Eton. I
was coming down Judy's passage when I met my form-
master Mr. Heygate striding away with the remark :
" I shall certainly take no school to-day." This was
charming behaviour on the part of any master, and there
was a cheer which swelled into execration when it was
noticed that a Boer flag had been hoisted from Broad-
bent's House. As a joke Delves-Broughton and Barclay
of that House had hung the enemy's emblem from the
windows of a boy called Paul (son of the historian of that
name and, of course, no relation to *Paul* Kruger). The
House was besieged and stoned by an angry crowd. Every
window was smashed and the garrison returned fire with
every conceivable comestible. Old " Broader," a bent
figure, popular, sarcastic, and the last eventually to
survive of the old Eton characters, stood surveying the
damage. He was too wise to protest. He grunted and
slowly wheeled back. It was a day of madness and we
passed on to Arthur Benson's whose boys cheerfully
emptied their bookshelves into the street. It was pleasant
to feel lexicons and dictionaries underfoot. There was no
such scene since the great Eton Rebellion, when every boy
(except Grenville, the famous book-collector) cast his
books over Windsor Bridge.

Mafeking was a day of surging relief and ridiculous
riot. We raised heavenly Cain all day and in the evening
we marched on Windsor amid a frenzied crowd. In those
days England was more definitely divided into " cads and
gents " than to-day. The outer world of cads (which
included the pro-Boers in Parliament) simply did not
count. The crowd received us with delirious delight and
we might have been the relieving column entering
Mafeking. From Eton we surveyed the subservient race
around us of cads, Jobies, touts, and dissenters. There

was no thought of social reform, of mixing the classes or of a Labour Government, which would have sounded as comic as putting the Jobies into the Governing Body of Eton. It is impossible in every way to recall the settled class-sentiment of those times. To-day there are a hundred divisions and interlooping compartments in the social structure. They are chiefly due to quick application of fresh wits or new wealth. Good clothes and heavy subscriptions cover all the rifts in Society itself. But while Queen Victoria reigned, there was a strong hereditary Society, the great company of English sportsmen and the rest were the Rest !

The Boer War was looked on as a gentleman's war, almost as an Old Etonian war. It was inevitable that Imperialism swelled, Kipling sang, and the Tory Party swept the polls. The country knew who were its leaders and masters and voted for them solid.

In March 1900 my brother and I were delighted to get War leave to see our fond father off to South Africa. There were many leaves obtainable at Eton then : Long leave, Short leave, Bisley leave, Henley leave, Fourth of of June leave, but War leave was a happy innovation. On the assumption that we would never see our parent again we spent a delightful week in London with the butler who took us all day and every day to the Westminster Aquarium. This palace of cheap amusements has been replaced by the Nonconformist Central Hall. Here we watched melancholy fish behind the dirty glass, educated fleas, women's all-day bicycling races, and Professor Finney diving wrapped in flames into a water-tank. Here the butler nervously interposed between us and some ladies who were anxious to enter into conversation. I had never met prostitutes before and I mistook them for housemaids dressed up for a spree.

Alas the blissful week came to an end and we gathered to take a tearful farewell of our parent at Bill Beresford's house in Carlton House Terrace. It turned out to be a merry affair. His duchess Lily was protesting that the

London cabmen objected to the back view of the Callipygian Venus in the dining-room window. Marcus Beresford insisted that his cabby had said it did not compare with the missus ! It was an odd twist of conversation to remember down the years.

At any rate we were in roaring spirits as we drove in horsecabs to Waterloo Station. The Frewens were waiting for us as they also shared in the War leave. My grandmother was smiling bravely and joyously as we steamed out. She had already seen him off to Tel-el-Kebir and her father had returned from Waterloo so she knew how to behave on these occasions. Troops went to the Boer War in a delirium of delight. Tears were reserved for those who could not get taken. The war seemed like a tremendous picnic far away on the veldt. There would be plenty of antelope to shoot and a few Boers for Christmas shooting. We boys travelled on the train to Southampton, but were very dishevelled by the time we arrived. On the way my father bequeathed his watch to me and his gold links to my brother. We decided to fight it out then and there for the watch. Nearly forty years have passed and I am glad to say that the watch is still ticking in its original possession.

We rushed round to the transport and amused the soldiers who were reading tracts on the unprepared state of their souls. Gloomy tract-distributors were moving amongst them, but we bought a crate of oranges which we scrambled amongst them like a children's school-treat. We had them cheering again as the transport slowly moved away. My father stood in a yachting cap wearing a pink flower in his smart overcoat while my mother took snap after snapshot . . . until there was only a blurred ship. . . .

Study at Eton forty years ago varied immensely in interest. I came across masters who were incapable of keeping order or conveying a fragment of knowledge. There was an instructor in French and another in Mathematics who appeared like " transient embarrassed phantoms." We carried one round his class-rooms shoulder high on the ground that he was the most popular master in the school. Another we treated as the honorary secretary of a mythical club (called after his name) which we used to do work for other masters or read fiction or merely for relaxation.

There were a few masters who exacted work, but were content with little. Their class-rooms were dull, decorous, and sleepy. Others were inspiring, no less.

But amid many wasted hours and a system which was often ridiculous I attained some of the most precious gifts that any system dares to promise. I learnt the wonder and beauty of the universe, the fascination of science, and the charm and power of literatures. Incredible as it seems, at Eton I learnt to love Greek. The Classics became my religion instead of the Catechism and the Old Testament. And I discerned the values and beauty latent in English writing. And all these came to me before I was seventeen and had to leave Eton prematurely.

I played no games. I made few friends. I never won a colour, but I found pearls of great price. Eton left me a literateur, desirous of letters and ready to appreciate the world of books. My knowledge was scrappy and my scholarship hazy. But I could never be bored again throughout life. Magical keys had been thrust into my keeping. I bless the old School library.

All miseries and loneliness and unpopularity were worth enduring for that. I had the good fortune to come under three of the most inspiring teachers that Eton has ever known. To be up to any one of the three in class was an education in itself. Amid the run of exemplary ushers and decent dominies there were three men of genius whose names and memory I will always revere as a Chinese student for ever reveres his teachers : Allen Beville Ramsay, Arthur Christopher Benson, and Hugh Vibart Macnaghten. I often wonder if Eton has had one teacher to touch them since. If she has, she is justified of herself.

M

I had four halves up to Macnaghten and two up to
Benson. They opened their minds to those who cared to
enter. From afar they pointed beyond the muddy playing
fields to Parnassus. They gave me and others that extra
sense which ensures that life has an escape, a hobby, a
drug, perhaps a vocation while sight lasts and ink runs.

I met Arthur Benson in Middle Fifth. The pity was
that he was not allowed to teach us English instead of
Latin : Ruskin and Pater instead of Cicero. Oh, to have
had his interpretation of Macaulay and Gibbon instead
of having to struggle through Thucydides with our noses
dipped in syntax and our thumbs in the lexicon. No
doubt Thucydides was a prince of historians, but he
should have been read aloud with cribs. As it was, a
class of thirty boys was made to hate a Greek author,
and a fine Englishman of letters was worn out in the
process. He threw us anecdotes and asides like sugar
plums out of the dough. When our editor remarked that
one of the typical speeches was " brief and soldierly,"
Benson drily pointed out that it was neither : and how we
laughed ! Wherever there was a gleam of poetry or a
chance to make a literary point he made it. He set up his
own poems to turn into Latin verse and two became
embedded in my mind. One was in memory of a carrier
pigeon carrying a love letter which he had accidentally
shot. Another was his resplendent lyric about the
Phœnix which represents him in the *Oxford Book of
English Verse*. It was a surprise to learn that he had
written it in his sleep :

> " Those ashes shine like ruby wine,
>   Like bag of Tyrian murex spilt :
>   The claw, the jowl of the flying fowl
>   Are with the glorious anguish gilt."

To me that stanza became a symbol not of the Phœnix,
but of the jewels of literature which could be discovered
by poking a bit in the ashes.

Working these jewelled lines into Latin gave me my
first sense of English verse. Would we could have had

more of modern poetry instead of an insufferable book called *Scriptores Romani* ! Still Benson made the best of them. He gave us the younger Pliny's account of the eruption of Vesuvius which buried Pompeii, and the Emperor Trajan's correspondence about the new sect of Christians. I am afraid we thought the Emperor had taken far too lenient a view and we much regretted that Christianity had survived the persecutions. It was curious to think of Christians as a small society of outlaws, far more sympathetic beings than the pompous bores who spoke to us out of pulpits on Sundays.

Benson showed his delicious touch of mingled humour and sarcasm in his school library lectures. One on Lewis Carroll was a revelation of word magic. It seemed impossible that any lecture about books could be so absorbing. He was really more amusing than Lewis Carroll. His power of quietly putting an author over the limelight was wonderful. At least he sometimes made us write English poetry. My first poem for him on the Gracchi (written with infinite care and metrical perplexity) was spoilt when other boys (jealous no doubt) discovered an unintended indecency in my first line. I was filled with agony and shame, but Arthur Benson saw nothing ill. He was wasted at Eton, as his self-torturing writings have shown. He made his success later as the Master of Magdalene at Cambridge. Had he become Eton Head, he could have lectured and preached divinely and inspired us *ex cathedra*, but alas we only knew him as a weary usher on the borderlands of sweet madness and poetic melancholy. Of him it could be said as was written of a Pope cut off in his papal prime : *Demonstratus magis quam nobis datus.*

My last year at Eton was spent under Hugh Macnaghten. Through him I acquired Greek as people acquire a sense of music or philosophy. The means were Sophocles and Plato. He confirmed my experience that Eton masters were either too ridiculous or too good to be true. Hugh Macnaghten could be compared only to William Johnson,

" Ionicus," who had remained a legend in the school. He also was a Greek and a poet and had discovered that favoritism is the secret of good teaching. The only difference was that Johnson was a pagan and Macnaghten retained an ascetical interpretation of the Christian creed.

The Greeks whom Macnaghten touched for us in class remained with us for ever more : Sophocles, Apollonius Rhodius and the Anthologists. I cannot read Sophocles without letting the translation assume his gentle accent in which the r took no part. Orestes and Electra I came to imagine almost as members of the Macnaghten family. Apollonius Rhodius' story of the Argo, that curious mixture of archaic epic and modern love story, lives as he expounded it. It was the first love story I could understand. Jason seemed to me perfectly right and sensible in jilting Medea after he had taken all he could out of her and Medea was worthy of slow torture. But Macnaghten always inspired pity for his characters ; and I realised that a woman's love deserved all pity.

Socrates swam into my ken and I wept over his fate. The sight or mention of hemlock brings back all that story and passion sophisticated by Plato in the Apologia and the Euthythro. Sometimes Hugh Macnaghten seemed like the great Greek himself : without the subtlety of Socrates but with his character for fairness and his courage to die.

From Macnaghten I learnt first ideas of Higher Criticism. The Bible was not to be taken too literally. " Of course God could have made the world in six days, but He preferred not to," was his wise summary. Like the saints, who strong in their own chastity could dispense themselves from prudery, he never minced or mystified matters. Any other master would have shocked us in explaining the furious play which St Paul made with the phrase " circumcision." The English version has of course slurred the meaning in the Greek.

Poor dear Hugh Macnaghten : great triumphs and great sorrows befell him. His House became the best in Eton

history and the best of the best. He became Vice-Provost
and lived saddened by the loss of so many pupils. The
flower of his House fell in France. And his last years were
saddened by a darkening of his spirit. The exquisite
matter in his brain became jarred but not blurred. Everything seemed withdrawn from one who had given
everything to others. In the end he sank under the
affliction of body and mind and became a man of sorrows.
On the Fourth of June, 1929, I saw him for the last
time on the old cricket playing field. Words failed him
and in the excess of grief tears failed me as well. In
August of that year he cast himself into the Thames
and died like Leander under the running water. The
Greeks would have approved. The mediævals would have
expected lilies to rise from the spot where he was drowned.

A third master who touched the highest functions of a
teacher was Dr Porter. He taught every branch of
science in a gaunt brick laboratory (now hewn down).
He was revered and was believed to have preached once :
on the probable gases let loose at Creation ! He lived in an
atmosphere of colour-photography, home-made gramo-
phones and weird experiments. Lower boys believed
he had resurrected a cat from the dead with the aid
of a galvanic battery. His teaching became legendary.
Certainly he revealed the elements and wonders of
creation to gaping youth like one that spoke having
authority. I learnt far more Theism or the actual workings of God from him than from all the chapel services.
Porter would have agreed with the well-known Mr Squeers
that : " She's a rum 'un is Natur." He was a pioneer
always dabbling on the edges of scientific discovery.
He was the first of all amateur photographers. He was
a good astronomer and read the Heavens like a book.
He used to take his class into South Meadow to study any
passing eclipse ; and after a lecture of his on the return of
the great meteoric showers in 1899, we sincerely expected
Eton to be pulverised before morning.

He made his laboratory a city of refuge for boys in search of peace from fagging or ragging. I spent many pleasant hours there out of the rushing Eton world. I renewed a taste for popular astronomy. I spent a Half trying to resolve a sixpence into its component parts, making test-tubes, evolving what can only be called the antithesis of perfumes and disgorging different types of gas. Some of my new knowledge has lasted. I still know that Argon is a gas which can be found in the mud on lake bottoms. Hitherto I had mistaken the unsavoury bubbles which rose in the lake at Glaslough for the breathings of eels !

Porter used to give an entertainment called G.B.L. or Good Boy Lecture to those who had kept the best notes in school. (I believe in later years he gave one for Good Masters, if there ever were any !) The G.B.L. was a singsong with wonderful lantern slides taken from his travels and illuminated by a run of yarns and ghost-stories which made us afraid afterwards of returning in the dark.

Two of his ghost stories bit into my memory like etchings. He remembered visiting an inn near Oxford. Here he once found a man watching and staring at an upper window. There was a haunted room behind in which no guest was allowed to sleep. One night when every room was full owing to a local fair a stranger had arrived and insisted against all advice in sleeping there. In the morning there was no answer when the maid called him. At last they broke down the door and a little gibbering creature ran out. This creature died twenty years later in an asylum without giving a clue to his name. The only clue to the story was that the room was panelled with the timbers of a ship which had been haunted by a species of blood-sucking spiders ! This was only the skeleton of a long drawn tale.

Another gruesome tale which Porter told with convincing power was of the man who accepted a bet to nail a nail into a coffin in the vaults of St Paul's while the clock was striking midnight. His friends waited in a coffee-house while he accomplished his wager. Unfortunately he found himself tightly held and was there found dead the next morning. He had nailed his own cloak to the coffin !

At the end of a ghost story Porter's face was always rubicund with a large sceptical smile. He took a pleasure in transfixing the credulous. I never heard ghost stories better told than by Porter. His only equals in gentle terrorising were Augustus Hare and Dr M. R. James. There are two concomitants to a good ghost thrill : lowered lights and hairs raised !

His intonation was perfect, and the art of anecdote I learnt from hearing him on these occasions. He had some humorous scraps taken from his travels in Ireland and France. During the Boer War he courageously sat down in a French café in days when *"conspuez les Anglais"* was a frequent Gallicism. He noticed that everybody noticed him and spoke in whispers. At last a man approached him newspaper in hand and said they had bad news for an Englishman. The Queen was dead ! He sat motionless. Worse, the British Army had been defeated by the Boers. He continued mute. There was worse to come : Milord Kitchener had committed suicide ! At this he broke into laughter and was given up as a hopeless lunatic.

Porter was unlucky in his House, which ran a little loosely. There were several similar Houses, and Warre was worried. He asked his masters to use a tighter rather than a looser rein. It was rumoured that he had asked his staff to be tight in preference to being loose ! Porter was one of those who refused to play policeman over boys and his House came to an end, but he was greatly consoled when Oxford made him a Doctor of Science. I was at Cambridge when his House was disbanded. His old pupils immediately signed a protest which I was also asked to sign. Hugh Frewen wrote the text and it must have touched the poor old Head on the raw.

He thanked us for our interest in the old school, but referred any action on his part to the day of judgment. I must confess we felt rather appalled at the idea of the Head appearing before any tribunal! Porter survived to head the masters' list and to become his own legend. He taught the sons and once the grandson of old pupils. I have often hoped that he has been allowed to satisfy his curiosity as to the other side of the moon. ·

Nevertheless Warre was one of the half-dozen great men I have met in my life. And I include Tolstoy, Pius X and President Theodore Roosevelt. He was nobly endowed in body and mind and he doubled the value of Eton. He was Zeus in the Eton world but he had his blind streaks and his Zeus-ship was limited. He looked out upon the Eton which he had fashioned and behold it was good. His greatness became more apparent in the succession of excellent men who succeeded him. None could pull his weight. None could wield Apollo's bow or shall we say Dr Warre's birch. His immediate successor was Edward Lyttelton : cricketer, Christian and cracknut. Then came Cyril Alington who must find his own historian and Mr Elliott not yet a Lower boy when I left. If all I hear is true I am inclined to say : long may he reign! The appointment of Lord Hugh Cecil as Provost instead of my old classical tutor, is one of those ingratitudes by which the academical job is still exercised in England.

The chapel is the appurtenance of the Provost who sits in the holy stall of King Henry VI. The Provost was preceded by a Holy Poker who also conducted the preachers to the pulpit. Great was the boys' delight if an anxious visitor made a bolt ahead of time followed by the Holy Poker who was never allowed to catch him up. Boys sitting on the knifeboard only had to thrust out their legs to turn a flat race into hurdles.

Upper Chapel remains a glowing memory. We hurried in every morning before the bell closed its familiar three or four final warning beats. The swells and " Pops "

arrived at the last moment in the garish kind of dress
Dan Leno or George Robey would wear on his wedding
day. The biggest swell was Harry Dalmeny. Any boy
who put on too much side was nicknamed " Dalmeny,"
I remember him playing at the Wall on St Andrew's Day,
1899, while his unathletic father Lord Rosebery watched
beside obsequious Tutors. Eton was Rosebery's spiritual
home, and he asked to die to the notes of the Eton Boating
Song.

Every morning Sixth Form entered to a light goose-step
from the organ. They were followed by Head, Provost and
Vice-Provost. This was Warre-Cornish whose House had
its own hymn (202 Ancient and Modern). Instead of the
words :

" Lift up your heart—Lift up your voices "

the school used to substitute :

" Play up Cornishes—Play up Cornishes."

That was before my time, but we still sang " Kinkering
Congs " and we had a habit of turning towards a boy
called Cope and solemnly singing :

" And Sion in her anguish
With Babylon must *cope*."

The Psalms 8, 23, and 121, were favourite chanteys
which could be chanted with a merry noise. The sermons
were dull or frothy. Exceptions I heard from Robert
Hugh Benson, Hensley Henson, and the present Bishop
of London. One old parson from Somerset (the Head's
home county) delivered an oration which was described
by Arthur Benson as the worst he had ever heard. When
he spoke of " scratching the rocks of eternity with our
fingernails," we thought he was trying to describe the
Wall Game. The great Doctor Butler of Trinity once
referred to Eton graves all over the world in the Latin
adaptation : *quae caret ora cruore vestro?* The *Eton
Chronicle* misprinted the word *cruore* so that it read in
translation " what shore lacks your amours ! " Butler

had preached in bygone years as head master of Harrow and made us the famous epigram : " We will look up to you from Harrow if you will not look down on us at Eton."

There was Stuart Donaldson's famous sermon against swearing, for which he suggested the patent remedy that a boy finding himself in a passion should start rapidly counting one—two—three ! For some days boys were dropping books or shinning themselves and then rapidly counting in class—one—two—three, etc., until normal expletives were restored.

The mighty carved canopies in chapel still concealed the beautiful mediæval frescoes, which Provost James uncovered to modern delight. They portray the romances of religion. Here was the knight on his road to tournament who delayed in order to say Office of Our Lady and found that Someone not only had taken his place, but won the tournament for him ! Here was the woman raised from the dead by Our Lord at His Mother's petition to confess an omitted sin to her Confessor amongst the living. Here was the painter who painted a picture of the Virgin and the devil and, being tempted to paint the devil less ugly than he was, refused, whereat the devil tilted the painter's ladder and he would have fallen had not the Virgin reached out her sweet hand to save him !

All this sounds like fairy lore compared to the bleak propositions set in the Catechism, but the English mind can always return to religion by way of antiquarianism. Compared to the beauty of the mediæval, the modern stained windows were ghastly. Belshazzar's Feast was represented by three toads on a plate and cans of lemonade, a most unsavoury repast. Protestantism had not improved religion at Eton.

Confirmation comes at the difficult time in a boy's life. It can be made deep and salutary, but with us it was like a daub of whitewash. It was not the Sacrament of the Mediævals, and it was not the Eleusinian mysteries of the Greeks. Confirmation was very badly managed at my House as we were sent to the Conduct or Chaplain who gave us dry lectures in chambers. We felt that so much extra work was being foisted on us.

The Englishman accepts religious views provided they are not tied up with moral questions. Confirmation was a better success in lay than in clerical hands. The moral or sexual side should be kept entirely separate from the mystical or dogmatic. Let the latter be explained by a clergyman, but all that pertains to the fruit of the body should be left to a competent doctor in his consulting-rooms. Otherwise what has been called " the Divine Physics " becomes too much of a mystery, is associated with goody-goodiness and reduced to a form of subvulgar joking. The Anglo-Saxon attitude towards sex has made it hopeless.

There were excellent clergymen at Eton : Lionel Ford (Dean of York), Henry Bowlby, and Cyril Alington (Dean of Durham). To the boys they personified the Three Persons of the Trinity in that order, but we were not taking our morals from them. The individual boy kept his own code. Sometimes it was superior and sometimes lower than the school's. Lionel Ford once preached a memorable sermon on the rather upsetting text : " Thou shalt not commit adultery." Ladies were cleared out for one evening Chapel and " Pi " Ford preached a sermon which pierced most of us like arrows. It was clear and courageous, and what is rare in such talks it was suitable for the ears of gentlemen.

Public school morality is much discussed, but a word can be said for Eton's fair fame which should apply to most of the great English schools. My own experiences certainly furnished me with a mild innoculation against the sordid side, but it is ridiculous to speak of vice at public schools. Vice simply doesn't exist. The curriculum of work and the slavery of games do not allow any per-version of puberty. There are always a few boys who are over-sexed, and a few with the unlucky gift of good looks. The former treat the latter to chaff or foolish affections. Friendships were distorted by gossip, but

the glamour was always dissipated by the arrival of
the first chorus girl in a boy's life. The atmosphere
in my time was rowdy, hearty, and masculine. Some
of the house masters used to cackle like hens over
their chickens, but I doubt if anybody's morals were
ever ruined at Eton. There were Houses where boys
passed their whole time at school innocently, and others
where they rarely underwent unpleasant experiences.
A boy's innocence is worth preserving as long as possible,
but not his ignorance. If everybody were kept innocent
all his life, the world would soon come to an end. The
State requires a supply of healthy fathers and family men
and Eton has played her part. If the older boys learnt
during holiday the way of a man with a maid, it was the
prelude to marriage not to decadence.

Mothers tremble at what they imagine passes behind
the scenes at a public school, but it is surely a part of
education to acquire knowledge of good and evil. Sooner
or later the tree of knowledge must be tasted. Happy
if it is prettily picked as in the Garden of Eden by a
woman's hands. Not so happily if it is ruthlessly stripped
by the other sex. Effeminacy arises from very different
sources than the public school. Public school men do not
appear to have the time or taste to devote themselves to
the toilette of Venus which is often a cult with Continental
youth. In consequence few (according to those who have
had the right to judge) come up to the standard of what
are known as "Latin lovers." Perhaps there would
be fewer divorces and more contented wives, if there were
more accomplished husbands.

I am writing from thirty and forty years ago, and not
a word of my present script need apply to the Eton or
public school men of to-day. I believe that the phrase,
"public school vice," is a contradiction in terms. The
thin line of effeminates is seldom recruited from the public
school. Boys with the "cissie" disposition generally had
the symptoms knocked out of them. As Mr Jorrocks
once observed : "Eton knocks and Eton kicks save many

a high-bred lad from ruin." At the same time a public school which has no place for the poetic or artistic boy, is a failure.

Popular actresses could make more moral influence than imagined. I doubt if film-stars can fill their place in the boyish imagination to-day. Edna May and Marie Studholme were worshipped from a distance. At least two of my Eton contemporaries believed they were going to marry Edna, whose loveliness was one of the rewards of long leave when she was playing the Belle of New York. The last time I saw her she was sitting in a box at the Opera wearing the long-braided hair of those days and making two tiers of Peeresses and subscribers' wives look like jewelled vegetables compared to her flower.

Once there was a concerted approach to a lady of the town, whose name I ought to have forgotten. It was believed that her favours were expensive or at least beyond a single boy's pocket-money. A group, most of them from my House, conducted a sweep with her permission. It has happened before and will happen again wherever youth is ardent but impecunious. The lady entered into the spirit of her admirers and permitted her charms to be symbolised by guinea tickets which were raffled in a boy's top hat. The winner was a youth in jackets who declined to sell his ticket in spite of the stern advice of the experienced. He was much envied and chaffed although I doubt if the lady gave him more than a good tea and good advice. But he certainly boasted when he returned to school.

Rightly or wrongly we were not pressed to work hard. Lower boys were swished for idleness, but nothing could hasten the steps of hardened loiterers in Fifth Form. About half the school did as little work as they felt inclined. The rest did a little more with the exception of the " Tugs " and the " saps." The happy relations between most masters and their pupils could be expressed in " live and let live." The only master who drove us hard was Kindersley. I was up to him for a Half and never incurred a word of praise or blame, but his Greek saying lessons gave me headaches. Kindersley was a massive oarsman and an early Rugby player. He was the cause of the rule in Rugby football that the player should drop the ball when tackled. In an international match he had carried three Welsh tacklers over the line ! He had rowed Exeter College up the river at Oxford in days when most of the crew were drunk. This was the Oxonian tradition and I give it for what it is worth. He was the only master who caused fear. His House suffered a disaster by fire in 1903, when two boys were suffocated in spite of his own heroic efforts to break the bars.

All my masters are dead with time, gone or forgotten. There is one survivor in the Vice-Provost Mr Marten, and I remember gratefully his comments on my first historical essay which I had worked into shape thanks to the combined erudition of the school librarian and the *Encyclopædia Britannica.*

Most of the masters had nicknames and the more absurd they were the more they were loved. There was a " Bunny " Hare who might have been the White Rabbit in Alice's Wonderland, grown old and grey, with his ears lopped and a master's gown tied to his shoulders. He looked incapable of keeping order, but his unwearied patience made him the ideal dominie for dunces. It seems impossible to think of Third Form and of all the empire-builders he helped to ascend from those lowly ranks without " Bunny " Hare. In old days there was a " Badger " Hale and in my time a " Bull " Hurst, who looked and sang like one in Chapel. He was one of Eton's highest Wranglers. Another was Cowell, who won the competition for fixing the return of Halley's Comet. His calculations brought him within two days of the right answer. It· was an international competition and was adjudicated at Berlin by the Imperial Russian astronomer. So presumably a little mathematics were taught at Eton.

A delightful master was " Babe " Booker and I enjoyed

being in his class. I think he was called the " Babe "
because of his artless remarks. He was an archæologist
who knew all about the Roman Wall. He talked with
great pride of a shoe he had excavated. His calves were
thicker than most men's shoulders.

The most astonishing mathematical master was
" Hoppy " Daman whom I attended in the last century.
There was evening school in those days. " Hoppy " was
a strange and gifted creature, bearded and ordained to
Holy Orders I think in recognition of the divine sense of
humour. When he and Warre proceeded up chapel
together it recalled Landseer's picture of " Dignity and
Impudence." Even stranger was their contrast in voices.
Warre thundered the Ten Commandments as though
they were new rules he had devised that morning for the
school. Daman's voice was entirely unsuitable for divine
worship. Once he read prayers in College, but the solemn
" Tugs " broke into Homeric laughter. That night no
prayers could be said nor curfew rung.

The mathematical masters were weary mind-grinders.
It was necessary to work hard at their dreary subjects to
get a good place in Trials. I learnt the first two books of
Euclid just as I learnt the Collects by heart in childhood
without knowing or caring what they meant. I understand Euclid has since been abolished and my hardly
acquired information is now obsolete. I always doubted
Euclid's definition of a Point as " position without
magnitude." That might apply to certain promotions
issuing from jobs, but to my mind non-magnitude implies
invisibility. A thousand Points, therefore, would not
occupy more room than one. If Space is the position of
the Universe, all Space could come under one Point.
" Perhaps I am wrong," as Provost James used to say.
Modern masters at Eton know something, for I consulted
one about Einstein's theory and he told me that it meant
that if one walked far enough into Space one would
eventually catch up with oneself !

By the end of my time I had sighted the Binomial

Theorem from which I flinched in mental terror. I do
not move freely amongst the Dimensions. The beauty of
mathematics means nothing to me. Decimals may be
decimated and fractions fractured eternally for all I care.
I learnt neatness and the contours of Euclid's propositions
from those many grievous hours : those unartistic and
unlovely shapes for which the blackboard seems to have
been invented.

After forty years one can revalue and estimate the
education we were given. French was the great flaw at
Eton. I am left with a memory of baffled pedagogues and
contemptuous pupils. The exception oddly enough was
Monsieur Hua, who was as pleasant in conversation with a
boy as with his friend King Edward VII. His select
class really led to knowledge ; but I remember two boys
who came to school with good accents and preferred to
lose them rather than be ragged as " Froggies." One of
these was once failed by Hua and quickly mobbed by a
jeering crowd inquiring " did he fail in his own language ? "
The French texts we read were dreary beyond belief.
There was a *History of the French People* of in-
superable dullness and the *Eton French Reader* led nowhere. Daudet's *Contes de Lundi* gave me a first glimmer
that French might have an interesting literature. We
read Daudet under our classical masters, a device of
Warre's for bolstering up French. There was a short
story about the Morgue which gave us a gruesome thrill.
I wish we could have had Guy de Maupassant's best. It
might have acted as an inducement to learn. The grace
of French idiom was hidden from us as much as the
audacities of the writers. Our Greek we learnt with
accent but our French without !

I do not believe in Bowdlerising the classics in any
language, neither in Shakespeare nor the Bible, if youth
is to be interested in literature. The Greek and Latin
classics could be made popular and memorable if they
were read wholesale from cribs, leaving the scholars to
garner the debris of grammar and to point the accents

which incidentally the Greeks themselves never used. We were allowed cribs for extra books, and oh the joy of hearing a book of Virgil or Homer read right through from translation. We naturally read the passages which had been excluded for impropriety and found them tame enough. I believe literature should be read as a whole. Castration is an insult to the classical and indeed to the Divine Author of the Bible. Why should the Song of Solomon be ignored ? Is it not the divine teaching to all lovers ? Instead of the poetical magnificences of Job we ploughed through dismal Books of Samuel and Judges. Instead of the Apocalypse and the Apocrypha, which gleam with glory in the rough quartz, we conned the Baedeker journeys of St Paul and wished he had been drowned off Malta.

It was the Victorian belief that religion was dull and therefore Bible-reading and sermons were kept dull. The pity was that so much opportunity was missed. There was an audience of eager, half-mocking yet generous-minded boys. They waited for the eloquence, romance and inspiration which never came. Youth refuses to be bored and the majority of Old Etonians avoid church for the rest of their lives. As for the Biblical conundrums called Sunday Qs which spoiled two hours of every Sunday—if only we could have been given Frazer's *Golden Bough* and his *Bible Folklore !* Job I never discovered till Cambridge and jumped with joy when I chanted his saga.

I would abolish the endless saying lessons which hardly left a single quotation in one's memory. Mr Pelman can supply all mnomonic defects later. Once I had Horace's *Carmen Sæculare* by heart, but all the Latin tags I remember are a few amusing mistranslations such as :

Lapsus calami, as the Latin for libel !
Incessu patuit Dea, " the goddess was open to incest."
Casus belli : " When a woman condemned to death pleads childbirth."

N

One should know enough to make a timely quotation from the Classics or be able to appreciate a slip in Latin. I found an unexpected pleasure in the Irish councillor who accused his opponent of acting *ultra virus !* A little Latin and less Greek enables one to enjoy subtleties in speech. I remember a Southern Irish paper which described the health of a worthy priest being drunk *ad mutos annos* (a mistake for *multos*). It did not add whether he had been " silenced " as they say.

A little Latin and less Greek is a precious gift and was abundantly bestowed at Eton. The biggest gap in the curriculum was the absence of English and the reading of English Classics ; or we should not have an Eton boy suggesting that Solomon wrote *Vanity Fair !* How few I read of worthwhile English all those years. Holiday tasks enforced Scott's *Fortunes of Nigel*, Kingsley's *Westward Ho !*, Macaulay's *Essay on Clive*, and Shakespeare's *Henry V* and *Macbeth*. They were appreciated, but what chance has an author against the distractions of the holidays ? We enjoyed Kingsley's novel and mobbed a boy called Parsons on the ground of his relationship with " Father Parsons."

The only English Classic which sank into my mind was Milton, thanks to my tutor's exquisite reading at Sunday Private. Slowly the magnificent vistas and rhythms of *Paradise Lost* grew like an organ cantata on my ears and remained with me for life. It sounds priggish but I can face any sleepless night or long journey by rail or sea if I have a Milton to mumble to myself.

The Eton schedule is probably much changed, and I could only suggest changes from the experiences of forty years ago. If I were asked what alterations I should like to have made in my own education I should say :

Instead of French (which can only be learnt in France) substitute a general knowledge of the Celtic dialects surviving in these Islands. An insight into Welsh, Gaelic and Irish and their literatures would be of life-value to those who live in sub-Celtic districts. At least they would learn something about their own lands before they became Teutonised. But I am afraid it will be a long time before Irish is taught even as an extra at Eton!

Instead of attempting the higher Mathematics I would give every boy a sound knowledge of Currency and the working of the whole Stock Exchange, of Investments and the perils and properties of Finance. The wealthier boys will then learn how to guard their family fortunes and the poorer will be able to enter Business and the City.

I should like to have found place for the English Classics to be learnt as minutely and grammatically as the Classics proper. No boy should leave the school without knowing Chaucer, Bacon, Shakespeare, Milton, Gibbon, Macaulay and Scott with perhaps Lamb and Miss Austen thrown in. And it should be a knowledge which lasts through life carrying a power of expression or at least an appreciation which is totally lacking in nine out of ten public school men.

Monsignor Barnes used to say that Warre had standardised Eton. She used to produce a breed of great men, but the time came when she preferred to produce men who were successful. There were no competition examinations in old days. The examination has become the axis of the Varsity and the Public School : and the result ? It has tended continually to raise third class minds to the second class but also to flatten first class minds to the same standard. Success in examinations of all kinds is due to a mixture of industry and cunning : the same qualities which avail at bridge or the Stock Exchange !

But this applies to every public school and there is no tempering the Examinations until the Varsities substitute true education for mere instruction. Symbolically the old Eton before Warre knew neither bounds nor the tyranny of compulsory games. The captain of games in each House leased a field from a farmer and the boys played if they wished. Better still in football-matches between Houses the whole House played ! This surely

was the true team spirit. And there were amusing
matches in those far away days, as for instance between
those who shaved and those who didn't !

The Eton and Harrow cricket matches reached their
highest pitch of interest and excitement in my time. In
those far away days Harrow defeated Eton regularly
and the alternative to a defeat was an excruciating draw.
No one in the school even remembered an Eton victory and
there was none until after I left. The pendulum then
began to swing crushingly against Harrow.

The heroes of both schools were cricketers. There were
Howard Smith and Lord Francis Scott who dared to
knock about the Harrow bowling. I often wondered what
happened to E. M. Dowson, the Harrow nipper, who
regularly bowled out Eton with his slows. And what
happened to E. G. Whately whom I saw take the hat-
trick in Harrow's second innings of 1900 ? That year was
a match of splendid cricket and sudden reversals of fate.
On the Saturday afternoon Eton were 100 runs ahead
with eight wickets in hand. Tod had reached 96 and K.
M. Carlisle threw him a full-toss which bowled him clean.
Eton then collapsed. But even so Harrow could only
just make the needed runs and win by one wicket. In
the midst of the excitement Whately took his memorable
hat-trick. I never prayed such genuine prayers nor shed
so much sweat as that hot afternoon in the Eton stand.
Beside me were two old gentlemen in a state of profane
and perspiring hysterics. Men wept like babes and boys
shouted like men. The Eton and Harrow stands are now
erections of the past. It was a heart-shaking sight to see
the whole Harrow stand to rise as one and cheer with hat
and cane as each Eton wicket fell. Terrible was the Eton
wrath when the match was over. We rushed towards
the pavilion in a running fight. The rival columns cut
down each other's colours tied to canes. It was give and
take the whole way with a hat sliced here and a brim
torn there. . . .

My friends were at one time in the thick of the scrum when suddenly a thickly built Harrovian danced in front of Hugh Frewen and cut his face open with a cross-cut, but added kindly : " You had better not take me on. I am Vibart the boxer." We retreated with our hats in a state of fluff from that engagement and Hugh had to have his cheek sewn up with a red-meat plaster. Vibart was believed to be " the Demon " in the Harrow novel, called *The Hill*, and it showed restraint on his part not to finish us off. The spirit of Lords was continued in hansom cabs down Baker Street whence the rivals still defied each other. The cheering and rioting only died down at Earl's Court at a late hour on those immortal Saturdays.

The old rivalry has rusted with the years and seems as distant as that of Montagues and Capulets. I remember a Roman princeling who announced after a year at Eton that he had added an implacable aversion for Harrow to the feuds of his noble House.

We never missed the chance of a riot. There was a merry outbreak at the opening of Queen's Eyot up-stream (May 11, 1901). In my first summer we used to row to Surley Hall : an old riparian hostelry beyond Boveney Lock where it was easier and pleasanter to become intoxicated than at Tap. It was abolished in favour of Queen's Eyot where rowing masters could read " Absence," and boys could avoid the rush to return. The opening day was memorable. Hundreds of thirsting and hungering boys arrived in every shape of ship. The commissariat broke down and the restaurant was merrily looted and pillaged. Everything was eaten and nothing was paid. We returned in uproarious mirth. I have never been there since.

Eton was much more picturesque in those days and not plagued by motors and buses. During school hours we were only interrupted by the hoof-beats of the tradesman's van. Ascot week was particularly picturesque, when all the coaches laden with London beauty and fashion bowled through Eton on the way to the Long Walk and the race-course. It was a tantalising sight to

the boys who were impeded by Special Schools and
Absences. It was very difficult to get to Ascot until the
motor-bike was invented. In my time the Grenfell twins
managed it because one could always answer at Absence
for the other. Even their tutor Walter Durnford could
never distinguish them. Miss Evans remembered when
boys were allowed to run behind the coaches and given
champagne on arrival at the course. And under a broiling
sun !

There was little traffic in the main street through Eton :
allowing space for such ceremonies as Parade and
Hoisting, now memories in the distant past.

The winners of river events were brought back in
triumph from Rafts. The magnificados of Pop, having
refreshed themselves with " Brews," condescended to
carry them shoulder-high between lines of cheering boys.
They were then hung out of their tutors' windows while
jugs of water were poured over their heads. On the same
theory, that the glass from which the King's health has
been drunk must be broken, so the jug from which such
heroes had been baptised was hurled to smithereeens
into the street below. It could never be allowed to return
to the duties of domestic crockery.

There were better reasons for abolishing Parade : an
amusing exhibition which took place every night in
summer in the half-hour before lock-up. To the strains
of a barrel-organ all the swells, semi-swells, and would-be
swells paraded up and down the narrow paving between
Barnes Pool Bridge and New and Lingwood's shop. To
attend Parade it was necessary to be well-dressed and
taken by a friend. It was rather like being presented at
Court, for the Captain of the Boats often attended and
passed nodding down the line. The masters objected to it
as pure advertisement and it was abolished by the boys
themselves. It was a miniature reflection of Sunday
Parade in Hyde Park, and a convenient means of making
engagements and exchanging gossip.

Brews and Hoisting are really to be regretted. " Brews "

was a simple distribution of champagne after a boat race to the victor, the defeated and their friends. It was abolished by a prohibitionist Captain of the Boats in my time. The Eleven were hoisted if they won at Lords and the Eight if they won at Henley. It seems a pity that Hoisting cannot be revived on the Fourth of June, in favour of Old Etonians who reach Viceregal or Cabinet rank or a Bishopric.

It was the old-fashioned Eton still. The old system of Praepostors was in full swing. Each boy became Praepostor for his Division in turn, and for a week had to keep a long thin book which had to be returned regularly during the day to the school office with the names of those

" staying out,"
" on leave,"
" in afresh."

He had to stand up and mark the absent in Chapel and afterwards collect medical excuses from various old dames. Only the Sixth Form Praepostors survive to summon, prepare and accompany culprits to execution.

The swishing over the time-honoured block should never be abolished. It used to be called " the Eton Confirmation." No doubt it will run danger of abolition should Eton ever come under Socialist conditions. When the sons of working men are allotted places at Eton no doubt " hereditary and aristocratic " punishments will be reduced or done away with.

There were some painful experiences such as a " cherry bum " (produced by the round handle of a toasting fork) and a " Pop-caning " which would have led to legal action in schools under the London County Council.

I am glad to say that bullies often ran into the Pop-caning. Some louts from my House once threw some smaller boys out of the Keepers' Fives Courts in order to play themselves. Unfortunately the Keepers had given the court to their little friends and heard of their treatment. I can only say that the bullies (much as we disliked them) took their punishment like men, stuffing handkerchiefs into their mouths not to betray their anguish. Their heads were pushed under a table and each Pop present used the peculiar knotted cane called the "Pop cane."

Here is the experience of a noble Earl, my contemporary at Bowlby's House. As a new boy the second captain ordered him to tell the captain he was "a damned fool." He did so, but left out the damnatory clause. For this lack of accuracy he received twelve with a toasting fork handle.

On the whole life was very free and pleasant, once the fagging had ceased, but any boy ran the risk of a severe experience. For boys born to a bed of roses and especially those who were thoughtless of animals it was salutary. Anyone who had really been thrashed at Eton would think twice in later life how he treated his horse or sentenced a prisoner in the dock.

The present modernising of Eton looks as though there will be a massacre of the old Houses and a disintegration of "old familiar places." Slowly Eton will become as sanitary and efficient as the London County Council could desire. Tradition and atmosphere are delicate plants and once destroyed can hardly be regrown. Stones are fossilised memories. How moving it was to drink from the old School pump in the Cloisters or to touch the stone on the wall outside Chapel on which Gladstone had cut his name (obliterated since by Tory thumbs) : or to pass the picturesque old House which had sheltered a fledgling Shelley : or to stand in Weston's Yard where Tennyson was once seen staring into the windows behind which Arthur Hallam had lived. All Eton recollections are carried by the two words, *In Memoriam*.

It is something to peep back into the nineteenth-century Eton and memorise the past. I recall the funeral of William Adolphus Carter, the last of the old Fellows of Eton elected on the original foundation of King Henry VI, before the Governing Body superseded the mediæval Fellows. The boys regarded the Governing Body (so a Lower boy once stated within hearing of a member) with "unmitigated contempt."

It was an Eton before the School Stores and the old school tie. It was once believed that old Etonians could be distinguished without reference to their neck-colours. A school tie is perhaps necessary in days when Eton must stand up to Giggleswick and Stowe.

The school stores have added to the health of the school. We used to depend entirely upon "sock-shops" and Jobies. I used to deal with a one-armed veteran who could imitate "Goody," the old Provost of my father's time. Jobies were links between the generations. I remember my father's delight on finding the same old Joby at the Wall, with a light blue ribbon round his straw, who had sold "sock" to him in 1870. The old lady who sat with a basket outside Upper School disappeared before the last of the dames, and who remembers Blake, the picturesque and eccentric school porter whose deafness made a slate the only means of conversation?

School cricket matches were still played in the playing fields bounded by enormous knobby elm trees half as old as the school herself. Agar's Plough was a dreary expanse recently saved by patriotic old Etonians from the jerry-builders of Slough. I first crossed it paper-chasing in March, 1899, and remember jumping the yawning holes out of which the present groves of elm and chestnut have since sprung. The new pavilion, with its disconcerting Latin warning to the batsman, had not been dreamed.

It is something to have lived to see three Provosts die in the Provost's Lodge. The present and reigning successor of the Founder was known to us as a brilliant member of the "Hughligan" gang in the House of Commons. Presumably he will have the unique privilege of celebrating the fifth centenary of the foundation of the college in 1940, which must be a year of immense solemnity and interest to Eton. Will it be celebrated by an Eton pageant of scenes through the ages, or by the long-deferred canonisation of King Henry VI ?

At Eton one is believed to make one's friends for life. But the friends of one's teens are seldom the associates of manhood, and those with whom one enter's life's first adventures and responsibilities do not remain the companions of middle age. Perhaps we shall all meet in the communal workhouses which the benevolent government of the future will provide for those who wear the old school tie. In old age one becomes a solitary survivor, or perhaps more happily one does not survive at all.

From my House I have since met very few : only two contemporaries, Sir Evelyn Wrench and Professor Carr-Saunders. Wrench was a senior when I arrived and the pleasantest boy in a rough crowd. He was already wide-awake to novel influences and had spent a convalescence watching Marconi experimenting in the Isle of Wight. He came under Northcliffe's influence I think for ambitious reasons and rejected the same for higher reasons. The schemes and societies, which he has founded, have made him an attractive figure in the English-speaking world. If he had not been such an idealist he would probably be a rich man.

Another member of my House whom I cherish, for we " sapped " together against much ragging and barricades, is Professor Carr-Saunders, who took a Science First at Oxford and became the leading authority on Heredity and Population : those twin sciences of which so little is known and on which so much of future planning depends.

We worked much harder than the Collegers as we were under the perpetual menace of interruption. The old School Library was our favourite city of refuge. The Library was then housed over New Schools beside the Sebastopol cannon. Hours of peace and happiness were procurable among the shelves. It was in this room that Gladstone, Ruskin and Morris lectured to the school. Over the seat where I usually sat hung a copy of Porson's *Bacchus* verses inscribed in his famous " missal " hand which first inspired me to cultivate script for script's sake. I began to collect autographs (as I believe an Oriental would collect them) not for the fame of the author but for the sheer beauty of the handwriting.

From this citadel, which was well furnished with keys to the Classics, and from my cupboard-bed, in which I used to read with a candle stub to all hours, I made every effort to surpass the Collegers in my division. During my last year I was up to Hugh Macnaghten in Select at the top of Upper Fifth. There was one imperturbable little Colleger who always remained at the head of the class : the future Monsignor Ronald Knox, a purveyor of many good detective stories. At the end of the Summer Half Macnaghten gave us each a double " send-up for good." It was a rare honour and I doubt if I really deserved it, for I was a poor second to Ronny Knox. The Head also doubted my merit, for when I handed him my two sets of Latin verses immaculately copper-plated on vellum he turned quite gruff. He refused to accept more than one and then insisted that the second copy was a hold-over from the previous Half. I had been imagining a splendid scene worthy of the finale of *Eric or Little by Little*. I hoped to hear my head master's encomium and to feel the shake of his massive hand and be commended for all my work. It was the only time that I felt like swimming to the surface of the Eton Pool. Alas, poor minnow ! I was barely noticed and I retreated with choking grief. A few days later I returned to fetch my Leaving Book which he handed me like an official doling out passports. It was customary to bring a photograph of the Head and to request his signature. He stretched out his pen once more, but photograph I proffered none. Then and not till then did he appear to notice my existence and our eyes met. I hope I did not quail. I turned and walked away in a state of genuine pique. I had been in Dr Warre's Academy for Young Gentlemen for three and a half years. During that time I had never been complained of by any master. I had

incurred exactly one yellow ticket. I had missed exactly
one School without a formal excuse. A blank stare was
all I received from the Head on leaving.

I realise now that he was far too great a man to have
noticed me. Perhaps it was better to be obscure in the
days of Warre than brilliant under his successors. At
least I recognised a very great and noble though one-sided
man of narrow views and broad chest. He possessed the
intangible greatness which made him seem a king amongst
men—like Agamemnon *anax andron*. Amongst all other
schoolmasters he was a salmon passing through a river
of chub and pickerel, not to mention the slimier eels.
Lord Darnley has told me of the scene of Warre's last
School at Eton when he heard the Sixth their saying lesson
for the last time. Darnley was last. When he had finished
he saw the Head close his book and sit back in the traditional chair, saying : " *Finis laborum meorum.*" It
remained the most memorable moment in Darnley's
life : too solemn for words and beyond tears.

His achievement was considerable, but what he achieved
showed how very much more he might have done with
that power and that influence which only a dictator has
wielded since. In one matter he set the example of
School Volunteers to all public schools, and if he had
had the foresight he might have made military training
compulsory instead of those wretched and useless games.
His Eton Volunteers in their famous uniform (before the
predominance of khaki) always lifted the heart of the
school as they swung through the playing fields to the
school band.

There was an amusing tradition in the school that the
Kaiser had inspected the Volunteers in the early Nineties
and that some dare-devil, for a bet, had fired his rifle to
frighten the Kaiser's horse and been expelled from the
school in consequence of His Majesty's representations
to his grandmother the Queen. Tradition said that the
hero struck the Imperial mount with a cork. It was
well known that chocolate beans from Rowland's " sock-

shop " could be made to fit the ·303 rifle on field days. In recent years the whole matter was mooted in the *Eton College Chronicle*, a copy of which I ventured to send the Kaiser in exile in order to obtain the historical account (which I think Thucydides would have done under the circumstances) I received a long letter from the Imperial Chamberlain which minutely corrected the tradition. This was translated and placed in the Eton archives. The Kaiser good-humouredly pointed out to posterity that :

" When, during the ' Manual ' exercises the shot went off, His Majesty's horse did *not* shy. It was His Majesty's own horse brought over from Germany, accustomed to manœuvres, rifle-shooting practice, and artillery fire : it stood quiet. The English horses, ridden by the English officers attached and the Prussian suite, seemed less used to gun-fire. They were startled— particularly those opposite the front line—reared up and brought their riders—unprepared as they were and at first hardly able to keep their saddles—into very uncomfortable but somewhat humorous positions. His Majesty was extremely amused at this *Schoolboy joke* and was laughing about it with his suite during the ride back to Windsor. At lunch the Emperor told the story to the Queen, his grandmother, and the other relatives who were present, amid much laughter, which was renewed when an officer of the English staff announced that the youthful delinquent was . . . . Before the inspection he had made a bet with a friend he would fire off a blank cartridge.

" At the end of the amusing article in the *Eton College Chronicle* the writer lets his imagination run riot. His Majesty was, of course, very far from being angry with the young culprit and did not dream of asking the Queen or Head Master to inflict punishment. His Majesty has enjoyed reading the account of the amusing incident—a regular Eton-boy joke."

Two blows befell me towards the end of my time at Eton. In February, 1902, Arthur Dunn died at the top of his form and the height of his success. Old age and decay he was happily never to know. It was the first gap made by death on my school horizon. How well I remember the exact spot in Judy's Passage where Leatham Major shouted to me in passing that " Your Mr Dunn is dead ! " I stood transfixed as by an arrow and crawled to school in the mutest agony. I had an idea that these tragedies only happened in Greek plays or novels. It was a quarter of a century before I could bring myself to visit his grave.

It was followed by a breakdown on my part, the result of overwork or rather of trying to read every night by firelight or candle-stub after hours. I was straining my optics into the watches of every night. One day in school I found I could not see straight, and laid my throbbing head on my books. I was taken back to my house and left in the sickroom with ice on my head. I remember spending two sleepless nights praying for sleep and wondering when my prayers would be answered. My grandmother descended upon the dame, and I think the dame met her match.

I was taken away for the rest of the half, and henceforth my Eton status could have been covered by a Bateman drawing of " the Etonian who had brain-fever." It seemed a ridiculous as well as a useless thing to do.

The last summer half passed like a dream, and I was allowed to do more or less work as I liked. I became a slow long-distance swimmer, which became an asset in life. I became a hermit between my room and the school library. Eton allowed me to live the life of an amphibian dreamer. Across the years I apologise to the boy sitting next to me at meals who told another that during the whole half I had never spoken once.

I left Eton on the last day of July, 1902. For twenty-four hours I had been running round in a curious awakenment of grief, saying to myself : " In so many hours I

shall cease to be an Eton boy." I questioned inwardly
the actual moment : was it the moment that I stepped
out of my house for the last time or while passing the
Shirking Stone with the College Arms near Barnes Pool
Bridge ? Some said that the actual passage from caddis-
hood to Old Etonian dignity takes place on Windsor
Bridge. That venerable structure had only been freed
recently from toll. There were still boys in the school
who had missed trains at the toll-gate. How prehistoric
it all seems !

My last morning was a poignant excitement. My
Classical tutor gave me Bodley's two splendid volumes on
France as a leaving gift. There was a last visit to the
poor old dame, full of sympathy and good wishes : " Be
a good laddie and respect the Holy Ghost," was her last
alarming injunction. Slowly I drove down the familiar
High Street with my Eton ottoman and neglected bath-
tub strapped to a fly. They were both serviceable for
packing clothes and books. Half-way down town I
passed Hugh Macnaghten and we waved. All who knew
him will know how much that meant to any who loved
him. Upon his soul be peace and serenity for ever !

There were a few boys leaving by the same train. I
remember arriving at Eton with Gordon Selwyn, and I
remember leaving in the same carriage with Stobart of
Miss Evans' House. Like me he had not succeeded in
collecting a single colour, when his popularity had brought
him past the sacred portals of " Pop." I have noticed
during my life that there are only three clubs really
worth belonging to : the Eton Society called " Pop," the
Supreme Bench of the United States and the Sacred
College of Cardinals : and in Etonian eyes the greatest of
these is " Pop."

France and the Latin Quarter

*

LIFE, ESPECIALLY LITERARY LIFE, SHOULD BE LIVED
in several compartments. It is true the great critics
of a literature from Hazlitt to Sainte-Beuve have only
known their own literatures. But for appreciation
(which is the *feminine* for criticism) a second language
should be known even unto idiom and idiosyncrasy. To
know too many languages is to know the literature of
none. Better learn Esperanto and transcribe the Encyclopædia into that hopeless system of verbal mechanics.

French is the obvious tongue-mate to add to English.
It was incredible how few Victorian Englishmen outside
diplomatists, exiles and a few gamblers troubled to know
French. In the eighteenth century English writers and
noblemen knew French often as well as English. The
only Englishman I ever knew whose French was as good
as or better than his English was John Edward Courtenay
Bodley. His splendid volumes on France accompanied
me from Eton when I was feeling more eager to learn
French than to do anything else on earth. I believe
that when one is young any wish, whatever it is, is
granted provided one feels the achieving power of desire.
Real desire is rare, but it is as strong as destiny. Like
destiny, desire may bring its own achievement but slay
the achiever.

Happy those whose adolescent desire is not seeded
with destruction. The handling of dead languages had
awakened this instant desire to know a living one. I set
out for France feeling like a bird-stuffer's apprentice
who sallies forth to catch a bird of paradise.

Paris was not unknown land. We had spent the Easter holidays of 1895 in the Avenue Kléber. Paris was more of a garden then and chiefly inhabited by Parisians. First impressions were abiding. I travelled over with my mother and Paderewski who had been the idol and protégé of the Jerome sisters. He was in full floraison then. I recognised his wonderful hair from the skits which were played at music halls by comedians with hearth-rugs attached to their heads. As we approached Paris, the great pianist began playing tunes in the air for his friends to guess. At last I had discovered one of the secret games played by grown-ups !

I remember looking out into the darkness and reading the name of the station in huge letters : AMIENS and falling back utterly puzzled. We always left Dublin from a station of that name. Were all big stations called the same ?

Every day in Paris we wandered to the Seine to contemplate the Eiffel Tower, which seemed crushingly enormous to a child. I used to watch the clouds moving against the summit and enjoy the delicious sensation that the tower was really moving though never falling. My Aunt Clara had been a friend of Monsieur Eiffel, and a signed certificate proved that she had been the first woman to stand on the very summit. People were already talking of pulling down a monstrosity which was of no real value save to suicides. In the days of my next visit to Paris it made a goal-mark for Santos Dumont's flying-machine, and since then wireless has made it an asset of France.

Easter of 1895 we attended Notre Dame. I heard a High Mass for the first time, and I recall old Cardinal Richard passing down the aisle and giving his Easter blessing. I felt deeply embarrassed when our Lutheran Fräulein stood rigidly still while all the faithful curtseyed to the ground. Bad manners are most insufferable when disguised by principles. I love the Pope's remark when a Scotch Protestant remained standing throughout an audience: "Oh, I see, an addition to our sculpture gallery!"

o

At Vespers we heard a Dominican—it must have been that prince of preachers Père Janvier. His clear-cut elocution held the rippling throng to absolute attention. I could only follow him by the dramatic gestures which he made under his white robe against the massive grey pillars. Very early in life I decided I preferred French to German religion. French churches were full of incense and lights and music. We used to be taken to German services by Fräulein in the Chapel Royal attached to Marlborough House. I have an amusing recollection of the clerk falling fast asleep during the sermon and snoring louder than the preacher who raised his voice in vain and finally desisted. He was literally snored under to our delight. But what a dreary service it always was. It is now fortunately abolished even as a memory of the Prince Consort.

In the *Champs-Élysées* I saw a new-fangled motor-car for the first time : rather like an ugly thunderbolt striking through the horse traffic. It equally lacked the deportment of the steam-roller and the speed of a train. It was curious to watch the long wake of bolting and rearing horses. The frenzy of the animals was only matched by the imprecations of their drivers. The car finally stopped dead while a pair of splendid steppers endeavoured to overstep the holiday crowd. This was in April of 1895.

At the *Palais de Glace* I saw and felt artificial ice for the first time. The corresponding place in London was Niagara, a fashionable ice-rink run by Hwfa Williams. Instructors floated about in astrakhan caps and black breeches. At Niagara I had the honour as a small boy of skating with the Duc d'Orléans. When I heard that he hoped one day to be King of France I induced him to promise to send me the first postage stamps bearing his head. My royalism remained unrewarded.

We shared the *Avenue Kléber* flat with Jennie Churchill, now passing through a becoming widowhood. With her black hair and glittering eyes she continued to draw endless attention. Looking back it seems a real pity that she did not marry the devoted Hungarian sportsman, Charles Kinsky, whose sole introduction to the English-speaking world was that he had won the Grand National of 1882 on his own horse. He had been a great friend of the family, and Uncle Moreton, who had ridden in the first flight at Melton, approved hugely of his riding. To Uncle Moreton winning the Grand National was greater than the Derby and the Garter combined. He had been waiting for a very late bride in Trinity Church, New York, when to distract him his best man whispered that Charles Kinsky had won at Aintree. He was so overcome that he withdrew to the vestry to give vent to his feelings and it was his bride's turn to do the waiting.

Aunty Clara had an odd admirer in the rather disreputable King Milan of Servia, whom she met in Paris in his days of voluntary exile. He followed her to London, where his presence was not appreciated by Queen Victoria. Her royal black list included him with Leopold II of Belgium and Victor Emmanuel I of Italy. Hearing that he paid a daily visit to the Frewen house in Aldford St, she sent Aunty Clara word that she wished her to use her influence to persuade Milan to quit England! Poor Aunty Clara's indignation that she could have this influence knew no bounds. Victorian ladies knew how to combine romance with convention. It was their secret and their art.

The stories about King Milan were worthy of Rudolph of Hentzau. He was always followed by a gigantic foster-brother who stood behind his chair whenever he fed and lay across the door-mat wherever he slept. There was a thrilling story which Aunty Clara told us of a deputation of Servian officers arriving in Paris to invite him to consider returning to his own country. He entertained them in great secrecy to dinner in a private room. All was very amicable and at the end of the meal the loving cup was handed to the King by the leading visitor asking him to taste the wine. As the King was lifting the

cup, his foster-brother whispered swiftly into his ear that
it was poisoned. " The honour is for you," said the King
and passed it back to the officer who drew himself up,
shouted, " God save Servia," drank the deadly potion
and fell dead. In those days a political scandal could
be hushed up, and one more nameless and mysterious
grave was added to Parisian soil.

My Aunt Jane also had adventures in Paris. She was in
great beauty and being painted by Hébert in his studio.
While sitting for him once she was overcome by an
odour far more unpleasant than any oils. The artist
himself was affected and finally climbed out and broke
into the window of the studio below. The corpse of a
fellow-artist had been lying dead for two weeks !

Another time she brought home a thrilling story from
the *Gare de Lyon* where she had seen one man pursue
another and fell him with a shot and plug him till he was
dead. I forget which was the husband and which was
the lover.

She was staying in the Hôtel Scribe and had retired to
bed when she woke to see a very corpulent gentleman
standing over her. He had unscrewed the jambs of the
separating doors and entered to make known his
Falstaffian passion. Love is distressing enough in lean
men, but to the fat it is absolutely fatal. My aunt coolly
awaited his approach and struck him as hard as she could
amidships. He doubled up and disappeared as suddenly
as he came. The next day she left the hotel, but as luck
would have it, the fat man was in the lift ! She had
acted wisely and successfully. Although Holy Scripture
mentions screaming as the proper course for a woman in
need of rescue, it is a fatal one to take in an hotel or in a
foreign land.

Early in that year, 1895, Dreyfus had been disgraced
and exiled, but not a whisper reached us in Paris. During
my later schooldays English homes were distracted, and
a great curtain of horror and mistrust fell between the
two countries. I remember my grandmother reading out

the result of the Rennes trial with a white countenance and then leaving the room. Like many things once too deep for tears the Dreyfus affair is now only film-fodder. Mr Bodley used to say with all his knowledge of France that the inward meaning of the *Affaire* Dreyfus must await the Day of Judgment. Dreyfus himself was utterly unimportant. It was on a hundred other points that the French nation divided and lacerated itself.

During the summer holidays of 1901 I persuaded my parents to send me to Tours to learn French for six weeks. I arrived alone in Paris, was taken in charge by a seedy Teuton who for five francs conducted me from the *Gare du Nord* to the *Gare d'Orsay*. There was time on the way to visit the Louvre and he showed me the nude statuary with special care, pointing out the tail ends of fauns and goddesses. I was much shocked, but I was greatly interested by the marble Hermaphrodite who could only be properly (or improperly) seen by slipping under the railings placed by the authorities. I certainly had my five francs' worth, but what has happened to all those solid five franc pieces of the French currency? Louis Philippe was generally on the coin, and there were real gold Napoleons in circulation.

A great friend of the Frewens was Edward Tuck, a freeman and benefactor of Paris. He and Uncle Moreton met on the congenial ground of bimetalism which, of course, means a silver currency with the same rights and standard as the gold. Old Tuck had received his Consular appointment from Abraham Lincoln and had endured the siege of 1870 in Paris. He lived out of America for sixty years, and through him started the legend that good Americans go to Paris when they die. For his pro-silver work the French oddly gave him a gold medal. He lived into his nineties, and on this occasion of my last visit sadly placed a five franc piece in my hands as a souvenir of better times when the currency had a silver lining. It was the last time I was tipped.

From the *Quai d'Orsay* I trained to Tours where

Monsieur Firmin Counort, a *frère Chrétien* turned family
man, awaited me and took me for the first time into a
café. After a drink, which was greener than grass and
sweeter than saccharine, we drove slowly to Rochecorbon,
five kilometres up the Loire. At Rochecorbon, amid vine-
yards and wine caves that had been carved in the cliffs,
I learnt to masticate French.

Monsieur Counort was a dear old Frenchman, very
devout and brimming with information about subjects
which registered blank with a British schoolboy : the
phylloxera disease which had destroyed the vines of
France, the war of 1870, the Catholic religion and the wine
of neighbouring Vonvray. He opened a new world, and I
spent happy afternoons with him at Blois, Tours and
Amboise. For the first time a man talked to me as though
I were a man. He had taught in religious schools all his
life, but left his Order and married. This had not prevented him from remaining on good terms with the Archbishop of Tours who christened his children including the
twins who arrived subsequent to my visit. The dear man
was ridiculed as a prodigy, for his was the only family of
four in the parish. He looked very like the prints of Louis
Napoleon. He attributed the defeats of 1870 to the
French desecration of the Sabbath. He showed me the
marks of German cannon on the *Hôtel de Ville* facing the
splendid bridge at Tours. For the first time I learnt of the
difference between the French and German people then
solidly united in their hatred of the English. In those days
the statue of Strasbourg in the *Place de la Concorde* was
covered with mourning wreaths, removed since 1918.

The Boer War was in process, and English tourists
were shocked by the grim caricatures which embellished
the kiosks : Highlanders bayoneting women, heaps of
English soldiers in their death-throes and everywhere the
cold-blooded Joe Chamberlain, in whose honour the Paris
boulevards rang with :

" *Chamberlin, Chamberlin ! Assassin, assassin ! "*
Early I learnt in life to discount propaganda and to

discard atrocities. As for the assaults alleged by Tommies on Boer women Winston had returned from South Africa and declared that the British soldiers' conduct was ordered partly by his innate chivalry and partly by the plainness of the Boer Frau.

As for the caricatures of Caran d'Ache, I believe that genius whispered into one ear and the demon into the other. What a draughtsman ! I remember his picture of Lord Roberts illuminating the Transvaal in honour of the Queen's birthday (and how ?) or of General Buller striking his head against a mountain, or the colossus of Death scything the English on Spion Kop. These wonderful caricatures were not allowed in England, and naturally disappeared in France after the Entente. Caran d'Ache was more devastating than Raemakers during the Great War, and no caricaturist has equalled his line or his imagination since.

European nations were always threatening to intervene. When the Boer prisoners were sent to St Helena, a gust of historical emotion swept France. The ordinary caricatures were fantastic. The *Monde Illustré* published a famous picture of the Guards advancing in kilts ! as well as a regiment described euphoniously as the " Irish-Killings."

So strong was the feeling that the Prince of Wales could not attend the Paris Exhibition. But the seeds of the Entente were working in the minds of statesmen. Even the arrival of the exiled Kruger did not turn back the tide. I watched the Boer generals being welcomed in Paris after the war. With pathetic dignity they announced they were now British subjects.

Monsieur Counort's admiration for England could not swallow the Boer War. Otherwise his admiration was complete. He thought it best for me to pass as an American. I preferred to claim Irish, and then Monsieur Counort broke to me that three generations back his name had been O'Connor. A descendant of the wild geese!

I learnt French by talking with peasants in the vine-yards and fields. I hired a canoe and paddled down the

Loire. I annexed an island and built a fish-trap. I
snared lizards and, most exciting of garden-sports, went
hornet-hunting with an old gardener. He exhibited the
greatest courage. The old fellow stood up in his *sabots*
outside the hornets' nest and singed them with wisps of
burning straw when they charged him. Remembering the
adage that one hornet's sting kills a man and three a horse,
I cowered behind a wall.

We went into Tours to visit the house of the Holy Man
of Tours. His waxen effigy lay on his deathbed surrounded
by the crutches of all whom he had cured. So the
miraculous had occurred since New Testament days!
Every Sunday we attended Mass in the lovely old church.
It was very different from English services. I ate *pain
bénit* and became deeply moved by the coloured Stations
of the Cross, and to a less extent by a little girl who
passed the collecting bag under the protection of a Swiss
Guard. The old *curé* was our perpetual joke. Are the
clergy a jest in all churches? He had one sermon only:
about a pilgrimage he had once made to Lourdes, and
invariably burst into tears. Perhaps he was a saint and
had the gift of divine lachrymation. I learnt from mystic
books there are always a few choice souls whose tears
move the Eternal.

On the Feast of the Assumption I heard High Mass in
Tours Cathedral. In years to come that corner of the
world was made alive for me by Balzac's *Curé de Tours*.
Tours was not a great cathedral among those of France,
but there was a west window of utter glory. Beneath the
Rose was a gallery of glass which the sun struck to ruby
and gold.

When I returned to France as a student I swung into
the orbit of Balzac. No one can touch French without
coming to some conclusion about Balzac.

There are men of letters like George Moore who boast
they have read Balzac through. It is commoner to meet
those who have really read Dickens, Scott or Macaulay to
the last dregs. As everyone has a favourite novel of

Scott or a chosen essay in Macaulay, perhaps it is a test to pick one's choice in Balzac. "The Atheist's Mass" is my favourite among the short stories, and amongst the novels—*Une affaire ténébreuse*, although I have never met an Englishman who had ever read it or could suggest the plot or texture of that absorbing volume.

In October, 1902, I settled in Paris in the *rue d'Assas*, where Synge, the Irish dramatist, had recently passed lonely days. I was in time to attend Zola's funeral. His defence of Dreyfus had made him a popular figure in England. Suddenly he had been asphyxiated in bed, and the grim headline appeared: "The Angel of Death strangles Zola in his sleep." The religious and anti-religious Press in France never minced matters. I used to read *La Croix* and *La Lanterne* with equal zest.

Zola's death caused deep excitement, and Monsieur Counort believed he had been divinely prevented from finishing his series of novels called *The Four Gospels*. Three had appeared, and were horribly dull. Even as literature the Apostles beat him every time.

I marched with the students from the Latin Quarter on the day of the funeral to the rue de Bruxelles in time to see the police removing the card from Dreyfus's wreath which was hanging on the side of the hearse. French *pompes funèbres* exceed an English undertaker's dreams. Dreyfus himself marched behind. The procession passed slowly through Paris to the cemetery in Montmartre. The marchers were hotly assailed by their political opponents at the corners. There were some hopes of driving the coffin into the Seine, and cries of "*A la charogne, à la charogne*"! Twilight was sinking over the distant heights by the time Anatole France began his oration over the body. He was then at the height of his fame as a dispenser of that idiomatic irony which has since disillusioned Gallic youth. There was wild excitement while he spoke, and at the end the students marched past the grave throwing wreaths into the air and shouting: "Germinal! Germinal!" Some may have brought their

flowers, but most of them rifled the tombs in the cemetery·
I have seldom felt such excitement at even an Irish
political meeting. As funerals go, I have never enjoyed
one more. (October 5, 1902.)

That winter I worked at the Sorbonne finding some
novel subjects. As soon as I could follow the slow, clear
diction of the professors, I began filling gaps in my Eton
education : Ernest Lavisse on French history, Professor
Michel Revon on Japanese poetry, and, most unexpected,
Professor de Jubainville on the Irish Epic ! Here was a
subject Eton masters had never heard of. For the first
time I learnt there was an old Irish language and that my
Ulster home was as rich in heroics as Avalon or Troyland.
It is extraordinary that generations pass through British
schools and universities without suspecting the old Celtic
Saga. Achilles and Aeneas have become real personages in
English culture. King Arthur has been left buried in
Glastonbury. As for the Ulster Epic, I heard from
French Philologists with growing wonder that there had
been greater heroes than William of Orange and "fighting"
Saunderson. I learnt to populate my Irish home with the
shadows of Cuchulain and Deirdre and the Red Branch
Knights. The ruins of Emain Macha were within walking
distance of my home, and Emain was the Irish Troy !
All I had known hitherto was briefly gathered from the
coachman driving into Armagh: "Yon's the Navan Fort."

The Paris of 1903 was different from the inter-
nationalised capital of modern France. The French
rested in the security of alliance with the Czar. A
magnificent bridge built with the kopecks of Russian
peasants lay new and glittering across the Seine. It was
better security for the future to welcome Edward VII
when that determined monarch pressed his Entente on a
French public still hoarse with cheering the Boers. But
necessity is a stern bed-maker. One of the English
attachés wore the uniform of the King's Royal Rifles
and was mistaken for a Boer officer. His reception was
uproarious.

From the Latin Quarter I shared in the excitements of his visit. The first reception was chilly. Frenchmen did not mind if *le bon roi Edouard* became a trump card in Delcassé's policy. But that he should become a Parisian among Parisians *ça c'était trop fort*. There were instant attacks chiefly from the pen of the veteran Nationalist, Henri Rochefort, whom I remember receiving a minor ovation in the *Champs Élysées*. Then the King went to Longchamps and offered a racing cup. Then he signed his name in French at the *Hôtel de Ville*. By the time he reached the gala at the Opera he had won. Nothing marred that occasion save that the ungallant authorities removed a noted courtesan from the stalls. How she obtained her ticket amid that plethora of the grand official world no one knew, but Frenchmen wittily suggested that the King had sent her his ! With no more exciting companion than Madame Combes, the King fell fast asleep during the performance. Naturally I was not at the Opera, but I applied for a ticket for the Sunday service in the English chapel in the *rue d'Aguesseau*. Dr Noyes, the chaplain, questioned me whether I was a Fenian and gave me my ticket. The whole English community were packed into the church. The French were deeply impressed when the King *walked* to church according to English custom. They would have been less edified had they seen the fashionable ladies mount their chairs to get a better view !

The King had the happy look of any man who has escaped for a long-desired holiday. No doubt he felt at ease finding himself in Paris without being reported to the old Queen. He enjoyed throwing over her beloved old Germany for a flirtation with France. In the end the very boulevards were cheering him, and the great European scene had been set for Fate. There was only one English statesman who appreciated the new Entente at its real values. The much vilified Mr Chamberlain remarked that it meant war. And he had had quite enough with one.

Nothing else happened in Paris that year. There were

little incidents. A daring and horrible monument was
erected to Baudelaire in the *Cimetière Montparnasse*.
His poems became as symbolic of one period of my life a
Mrs Alexander's hymns of another. I have only to re-read
them to find myself tripping to the Morgue which used to
offer a pleasant visit on a spring morning. The Morgue
has since been withdrawn into privacy, but it used to be
a public building, low and damp, ever dripping behind the
apse of Notre Dame. Behind plate glass windows the
living could stare at the dead.

I watched the astronomer Flammarion experimenting
in the Pantheon with a pendulum hanging from the roof
to prove the rotation of the earth.

In these days of disappearing streets one must remember
cities by their public statuary. Two marked the Paris
of my time : Comte was placed in front of the Sorbonne
Chapel and Victor Hugo was given a monument of vulgar
pretension. In a big city the long streets flow like
sentences, the squares are set like paragraphs and the
statues act as punctua'ion, like commas between streets. But
the Victor Hugo statue resembles a note of exclamation !

There were some historical deaths while I lived in Paris.
The old Queen of Spain, Isabella, died in her palace in the
Avenue Kléber. I was interested because I had collected
Spanish stamps with her podgy and imperious head. And
while Père Loubet was returning King Edward's call,
Pope Leo XIII died after breaking all Papal records.
Vidit annos Petri : in other words he had reigned for a
quarter of a century, although the pontifical ritual had
told him he would never outlive the years of Peter. The
great Cardinal Rampolla resigned and the papers an-
nounced that his place was taken by his understudy,
Mgr de la Chiesa. Rampolla's name blazed like a rocket
during the Conclave and then died down for ever. De la
Chiesa was forgotten. The name meant nothing then, and
I little dreamed that when I attended his funeral twenty
years later he would be a Pope.

I settled down in the rue Servandoni near the Church of

St Sulpice. Oh, the peace of those quiet streets, broken only by the hum of human voices and the street cries of Paris. They became familiar snatches of melody: *"J'aime la cerise!"* *"Marchand d'habits!"* *"Tonneaux! Tonneaux!"* How slowly the world turned then under the slowly opening chestnut trees!

French came rapidly, especially as I used to read aloud for three hours a day. I read Zola's *Rome* whole. I tuned my ear in the lecture-room and theatre. My education was becoming mixed as I tested my French by learning other subjects in French. Their variety was amusing. I took up old Irish under de Jubainville and Japanese poetry under Revon. Hugh Frewen joined me in the rue Servandoni and we attended Revon's lectures assiduously. Apart from our curiosity for things Japanese, we enjoyed his exquisite French diction. He was puzzled by our perseverance and invited us one Sunday to his house in the country full of charming children. It was the first time we received French hospitality (and almost the last), for hospitality in France is almost entirely a perquisite of Americans. Years later we were happy to entertain Professor Revon when we were undergraduates at Cambridge.

Gaston Paris also died in this year, just as I had begun to be interested in the legends of the Middle Ages. He opened to me the thirteenth century and all the romance of mediæval terror and beauty which was missed in the textbooks. Henceforth I took Huysmans to my heart instead of Zola. Balzac passed into the background of his own century for me—stifled by his own characters. I struggled as long as I could with Zola's family of Rougon-Macquart, but one cannot chew dried dung and wash it down with whitewash in buckets for ever. In Huysmans' novels *En route* and *La Cathédrale* I found a sign-post in life. The very idea of making Chartres Cathedral the heroine of a novel enchanted me. Huysmans was the first modern author I collected and annotated. He had just returned from his Benedictine pilgrimage and was living near the convent in the rue Monsieur. I never met him, but after his death I used to listen to the exquisite plain chant dropping like crystal drops behind that convent grille—and thus remember as in prayer the writer of my choice.

I learnt to read methodically, in a manner I have never departed from. I made a point of indexing books that interested me and filling the flyleaves with notes and queries. Rare words and idioms were worth scribbling out. This habit I transferred from French to English books. I know no better advice to those who wish for a literary career. Never read a book without extracting at least one phrase or one item of information. Notes, references, indexes form the pleasant fruit, the mind's trophies from a lifetime of reading. Otherwise collect butterflies or postage stamps, if the intellectual strain is too great.

Two Russian novels which I read in French impressioned me deeply: Tolstoy's *Resurrection* and Dostoevsky's *Crime and Punishment.* They were a sweeping change from the novels of Rider Haggard and Guy Boothby in the House library at Eton. For the first time I quaffed the despair and melancholy in which Russian novelists revel. The names of Marmelodoff and Raskolnikoff sank into my soul as I slowly made my way. I began to notice and mark what I considered "sublime passages." I had found several in Zola's *Rome :* for instance, the picture of the living Pope being carried down the lines of the dead gods and goddesses in the Vatican Museum, and the wonderful scene when the lovers die in each other's arms.

In *Crime and Punishment* there was the pathetic scene when Raskolnikoff asks Sonia if her sister is to follow Sonia's pitiable calling on the streets, and Sonia replies : "No! God will not allow that," and Raskolnikoff kneels to kiss her feet.

As for Tolstoy's *Resurrection* I lived the hero's part in my dreams. The book's influence was unshakable. I vowed never to add the least necessity for the world of prostitution; and the idea of rescuing those who were only fallen women in that they had fallen to men's selfishness took root in my social conceptions.

Hugh Frewen and I lived in a pension with a Japanese comrade, Monsieur Hyashi. We used to consult him about writing English Tonkas (the Japanese dwarf-poems in eleven syllables). No metre or rhyme was needed and Tonkas were a relief after Latin verses at Eton. Hyashi astonished us by his industry, working ten or twelve hours a day. The day after he had learnt French he started learning English. He was never tired and always ready to practise English syllables on us, punctuated with hollow rippling laughter. Dear little Japs! as Monsieur Revon said, quoting Francis Xavier: *Populus iste deliciae meae.* Deeply we sympathised with them when they became involved in war with big black-bearded Russians. Was it not Aubrey Beardsley who suffered agonies of apprehension at the idea they were risking a battleship made of lacquer in their Chinese war?

The *rue Servandoni* is a narrow twisting street between the Luxembourg Gardens and the *Place St Sulpice.* Widor, the organist of St Sulpice, told me Servandoni had been one of the architects of the church. The bells of St Sulpice made a melodious regulator of hours. I soon exchanged the dull little English church in the *rue d'Aguesseau* for services in the magnificent unfinished pile shadowing our street. The last of the race of female pew-openers lived in the English church. In my youth every London church kept one of these Victorian virgins, a species of vestal house-keeper, flitting about in lace caps and unlocking and closing pews from which children felt there could be no escape.

I preferred the picturesque Swiss Guards at St Sulpice with their heavy halberts and big cocked hats. The choir of the Seminary sang Vespers and High Mass every Sunday. The fine Seminary was on the point of confiscation, but the chant of the seminarians was still the life of St Sulpice. The organist, Charles Marie Widor, had been

a friend of my mother and invited me to his organ loft,
where he performed musical miracles with his legs and
arms. It was thrilling to sit on his organ board and help
him pull the stops and listen for the voices rising out of
the depths below. Widor was the *doyen* of French
organists. He had come to St Sulpice during the war of
1870. He had succeeded César Franck at the Conserva-
toire and long survived the Great War. He and his
organ had become one flesh, one soul and one bag of
winds. So completely had he mastered the keys that
while he played he could converse with the fashionable
ladies who flocked to the *salon* he held at the top of those
dark and crushing stairways.

From the organ-loft there was a bird's-eye view of the
High Altar with twinkling lights and tiny figures moving
round in gold vestments. I can see Widor exchanging
animated gossip with his visitors . . . the Princesse Murat
has arrived in sheer scarlet from her neck to her sweeping
skirts . . . more animation and compliments . . . a pause,
and Widor wakes up to the service below. . . . *Tiens,
qu'est ce qu'on fait ?* A few quick manipulations, a creak
from the organ and the great harmony is under way . . .
" *Introibo ad altare dei.* . . . "

Every day of his life Widor dined in the old *Café Foyot*
at the corner of the *Palais du Luxembourg.* There I
glimpsed famous actors, senators and the most famous
waiter in Paris, who is better remembered than many
whom he served.

Another café I frequented was the Bonaparte, facing
the church of *St Germain des Prés.* It glowed in those
days with Willette's famous signboard, long since withdrawn in favour of the Entente, for it showed the English
flag amongst others trampled under Napoleon's horse
hoofs, while Fame, naked and unashamed, whispered into
his ears. No doubt it was too poignant for the tourist traffic.

There were still living links with the Napoleonic past.
In this year the Empress Eugenie passed through Paris.
It was the fiftieth anniversary of her glittering marriage

with the Emperor Louis Napoleon. I would have given anything to have seen the old lady wandering in the garden of the Tuileries and overhearing the zealous park-keeper ask her if she had been there before !

The Princess Mathilde was also living : a link with the first Emperor. She was his niece ! Sarah Bernhardt was playing *L'Aiglon* (the second pitiful successor to the dynasty), but the Princess refused to go, as she said, for the sake of hearing her deceased cousin talking rubbish to Metternich.

Sarah, playing in her full prestige, was one of the sights of my Paris. To play the part of this slim, unhappy princeling she had cut her hair and slept for weeks in military boots. Here was the illusionary power of the real actress : a plump middle-aged woman bringing to life this haphazard youth born of the Hapsburgs by the French Revolution. The impression was overwhelming. The audience felt that if Sarah was not like L'Aiglon it was his business to have resembled her. Only to her appeal could the corpses have answered as they did from the field of Wagram. They had waited for her to come to life.

There was another unforgettable production at this time : *Louise*, at the *Opéra Comique*. It was the apotheosis of Paris and of the life around the Latin Quarter. The scene opened with all the familiar street cries breaking through the mists of dawn. Coquelin *aîné* I saw at the *Comédie française*. The only other play I remember was Tolstoy's *Resurrection*, played movingly at the *Odéon*. It was seen and heard with the hush with which a Passion Play is followed.

About this time Isadora Duncan arrived in Paris and danced at Sarah's theatre to the delight of students. The names of dancers and courtesans automatically drifted from the posters to the memory of passers-by. These were the days of Cleo de Mérode and *la belle Otero*. Names die down in memory, but there was one whose last name at least was lit suddenly in the coming years, lit indeed by the flash of a firing-squad. At the *Cirque Molier* a

P

fascinating creature was dancing Hindoo dances, and her name was posted as " Lady Macleod Matahari ! " I often wonder were they the same, the dancer and the spy ?

Great excitement over the death and funeral of Louise Michel about this time. She had been a *pétroleuse* under the Commune. She seemed the Boadicea of a Lost Cause, but she would have found herself to-day. Society was so secure and petrified that the first motor-race from Paris to Madrid caused a real shudder in 1903. Hour by hour news of the road casualties came in, until a humanitarian government stopped the race. Seven were killed, and Europe was shocked. I remember the murderous cars (like old crocks they would seem to-day) and chauffeurs dressed like Arctic explorers. Amid storms of dust they ploughed through France like threshing machines mounted on old horse brakes. Twice as many are killed every single day now, but this seemed a holocaust.

There was much to be seen and heard in Paris apart from the so-called life of pleasure which is an artificial world prepared for tourists. Paris is supposedly the City of Prostitutes, but they did not enter into the lives of students. Students were poor and lived from hand to mouth. In this way the Sorbonne resembled a mediæval University far more than Oxford or Cambridge. At the *Bal Bulier* students danced with artists' models, and schools of painting like the *Salon Julien* gave balls where the models danced without a stitch except their shoes and stockings. It was not upsetting when one recollected that their partners had been painting them in the daytime with even less covering. The strictest order was kept at these balls, and familiarity was met with the back of a girl's hand.

The Latin Quarter was not an insidious part of Paris for a young man to live. The French youth of those days boasted no athletics. They toiled at desk or easel or in the medical schools all day. Only in the evening did students sit in the cafés, especially the *Café d'Harcourt,* where they could drink beer, scribble letters and poems, play chess and sometimes sing a chorus. All the simple Bohemian life has since disappeared with the Americanisation of Paris. The only possible exercise was fencing. Three times a week I fenced with a *maître d'armes* for an absurdly small sum. Fencing is a lighter, quicker and more lasting sport than the cricket and rowing on which English youth is bred. It touches every muscle in the body, and a good fencer can fence till sixty.

I do not think that women were the danger of young men. French girls made easy and shrewd companions. One learnt by living in French families that though the French have rejected prudery they keep a strict morality. They kept their code, but they made no hypocrisy over any lapse. They had no objection to the English code except that the English would insist that things were not what they were. The French preferred to stress the realism of life. The English, of course, cloaked things as they were. Drama, newspaper and books showed the same division between the national mentalities.

The women of France kept within two codes and made no effort to cross from one to another : wives and mistresses. But the wives had toleration for a class who they knew would never dream of subverting them. There were no shades or shady mixtures as in England. The demi-world was a world to itself.

For young foreigners there was a real danger not from women, but from a society of secret decadence which made the English public school look like a girls' school. No youth of sixteen to twenty could live long in Paris without being approached on the part of a colony whose types have been sketched in masterwise by Proust. They were wealthy, of no particular age or country, generally artistic and very agreeable socially.

I had American friends who counselled me after passing through similar experiences. The most prominent at the Sorbonne was Jo Stickney, who was about to take a Greek Chair at Harvard. He stood six feet four and much resembled a Greek god, in spite of his curious staring eyes.

Six years older, he was an invaluable guide and protector.
I was in and out of his rooms in the rue d'Assas, and from
him I learnt what was to be said about Oriental China,
Japanese script and the Renaissance. He wrote a most
exquisite handwriting on thin vellum sheets. And as
part of my education he revealed to me the secrets and
addicts of that decadent world which met its first catas-
trophe among the Cities of the Plain. Here they were
flourishing in Paris with their own newspaper, their own
parties and balls, in fact a whole section of life which was
as clear of ladies as an ecclesiastical seminary.

Stickney and I used to roar with laughter over the
efforts made by some absurd creatures to add us to their
number. But it was very tempting to mingle where the
Arts were understood and perfect French was spoken.
Curiously enough I never met any Frenchmen amongst
them, although they included escapes from London and
Berlin. I was invited by a famous composer, a great
friend of Melba, to hear him play his own songs in his
apartment. This was an opening to French literature,
for Anatole France and Proust frequented his rooms.
Proust, of course, meant nothing then, but I should
like to have known him. No doubt he was already
studying these courteous bisexual creatures like insects.
As for the *maître Anatole* he went wherever a Muse opened
a door. I knew I had no right to be there, but at seventeen
I felt flattered at even finding myself in the same room as
men of art or letters.

It was very difficult to avoid their attentions. I used to
dine with the Millington Drakes, who offered a centre of
hospitality which those who enjoyed it could never forget.
After dinner one evening a famous musician called
unexpectedly from an adjoining apartment and entertained the whole party to a late hour. At midnight I
prepared to return to the Latin Quarter, but the Drakes
for some reason would not let me go, and I slept in Mr
Drake's dressing-room. In the morning the kind Drakes
explained that their musical friend had waited on the stairs

to take me to see the night life of Paris, for which they judged I was not sufficiently mature.

In the same *Avenue du Bois de Boulogne* (now called after Foch) lived the wisest and most cynical of Americans, the great Henry Adams. To his feet I was brought by Jo Stickney and had the sense to listen with a delight which touched the old man. In 1903 he was at his zenith, talking exquisitely about blue China, the modern dynamo, Chartres Cathedral and the Latin mediæval hymns. His rich personality has been since revealed to a wondering America in his Autobiography. But I knew the book called *The Education of Henry Adams* as conversation. I had only to listen to hear it all while he conversed with Stickney.

The first time we met he was very interested at the first appearance of the telephone in a crime drama. Paris had been thrilled by listening to a murder through the telephone. "Uncle Henry" had a formula connecting the ages whereby the modern machine had taken the creative powers of the Virgin in the Middle Ages. The Paris Exhibition of 1900 had convinced him that all progress was going in the wrong direction : that man would destroy first his soul and then his body with his own machines. The most upsetting of all his doctrines was that Democracy was a failure, and that the White House itself would become a cage for thwarted statesmen. He was convinced that the second term in the Presidency always brought disaster. Russia and America he foretold would cut themselves away from Western Europe, and if they returned would only undermine the old civilisation from which they had once grafted their own.

As for the Virgin, who inspired the great cathedrals, she was once the dynamo of European man. "You must come to a conclusion sooner or later," he said to me in awe-inspiring tones, " whether the centre of the universe is masculine or feminine." I could not conceive that it was not masculine, but Uncle Henry doubted if I were right.

Grandson and great-grandson of Presidents, he was a survivor of the Sixties which he had spent in London

with his father struggling to prevent England's interference in the Civil War.   The *Alabama* had slipped out
of the English yards, and there were Rams, which were
only not launched because the Adams family gave
Palmerston the choice of war.

He was a very little old man, but chirpy as a cricket.
He had satirised American Society in an anonymous novel,
Democracy, and he had devised a science of History.
By linking the trend of forces in different ages he believed
that the course of History could be foreshown. Long before
the Great War he foretold that Germany must divide
world-interests with England or else destroy England and
France.   He was a traveller who had quested the Southern
Seas, found Stevenson in Samoa and sat under the tree
of Buddha.   When his wife committed suicide, he com-
missioned St Gaudens to sculpt a famous Nirvana
under which he and his wife lie to-day at Washington.

I was too young and ignorant to profit from this wise
and weird old man.   Anyone who has read *The Education
of Henry Adams* can conceive what an education it was to
become familiar with Adams himself.   Stickney had the
entry to his apartment, and in their company I felt as one
walking in the groves of Greece with Plato and some young
Greek disciple.

Memory is a jade.   So much real wisdom slipped me
by for ever, and it is only the gossip and stories which I
recall from those Attic evenings and days.   One story
always sticks, and I can hear Stickney's recitative voice
and Uncle Henry's ironical comments.   A wonderful case
of crime had been tried in the French Courts.   A lady of
easy virtue (so called because her path is hard) had been
visited by a wealthy friend while she was lying indisposed
in bed.   There had been no quarrel between the friends,
but for some reason she had shown him the loaded revolver
which she kept under her pillow (no doubt in defence of
her virtue).   Unluckily it went off and the bullet pierced
his eye.   She was tried for murder and acquitted because
it was shown that the bullet had not broken the eyelid.

He had not had time to blink! Therefore she had not menaced him nor caused him the least apprehension. Therefore it was an accident.

I regret I had not the sense to write down all I heard fall from these perfect conversationalists. In life there are plenty of Doctor Johnsons, but alas, the Boswells are few. Stickney returned to Harvard as America's most promising scholar and died the next year. Will none recall him save his youthful disciple? How often I remembered how often we had tired the sun with talking and sent him down the sky. His parting gift to me was the Greek Anthology. But later I wrote a poem which contained as much anguish as a young man could feel for another :

A DEAD FRIEND

I drew him then unto my knee, my friend who was dead,
And I set my live lips over his, and my heart by his head.

I thought of an unrippled love and a passion unsaid,
And the years he was living by me, my friend who was dead ;

And the white morning ways that we went, and how oft we had fed
And drunk with the sunset for lamp—my friend who was dead ;

Now never the draught at my lips would thrill to my head—
For the last vintage ebbed in my heart ; my friend he was dead.

Then I spake unto God in my grief : My wine and my bread
And my staff Thou hast taken from me—my friend who is dead.

Are the heavens yet friendless to Thee, and lone to Thy head,
That Thy desolate heart must have need of my friend who is dead?

To God then I spake yet again : not Peter instead
Would I take, nor Philip nor John, for my friend who is dead.

As for Henry Adams he needs not my pen nor the pen of other. When his book was published he proved to be his own Boswell !

They were a wonderful pair of intellectuals for a young man to meet. Stickney was a pure pagan and wished to dissuade me against the Catholic Church which fascinated my Sundays. But Uncle Henry was an authority on

cathedrals and the hymns of Adam of St Victor : and the
Porta Latina lay beyond.

I met other interesting people. Charles Kinsky was
at the Austrian Embassy. He was my brother's godfather, and the Great War never broke the link between
him and the England which honoured him as a great
sportsman. He always kept horses in England. The fatal
outbreak of war found him in Austria. He had already
telegraphed to his English groom to shoot all his stud,
which very sensibly he refused to do. I am certain
Kinsky never wished their destruction, but he was
anxious to prove his loyalty to his own Emperor.

The Austrian Embassy was great in the world of
diplomacy. It still represented an Emperor who still
figured as the Holy Roman. Count Wolkenstein was
Ambassador. His old Countess had been a patroness of
Wagner. Our concierge could not believe it when an
attaché left their cards on so humble a student as myself.
Talking with her was like conversing with the past century.
The Ambassador was subject to a state of moody despair
for which the mediævals kept the word *accidia*. She
used to beg me to cheer him up with the enthusiasm of
youth, but our walks in the Austrian Embassy gardens
were as silent as death. He peered at me as sombrely as
Randolph in his last stage. Unhappy must be the lives of
old men who have not taught themselves an art or a
hobby in their youth, or better still a philosophy like
Henry Adams. When I found Uncle Henry fifteen years
later living in great old age in his city of Washington he
was never dull nor disagreeable nor dismayed. He could
still flash the vital spark from brain to brain.

These days in France were the days when laws were
fashioned against the Church. The Religious Orders were
being scattered. I saw some Franciscans leaving and met
Jesuits compelled to associate in twos or threes. To my
great disappointment I could not reach the *Grande
Chartreuse* while the monks were there. The whole
country surrounding the monastery had become dead

after the passing of the noblest and most austere of the Orders. We were told that the abbot, when he emerged from his abbey for the last time, very simply summoned the French Premier to meet him on the Day of Judgment. I never failed to visit a Carthusian monastery. They seem to preserve the mystery as well as the beauty of holiness like silent power-generators of the spirit.

Mediæval studies meant taking a living interest in the one great survivor of Christendom : the Roman Church. Monsieur Counort introduced me to Mgr Pêchenard, the Rector of the Catholic Institute in the *rue de Vaugirard*. Evenings I spent in his company, and through him I started a new line of historical studies. Under his roof I met the Catholic poet, François Coppée, who spoke with the tremendous prestige of a member of the French Academy. He was Dionysian in his frenzy against the injustices done to the Church. He was full of life and humour and that vital irony which is part of a French writer's make-up.

Time rushes away, bearing all her children. I felt saddened to find my Immortal, when I last visited Paris, had been mortalised in a public statue not far from the Invalides. My poor friend Pêchenard was made Bishop of Soissons and lived to see his cathedral crumbled by the German guns.

All the distinguished Frenchmen I met have passed, including my lecturers at the Sorbonne : Gaston Paris, Ernest Lavisse, Leroy Boileau and Monsieur Faguet, who had been recently received at the Academy. At his reception occurred a famous scene : the reappearance, as it were from the dead, of Emile Ollivier, the Liberal Prime Minister who had gone into the War of 1870 " with a light heart." That phrase about " *un cœur léger* " had snuffed him out for a generation. But at Faguet's inauguration he returned like a ghost and made mention that the great melancholias of history were reserved for those who raise human beings to the divine. It was a wonderful sentence which will never be out of date.

Cambridge and King's

*

MY ASSOCIATION WITH CAMBRIDGE I DATE WITH
two fairly permanent foundations. My first year, 1904,
was the date that the Letchworth Garden City came into
being, and that King Edward VII came to open the new
science schools in the University.

I spent some preliminary months reading at Trumpington Rectory with Robert Bury, a brother of John Bury
who had just succeeded Lord Acton in the Chair of
Modern History. Driving slowly through the Cambridge
suburbs in October of 1903 I felt the same thrill which
Arthur Balfour recorded the first time he passed the Fitz-
william Museum which stands like a pillared gateway to
the University. In the twilight every figure seemed a
Don and every shop boy returning home some laborious
scholar without his gown.

The surrounding country had not been given that
commercial aspect which is now worthy of the more
practical teaching of Cambridge. Roads were not
macadamised and tarred : traffic was unmechanised.
Human beings could behave as such without running
risks of injury. Trumpington and its sister Grandchester
were still isolated and timbered from the world. They
were separated by the stream which had turned the mill
for Chaucer's Miller of Trumpington. The church was
famous for a Crusader's Brass which archæologists used
to rub endlessly to make transfers. The Rectory was a
rambling old house set in an old-fashioned garden of
roses and pawky apple trees overhung by great elms,
cadaverous in winter, but dropping green curtains in

234

summertime. The windows had been designed and glazed by Grote the Philosopher to keep out the sound of nightingales. Here indeed was peace.

Robert Bury was the finest Platonist in the Church of England, as his editions of the Symposium, the Timaeus and the Laws have shown. I soon learnt the truth that every man is an Aristotelian or a Platonist in all matters that count. I plunged for Plato. I became as anti-Aristotelian as I had been anti-Harrovian. I took up sides rather than a philosophy. Plato seemed to offer a background to the High Church mysticism I was anxious to cultivate. Looking back across the years, I ask if anyone can know politics who has not read the Republic of Plato or can understand Love without kenning the Symposium ? As for philosophy, I used to set up Comte and Herbert Spencer in order to ridicule them like dummies or pierce them with arrows from Plato's bow. Not that I could wield it, but Robert Bury could, and from him I began to learn that patient sense of language and of meaning which wings a scholar's soul.

Our first visit to Cambridge was to hear a lecture from his brother the Professor. I was sorry to think I had missed Lord Acton in the Regius Chair. Cambridge still spoke of him in hushed whispers : the most learned man in Europe if not in Cambridge ! He had created a wide reputation by constantly quoting from a book he had never written—the History of Liberty ! It was perhaps better than losing one's historical repute by writing one. I was deeply impressed later to find his disciples like Laurence and Figgis still murmuring about this book which, of course, could never appear. It has since taken its place on that phantom shelf which is adorned by Dr Mayor's Martial and Dr Headlam's Æschylus, for both of which all scholars were pining in my time.

Jack Bury was a great contrast to Lord Acton. He perpetually wrote books and he talked very little. His pupils could never come into touch with him, but I always found him amenable, as we were Monaghan men together.

The Burys were sons of the scholarly old Rector of Clontibret within a short horse-drive from Glaslough. Clontibret is one of those parishes which lie, as the Irish say, very comfortably at the back of God's Beyond. Tourists often pass through the County of Monaghan in trains, but who has ever reached the back bogs of Clontibret even in a jaunting car ? It was a sad and lonesome place, and we believed that the Bury family used Greek as the language of their household. It was curious, but I could never find trace of anybody from County Monaghan going to Cambridge except the Burys and myself.

At Trumpington I lay low and read rapidly. After a few months I took the "Little Go" Examination. I never felt so keen and exalted as I walked in three miles every morning to the Corn Exchange and made hay of the papers before striding back in the afternoon. French and Greek now came easily. I had a choice between Paley's *Evidences of Christianity* and Logic. Paley is now obsolete and a gibbering figure in limbo. He was described as "tedious to man and an insult to God." His theological demonstrations, the epitome of the eighteenth-century rationalism in a Rectory, were supposed to have laid the foundation of the whole Cambridge school of Agnosticism. I preferred Jevons' *Logic* and have always wondered since why the elements of logic are not taught in public schools. There is no quicker way to teach reasoning, and it covers the ground very prettily where mathematics and letters meet. It can be studied hand in hand with Alice's adventures "Through the Looking Glass."

Having conquered the "Little Go," I read right through Lucretius, described by Jack Bury as "the only original author produced by Rome." Even so his theory of atoms was borrowed from the Greeks, but his masterly hexameters hammered out like iron made a new music in my skull. For the first time I had the feeling that I was eating into an author's marrow. I have never known or really cared whether his atomic theory was right or not. Every thousand years the scientists come round to it again. Is the whole universe made of atoms as indivisible as the Persons of the Holy Trinity ? Although the scientist cleaves the atom I feel that Lucretius stands. A comet seems to me a wonderful instance of the subtility of Lucretian matter raining through space.

For the first time I began to get Latin into my blood and to chant it on lonely walks on the Royston Road. What a splendid language it was before Virgil polished it up for Court use and Ovid tessellated it into an amorous kindergarten ! Lucretius delighted me because he had a reason for everything : a theory of space and an explanation of the process of tickling ! Modern discovery often finds a hint of prophecy or at least a suitable phrase amid that rugged sea of words. Here I spotted vaguely the Plurality of Worlds, the Theory of Light, the Survival of the Fittest and even Saltation in Nature : " You just and only just can call it a change of inclination." However much he disapproved the survival of the soul, here were the first ideas of all psychical research : " The existence of things like films peeled off from the surface of things."

What a writer—half a poet, half a laboratory assistant and an encyclopædist all the time ! He dealt with sleep, dreams, shadows and echoes as phases of the working of atoms. There was a meticulous reason for everything. I still see a Turner sunset or a Freudian dream in terms of Lucretius. I was perfectly satisfied with his analysis of Love and Lust (into which every youth of eighteen needs to inquire). As for that glorious enemy and seductive mother of men, Woman, I found three terrible passages which made a threefold lamp upon the path of the adolescent male. The seventh chapter in the Book of Proverbs : a certain poem by Dean Swift and a cutting from the Fourth Book of Lucretius. The first two are well-known, but only the Latinists quote the Lucretius. Even in English it makes rare stuff for dealing with womankind. Once a man is in their toils :

" Lo man's life is passed at another's finger-call.
His estate is melted to furnish her with the coverlets of

Babylon. His duty is all undone and his good name
sickens and staggers.

The lovely shoes of Sicyon laugh upon her feet ;
her great green-lit emeralds sink into the gold and the
moisture of her body soaketh dresses as wine-coloured
as the sea.

Her father's noble pile of earnings maketh ribbons
for her hair and tiring unto her head.

Feasting is hers with rich cushions and dishes. Many
are the cups, but unguents and coronals are all in
vain ; for from the very well-spring of delight ariseth
something rather bitter ! "

That *amari aliquid*, how often it leaps to the mind in the
midst of the so-called dissipations and delights of life.

I made Lucretius my prophet and my friend much as
men of the Nineties absorbed Omar Khayyám and the
Latin Quarter used to sup on Baudelaire. Apart from
his philosophy I made him a measuring rod in literature.
I had his metre and his phrase under my skin as a French
mistress says of her lover. Later I tried my pen on a
prize poem for the University in Lucretian style. The
subject was excellent : Siberia. It puzzled and pleased
my college tutor who sent for me. It was the only piece
of work for which I received commendation during my
whole three years at Cambridge.

I used to visit Cambridge from Trumpington like a
Moslem tripping into Mecca. I came to see King
Edward VII open the new schools in Downing Lane.
The whole University was in attendance. Of all the Dons,
Masters and Heads of college, who hailed the royal entry,
not one survives the third of a century which has passed.
Unforgettable was a king who looked a king. Genial,
round-bodied and richly bearded, he looked like a gelded
Henry VIII, bluff and affable without the disfiguring
elements which made the Tudor so sinister amongst
Cambridge Founders. I wondered what memories Cam-
bridge still held for him. Here he gathered his first sheaves
of knowledge and here he had garnered his first wild oats.

I was still thinking of going to Trinity, Dublin, under the ægis of Mahaffy, but Jack Bury persuaded me to come to Cambridge. And the attraction of King's was magnetic. The same holy Founder of Eton was beckoning me. There was the most glorious chapel in Europe, and there was rumour of keen intellectual life. I applied for entry and found myself sitting for examination. Dr Dent of musical fame was presiding. A few days later Mr Macaulay (later Vice-Provost) took the trouble to ride his horse to Trumpington to inform me I was a Kingsman.

The next time I walked through Cambridge I felt as Wordsworth felt when he wrote his " Prelude." Everyone, who has felt the thought, will claim the words :

> " I could not always lightly pass
> Through the same gateways, sleep where they had slept
> Wake where they waked, range that inclosure old,
> That garden of great intellects, undisturbed."

Cambridge in the new century was full of famous Heads of colleges. Old Montagu Butler was Master of Trinity, lived in his enveloping gown and retained the academical manners of the past. He had been heard saying to a fellow-master in a London bus to the amazement of the travellers :

" Master of Jesus, shall we alight ? "

And old Morgan replying :

" Master of Trinity, are you sure we have reached our destination ? "

He looked like the God of Abraham and Isaac and Jacob as he sat in Trinity Chapel under his canopy. The only chance I had to meet him under his roof amid the pictures of the Master's Lodge was with a group whom he addressed on social purity. He entertained us charmingly, and his anecdotes drifted sonorously through the rooms. When we returned to King's, Sir Charles Waldstein burst into fury at the idea of an old man with a young wife presuming to tell undergraduates to keep straight. It was true the old man had both sons and grandsons among the undergraduates, but he came under the heading of Patriarch and if he had begotten fifty sons he would not have made a less admirable Master of Trinity.

He had a wonderful soft lucidity of after-dinner speech, and never lost an occasion to allude to the prowess and prominence of the College. A Varsity wit reported that he had dreamed of the day of Judgment and overheard the Master of Trinity returning thanks to the Most High after the very difficult proceedings of the day, not without a suggestion that the Eternal might be willing to be considered a Trinity man himself !

The ruling masters of Clare and Magdalene had actually become Masters of their colleges in the Fifties. Dr Atkinson's jubilee came in 1906, and he only missed a diamond jubilee by one year. Lord Braybrooke became Master of Magdalene in 1853 and was still there. The master's garden supported his cows, and the whole college was rural rather than academical. In my Uncle Moreton's time it had been considered a very good college to hunt from. As at Saint Catharine's there was only a handful of undergraduates. Saint Catharine's was still under the mastership of Dr Robinson, who was rightly or wrongly supposed to have voted himself into office and had been boycotted by the University ever since.

Magdalene received a wonderful renaissance when Stuart Donaldson and Arthur Benson arrived from Eton as Masters in succession to Lord Braybrooke. Benson had come to mental grief at Eton, trying to make up his mind whether to take Holy Orders and aspire to Warre's mantle or not. He preferred not to risk failure and unhappiness, avenging the procrastinations of his mind in the pages of his diary. He intended to make short work of Latin and Greek at Eton, introducing the future rulers, legislators, squires and sportsmen of the Empire to a sound study of modern history and languages. He would probably have lost half his staff, all his friends and his mind. At Cambridge he found himself secure, and I felt all the charm of letters and humours of biography again when I heard him lecture on Charles Kingsley, an old

Magdalene man. In its way it was perfection. In a town of arid and perfunctory lecturing it remains a flower fresh blooming in memory. It simply quelled some of the irreverent who were listening.

My first nights at King's were spent in Gilbert Cannan's rooms and I admired the humorous illustration with which he had painted his fire-place. He was one of the King's College school of novelists which included " Dodo " Benson and E. M. Forster. We passed like ships in the night, for he was leaving just as I reached his moorings. His career was always of interest to me, but the promise of his pen was not fulfilled. He married Sir James Barrie's beautiful wife and later he passed into African jungles where he met an even more romantic adventure. And his end was sad. The fates of Kingsmen are said to be very strange and varied.

My first year I lived out of college in lodgings under the tower of St Benet's Church, the oldest in Cambridge. Later I lived over the Porter's Lodge at King's and my last year I passed in Bodley's, the new building over the Backs, overlooking the green and tideless reaches of the Cam.

The Cambridge Backs are famous and are always contrasted with the Fronts at Oxford.

There are a number of subtle differences between the two Universities which we used to take a simple pleasure in recording. From Doctor Johnson's conversation with King George III of happy agricultural memory it may be gathered that although Oxford had the more books, Cambridge made the better use of her smaller store !

Oxford was known as " the home of lost causes." Cambridge was rightly, with Newton and Harvey, considered the home of discovered ones.

At Oxford we believed that the Dons wore evening dress at dinner. This was reserved for the waiters at Cambridge.

Oxford was supplied (before the Morris era) with trams drawn by pairs of horses. The tram which I recall

Q

plying between the Station and King's at Cambridge was harnessed to a single quadruped.

We were also told that ladies of pleasure could be found domiciled at Oxford, but Cambridge men in search of pavement romance had to go to London.

Oxford is celebrated for a manner : Cambridge priding herself on her manners.

Oxford is a University in a city: Cambridge a University with a city attached.

At Oxford you take your napkin but not your gown into the *Common* Room. At Cambridge you take your gown but not your napkin into the *Combination* Room.

The speakers differed at the two Universities. At Cambridge they were dramatic : at Oxford theatrical. Cambridge produced personalities whereas Oxford inclined to personages.

Finally the Oxonians parted their hair in the middle whereas the Cantabs divided theirs on the side.

But I always felt the real distinction lay in the manner of the undergraduates in the street. At Oxford they walked as though the street belonged to them. At Cambridge they walked as though they didn't care to whom it belonged.

Wherever one lodged at King's one came under the shadow of the Chapel. It hung upon us like a cathedral. No building in Cambridge lifted a roof to half its height. It had inspired both Milton and Wordsworth. Entering in sunshine one was smitten by the glory of the painted glaze. In the evening one's soul was suffused by the mellow candlelight. The walls were rich with gigantic carved heraldry—the rouge dragon of Wales, the white greyhound of the Nevilles and blistered right and left with the red rose of Lancaster. Like great bulbs of carved stone darkened by the fogs of centuries. This was the red rose of England. At King's it stood for the family of our Founder, but there was a legend and a descent too beautiful to be historical.

Not without reason or romance could that floral symbol have come to be the English badge. To the House of Lancaster it came through Edmund Crouchback who married the widow of the grandson of *La Reine Blanche*, the White Queen to whom Thibaut the Troubadour had brought it from the Holy Land. It had become the Rose of Provence, but in former days in Palestine it had been the Rose of Sharon, the lovely flower stained by the blood-stained Venus in her search for Adonis.

In this superb chapel, said to be the exact measurements of Noah's Ark and indeed exhibiting a number of fossilised animals which might have accompanied that primitive navigator, we heard service on Sundays rendered by the best choir of boys in England. On week-days the chaplain and a handful of undergraduates held the fort for mattins. Vespers were sung by the choir with gentle perfection. I seldom missed stepping into the Chapel day by day. It became like a mould upon my callow soul. And again and again Wordsworth's splendid sonnet seemed to float from the pinnacles which once evoked it. In my time the pinnacles were the resort of a cormorant which roosted there by night to the delight and amusement of all who loved birds. Some low-minded sportsman shot and stuffed the noble bird. I am glad that the Vice-Provost Whiting visited the culprit and indignantly claimed the body on behalf of the college. The tragedy went to my heart and I dashed off some lines for the *Cambridge Review* : the first poem, I ever saw of my own in print. After the years I recall them in their simplicity :

> " Scaly legate from the termless Ocean
> For a while our College guest :
> I am sorry that the Cambridge gunners
> Killed thee on thy harmless quest,
> That the muddy minnows here are grudged thee
> And a Fleur-de-lys for nest.

> " Still to hear the flooding tide of anthem
> And the chants that ebbed to thee,
> Cheaply hast thou put away thy fishing
> And thy birthright of the sea ! "

I had a passionate love for birds. One day I found the
porters removing the swallows' nests in the front porch.
I hastily wrote an entreaty to the Provost from the
swallows in my best Greek. The swallows nest there to
this day.

Calling an old cormorant " scaly legate from the ocean "
is good. It recalls the Irish journalist who called pitch
and toss " the Baccarat of the Bucolic," but such is the
fustian of poetry !

Although all the poets of England but one seem to have
preferred Cambridge to Oxford, Wordsworth's " Prelude "
makes him peculiarly the bard of the Cam. How well he
recalled the whimsical and eccentric old Dons who
flourished in every college :

> ". . . and having almost in my mind put off
>   Their human names, have into phantoms passed
>   Of texture midway between life and books."

Like Nicholas Nickleby we hesitated between the respect
we ought to assume towards the venerable and our natural
love for the whimsical. The colleges chose super-scholars
as Fellows of the colleges, or such harmless eccentrics
as they thought unsuitable for other professions. There
was no other explanation for some of those marvellous
types who have been served up in memoirs and embellished
in fiction. We were not without memorable specimens at
King's.

The most remarkable figure at King's was Oscar
Browning the O.B. No Don ever created such a legend
in his own lifetime, and it was one to which we added
laughably and libellously every week. During his
tempestuous career he was sacked as an Eton master
and later as a Don from King's. Yet he had adorned
both foundations. Mr Wortham has given him an
admirable biography, Arthur Benson a cruel but living
essay, Lord Birkenhead the finest laudation and
J. K. Stephen one of the most ingenious epigrams in
English.

" O.B. O be obedient
To Nature's stern decrees
For though there be but one O.B.
He may be two O.B.'s (too obese) "

Even so the enormity of his character has never been properly described.

The O.B. hung like a millstone round the neck of the college, but he was the target of our gossip. Freshmen and Seniors found common ground in discussing the O.B. Even Dons could be rallied out of torpitude by queries concerning his past. They broke into Homeric laughter or hostile undertones. They all agreed that he was an ornament from outside, but the greatest nuisance within the college. For twenty years it had been impossible to conceive Cambridge without the O.B. in the streets, on the boards, in the societies, in the limelight or actually in the Cam, for he was a great swimmer all the year round.

The same man, who could patronise royalty, could be gushing to the Freshman. He could be equally tactless and sympathetic. As a debater at the Union or as a Proctor he was a great success. He could not speak without being the lion of the evening. As a Proctor he remained human. He told me his most difficult case had been with an undergraduate who had offered a passing tramp a bottle of whisky on condition he swallowed it neat. Of course the tramp gulped it and fell dead. It was a case of stupidity not of manslaughter.

The O.B. was stocky and immensely broad. His brow gave the impression equally of faculties high and low. He had an enormous head and a huge paunch which literally swung in front of him when he waddled. Lord Birkenhead was probably right in asserting that the real difference between the two Universities was the existence of the O.B. at one of them. He failed to become at Cambridge what Benjamin Jowett had been at Oxford. Like Jowett he was a colossal snob, but he was never smng. He was always ready for a romp. What could you make of a man who revelled with the undergraduates and

quarrelled with the Dons ? A man who went into mourning for a German Grand Duke and dined the sailor lads
whom he started in life, each carrying a locket from his
benefactor ?

As was only right it was Oscar Browning who introduced
Oscar Wilde to Cambridge. Oxford's great wit was
lodged at King's and his memory was still vivid among the
sedate Dons, who had delightedly heard their little wise-
cracks caught up and improved on the return-sally.
There was a grand saying of his remembered, which I do
not remember to have seen in a book. " The English,"
he said, " were always boasting of their Bard, their Bible
and their Bradshaw, none of which they could ever
understand ! "

The O.B. was a Christian Scientist in his old age, but
he used to insist on the infallibility of the Pope. He could
sing a comic song and he could write a mediæval Ballad
to the Blessed Virgin. He was the presiding genius of
the Liberal Society, all of whose offices he had slowly
absorbed by the time it was necessary to dethrone him.
He was fated to wreck in the long run whatever he touched.
There was a famous caricature of his leaving the treasurer-
ship of the Union based on Tenniel's " dropping the
Pilot." It was rumoured that the River authorities had
protested against his remaining in the swimming club on
the ground that he was gradually washing away the
banks !

Nicholas Wedd, a Fellow of King's, could only define
him to some visitors as " the sort of man who would have
trout for tea." They called on the O.B. and by an
extraordinary chance they found that he was devouring
a trout in solitude. Wedd had only chosen the simile
to give an idea of the impossible. It must always be
remembered that the O.B. introduced the first private
bathroom into a Cambridge college. While he was
proudly showing the late Duke of Clarence over the scene
of his ablutions, Leo Maxse, late editor of the *National
Review*, locked the door upon him and his royal visitor.

Poor O.B.—he was finally dispensed and dispersed by his ungrateful college. Nobody had been more loyal to King's, and while he was an examiner in the History Tripos few Kingsmen ever failed of a First. In later years he said to Provost Sheppard : " You have made King's the premier classical college as I made her the premier historical one. I hope they won't sack you ! "

Once he described a delightful friend of his, recounting his many charms, but added absent-mindedly : " He is always being mistaken for me ! "

In the Eighties he had been seriously considered as a Minister for Education, but he failed at elections in the constituencies because, as he told us, he was perpetually mistaken for the poet Browning ! In his final exile he dragged himself away to Rome whence he was brought back, a handful of grey ashes, to be laid under the Chapel at King's. He was one of those human puzzles whom the Creator seems to have reserved for his own solution on the day of general judgment.

The first time I met him, the wind was blowing through his gown and he looked more swollen than the reality. He immediately dragged me into his famous rooms : " It's your duty to come here on Sunday evenings. You will meet everybody here." How describe the rooms which were decorated to suit their occupant—the photographs of royalty, the Arundel prints, the preposterous gold wall-paper, the oily portrait by Zuluoga and the gross, hearty, amphibious creature who seemed composed equally of brain and heart and fat !

There was a change in the Provostship my first year. I had barely made acquaintance with Augustus Austen Leigh before his career drew to a close. He was the brother of the formidable " Flea " at Eton, and under his guidance King's had ceased to be an Eton close. The scholarships were now opened to the world and the Fellows allowed to offer their ink-stained hands in marriage. In the old celibate days King's had not been

troubled by examinations or morals. Unbelievable
stories were told of the old men who had included some
amusing sinners and one serious Saint, Mr Simeon. Apart
from his benign portrait hanging in Hall his only memorial
was a hand-rail half-way to his rooms traditionally called
the "Saints' Rest." What Newman had been to Oxford
old Simeon had been to Cambridge. It was curious that
a much more striking memorial remained to a Fellow
who had had to leave the college. It was a long and lurid
story, but nobody knew the details except Provost
Montagu James and the Master of Jesus who told it to me
one evening after the Port. This Fellow had led a younger
Fellow into temptation from which the younger did not
return alive. His body was brought back quietly to
King's, which being a Royal foundation was not liable to
an inquest. It was all hushed up and the delinquent
disappeared into Australia for ever. But after his death
his savings returned to the college to fill the empty west
window with coloured glass. It was known as "S——'s
Repentance." The moral seemed to me to have some
significance. Out of passing sin and tragedy the House of
the Eternal was beautified. But what a short story for
Maupassant !

One afternoon the Dean rushed into Chapel with the
sad words : "The Provost is dead." It seemed a full
stop to college life, but a college has a hydra-existence,
and there were several heads hidden in our ranks who
could little have dreamed of becoming Provost. In spite
of a hurried and I am afraid mocking placard "Vote
for the O.B.," the Fellows elected Monty James. In
the summer of 1905 he was installed, and I remember the
delight with which I listened to the peals played on the
bells of Great St Mary's. Our only disappointment was
that he refrained from parading through the lesser colleges
in the state coach which belongs to King's and to no
other.

In later years Dr James became the most learned, most
affable and popular of Eton Provosts. I only knew him

in benign Olympianhood at King's. Every Sunday the Provost's Lodge was open to all who dared intrude. I have heard him in his most exquisite moments such as reading a freshly concocted ghost-story or reciting the trial scene from *Pickwick* until his audience felt that Mrs Bardell was a Cambridge landlady and Mr Buzfuz the finished legal product of Trinity Hall!

Monty James had an infallible memory, perhaps the most wonderful of our time. And as a scholar he never made mistakes. The only general knowledge question he failed to answer once was " Who was Pontius Pilate's wife ? " The name is known though it is not recorded in Scripture. I may add one slip gleaned from all his works. He derived the name of the Irish County Clare from the same source as the family or college of Clare, but the Irish Clare is derived from the Gaelic *clar*, a smooth board or plain. This slip occurs in his book on East Anglian churches.

His memory held good for figures as well as names. I remember when some Yorkshire Abbey was burnt he immediately quoted the exact dimensions. He became uncanny when an illuminated missal was placed in his hand. He would give the date, the school, the diocese and sometimes the very monastery where it had been written. Very simple, deeply learned, and inwardly humorous he floated above the planet. He never revealed his profoundest thought nor did he write the immensely great book he could have written on the Middle Ages. He kept much that he knew to himself. Perhaps he was wisest in this.

I wriggled out of the O.B.'s clutches when he wished me to read History. The classical staff at King's was too tempting. The teaching at that time was incredibly good with Dimsdale teaching Latin poetry, Headlam Greek poetry, Wedd Classical History and Sills lecturing on Thucydides.

Sir Charles Waldstein was at King's : the most inspiring teacher of Classical Archæology we ever knew. He could

make the dead statues live, and spoke of the great Greek
sculptors as though they were exhibiting in Burlington
House. He had lapses of knowledge and was rumoured
ignorant of the Bible. In fact he had asked the Provost
if he had ever come across a story about some " talking
donkey."

The classical teaching was as remarkable in the University at large. I went for lectures to Henry Jackson on
Aristotle, to Sir Richard Jebb on Sophocles and Adam
on Plato. I ought to have become a real scholar under
such instructors instead of dilettante.

Nicholas Wedd was the best teacher in King's. It was
said that he was " educated, not begotten." He was crisp,
clear and humorous, and had the pleasantest way of
assuming you knew as much as he did. His endless half-
lighted pipes, his quick asides and unfailing sense of Latin
were a delight to his pupils. He amused us by his anti-
clericalism, and attributed the Isle of Wight disease
amongst bees to the presence of too many clergy in the
Island. Kingsmen were fond of talking and working
through the night. Wedd had been famous for nocturnal
hours. Once he had been dragged out of bed on a summer
morning and only observed : " I believed it always snowed
at this hour." Like Mrs Clennam in *Little Dorrit*, he never
knew the difference between summer and winter.

It was an intellectual treat to read Cicero's correspondence with him in the winter evenings before hall. It
revealed the whole art of letter-writing. I remember how
much I valued those sessions when I found myself
punctured once near the Caxton gibbet an hour before I
was due in Wedd's room. I left my bicycle in a farm-
house and ran the eight miles. There were lecturers one
would have run the same distance to avoid.

Walter Headlam has become a legend. He lived for
Æschylus, and he must have imagined he was Æschylus
just as the O.B. gave history lectures on the assumption
(which he did not press) that he was Napoleon reborn.
Headlam's delicacy of ear and immense knowledge of

Greek made him an arbiter of the phrase. He restored the corrupt choruses of Æschylus as though he had originally written them. He taught me two things for certain :

1. The right way to step into a hansom.
2. How to write the Greek characters.

A specimen of his script was as well worth framing as any piece of Chinese penmanship.

To elucidate Æschylus he read entirely through Greek, including all the later authors and some so feeble that he compared them to Anglican hymn-writers !

Another of our teachers was equally industrious. There was a story that a German professor had counted the number of times each of the two negatives *ou* and *me* occurred in Homer. But our industrious one counted them over again to see if the other was correct !

Walter Headlam was really inspiring and left one with an idea of that heavenly scholarship which is not achieved by textbooks nor measured in examination rooms. He made Æschylus as great a possession of one's mind as Shakespeare. There was a tremendous controversy between Headlam and Dr Verrall of Trinity which has been preserved in pamphlets. Verrall was also a master of Æschylus and inspired the brilliant phrase, " *splendide emendax*," for classical emendators. How true or false the great emendations must be will never be known. Dr Giles, Master of Emmanuel, told us that one of the most emended lines in Euripides turned up at last in an Egyptian papyrus ! By that time all the principal scholars had had a trial at rewriting the corrupt original. Here was a wonderful chance to test the emenders. It was then discovered that only one of the editors had made the right guess, but that he had afterwards withdrawn it as over-rash !

For years scholars had been looking forward to Headlam's edition of Herodas, of which the *Classical Review* published tantalising hints. I enjoyed reading Herodas with Headlam himself in his rooms, for he refused to enter anything so prosaic as a lecture-room. In prehistoric days Etonians used to draw out Dr Keate when reading Horace by referring to a certain editor he detested. The draw was as certain as the words of the formula which instantly fell from Keate : " Baxter as usual mistakes the sense." But Headlam was not so mild when we mentioned Dr Nairn, who had had the effrontery to edit an edition of Herodas before Headlam was ready with his. Before the end of every session we used to throw him Nairn for the pleasure of hearing a schoolmaster cut up by a scholar.

The only outside lecturer to impress me was Henry Jackson, who looked very like Socrates. If he had stood in the market-place and allowed some Sophists to heckle him, we should have had a perfect representation of a scene from ancient Greece. He helped me to nibble at Aristotle when my soul was set on Plato. I found Aristotle the stuffiest stuff I ever tackled, and it was a relief to hear Jackson say that we have only his lecture-notes which must have been expanded in discourse. "And the metaphor about the spear must have been taken from an actual spear standing in a corner of the lecture-room." That made it vivid. But unforgettable was his slow transcript of Plato's famous myth concerning the Cave. What an allegory ! What a parable ! I have always taken all science and fresh discovery to the test of Plato's Cave and found the experience most refreshing. Jackson was not all Greek and philosopher. He held strong views on all modern literature and was as strong in their delivery as Mahaffy. He prevented my reading Kipling for years because he insisted that he had debased the coinage of English. I loved his simple comment on De Morgan's novel, *It Never Can Happen Again*. All he said was : " I am heartily glad it cannot."

Many of the old Dons were as simple and quaint as the God of Books ever made them. Many could have fitted into Alice's Wonderland. Indeed the wonder was that they were not in Lewis Carroll's pages but living in our midst. They were funny yet extremely sedate, and they had what might be called the Melchizedekian touch. That is, it seemed impossible to believe they had father or mother. They were generated out of odds and ends, chiefly odds! Johnny Nixon of King's was said by Provost James to have been composed out of the fragments of two promising young Dons who had been smashed in an early Victorian railway accident. His actual stomach had been hurriedly borrowed from the engine! Nixon was a subject of constant curiosity in the College as it was never decided how much or less of him was artificial! He had several false hands devised to hold pens or cards, and the minimum of optic nerve. His buoyancy was attributed to a constitution of cork, and the voice with which he chortled madrigals (his principal hobby) was believed to be another part of the legendary locomotive. One night his place was unfilled in Hall and the Dons at the high table amused themselves by inventing new deficiencies. " I don't believe he had any real ears," said one, and : " His gyp keeps his spare ribs in a box," added another. Suddenly Nixon appeared, and there was a dead silence while he took his seat. The Vice-Provost asked him to take some soup. " I am afraid I have no taste," said Nixon innocently. There was a suppressed quake in every breast, for the palate was the only part of him they had forgotten.

Nixon could be grumpy and gruff to other dons, but to young men he was charming. Of course, his charm lay in their sense of ridicule. He was unwilling to survive the loss of so many of his dear pupils. During the War he turned his head to the wall and died. For this old man we wept.

The undergraduates became typical of King's in a very short time after arrival. By the rest of the University we were considered " freaks," and we were freakish enough to ignore the rest of the University. I rarely set foot in any other college except Trinity or Magdalene. I went once to Corpus, but that was to exorcise a ghost. I went once to St John's to attend an Irish dinner. I went once to Selwyn to see the astonishing sight of a *prie-dieu* in an undergraduate's room. I attended a Gaelic class in Pembroke. Kingsmen kept to themselves and were allowed to be as unconventional as they liked. We practised Oriental theosophy, muscular Christianity, psychical research, high ritualism and social reform in turn.

We were very hearty in groups, not without more exquisite moments. We encouraged a number of college sports such as tricycle-riding, roof-climbing and midnight swimming. There were several old Dons who kept old-fashioned tricycles in college. These iron mistresses of the road we used to bestride ourselves at night and ride round the courts. Racing dress consisted of undergraduate's gown and bare skin. The noblest athletic effort ever seen at King's we owed to a challenge made by William Hope-Jones. Though there were poets in the college, there were no effeminates. Unfortunately it became known that a third-year man was indulging in a hot-water bottle at nights. This was considered a disgrace to the college, and Hope-Jones challenged its owner to run the quarter mile round the front court on a wintry dawn. It was agreed that the challenger should run stark while the challenged wore as much clothing as he wished. The race was won by the less encumbered party and the offending hot-water bottle was duly confiscated and sent to Doctor Barnardo with the compliments of the Provost, the Fellows and Scholars of the college.

I much enjoyed rowing for the college in various boats with Hope-Jones. His prodigious strength always helped me out. He could row one afternoon, bicycle all night and row a full course the following day without missing the morning lectures between.

We rowing men entertained ourselves to tea in turn. Taking tea with Hope-Jones it was necessary to wear an overcoat, for he lived in a blast of wind or at least a good draught. An enormous teapot was set brewing on the floor, round which his friends sat munching apples, oranges and bananas. The skins and cores were thrown into the yawning teapot to stew : and it was not a bad beverage which emerged.

He used to organise rows to Ely and back (a matter of thirty-four miles), but he alone returned fresh and warbling. They were splendid and strenuous days. After a merry meal at the Cutter Inn we used to attend Ely Cathedral in our shorts and return slogging and slicing the water, for we had no eagle-eyed coach watching from the bank. Hope-Jones, being a mathematical wrangler, counted every stroke. Past the dreary and desolate Fens, past the public-house inscribed " Five Miles from Nowhere," till we reached the lock above Clayhithe. On a winter's night we carried an acetylene lamp in the bows, and must have looked like the ghosts of dead oarsmen permitted to revisit their old haunts on the Cam.

Once in summer we stopped half-way back. We were parched and stiff : dry within and dripping without. We brought the boat into the rushes and then dropped the eight of us into the water. I never felt such sensuous delight in any bath before or since. The water enfolded us like ice-chilled velvet, and for that moment drowning would have been bliss. We dried ourselves with cox's scarf standing in the sinking sun ; and then arose the difficulty of embarking in our outrigged craft. It was settled by Hope-Jones, who turned himself into a human landing-stage. We walked heavily over him one by one and so rowed home.

Rowing filled college life to the exclusion of almost all else. It was a form of slavery, but it upheld one against the aguish damps of winter and seducing slack of summer. Twice a year we trained for the college races and sat at a special training table absorbing those special foods which I imagine are eaten by pugilists or the fat lady at the show.

How well I remember the last race I rowed in May week, and the curious anguish I felt getting out of an eight-oar for the last time. On the bank at Ditton stood a wonderful trio watching us : Provost James, Walter Headlam and Wilamowitz, the German editor of *Æschylus*, whose long desire had been to visit Headlam, then, alas, within a few weeks of death.

Rowing has great assets in spite of all that is brought against it in theory or practice. Rowing men do not invariably die of heart trouble in middle-age. We learnt rhythm, good companionship and at times singing in chorus. We felt divinely well when we emerged from training hall and swept arm in arm down the street or strove to rock the horse-team off the line by swinging together from the roof-seats. How important was one's swing and the finish in the boat ! Coaches used to tell us to swing forward to meet our stretchers as we hoped one day to meet our God ! What coaches were allowed to say on the river would have filled Swift's *Swearers' Bank* to repletion. I once plucked a delightful euphemism from a pamphlet of the time of Queen Anne which I intended to use as the title for a treatise on Rowing. It is still too good to lose : " Kind cautions to watermen ! "

The greatest of all coaches, Steve Fairbairn, had recently returned to prominence on the river, and colleges were copying the violent style to which he trained the Jesus College crews. At King's and Third Trinity (the Etonian Rowing Club) we held out against such savagery. But Steve conquered the Cam in time and the Thames no less. His death is recorded while I am writing and I cast a wreath upon the great oarsman's grave : a poem I wrote for the *Granta* thirty years ago !

" STEVE "

(" Jesus paddled home—Steve Fairbairn coached them all the way."—*Cambridge Review*, November 5, 1908.)

> The day I joined the Freshers' rank,
>   Where tides of Camus flow,
> Great Steve was on the towing bank,
>   And that was years ago,
> And men of antiquated mien
>   Then whispered of his fame—

" Long, long before we rowed, he'd been
    Here tubbing men the same."
That very minute past he swept,
    And filled our reverent gaze,
The one and only relic left
    Of Georgian coaching days ;
And like an organ strapped to wheels,
    We heard him through the fog—
" Now shove like kine and slip like eels
    And thus the water flog."
'Twas in prehistoric dream
    That first he took an oar,
And his rowing on a rising stream
    Was useful unto Noah.
And he later trained the Argo,
    And he won the match
When he stroked both crew and cargo
    As Medea's scratch.
With Persians once he dipped a blade,
    Before he won his blue ;
He sorted satraps out and made
    A record trireme crew.
'Twas he on Hellespontine bay
    Set up Leander club,
And coached Diogenes, they say,
    To sit his famous tub.
And every Jesus college eight
    That ever rigged in May,
Or sailed the sea in search of plate,
    He taught them how to stay
Or go, as might the case require,
    And his the voice they know,
So sleep begetting when they tire,
    So soothing when they row.
He trains them long, and fills them well
    With draughts of steaming Oxo,
Sole reason why (the posters tell)
    His Mayboat never crocks, oh !
His men he watcheth from the marge,
    So hairy, thick, and browned
Like haystacks sitting in a barge
    Where needles are not found.
And I am sure those men and Stee
    One day will try the Styx,
And Lethe not forgetful be
    Of their good stretcher-kicks.
And they will one day shoot past Charon
    Like a breath of wind.
And laugh to hear him put a fare on
    Men who use his grind.

R

" The needle " was the expressive term for the sinking which all rowing men experience in the stomach shortly before the starting gun.   " The needle " I believe also plays a part during the marriage service and before executions.

Rowing left no time or energy for any other exercise. I had an occasional chance to play the famous Wall Game at Eton when King's sent teams to play College. On such occasions when the two foundations of King Henry met, such stalwart and eminent players took the field for King's as Sir Stephen Gaselee, Professor J. M. Keynes, Bishop Philip Loyd and the present Dean of Winchester. Proud they were to assume the sacking and padding needed in that most difficult and dangerous game : the mediæval Eton Wall Game, whose rules are sometimes known to the umpires, seldom to the players and never to spectators !

There was a brilliant intellectual life at King's in which rowing men hardly shared. The scholars had produced a brilliant paper called the *Basileon*, a hardy annual which fell to my editorship in number eleven, " the Fourth Book of King's." Looking through old pages the old college life drifts vividly back before my eyes. What good stuff could be turned out ; and after the years how strange to read two prophetic accounts of war with Germany which were written in 1908.   One was called " a Kingsman's Home." It was a skit on the famous " Englishman's Home " which had been recently received at the New Theatre with laughter and derision by a generation of undergraduates, most of whom were to die in defence of that same Home.

My *Basileon* was marked by a versified attack written by a young Fellow Esmé Wingfield-Stratford, against the Carbonari. The Carbonari were founded by Eric Holt in my second year and included all the young intellectuals. I can only think of Rupert Brooke and Hugh Dalton (now a pillar of the Labour Party). To the Conservatives and churchmen they were distasteful, and "Wingers" launched a furious satire against them as "Atheist Exquisites and Anarchist Bedlamites." They were caricatured dining in Hall and proposing toasts so Red that the college worthies (Sir Robert Walpole, Archbishop Sumner, Lord Chancellor Camden) descended in protest from their frames. The next scene showed the worthies being ducked by the Reds in the college fountain :

> " Thrice happy is the shameless Redcaps' lot
> All Kings forgetting, by all King's forgot."

In the same number I printed two sonnets by Rupert Brooke, whose first poetical ventures were filling the College with mild admiration. Curiously enough it was Donald Corrie to whom we looked to be our bard, as he had won the University Prize for verse.

I also published a King's Pageant chiefly for the purpose of ridiculing the O.B., who was made to appear successively as the River Camus, King Henry the Founder and the Goddess Hygeia. It was good fun and the O.B. only beamed when I apologised for the lengths of our caricature. Curiously enough an uncle of mine, Murray Guthrie, while an undergraduate at Trinity Hall, started a libellous sheet called the *Gadfly* for the sole purpose of deriding the O.B. After threats of legal action he started the *Granta* instead, which has flourished till this day. The *Granta* was the title of a magazine O.B. was meditating himself. When he disclosed the name in confidence, it was considered an immense joke to snatch the copyright by appearing first with the name.

The centenary of the O.B.'s birth has come and gone, for he belonged to the splendid vintage of 1837. In his dying days the Government graciously made him an O.B.E. Perhaps it was a joke but he received it with prodigious gratitude. He might have been an Eton Head, a Provost of King's or a Minister of Education, had he only added tact to his many gifts and furious energy.

My only interest outside the college was the Hibernian

Society, which arranged a few lectures and a lively dinner during the year. Sir Norman Moore gave us a good paper on Brian Boroo and once delivered an hour of mediæval Irish. Sir Norman was Chief at St Bartholomew's Hospital and a Fellow of Cat's. We used to say a Cat's man could look at a Kingsman. He passed to me a direct tradition of the man he had most admired in life, Henry Bradshaw, the University librarian, who had died at King's soon after my birth. He had died with a book written in Irish under his hand and he had left a collection of Irish books to the University in which I learnt to revel. His impressive dreamy features looked upon us from a Herkomer picture in Hall and so well I knew his Irish books and his mind that I think I could (greatly daring and greatly unworthy) begin an intimate conversation should I met him in the libraries of Heaven. He was the patriarch and progenitor of all modern Bibliophiles. He showed that a bookworm could become a glow-worm.

I became secretary to the Hibernians during my last year and it was my duty to provide a famous speaker at the annual dinner. Failing poor old Justin McCarthy, I invited Tim Healy. Thereupon arose a schism and shindy amongst the Hibernians as to whether the King's health should be drunk in the presence of "Tiger Tim." Some said it would offend Tim and others said they would be offended by its omission. I suggested the toast of "The King of Ireland" and the toasters could decide inwardly who was *de jure* King of Ireland : the Stuart Claimant, Lord Inchiquin for Brian Boroo, the O'Conor Don for the Connaught dynasty or King Edward VII. In the end Tim came not and the Society of Hibernians broke into two. Many years later I passed through Dublin when Tim occupied the Vice-Regal Lodge as Governor and representative of the King. The wheel had come full circle as it always will when left to itself. He was then being boycotted himself because "God save the King" accompanied his own dinners and progresses.

There was a great contrast between Irish dinners at

Oxford and Cambridge. Ours were noisy and happy-go-lucky. There was record of one held in a lecture room lacking ventilation save from a skylight. Before the evening was over, every chair and plate, in fact the whole paraphernalia, had passed through the skylight except a fat waiter who had stuck halfway. When we attended the Irish dinner at Oxford we met Lord Bryce, then Irish Secretary, as the guest of honour. It was all so formal that the Irish brogue retreated before the Oxford accent.

It was in the early days of the Gaelic League, and an Irish Class was started at Cambridge which was attended by a half-dozen enthusiasts. We were fortunate in finding a Manxman, who had studied Irish in the wilds of Donegal, Dr Quiggin of Caius. He had written a book on the dialect of Meenawallia in the recesses of that county and the University had printed it. The class was taken in Dr E. G. Browne's rooms in Pembroke.

Cambridge possessed an extraordinary Irish character, Sir William Ridgeway, a quarrelsome, embittered, brilliant, blind archæologist who lived at Fen Ditton, and appeared to dress in suits taken from corpses drowned in the river. He was a world authority on the Homeric horse, on the hero-tomb, on the origin of coinage and the Irish epic. He knew all about Cuchulain, but he was unapproachable on account of his violent Irish politics. He was in favour of the real conquest of Ireland. He was a Cromwellian throw-back but very stimulating.

Climbing has, I believe, advanced and improved vastly since my day. Membership in the old Cambridge Alpine Club could only be obtained by climbing fairly into every college after the gates had been closed. There was one which was practically impossible. The Alpine Society dined once a term with a rope laid down the table as the symbol of their craft. When a curious tutor once made inquiries, he was informed that the men studying criminal law were entertaining the Public Executioner.

I never had cause to climb into King's, which was easily entered from the top of a hansom-cab driven

down King's Lane and moored to the wall. Trinity was
frequently entered after ten by scaling some tall iron
palings surmounted by revolving spikes. It was necessary
to roll one's gown into a ball and impale it on the spikes
while they turned over. Trinity Hall was really difficult.
It could be entered by swarming up the angle of a twenty-
foot brick wall in Garret's Hostel Lane. But there were
spikes to be manœuvred on the way and the drop on the
other side was a bone-shaker. I managed it once from a
friend's shoulders on the night the Hall went head of the
river, in 1907. There was a huge bonfire in the front
court of blazing furniture, understood to belong to the
Dons ! Duggie Stuart (the oarsman, not the book-maker)
was being carried round the flames by the crew he had
stroked to victory. To row one's college to the headship
of the river seemed a greater achievement than any that
life could offer.

I expect the undergraduates were hardier and heartier
in those days. The railway companies were subject to
constant practical joking. On one occasion we ordered
a saloon carriage to take a football team to Oxford and
back. The railway company unwisely provided two third-
class carriages with a partition. By the time they
returned to Cambridge they had been converted into a
home-made saloon !

I was fortunate to watch the most famous of hoaxes
in October 1905 when the Sultan of Zanzibar and his
suite were believed to have visited the University in
state. Instigated by Horace Cole, a handful of Trinity
men (some said to be Ordinands) travelled to London,
visited Clarkson's, the theatrical wigman, and returned in
a Royal saloon carriage. How proudly the Mayor lent
his carriage to the visitors and how obsequiously the
college porters rushed to admit the distinguished visitors !
I witnessed their entry through the great gates at King's
and was completely deceived. The tall swarthy sons of
the Prophet in their splendid turbans, their portly tread

and the polite gesticulation with which they lifted their arms in mild amazement at all the sights they were shown, made a lasting picture.

The University enjoyed a nine days' laugh and though the names of the visitors became an open secret, no proceedings were taken. We were told the hoaxers had two bad moments. Half-way to Cambridge in the saloon they were seized with panic, but when they looked out of the windows and saw the Mayor of Cambridge in his robes they knew that all was well. Later in the day they were taken to a missionary bazaar where an elderly lady professed to speak their language. This they had disguised by means of an interpreter summoned from Oxford for the occasion. The interpreter saved the situation by explaining hastily that his master could not possibly meet any lady unless she had thoughts of entering his harem !

The success of this hoax was so widespread that Horace Cole devoted the rest of his life to a series of carefully planned incidents, most of which became celebrated in the Press.

One of these incidents was of some public service. While staying at Dublin Castle with the Aberdeens he decided to test the detective service by secreting himself behind a bush. When the unsuspecting Viceroy passed, he transfixed his coat-tails with a rapier and waited, watch in hand, for the arrival of the police, who were told how many minutes and seconds they were too late to save the Viceroy's valuable life !

I had made great friends with an Italian Count in Rome who married an American wife. It was a " mixed " marriage in every way. She was vivacious and Horace Cole found her dying of boredom. They met at some party and she confided her troubles to this English-speaking stranger who decided that a sham elopement would suit the situation. He carried her off in the old style, she descending secretly from a window with only her jewels, but on condition that she shipped home to her mother

as soon as he brought her to London. The whole episode
was carried out with complete chivalry.

King's was a Royal foundation and therefore not subject
to the entry of police or control by Proctors, as I discovered to my good fortune when the Proctors wished to
send me down and my College interposed her *obstat*.
My misfortune occurred most unexpectedly. There was a
tremendous rag on Midsummer Common after the match
against the New Zealanders in 1906. This was the first
visit of the " All Blacks," and though the Varsity lost
the game they held a magnificent team at bay. The
visitors made a new departure in Rugby football. Their
placing was novel and ingenious. It was reported that
they quartered the ground into three halves, but then
their gallant captain bore an Irish name ! Their speed
enabled them to run round and round the Cantabs who
only held them up by sheer force and tackling. Cambridge
included the redoubtable John Hopley, the finest human
specimen of my generation.

The match was a moral victory from the point of view
of the Varsity, and it was celebrated by a large bonfire
on the Common. By the time I arrived, men were carrying
whole hoardings, outhouses, palings and even a garden-
roller to the fire. There must have been hundreds of men
carting fuel, but I was the only one foolish enough to hand
a plank to a Proctor.

John Hopley looked as formidable on the field as in the
Ring. He was at one time favoured as a white hope
against the heavyweight Jack Johnson who later gave
his name to a large calibre shell. Hopley always won his
fight against Oxford with fantastic ease. His chief care
was not to kill the opposing sportsman. He was believed
to have practised once against a professional who, as a
result, was unable to practise again. After which Hopley
was persuaded by his father to leave the Ring. I do not
think he could have been beaten.

I never had time to attend the debates at the Union nor

join the dramatic societies, though I worked hard to learn parts in the Greek plays. There was a good run of those fascinating revivals from the past. I first saw our present and venerable Provost in the Greek play of 1903. Never were the leading parts in Aristophanes' *Birds* given a more spirited rendering than by Provost Sheppard and Professor O. L. Richmond. Their efforts to learn to fly before the days of flying were as laughable as possible. Prometheus was ludicrously played by an undergraduate of sturdy build and brow, waving a red parasol. Twenty years later I met him and reminded him of his dramatic antics. Casually inquiring his present position in life I learnt that he was seated in the chair of Pontius Pilate. Apparently this was quite true, as Sir Ronald Storrs was then administering the Province of Palestine, which the British as well as the Romans have found insufferably difficult.

In my last year the *Furies* of Æschylus was acted at the New Theatre. I still believe I could have brought down the house in the part of Clytemnestra's ghost which was given to Gordon Selwyn. Orestes was movingly portrayed by A. F. Schofield, the present University librarian. I can see him still running and almost diving with ghastly agility between and betwixt the horrible Furies, those " beldames with whom neither man nor beast could mate." Since those days the King's School of Ancient Acting has produced the whole Orestcia of Agamemnon in one performance. It was the Oresteia to which Headlam devoted his short life, dying untimely in my fourth year to be mourned with Lycidas and Rupert Brooke and all beautiful promise cut short by the hateful shears. Headlam wished to dedicate his final version to Swinburne, who gracefully replied that he thought the Oresteia the finest spiritual work of man.

It was disappointing not to find a place in a Greek play, but I was amused to receive an emergency call to appear as Romeo in the Imperial Theatre. This was a luxurious little theatre built for Mrs Langtry where the old Aquarium used to stand. It has since disappeared, and

I wonder if I am the only survivor of those who ever appeared on its boards. I must admit that it was only in a *tableau vivant* for charity. I was arrayed in the beautiful suit which Murray Guthrie had worn as Romeo at the famous Devonshire House ball in Jubilee year. My Juliet was my beautiful aunt Dosia Bagot arranged by her admirer Frank Dicksee, President of the Royal Academy. I was disappointed at having no lines to recite, but I achieved as good a corpse as I could. Unfortunately the curtain rose before I was stiffened and I was pushed down amid a roar of laughter. Dosia was also caught unawares, but I believe we looked very striking together : and with that glimpse of my Shakespearean powers the theatre-going world must rest content.

Cambridge days were too full to remember separately, but many a scene and corner, many a strange hour and many a passing friend rise up to picture me a Cambridge which is utterly gone :

The ragged elms with an odd rook's nest which once stood outside St Catharine's, betwixt the gates and the road, and many a magnificent tree that lined the road behind the King's Backs.

Old Johnny Mayor and MacTaggart the philosopher (looking like the village idiot) and the magnificent Adolphus Ward of Peterhouse abroad in the streets.

David the bookseller sitting over his bookstall in the market-place.

Sir Richard Jebb gingerly passing through Trinity wearing an affectation of spats.

The one-eyed Tout, a pathetic relic of humanity, offering his services to alarmed tourists.

Walter the sublime Beadle, Holy Poker and Cicerone of King's College Chapel.

E. G. Browne, the Professor of Arabic, guiding Persian patriots through Pembroke.

Sir Stephen Gaselee playing tennis in a hair-net.

Walter Headlam competing for the Greek Chair in the Senate House amid an enthusiastic gallery of his pupils.

Father Robert Hugh Benson preaching dramatically in the Catholic Church on his return from Rome.

John R. Mott leading an Evangelistic service of men in the Guildhall.

The thrilling first sermon and service of the Church Society in Great St Mary's.

And the descent of the Wooden Spoon in the Senate House during the reading of the lists in the Mathematical Tripos.

The delivery of degrees to the Chinese visitors.

Mr Keir Hardie's address in the Guildhall amid much disorder evoked by rowing men.

And amongst lovely nights and days: a swimming party given in the Trinity Gardens to which the uninvited guests arrived propelling tea in a bath.

Days spent upon Wicken Fen watching the sulphur-coloured swallow-tails dancing in one of their last English haunts.

King's stood for free thought, free speech and free ethics, nor were those freedoms abused. Some of the King's Dons had protested against giving an honorary degree to the Duke of York (later King George V) on the sound, but not loyal, ground that he had not earned it. I think the protesters included Berry, a Senior Wrangler, and Lowes Dickinson, who achieved fame as an international Pacifist. Dickinson was the nearest we had to a prophet albeit a minor one. He had the literary style without the mystic inspiration, but he was most sincere, most talented and most lovable. He lived to sink into an abyss of pessimism. In happier days before the War he led the intellectual column.

The Agnostic was predominant at King's, but the College never lacked Tories, High Churchmen and even Jacobites. At one time there was a fierce division in our ranks on the harmless subject of supporting a college mission. The College could never decide like other colleges what was to be done. In the opinion of most of the colleges King's needed a mission herself!

The Ritualists were gathered into the S.T.C. or Confraternity of the Holy Trinity from all colleges.

With immense trouble a High Mass was celebrated once a term at St Giles's. If the Bishop could be induced to be present, the vestments were discarded and the service held in St Michael's.

King's had been a preserve for centuries devoted to erudite Old Etonians with a taste for academical life, and to imperturbable Churchmen. It was natural for the pendulum to swing in the other direction. It was excellent for the Etonian atmosphere to be broken up and for Churchmen to discover that Nonconformists were human beings. Of all the sects the most impressive and the pleasantest companions were the Quakers. So much has been rightly written in praise of their principles and charming Christianity that I will only say that the best coxing that I ever rowed to, proceeded from a Quaker. Never will I forget his coolness and resource in the bumping races when we were unsuccessfully pursued and overlapped. His name was Alexander.

The Agnosticism of the College was tolerant but faintly contemptuous or perhaps pitying of all who held religious beliefs. There was a definite stand against High Churchmen as such which history is bound to record, for the results were important. We understood that the Provost had advised a definite Churchman not to attempt to stand for a Fellowship. While the College was adding first-class science-men to her High Table she was dispensing with first-class men like William Spens, Stephen Gaselee, Ernest Edghill and Gordon Selwyn. It seems incredible that any college should have discarded such talent. They were all High Churchmen in various degrees. Spens has become Master of Corpus, Selwyn Dean of Winchester, Gaselee Fellow of Magdalene. Edghill, the most brilliant of the bunch, died young after taking his Divinity Degree at London. His Cambridge thesis was on the Prophetic Agency ; and examiners, to whom it was submitted, could not believe so young a man could have written it ! It was, perhaps, typical of King's that the agnostic element favoured a brilliance in him of which conservative Churchmen were afraid.

His influence as a militant High Churchman was considerable. He was a prodigious worker : the hardest I ever met. At Eton his industry was so phenomenal that he complained deeply of the amount of time wasted in walking between the class-rooms. In fact he was in favour of non-stop lessons. He missed the Newcastle at Eton and his Fellowship at King's by a short neck. He showed the same restless energy in whatever subject he took up: Justin Martyr, Boys' Clubs, Slums, Morris Dancing or Hulsean Lectures. He was a sort of Toynbee in a cassock.

He transferred his work from Cambridge to South London and there he slowly undermined his strength. In the parish he was adventurous and experimental. He scorned Settlement work in his famous phrase as " an expensive way of showing the poor how the rich lived." Whether he was right or wrong, he exhibited in his own person the life of the poor. Few friends suspected the poverty and hunger which he endured, though sometimes a Latin telegram to Cambridge announced he was at the end of his tether.

Though his name remained unknown and his memory is unsung, he was a strong influence upon his friends. Out of his influence the pervading High Church Movement could be traced. We used to join him for week-ends in his parishes. On one occasion when a boys' service was becoming a little dull, Edghill ceased and ordered an advance to a neighbouring Common, where he challenged an anti-religious orator. A vigorous squabble followed amid cheering and counter-cheering. In the end a pale spectacled curate in a ragged cassock made his humorous appeal to the crowd. How else, he explained afterwards, could the rising youth be induced to take an interest in Church defence ?

Edghill must have been the pioneer of outdoor apologetics which are now a feature of the Hyde Park soap-boxing. He died owing to an accident in Camp in 1912. He severed an artery with an axe and spent his last hours reading to his boys aloud before a doctor could arrive to tend what proved to be a mortal wound.

Had he lived, he would have given the Labour Movement the Christian complexion it had begun to assume under Victorian leaders like Lord Shaftesbury and Charles Kingsley. Edghill saw the dangerous drift and realised that neither Socialism nor Christianity could realise itself without the other. He had discovered an evident crack in the social fabric, which he was striving after his manner to remedy—even when night befell him.

That so brilliant a scholar, so deep a theologian and so inspiring a leader and friend should be so feebly employed and so tragically forgotten has never ceased to rankle in my memory. He was one of the guiding lights, perhaps one of the great souls in my generation, but how many who read these words will recall the name of Ernest Edghill ?

It is true that the names we fancied would be great disappeared in after-life : apart from the War which not merely pruned but lopped the hope of a whole generation. My generation at King's will have to live on the fame of Keynes and Rupert Brooke. Their international fame was not then apparent. No doubt we should have cultivated them, but we were nervous of both. One was reported agnostic and the other æsthetic. No one at King's dreamed that their names would be wafted through hemispheres where J. K. Stephen was unquoted and the O.B. simply unknown !

Rupert Brooke lived in charming self-possession and budding poesy amongst us. He owned to no school of writing and seemed aware that he had only to march to his future. He laid himself out to achieve Poetry from the beginning. He had a healthy sense of parody and used some of Tennyson's most sacred lines to describe the cooking of sausages in a Rugby study on a Saturday night. Though they have survived they would only distress those who place the poets less than a little lower than the angels.

Gordon Selwyn was certainly the most prominent man of my year and the best Classical Scholar to judge by his prizes. To him was due the Church Movement, which disputed ground with the " Ciccu " or Low Church praying organisation. Oxford has the whole world to advertise her religious movements : Wesley, Newman and Buchman. It is forgotten or rather unrecorded in literary books how much Cambridge contributed to the Evangelical Revival, to the war against Slavery and to missionary work. " The Cambridge Seven," who had left glittering prospects to go to China, were still a memory and when I met one of the survivors in recent years it was like meeting a character out of a legend.

There was no commanding character nor leader at Cambridge. We looked to Oxford-bred bishops like Gore of Birmingham and Edward King of Lincoln. For a moment my heart stood still when Gore, accompanied by Gordon Selwyn, stood in my doorway. It used to be said that even the mildest Low Churchman was anxious to " shed Gore " in those days. But Gore refused to be shed and remained the buttress of the High Church. Bishop King was Visitor of King's, which by a curious mediæval survival had remained in the diocese of Lincoln. The rest of the University was in Ely. From Dr King we procured a written dispensation to eat meat while training for the Lent Races. This proved edifying to the High Churchman but was eyed askance by the Low Church coaches.

Spare afternoons, which were rare in the week, were spent scouring the countryside of Cambridgeshire and far into Suffolk visiting old churches. Every church had some memento of the old Catholic past : a broken screen, a rood-loft door, a quarry of stained glass or a faint fresco showing under the whitewash. Whenever we found a church locked, we left a written protest on

the doors, a quatrain we composed and which has no
doubt been added to several parish registers :

> " A traveller came to pray.
> Then open wide your door !
> Lest Christ may pass this way
> And pass for evermore."

Time was drawing short and in May, 1907, I sat for
the Classical Tripos. The harvest of three years' work
was gathered during six very harassing days. On the Saturday before the Tripos I found myself with a blank
headache. I was induced to spend the day on the Devil's
Dyke with two others in the same plight : Parker Smith
and Fry. We lazed on that fascinating boundary of
ancient kingdoms and wondered what the world was like
when free of examinations. My two companions were
alas ! to perish in the War. The same evening I rowed
a lock to lock course in the college boat.

In June the Tripos lists were read in the Senate House.
The men of my year stood grimly looking at each other's
faces. You could almost tell the first, seconds and thirds
by their expressions. Three days later I took my
Bachelor's Degree and celebrated by going with two others
to the Grand Opera at Covent Garden.

After three years of harmony and companionship
my year scattered for ever. Long after the War had
taken its toll, we met again with the survivals of other
years at a college dinner in the old surroundings. What
happens to Kingsmen ? had been a question we often
asked each other. We could now begin to judge for
ourselves. A number had quietly side-stepped and
become schoolmasters and parsons. A few impeccable
solicitors and at least one unimpeached Minister. Some
officials in the Foreign Office, a few doctors. One had
become a dean and another an earl. But it was not fair
to judge since so much promise had passed away untimely.

The exquisite memorial chapel was filled with the names of
the dead, including the name of an Austrian who had died
on the other side. That was typical of a noble old college.

Rome and Mary Crawshay

★

CHRISTMAS OF 1902 I SPENT IN THE ETERNAL CITY.
Three delirious weeks were lived in the Classics with all
my dead Latin germinating and dry textbooks of History
finding life. Rome should be visited betwixt school and
university, while the legends of Rome are still a fairy
story.

My aunt, Mary Crawshay, was living in Rome at the
Quatre Fontane overlooking the Quirinal Gardens, so much
so that the new king (now the venerable Victor Emmanuel)
had built an enormous wall to block the view. Still by
climbing the roof we could see the dome of St Peter's
sinking like a big black bubble every night into the
sulphurous sunset. My hostess had married a Welsh
magnate with the taste of a Renaissance collector. The
Palace was full of superb furniture. He possessed the
famous Borghese chairs and one of the most beautiful
of Crevellis. Bob Crawshay, although very delicate, was
a daring motor-driver in days when cars were rare and
roads unfitted for speed. As soon as the car left Rome we
shot through a cloud of dust, poultry and picturesque
peasants, all in a state of swirling agitation. Had the
reigning Pope Leo XIII been told that in thirty years his
successor would be driving out of Rome in one of these
cars, he would not have credited the report. A high
trapeze for cardinals in St Peter's would have seemed less
astonishing.

Everyone can recall but none can describe his first
glimpses of Rome. Mine was the Rome of Pope Leo XIII.
Well up in his nineties he survived like a flickering wick

S   273

in an alabaster lamp. He had seen the whole nineteenth century. He had been ordained in the year of Queen Victoria's accession. As a cardinal he had governed States of the Church. He was now a few months from his honoured grave.

Rome still bore traces of being the sleepy dusty city of the popes. The city had not been modernised and Mussolini was an unknown youth somewhere. Church and State were not on speaking terms.

I can date my first visit to Rome, for I visited the Pantheon on the twenty-fifth anniversary of King Victor Emmanuel's death (Jan 9, 1903). The streets were full of straggling Garibaldian veterans in their red shirts. The fiftieth anniversary has since been celebrated in shirts that were black. Nineteen hundred and three was also the year in which the French celebrated the centenary of their occupation of the Villa Medici.

Days of bliss were spent at the Villa d'Este and Hadrian's villa at Tivoli. I made friends with the monks who guard the catacombs and at their invitation rose early one morning and hurried out to the catacombs of St Calixtus to hear an early Mass in those sacred depths. It was dark when I left Rome and I felt like an early Christian escaping from Nero. My first vivid dreaming was broken by the sudden passing of the king in his motor. We believed his whole life was spent in a feverish imitation of the German Emperor.

The greatest impression made on my historical soul was made by the Colosseum—the Flavian Amphitheatre. Mary Crawshay had felt a stranger impression a few months previously, when the lions presented by the Emperor of Abyssinia had been lodged in that direction and could be heard roaring at evening time whence their shaggy ancestors had roared before the approaching games.

Professor Richard Norton was lecturing at the Pantheon. I attended his open-air talks and we made great friends. Like all the intelligent and amusing

Americans and Englishmen he was drawn to Mary Crawshay's *salon*. Many years later we met again in France and drove ambulances together in 1914.

Rome was full of delightful people who arrived at Mary's tea-parties : Doctor Axel Munthe, who treated sick animals and nervous women with the same understanding, and Henry Brewster, who wrote *l'âme païenne* and inspired Ethel Smyth's music, and Maurice Baring then in his promising diplomatic career.

Maurice, surprising to say, was then considered a diplomatist with a great future. With him was Esmé Howard, a young attaché, who has since achieved the Washington Embassy. Maurice undoubtedly devoted too much of the time he owed the Foreign Office to practical jokes and children's parties. Mary's boy, Jack, had christened him " the children's friend," but the Romans, though sometimes puzzled, mistook him for a typical English sporting nobleman ! Maurice cared for nothing except his friends and his jokes and the delightful scrap-book of poems and perfect passages which even then he was collecting by wilfully cutting up printed books.

One of Mary's friends had been Burne-Jones, the painter. She had immensely cheered his last afternoon on earth by a story of the small boy aforesaid. At his prayers on the previous night he had very properly remarked : " I love Jesus," and then with a passing allusion to his godfather, Lord Grenfell : " And who is that other smart gentleman whom I love ? "

Jack was, of course, one of the Christmas party. We used to mystify Mary's Roman friends by acting Biblical charades. On one occasion I paddled myself as Noah in a bath into the middle of the drawing-room while Jack poured water over my open umbrella. The Romans were politely mystified. They sat still and murmured their appreciation. Either they were trying to be polite or more likely they had no knowledge of the Old Testament. Jack and I were once trying them with a charade we thought they were more likely to guess than representations of Jezebel and Elijah the Tishbite when Mary interfered in an agony lest they would be shocked. We had just seen the Sacred Bambino in the *Ara Coeli* and it was easy to dress Jack up with a tiara and a poker as the favourite image of Rome while I imitated the sacristan and lit up candles.

The Romans were deeply interested in all customs and games and sports to do with " *vecchia Inghilterra.*" The English have only one out and out and constant admirer on the Continent : Italy at heart has been Anglophile through thick and thin.

At Christmas accordingly we determined to show Rome some old English ways. The faithful and enthusiastic Italian servants were coached into lighting a Christmas tree and performing the ritual of snapdragon. A crowd of Roman society were invited with their children and all went joyously. Maurice Baring was master of the revels and I officiated as Santa Claus. For days there had been talk and expectation of this famous English custom. Apparently " *il snapdragone* " was a kind of sacrament at the English Christmas. The great moment arrived and enormous dishes full of raisins were soon burning with brandy, and prompt to our instructions the guests rushed forward to pick and eat the plums. Simultaneously, alas ! the Italian butler, Alessandro, lost his head and threw in the salt as he supposed by way of condiment. The salt was of course intended to give the final lighting effect, after the raisins had been eaten, of faces turning green. Unfortunately Alessandro had mistaken his cue and before they could be stopped the guests were wrily munching raisins mixed with kitchen salt and brandy ! We turned in fury on Alessandro who uttered one cry of grief and disappeared.

It was a terrible fiasco which only Mary's popularity could survive. Snapdragon was taken to be one of those terrible English customs which are better admired than imitated.

Amongst Mary's guests were the Pasolinis, including

the dear old Count, the historian of Ravenna, and Barrère the French ambassador, whose dislike of England was attributed to his father's mastership at Woolwich in days when French masters were relentlessly ragged.

My only entry into Roman Society was at a ball given by Prince Colonna for his radiant daughter, now the Princess Sermoneta. I was enormously intrigued to meet a lady member of the Pecchi family ; and Mary could not decide whether the Protestants or the Catholics at home in Ireland would be the more shocked at the idea of my dancing with the Pope's niece !

Mary Crawshay was always able to make herself a *salon* as near the French model as any London hostess could boast. Without good looks save a wistfulness disarming the visitor, without wealth, though her connoisseur husband allowed her sometimes to wear the finest sapphires in London ; without any rich entertaining save a form of schoolroom tea, she made more than a social mark in two capitals. Through her I constantly met distinguished men and heard conversation that was witty, pleasant or thrilling, according to the moods she evoked at her table. Here I met Sir Norman Moore of Barts, Sir Almroth Wright and Dr Munthe, all physicians. In old days such different types as Field-Marshal Lord Grenfell and Lord Llandaff revelled in her wit. In her last days no one was closer to her than Sir Wallis Budge, the Egyptologist.

The social hostess of to-day entertains as many famous or infamous people as she can collect in a nervous frenzy. Her entertaining is parallel to the American idea of travelling which is to reach everywhere if only for ten minutes. The true *salon* only draws the regular *habitués de la maison*. This was certainly Mary's case, and neither her wit nor her charm was wasted nor wearied with the years.

Lord Grenfell had been Sirdar in Egypt, which had thrown open a new country to her. I well remember the lecture she gave in the Glaslough Schoolhouse on her return in the early Nineties. It was my duty to pass round exhibits of Egyptian produce which the excited audience generally ate before they had completed the round. Henry Mathews, who became Lord Llandaff, was devoted to her. He was a lawyer, linguist, conversationalist, Welsh Roman Catholic and Tory Home Secretary. He was able to conduct cross-examinations in half the Mediterranean tongues. Mary accompanied him on a yachting trip to Greece, but when he addressed the natives in Homeric Greek, alas, they understood him not a word! It was in accent not in syntax that he failed.

He was on two sticks by the time he passed into my admiring view, but I found him more fascinating than any actor on the stage. In his youth he had been brought up abroad and frequented the *salon* of Madame Récamier. He had dealt in famous cases (which for some reason we call *causes célèbres*). He used to take the floor and talk vigorously like a lawyer in court, while Mary checked him with an occassional aside which he instantly capped. His reminiscences were on tap. He used to describe his first great triumph in the Slade case when no English lawyer knew the languages nor sufficient Canon law to carry the case to Italy. A fortune depended on the legality of a marriage which had been performed by a camp-chaplain on the march. What interested him most was that the opposing Italian lawyer was the image of the great Napoleon. At the end of the trial Mathews could not help mentioning this to his rival and received the startling reply that he was the Emperor's son!

Mathews' family were Welsh Protestant and it was resented when Henry was brought up abroad as a Catholic. Old Mathews had sold the family place at Belmont to prevent its falling into Catholic hands but it passed eventually to the Benedictines. And the lad, who was brought up in Paris under such teachers as Guizot, returned to revive the old family title of Llandaff. At first he had wished to air himself as Monmouth, but that was discovered to be a Royal title. He had a mystical strain and used to refer to his prehistoric origin : " I am of the dark Silures." His wonderful letters to Mary always began " my dear Celt."

The late Lord Darling had a great admiration for him and used to mimic his expansive and fussy rhetoric. The judge was staying with him and once offered to accompany him to Mass at the Catholic chapel. Llandaff drew himself up and uttered with scorn : " Chapel ? That is the cathedral of Newport and Menevia ! " His political fortunes in England were made on the Dilke case. As the opposing counsel he issued a scathing attack on Dilke who was then the rising hope of the Radicals. Mathews halted at one point and allowed himself to compare Dilke's morals to those of the flies crawling up the window-pane. His attack naturally pleased the Tories and Queen Victoria, who looked on Dilke as a dangerous subverter of the realm because he had suggested that she should pay income-tax.

His niece, Miss de la Chère, was violently jealous of Mary and conceived that her influence would be used to turn Llandaff Anglican, but Mary sweetly asserted that she would never do anything to upset one of her dear " Roman Candlesticks." Miss de la Chère's wrath when she learnt that Llandaff had left Mary a thousand a year in his will was uncontrollable. Llandaff was much amused and related the scene to Mary, whose wrath swelled no less until he promised to remove the offending clause from his testament.

Llandaff was certainly the most brilliant man I ever met. Amongst British statesmen he was unique. To the Papal community he was a glittering exhibit. Miss de la Chère made the arrangements for his biography to be written, but it fell through lamentably. Mary would not surrender what had been the most intimate correspondence of his life, chiefly, she remarked, because Miss de la Chère would die of rage on reading it. The well-

known publicist, W. S. Lilley, was chosen. Mr Lilley
secured his fee and proceeded to write a book about the
absurd Catholic Union and his own absurder self. The
subject of the biography was not mentioned until late
in the book, which proved to be unpublishable.

Sir Wallis Budge came almost daily in his retired days
and wrote Mary a letter every day that he failed to come.
I have attended lunch at Mary's to meet him when the
company sat through the afternoon until past tea-time, so
enthralling could he be. In spite of his strong scepticism
he could spin a wonderful set of ghost stories. They
would have filled a small book and I think were due to
his Cornish descent. He used to begin with stories drawn
from his Celtic home : how the pilchards failed Cornwall
for many years until a wise woman—whom he knew—
spent a night at a holy well whence she returned and
prophesied the return of the pilchards. What was
astonishing was that they did come the next day.

Then there was a wedding and he was taken as a boy
with others in a buggy to the wedding feast a long way
off. On the way the wise woman sitting with them advised
them to return. She had just seen the bridegroom's
wraith riding past them ! She was right, for he had been
killed.

Sir Wallis' whole prospects had depended on his taking
a scholarship at Cambridge in Assyrian ! Mary had a
story that he used to pick up his oriental beginnings by
turning over the leaves of second-hand books : and had
in some way attracted Mr Gladstone's attention. He
was given his chance to enter Christ's College, Cambridge,
but no one in the University had sufficient Assyriology
to examine him, so the renowned Professor Sayce was
borrowed from Oxford.

Sir Wallis arrived and took rooms at the Castle Inn.
In his great nervousness he woke three times during the
night before the examination. Each time he remembered
a vivid dream. The dream was the same each time : he
found himself entering the gateway of Christ's, he was

being conducted into a small examination-room where he was locked up with the paper on Assyrian. Every question was left clearly on his mind and they were not questions which he knew too well. But what struck him most was that the examination paper was tinted a distinct green. He rose after the third dream and looked up the questions, providing himself with perfect replies. In the morning he made his way to Christ's and was conducted exactly as he had dreamed into an empty room where he was locked up with the paper. There were his sheets of green paper all right and there were all the questions ! The explanation was simple. Professor Sayce suffered from an ocular affection and could only read comfortably from tinted paper !

And at Christ's there was an Indian student who appeared to Sir Wallis in St. Paul's Cathedral after he had committed suicide presumably in Cambridge.

Another ghost-story which he told admirably related to the horrible haunting of Dauncy in Wilts by the " bloody parson." In the Middle Ages it was discovered that a priest had run amok and killed half a dozen people. Only a boy who hid himself in a barrel had escaped.

In the end Sir Wallis became a collector of mummies and Curator of the Egyptian department in the British Museum. He should have become the medium of countless mummy stories, but he only became more and more sceptical. He dug up mummies like potatoes. He dissected and labelled them like specimens. Nothing terrible ever happened to him. He analysed and exploded mummy stories. He told us of one famous mummy behind a glass case in the Museum. He saw one day two ladies consulting the mummy and asked them if they would enjoy hearing its history. They were delighted, for it appeared to be a close friend of theirs. They confessed that they consulted it on all daily concerns of life. Sir Wallis remained polite and learnt that the mummy answered yes to questions by nodding her head. When the answer was in the negative the action was also

negative. The ladies withdrew and Sir Wallis, convinced
of their sanity, decided to remain in the mummy-room that
night. After considerable thought he sent for the night
watchmen and ordered them to walk about in the next
rooms and in different corners. It was as he suspected.
When a heavy tread was laid on the threshold, the vibration caused the mummy's head to incline very slightly
but perceptibly.

There was only one incident which remained unex-
plained in Sir Wallis' memories : exactly one. A stranger
once called and asked if he cared to possess a coffin
board painted from the *Book of the Dead*. Sir Wallis went
round to his house and immediately recognised a valuable
find. This he wished to purchase, but the man refused.
He wished to present it, but on condition it was moved to
the Museum then and there. Although it was after hours
Sir Wallis arranged for the Museum van and men to come
round and fetch it. He then learnt that the coffin plank
was uncanny and that an unpleasant face was liable to
appear in the wood. Some spiritualists were intensely
interested and anxious to take a photograph, but the
owner was so alarmed and nervous that to be rid of
the whole concern he had offered it to the Museum on
the conditions aforesaid.

The spiritualists naturally followed their quarry to the
Museum and asked leave to take the photograph. Sir
Wallis consented, but on terms which would obviate the
least suspicion of a fake. He communicated with his
own photographer and arranged for six photographs to
be taken in the presence of witnesses. The head of the
firm was sufficiently interested to prepare the glass plates
under his own supervision and to keep each in a sealed
packet. The photographs were taken and the plates
developed. They were kept in a special box in the firm's
safe. Sir Wallis went round to see the plates. A strange
story awaited him. In spite of their most genuine precau-
tions the photographs were not available. In place of the
glass was a heap of powdered dust. It could never be

explained. Sir Wallis accounted this the only happening in his life which showed the workings of an unknown force —supernormal if not supernatural.

Mary's wit had been part of our schoolroom life. Her witticisms flowed as easily as oil from a well, leaving everyone in the room sorry they had not said it themselves. She had the quickest way of flashlighting her opinion or sending up an epigram like a baby rocket. But even when the rocket-stick came down—it stuck !

I can remember a score to her wit.

She described Maurice Baring's pictures as " Penny Whistlers," and when Fletcher introduced the chewing system for health she announced she was joining " the Salivation Army." She defined a Materialist as the sort of person who sends you a *paté de fois gras* when your mother dies !

When a famous musical hostess remarked : " How I love those disappearing fifths," Mary simply suggested : " I prefer the submerged tenth."

There was a Dr Emil Reich, who amongst his social talents used to lecture a little to ladies about Plato. Mary described him as an " Electroplatonist," which Arthur Balfour thought one of the best puns in existence. For Balfour she made afresh the famous epigram during his campaign for Protection : " England expects every land to pay her duty."

Among her Italian friends was Berensen, the great art critic, who very seldom accepted an attributed picture. Mary introduced him to her mother and afterwards insisted that he had said : " Quite delightful and most ornamental. Of the period but not genuinely your mother ! "

She was very good with nicknames. The old Duchess of Devonshire, who was very keen on Bridge, she called *Ponte Vecchia*. The Charlie Beresfords were " the Windbag and the Ragbag."

A friend of hers was accused of talking interminably

about his insides. She said : " Be patient. I find that when the organ recital is over, he is very pleasant."

In the old days in Dublin during the social rivalry which arose between Lady Zetland as wife of the Viceroy and Lady Iveagh of the House of Guinness, Mary said : " Their difference is so simple. It lies between Her Ex. and Double X."

She could be very original in naming a horse. Asked to name a filly by " Common " out of " Quick," she said " Mushroom."

Lord Westbury made the mistake of calling a mare Cymbeline which he believed was feminine. When Cymbeline foaled, he appealed to Mary for a name. She suggested " Enfant du miracle."

All these came as fast as thought. In Rome once Mrs Jack Gardner of Boston looked in at a party to which she was not invited. She was wearing ermine at the time, and as she seemed to hesitate, Mary whipped out : " Enter, Lady Ermintrude ! "

Most of her quick suggestions had the eighteenth-century note which could have made them worthy of Sheridan or Sydney Smith.

On hearing that the daughter of a baker had taken to grand opera, she observed that she would have no difficulty with her rôles !

And likewise of a cricketer, whose father had been a builder, that he would be a good stone-waller.

Mary's letters may some day be collected for they are on a par with her conversation. Her pen was always equal to a parody or a skit. Famous was the Baby Show she gave in Mansfield Street (July 4, 1895) for which she printed some necessary rules and nursery proverbs :

" Each exhibit to be under two years old.

" All exhibits to come in every-day nursery garb and accompanied by nurse and mother.

" All exhibitors to agree that the decision of judges

should be considered final when favourable, but should not be resented, resisted or remembered if the reverse.

"Accomplishments. Jumping, crawling, singing (audible to two) unaided pat-a-cake, familiarity with market-going pigs and the simpler forms of Thank you and Good-bye.

Nursery Proverbs

" One swallow does not make a Supper.
" Slide goes before a Fall.
" The Child says Father to the Odd Man.
" It's no use crying over Swiss Milk."

The most famous skit from her pen was a parody on one of the popular Oriental extravaganzas which were being written at the time : " The Heifer of the Dawn." Mary wrote an account of the Creation of Man as made for the recreation of Woman :

"Light dawned at last upon Washitub and he bravely took :

> the Pride of the Morning,
> the Coolness of the Evening,
> the Height of the Ridiculous,
> and the Breadth of the Plain.

To this he added :

> the Backing of the Favorite,
> the Putting of a Good Face on it,
> and the Lap of the Tide.

Proud of this beginning, he chose :

> the Weeping of the Willows,
> the Laughter of Gas,
> the Curse of Heredity,
> and the Resignation of a Prime Minister.

He took the Silence of Dean Maitland
and the Patience of Miss Milligan.

He then borrowed :

the Wisdom of Teeth,
the Swearing of Colours,
the Strength of a Conviction,
the Refinement of Sugar,
the Rescue of Cavalry,
and the Honour of making your acquaintance.

These deemed he sufficient and he blended and put
them forth in tweed which when Woman lifted up her
eyes and beheld, she sang joyfully aloud : Great art
thou, oh Washitub, behold thou hast fashioned here a
Perfect Man ! ''

Mary died at Easter, 1936.   Her light had not really
been left under a bushel. *The Times* printed some remarkable tributes, but it was astonishing to learn that her
death had drawn more such letters than any great public
character of the time.

Russia and Tolstoy

★

IN FAR OFF DAYS BEFORE THE APPALLING GROWTH OF world problems we turned our attention much more closely to insular things. There was no League of Nations, no Soviet Russia, no Fascism, no dividing gulf between Democratic and Totalitarian States.

We were interested in the conflict between Conservatives and Liberals. During my second year the Liberals won a sweeping General Election. The walls were covered with posters about " Chinese Slavery." It was a convenient battleground and nothing to do with China or Slavery. The question was whether Chinese workmen should be penned in immoral conditions at the mines in South Africa. English political history was changed by the slogan.

The new Liberal member for Cambridge was Buckmaster, one of the few eloquent Englishmen I have ever heard. He became Lord Chancellor. He was very popular at Cambridge as he was supposed by the smart set to be related to polo playing. I always loved him as he was to my mind right on the only two questions I cared for : Freedom of Ireland and Freedom of Birds.

On these two subjects alone I even ventured to speak in public. I was impressed to lecture in the small Guildhall (one of Cambridge's lost monuments) on Sinn Fein and the Irish Question. Kingsmen led by Professor Charles Webster amused themselves as bearded sandwichmen in the King's Parade. The present Provost Sheppard took the chair. This was in 1908 when the Liberal Party were slowly achieving Home Rule for Ireland once and for

all. In those days the English Liberal Party practically
represented the League of Nations in the world. That is
the small nations were leagued round England.

When Bulgarians or Armenians were massacred, the
voice of Gladstone had sounded upon the earth. Late in
time this tradition was now being exerted in favour of
Ireland.

We did what we could from King's, which was always
the intellectual front. Gordon Selwyn became President
of the Union and initiated a famous Irish debate, at which
Stephen Gwynn opposed the present Lord Londonderry.
I arranged papers on Irish subjects of which the best were
read by Sir Norman Moore and Oscar Browning.

So much for Irish politics. There were also Fabians
and Carbonari. Socialism as at Oxford was strongly
associated with the devoted High Church and the slum
priests for whom I conceived a devotion amounting to
hero-worship. When we had spare week-ends or were
passing through London we visited the Anglo-Catholic
outposts. There was Father Stanton at St Alban's,
Holborn, Father Wainwright in St Peter's, London docks,
and there was the memory of Father Dolling at Poplar.
Father Dolling's life and career had moved us deeply in
Osborne's Biography. I am sure I read it twenty times.
He had combined Christian Socialism with picturesque
ritual. He had made the Winchester College Mission a
wonderful success in the Portsea slums and had been
persecuted by Archbishop Davidson on the question of
all questions of Prayers for the Dead. Since the Great
War the Church of England has learnt to pray for the
dead.

Archbishop Alexander was staying at Lambeth and
invited me to tea. Archbishop Davidson entered and
remembering Dolling I avoided kissing his ring. No
doubt he mistook my aversion for shyness.

Father Stanton's sermons were filling St Alban's.
Whenever I spent Sunday in London I used to run down
an empty Oxford Street on foot from Marble Arch on

the chance of hearing him. Of all preachers I ever heard his sermons were the most poignant, witty and evangelical. He gave me a keynote to slum work : " There are plenty to look after the deserving poor. It is the undeserving poor who need our love."

We were intensely interested in things ecclesiastical. It was an age of controversies which have since gone to the dust. The endless discussion about Anglican Orders had survived Pope Leo XIII's reluctant declaration that they were invalid. This disquieting statement (though very few people knew what it meant) had upset many good men. The public of course did not care in the least whether Anglicans were valid or invalid. Good Protestants would have supported the Pope, who only meant that English clergymen had not acquired the same spiritual powers as " clerks in Holy Orders of the Church of Rome." But the High Church minded, especially dear Lord Halifax. I was interested enough to consult him and was invited to a dinner at his house at which Lord Milner and Father Waggett of Cowley were present. I revelled in their fine uplifting talk. To be present at the dinner I had bicycled from Brede Place to Robertsbridge in Sussex (nine miles in thirty-five minutes) and caught the train as it was leaving the station. On Anglican Orders Lord Halifax assured me that the new Pope Pius X had told him that the decision against them was not infallible. I found myself suddenly taken ill. Lord Halifax sent his butler home with me.

The *Ecclesia Anglicana* is one of the puzzles of history. Historical and unique it had survived the storms of the Reformation. It was quite clear that the old Catholic Hierarchy of Queen Mary had died out. The apostolic succession had been continued by Queen Elizabeth through Archbishop Parker who had been touched by Bishop Barlow, who had been a Catholic bishop under Henry VIII. From Archbishop Parker every Church of England ordination derived. There was a great question which kept us up of nights. Was Parker a real bishop

T

and had the magic of episcopacy taken like vaccination
in his case ? We debated the apostolical succession
amongst ourselves and our critics. One Kingsman
declared against it bluntly unless the successors of the
Apostles could perform what the Apostles performed—
miracles ! We clung to straws. We were much influenced
by a story told us by Father Hugh Benson, whose father,
when Archbishop of Canterbury, visited a French
cathedral incognito and was shown a vestment of St
Thomas à Becket. The sacristan without any idea of his
visitor's identity threw the vestment suddenly over his
shoulders. We accepted this as a sign that Anglican
Orders were valid and that Dr Benson was the lineal
descendant of the Martyr.

There was nothing to do but to read and re-read the
books written for or against Anglican Orders : Milner,
Luke Rivington, Arthur Stapylton Barnes and Abbot
Gasquet on the Invalid side while Littledale, Pusey, Gore
and Lacey upheld the Anglican claim. I imagine that
Cambridge youth have other and broader problems to
worry them to-day. But it kept High Churchmen worry-
ing as with a worm at heart. Papal bats began to fly
into sound Anglican belfries. The question was whether
Anglican clergy could convey Absolution in Confession
and above all, when they said Mass or the Communion
Service, did the Real Presence ensue ? By their works
in the slums, by the sanctity of their lives, by the hard,
unselfish existences in country rectories, by the revival
of English monks and friars at Mirfield and at Cowley, it
was certain that the Grace of God was with them.

Anglican Orders seemed a quibble of Church Law. The
Canon lawyers could say as much on one side as the other.
We believed that Leo XIII and Duchesne, to say nothing
of many Roman priests, held Anglican validity possible,
but the violence of Cardinal Vaughan and the Franciscan
Fleming backed by Gasquet's historical knowledge had
over-persuaded the Pope, whose dream had been to
gather the Church of England into honorary reunion,

Later popes allowed the same hopes to take a different line, hence the Conferences carried on at Malines between High Anglicans and Cardinal Mercier. But sufficient unto the day is the controversy thereof.

There was always an interesting test · the Greek Orthodox Church, whose Orders were recognised by Rome. Would Constantinople, Moscow and the Holy Synod recognise Anglican Orders ? We were told that they did. On the other hand we were told that the Greek Church could only consider the Church of England as a broken branch of the Latin. It was no use translating the Greek Mass into English or making Archimandrites process with archdeacons in English churches. It was wine and oil.

It seemed nevertheless that our last ditch was Russia ; and I eagerly snatched a chance to make the test. When I was given the opportunity to visit Russia in 1907 I kept this in mind. Many pilgrims have found their way since to Moscow, but generally to visit the Mecca of the Soviet. I wonder if any since my humble visit have gone that long journey seeking Communion, not Communism ?

This made a side-issue to a delightful visit for which I had to thank Count Benckendorff, the last ambassador of the Czars to the Court of St James. It is now something to remember and almost to boast : to have travelled through Imperial Russia before Lenin or Stalin were heard of. The great lodestone to the intellectual world was, of course, Leo Tolstoy, who was the most attractive and noble figure in Europe thirty years ago.

I left Charing Cross on October 12, 1907 in my father's fur coat and reached Berlin the next morning. I heard Mass in the Catholic cathedral and rushed round the galleries and felt entranced by Murillo's " Anthony of Padua." I reached Warsaw the next morning, drove across the town and started for Moscow with an English commercial traveller I met on the journey. On the boundary we were pulled out in the middle of the night, and the bagman's samples most unkindly scattered up and down the platform. Just as the train was starting an armful of his wares was thrust into his arms and he himself was pushed into the train. As he had taken a berth on the Trans-Siberian and had to leave the bulk of his stuff behind, his anguish can be imagined. It was my first taste of autocratic government ! I was allowed to enter the dominions of the Czar on the understanding that I was neither Jew nor Jesuit, which was duly stated on my passport.

White snow-clad plains followed, frozen rivers and little villages each with a church dome painted blue or green while the orthodox cross glistened in the sunlight. In the afternoon the train drew into Moscow and I was met by a retainer of the Benckendorffs. It was like a city of dream under the vividness of colouring and the clearness of atmosphere. Even the street crows looked a dazzling jet against the crystal snows. There were *moujiks* and priests in plenty in the streets and a struggling line of convicts in chains with half their heads shaved.

The next day I spent rushing about the Kremlin, visiting cathedrals and getting arrested, but I was always ceremoniously saluted, thanks to a passport signed by Sir Edward Grey, then Foreign Secretary. The cannon left behind by Napoleon with his initial N. lay thickly on the ramparts. I visited a picture gallery showing a portrait of the Czar Alexander II, the liberator of the serfs, painted after his assassination.

The following day was a Holy day (October 17, 1907), and the Kremlin was in ecclesiastical fête. I heard Vespers sung to the Blessed Virgin on a musical scale I did not believe possible to human organs of song. The Cathedral literally vibrated to the sound of the priests singing and the windows trembled. It was an occasion of high ceremony, for three Bishops were present. Their long, well-combed hair falling under their jewel-studded crowns made them resemble the Holy Trinity rather than three mortal men. This service took place in the Cathedral of the Annunciation. I stood transported with a heavenly delight, but my raptures did not prevent my feeling something moving like a mouse in my overcoat pocket : the pocket containing my precious passport and my entire stock of roubles. I glanced very carefully to the right and noticed a lady of considerable beauty clad in the richest furs. Nevertheless the conviction remained that her hand was deep in my coat pocket. I had to make an instant decision under difficult circumstances. Not knowing the lingo I could not give her in charge. Naturally I could not cause a scene of any kind, but I could not suffer the loss of purse and passport. That night I was due to take a train south to Sosnofka, the seat of the Benckendorffs. There was nothing to do but to drop my hand on the little intruder and squeeze her hand with mine until I felt the release of my valuables. I then drew out her white and exquisite fingers which I kissed and returned to the owner, who never turned round nor waved an eyelash during the process.

Was she a spy or a police agent or a professional thief or a professional of another kind ? I never knew, for that evening I was placed on a midnight train meandering south.

Railway travelling in Russia is slow and sometimes uncertain. At midnight there was a crash and the train left the line without rolling down the bank. The neighbouring community immediately rushed out of their houses not to give material assistance but to enjoy the conversation of the travellers. The passengers seemed equally pleased at the opportunity. The officials walked away and left the engine to its fate. There was nothing to be done but to make delicious tea out of the hot water. Russians always took a *samovar* or tea-strainer in their baggage. Political discussion, not being permitted in public, depended then on such accidents.

I felt very bewildered until students in student dress discovered my nationality and began in French trying to discover all about the great Darwin, whose theories, by the way, had begun to lose savour at Cambridge in my time with the coming of Mendel. All the students I met

in Russia were advanced thinkers ; and I felt this was no
occasion to refer to Anglican Orders.   I never once met
an ecclesiastic travelling in Russia.   So the night passed
thanks to the hot water supply from the engine.   Towards
dawn we all started walking with our luggage on our
backs.   We reached the next station and there awaited
the next train.

Meantime my destinies were in the hands of a committee
of voluble students, who had a hundred questions to ask
me.   I reiterated my destination and was finally shipped
on a train which travelled very leisurely all day and
brought me the following afternoon to a place called
Kaslof.   I was escorted to the platform and left alone.
From the departing train many friendly caps and hands
were waved and we parted for ever.   Night was falling
and also the snow.   I did not know within hundreds of
miles where I was on the map.   I wandered into the
town collecting both sympathy and attention, but all
communications had to take place by signs.   My imitation of a Western European lavatory was received at
first with incredulity and then with appreciative laughter.
A German teacher was found with whom I could converse
with the limited stores of Teutonic conferred on me by
my governess.   I explained my plight.   He was duly
pessimistic.   He discovered for me that Sosnofka was
fifty miles away across the plains and that my only chance
was driving.   His advice was simple "*mit Pferde.*"   I
leaped at the idea for I was feeling very desolate and lost
by now.   "*Ja, mit Pferde, mit Pferde !* "   He disappeared
into a stable and in twenty minutes reappeared with a
broken-down *troitska* attached to three ponies of varying
sizes.   It was more like a perambulator on a sledge.   The
owner was anxious to make his bargain, but my sole
knowledge of Russian consisted of the words, *Gospodi
pamilui* (God have mercy on us).   These I sometimes
repeated with little success.   My German friend was now
counting the necessary roubles I had to pay for a drive to
Sosnofka.   This was calculated in turn on the fingers of

all three of us, the sum was paid and I was allowed to take my seat with my bag between my knees. A post-boy swathed in sheepskins drove the ponies out into the starry night. We drove and drove and drove into the Russian forest in and out of the enormous ruts which almost swallowed the smallest of the three ponies. After several hours we lost our way and I was left frozen to the *troitska* while my driver threw stones at windows to waken sleepers and inquire his road. I composed myself to the despair of dereliction and wished I had never heard of Anglican Orders. We altered course and drove on again until to my relief we were hailed by a party of horsemen whom I mistook for bandits. They were a relief party sent by Count Benckendorff to search the steppes for me. By midnight I rode escorted into the courtyard of a pleasant country house built entirely of wood. To my amazement I heard a familiar English voice. On the doorstep stood Maurice Baring !

It was a glorious relief : something like being lost in Tartary and suddenly meeting somebody as refreshing as Dan Leno or one's college tutor.

I remained until December in the hospitable circle of the Benckendorffs. I indulged in winter sports : duck-shooting, wolf-hunting. Amusements included seeing a church bell cast and throwing coins into the liquid metal, sledge-driving, attending Church services and arguing the Irish question with Maurice Baring. Conversation at meals consisted of intensive arguments between Maurice and the deeply read Countess. Count Benckendorff was one of the last of the diplomatists of the old school and anxious to resign his position. Only the personal entreaty of the Czar kept him at the Court of St James. Curiously he was a Roman Catholic, being descended from an old German family.

The wolf-hunt was enthralling. A peasant, who had been bitten by a wolf in childhood and could therefore speak the wolf-language, was sent to howl in the woods the previous night. His lupine relations answered him

and were located some five miles away. The next day
we took guns and were posted outside a wood, while
hundreds of *moujiks* beat out the country. The wolves
were shot down with shot-guns and finished off with
revolvers. I can only say that Maurice and myself
concealed the fear though not the cold from which we
were suffering.

I returned to Western Europe by St Petersburg, but
first I paid a visit to Leo Tolstoy, fulfilling a desire as
great as my interest in Anglican Orders. From Moscow
I made my way to Tula, and though I managed to lose
my ticket and failed in pronouncing the name of my
destination, Isnaya Polyana, the name of Tolstoy was
sufficient, for porters and station-masters pushed me into
trains or led me down platforms. At last I was conducted
to a sledge where I sat in the straw and was driven to the
home of the great one.

The old patriarch, short, sturdy and bearded, received
me at his table where he and his family and a few disciples
were enjoying a vegetarian meal. There were some good
family portraits on the walls, but no carpet underfoot.
The great man rose and I could see he was really a fair-
sized dwarf in stature. His black flashing eyes and tangled
beard made him gnomelike. He motioned me to a seat
at his board, but first of all he subjected me to some
disconcerting questions :

Was I a Christian ?

Was I pure towards women ?

Was I a vegetarian ?

This last question the Countess answered for me in a
quick negative : " No : can you not see—he is too strong
and big ? " The Count grunted a little but became
charming and considerate to his uninvited guest. The
visit passed like a dream and I became friends with the
good Countess who was swathed in peasants' dress for his
sake, but hinted to me that she had lived luxurious days
in her youth. Everything had been sacrificed to Tolstoy's
ideas.

I slept in a room full of desks which was devoted to the village children. Tolstoy was up and working in his farm before dawn, in fact, two hours before I was dressed. He took me aside and talked of his philosophy. It was so simple. Every man, even men of letters, were bound to carry out some labour in the fields or workshop.

He talked to me in French. As far as I could judge, his English reading was limited to the works of Henry George and William Stead's *Review of Reviews*, which I noticed had been severely blacked by the Imperial censor. In the intervals I used to scribble down his words. Here is a sheaf of notes written and translated under his roof :

" Look at the evil which patriotism has accomplished. Patriotism is the egotism of the many. Egotism is sin.

" You must not resist evil.

" You must not hate the factory owners. You must show them the error of their ways. Perhaps they are self-deceivers.

" You must pray not only when you are alone but whenever you meet another man : that you may feel you are both sons of God.

" What you desire for Ireland you must desire for the whole world.

" You must never cast away a woman.

" You must read Henry George. I fear his ideas do not make progress.

" You have no right to preach to anyone : to your own family or to a tramp. You must not go into the slums through pride.

" There are only two lives. One is to live as the world lives and the other as a Christian.

" Once I thought my vocation was military, but it has turned out otherwise.

" I find a great contradiction in my life, against which I am always striving.

" It is a struggle always, but I have to await the Will of God. . . ."

Speaking of the state of Russia he showed me a picture of a priest blessing a new vodka-shop with the words :
" That is what is wrong with Russia."

On the state of Europe he had only one formula : " Sooner or later they must choose between me and the bayonets." This was seven years before the outbreak of the Great War.

The Countess gave me a photograph she had taken of him standing in the snow, and he kindly wrote my name and his across.

My last glimpse was at evening. His crumpled figure stood in silhouette against the light as he ushered me from his door. Three years later he fled from his grieving family and died in a railway station.

I returned to Moscow and visited the magnificent Cathedral of St Saviour, built as a votive offering for the defeat and retreat of Napoleon. It has since been dismantled stone by stone.

I visited the great monasteries : the Novodevitchy, the Novospasky and the Strasnoy.

The Benckendorffs arrived and took me to the famous Moscow Theatre, where the acting was so good it was hardly necessary to know the words. Maurice Baring, of course, could follow every line of the play. It was always pleasant travelling with him as he had a facility for conversation with Russian engine-drivers and could often find out where the train was going. We went to the most famous restaurant of the Moscow merchants where the waiters were all specially imported from Tartary. They wore dazzling white and little golden beards.

And thence to St Petersburg. I saw all the pictures in the Hermitage, attended a meeting of the Duma and visited the fortress-prison of Peter and Paul. Here I stood by the tomb of Peter the Great. It gave me a curious thrill in later years when I read of the opening and despoiling of the coffins of the Czars and how living men opened the silver shroud and for a while gazed upon the great Peter, who was Lenin and Stalin before their time and whose work may yet prove the more enduring. Visitors from England to Russia were rare in those days. The only other visitor I heard of that winter from England was the eminent critic Dr Kirsopp Lake (who had been runner-up to Dr Inge for the Deanery of St Paul's). Dr Lake had come to St Petersburg to see the Sinaitic Codex : the ancient vellum manuscript of the Bible. I afterwards cursed myself for not getting a glimpse of this famous Biblical manuscript actually written in the fourth century by men within historical memory of the Founder of Christianity. Thirty years later I was relieved of my remorse when I beheld it in the British Museum where it should last another 5000 years. It always amazed me why Russia sold it to England for such a flea-bite as £100,000 when Dr Rosenbach (as he told me) was offering ten times as much from a committee of American millionaires with a view to placing the supreme written relic of Christianity in the Library of Congress. When I first heard of the *Sinaiticus* in Sunday Qs at Eton I had an idea that it was the book Moses brought down from Sinai. A fairly intelligent " howler," I think.

In St Petersburg I came across fresh student friends. Some of them conducted me to their attics and I asked the subject of their studies. The answer was Chinese ! I could only gasp with admiration at their textbooks piled on the floor. Imagine working for a Chinese Tripos at Cambridge or writing classical Chinese verses at Eton !

While at St Petersburg a strange incident occurred to me. I found myself by my mistake or that of my companions unable to leave one of the courts around St Peter and Paul (a mixture of prison, Cathedral and imperial cemetery). Every gate was closed and finding myself alone I could not explain why I was there or ask my way out. A mist was spreading from the Neva and I felt desperate, but I noticed that the wall was scalable. It was spiked on top, but not so heavily as the railings I

used to surmount when entering Trinity College at
Cambridge. It took me a very few seconds to pull myself
to the top. I peeped over and saw a sentry disappearing in
the mist. I waited to calculate how soon he would return
and how soon he was likely to disappear again. When he
made his next disappearance I made mine. I simply
dropped and ran into the fog. There was another wall
but I surmounted it. Count Benckendorff was much
disturbed and said I had run a fair chance of being shot.
It was an odd adventure and gave me an excuse for
pretending I had climbed out of the mighty fortress.
Perhaps I did. I never returned to trace my steps.

Very soon I found myself on the edge of trouble.
Mornings were always spent in churches or monasteries
buying ikons, interviewing Archimandrites and querying
Anglican Orders. I found that I was not permitted to be
a communicant in the Orthodox Church, but I was invited
to a service where I saw Holy Communion administered
to an infant in arms through the medium of a spoon. But
my afternoons were spent with students, always a sub-
versive force in Russia. I attended a forbidden meeting
in a class-room at the University as the self-appointed
representative of Cambridge. The meeting was tumul-
tuous and enthusiastic, but was brought to a conclusion by
the police. That evening I left by a night train for Vilna
in Poland where I was anxious to express Irish sympathies
in patriotic circles.

I have not since crossed the Russian boundaries where
changes have been considerable and as yet inestimable.
Russia has been used as a social laboratory for the rest
of the world. Violent experiments and reactions :
rainbows in test-tubes : precipitate of bloodshed : and
a slow final deposit that only the historians in the year
2000 will be able to gauge.

Poland under Russian rule suggested analogies with
Ireland. I was shown Polish schools where language and
religion were kept alive despite the heavy hand of
Muscovy. I was advised not to approach the statue of

a Russian Empress which required the attentions of a
sentry by day and night for fear of a patriot's bomb. In
those days Imperial Russia was strewn with sentries.
I noticed one every fifty yards all the way from Moscow
to St Petersburg. Perhaps there had been a Grand Duke
in the train. I was told there were two sentries in the
Royal grounds : one standing on the exact spot where a
Czar had once observed the first primrose of spring and
placed a guard to protect it and where a Czarina had once
kept a tethered bear. Primrose and bear had passed with
a century of years, but the sentries never ceased to be
relieved.

The Poles were really persecuted and I remember the
valiant Archbishop Kopp left Vilna for Siberia the day
of my arrival. I often wondered what happened to him.

I was very happy in Poland visiting shrines and hearing
Mass in the street under a famous ikon of Our Lady
exhibited in a glass gallery over the people's heads. As
one trudged up the street and caught sight of the glimmer-
ing candles and the vested priest shuffling to and fro at
the mid-air altar one could hear Mass in the process. I
was lifted with enthusiasm for the cause of Poland as I
have never felt a cause in my blood. Years afterwards
I came across an unexpected reason which had been
kept a dead secret from me. Many generations ago there
had been a lapse on my English grandmother's side.
A member of the famous Polish family, Zamorysky, had
been involved in a love affair, and the result had been a
distant infusion of Polish blood. Zamorysky had been a
foreign secretary in London and his family had recognised,
or at least remembered, the liaison. After a hundred
years every scandal is as dead as the love-making in last
year's rookery. It is only interesting to me, as everyone
has a right to be interested in his blood mixtures. It
accounts to me for my frenzy of enthusiasm for the Polish
cause. When I returned to Ireland I collected thousands
of signatures from Irish children which I sent to the
children whose schools I had visited in Poland.

I stayed in odd hotels in Poland. I was received with the greatest courtesy, but in one my high mission was not recognised. I must have been mistaken for a travelling bagman. I was fast asleep one night when there was knocking on the door and I switched on the light. A gentleman with long ringlets and greasy demeanour was bowing and scraping before me. For a moment I thought it was the mayor or some civic dignitary. But no—with one hand he was counting and with the other pointing to a girl in Polish dress. After he had explained her charms in voluble German he proposed to leave her in my arms. It was her desire to meet " *der grosse Irlander.*" Unfortunately I was not feeling very gross and explained as well as I could that I could not dream of assaulting the honour of a Polish virgin. Much volubility followed and the young lady stood staring pathetically without a word. She wore a fanciful native costume. I suspected her proprietor was a white-slaver, and addressed him with contempt. He was still insistent and the poor girl lifted her arms mechanically. This was two much. I rose from my blankets, made a huge Sign of the Cross and hissed :

" *Ego sum sacerdos in æternum.*"

The effect was instantaneous. Everybody disappeared. There was a sound of wailing in the corridor and I returned to my slumbers feeling like " little Jack Horner." It was a happy way out of an embarrassing situation.

Hiking and Llandaff House

★

Rowing is not a sport that one can carry from the college boathouse into life. I sat in an eight-oar for the last time in June, 1908, after the last night of the May races.

As the boat we paddled slowly home came to rest for the last time outside the King's College boathouse I felt a curious nostalgia. Under the great poplar tree the cox summoned us in pairs to leave the boat and carry in our oars and then to lift and raise the shell which we had driven so often along the green and dreary reaches of the Cam. Farewell to Harry the boatsman, who had served us so faithfully all these years. A delicate hand and perfect judgment he always showed at the starts of the bumping race when our hearts were beating between the minute gun and the actual signal for start. Harry was the only antidote I ever knew to the " needle." In dreams I can hear the minute gun far away at Baitsbite Lock and the nervous coaches counting in different times to their more nervous crews all down the river bank. We swing out against the stream . . . twenty seconds more . . . touch her two and four . . . ten seconds more . . . nine, eight, seven, six . . . Bang ! Never again : and the great poplar is gone from the King's boathouse and the faithful Harry has taken service with Charon.

Hiking—long distance walking—was fairly popular, especially amongst the rowing men. It became a favourite life-long pastime and pass-space with me. Men walked from London to Cambridge and from Cambridge to

Oxford. My longest walk was from Cambridge to Berk-hampstead on Good Friday, 1904. I never stopped for a meal during the fifty-five miles. It looks a respectable jaunt on the map.

Oxford was always a city of my dreams and I decided to await the right moment and approach the city of the Oxford Movement on foot. I waited as a pilgrim for the right moment and arranged to spend a week at the end of my walk at Cowley St John amongst the Cowley Fathers. Oxford was still full of memories of Newman and Pusey and the Catholic Rivival. Father R. M. Benson, the founder of Cowley, was still alive, and the first Anglican nun since the Reformation, Mother Marian, was living in the Woodstock Road. They were both nonagenarians. These were indeed thrilling thoughts for the ecclesiastical-minded.

It was a fine and frosty evening as I came into Oxford for the first time on foot from Aylesbury way. Litanies were on my lips, but I grew very footsore and struck Oxford on the opposite side to Cowley. It was a painful trudge coming through St Giles. I was stiff and almost speechless when I reached Cowley. I had only glimpsed the magical colleges in the half light. Kind Father Lang-ridge knelt and pulled off my blood-stained boots, but the glimpse of Oxford had left me ecstatic. I had read so much about Oxford. All my literary heroes, all my leaders were Oxford. Pusey's ghost seemed to await me at the portals of Pusey House. Newman had crossed before me into Oriel Lane where my grandfather had watched him in the Forties. A New Oxford was arising. The Rhodes scholars were just beginning and Lord Nuffield was mending bicycles round the corner. . . .

When later I could wander through the buildings I discovered Cox, the old porter at Trinity, and had a long talk. He remembered escorting Cardinal Newman back to his old rooms and had seen him search the outside wall for the snapdragon the Cardinal remembered of old. It was still there ; and the Cardinal had stood by the window where he used to stand and read as a dreamy young man.

It is difficult to explain the exhilaration there is in walking through new country. The long walk is the finest and final form of exercise and leaves the passing scenery imprinted in the album of the mind. Twilight, starlight, moonlight and dawn are best known upon the lonely road. In those days there was no traffic by night, no blighting motors, no blinding lights. The night air pours like cold champagne into the weary lungs. The hardest time during a night walk is always between two and four of a morning. The spirits have sunk and the legs will not swing until the first gusts of dawn. It is like a slow resurrection heading into the tinted light and breathing the swift cold airs that have been wafted by the wings of the morning. Birds are astir at that hour and every wild animal that moves before man is abroad. The creaks of civilisation are unheard. Second wind and second strength come quickly to those who have made the determination to walk their way through the night.

To enjoy perfect happiness, it was necessary to reach a friendly house before breakfast, to fall into a hot bath and rest till mid-day. At one time I never sought or accepted invitations in the country unless I could arrive on foot, generally travelling through the previous night. This entailed sending luggage or rather samples of luggage by parcel post and not always finding them on arrival. Hostesses were kind enough to allow me to keep small supplies in their housekeeper's cupboards. A number of pairs of mouldering boots of late Victorian pattern marked the places where I was welcomed.

My distaste for railways and hatred for motors gave me a sense of the road and a memory of an England which no modern hikers will ever retake. But I regret that I missed visiting a number of old country houses which have since been destroyed, sold or turned into schools or clubs. There seemed to be a plethora of them in those days

U

and they seemed permanently in the hands of the old families, but the survivors in any county can now be counted on the fingers. There was a world of country houses which accepted anyone who had a repute for safe shooting and conventional clothes. Good dancing was a rarer asset, and lawn tennis was left to eager curates and heavy-skirted Amazons.

The memory of a long walk abides when a hundred railway journeys have disappeared in smoke. I pushed my way into remote parts. I walked across the island of Mull from Duart to Iona, took boat to the sacred island, there slept and walked back the next day : thirty-seven miles each way. In Ireland I walked from Glaslough in Monaghan to Pettigo in Donegal, some fifty-six miles, in a night and from Dublin to Gorey in another. How many extra miles I walked I never knew for I missed my way and found myself at two in the morning staggering in a bog near Wicklow without a star or a slip of the moon to guide me. Once I attempted to walk home from Dublin and only reached as far as Castleblayney in the night. I had foolishly donned new shoes for the occasion, and as a result I had to crawl into Castleblayney barefoot with my soles tingling under the bastinado of the road.

Ireland must still be the hiker's paradise. From the great old veteran Standish O'Grady I learnt that by walking round the sea-road of Ireland all her history legend and myth could be compassed. There were few sea-counties through which I did not set foot. I found the perfect approach to Killarney was not by train from Dublin but on foot over the mountains from Kenmare. On a sunny day the Kerry peaks seem to rip the white cloudy blankets off the sky and the passing of the Upper Lake is only magical in the twilight when tourists are abed.

Now that the eagles are extinct the chief attraction in Kerry is the half-tropical flora : the lovely bog violet and the elegant plants called St Patrick's cabbage which can be picked off the rocks. I was told that the famous Killarney Fern was extinct owing to the rapacity of tourists ; but I searched Torc Mountain with guides until I had the botanical delight of spying a film of split emerald growing under a dripping rock. I replaced the rocks carefully and trust that no one has found my specimen since.

The finest walking county in Ireland is Donegal. My first visit was to Mrs Adair at Glenbeigh Castle in 1903. Glenbeigh is a long narrow lake set between mountain walls towards Muckish. I came up through Finntown, but took a wrong turn and found myself on the Dungloe Road before the old Constabulary put me right. Rather than retrace twenty miles I preferred to climb straight through bog and mountainous country, making the distant peak of Errigal my goal. For six hours I went as hard as I could without seeing a human being or even raising a grouse. I struck one cabin in the mountains away from any road. An old man came out and directed me in Irish. If it had not been for the chickens pecking his mattress I should hardly have believed I was in human company. Even now it seems uncanny to look back to. Who was the old man living alone and ten miles from the next house ? He was unforgettable and I could never quite explain it.

Fortunately I was in fine fettle and it was a superb day with all the fresh air of the ocean warming in the sun and washing the mountain-sides. But every height I climbed, there was always another beyond. At last night began to fall in purple shadowings through the dips and I began to feel exhausted. I passed down what I afterwards learnt was the Poisoned Glen. I wandered in the half-dark till I struck Dunlewy Lake. At the lodge I saw a light and was compelled not only to ask my way but to demonstrate my physical inability to take it. I had missed Glenbeigh by sixteen miles and had to accept Irish hospitality for the night. The next morning I was as stiff as many pokers in an Arctic frost and I had to drive the rest of my journey by Irish jaunting-car : one of the lost delights of Irish life. The greatest difference between the old Dublin and the new has been the disappearance of that elegant vehicle which was as typical of the Liffey's quays as the hansom cab was of Piccadilly.

Apart from railways all Irish distances had to be covered behind a horse. Dublin was alive with inside and outside cars. The Irish Jarvey was a wit and a philosopher. Ladies attending the amusing and meretricious splendours of the Castle used to patronise the inside car which has been described as something between a short hearse and governess cart. When the fine ladies wished to leave, stentorian voices could be heard shouting : " Lady So and So's Insides coming up ! " The sham court at Dublin was a merry farce and put a galvanised life into the dead eighteenth-century city. When a Dudley or a Wimborne upheld the position in the grand manner, there was a welcome distribution of funds. But Aberdeen Viceroyalties lived up to the name of Aberdeen.

While staying at Glenbeigh I enjoyed my first cross-country drive in a motor. A fearsome machine it was : an old-fashioned horse-brake to look at with high seats and railing and an engine attached. It was a delightfully new experience crossing the mountains in the dark and seeing for the first time birds and moths flying bewildered through the acetylene light. About this time was manufactured the famous comparison between horse and motor traffic. The former required a " set o' lean " horses.

Motoring has deprived the highroad of all the pleasures of hiking which can now only be enjoyed in lanes and bye-roads or over open downs and moors. I still believe that no games give the mental satisfaction and physical pleasure that comes from a conquest of new country by an honest hike. My first long walk was from Orléans to Tours in July 1903 down the Loire in two days from cathedral to cathedral. I learnt the charm of starting at twilight, walking through the summer night and always resting through the heat of the day. A walk down a river is always a pleasant journey. There is generally a tow-path. A river bank is a cool and pleasant path and every big river is studded by historic cities and bridges. Thus much I learnt early. It is very seldom that a rowing race or a game of golf or a day's shooting is wonderful enough to leave a memory. But every long walk leaves memories that are ineradicable even across the arches of the years. The places, trees and even passing clouds and storms I met in the open as one wild creature amongst others are an indescribable and to me most valuable part of my life's harvest. Without hiking I do not think this would have been possible.

A whole generation has come since within danger of losing their leg muscles. The sight and scenery of England will never be known to motorists. More can be seen and sensed from any third-class carriage on the line. There has been a certain reaction to hiking which is the last chance the rising generation have of seeing England or retaining their leg-power.

The bicycle has also returned after a longish eclipse. At one time the bicycle was the only instrument of speedy or lengthy road travel. In the early Nineties I remember an Irish curate balancing himself on one enormous wheel with a small wheel running behind. The bicycle was in full use before 1900 with the invention of the pneumatic tyre. At Eton we used bicycles to slip off to Ascot. Heroes rode up to London tandem-wise. Returning to Ireland for holidays by a passenger boat which no longer runs to Greenore I used to abandon my luggage to the honesty of the Irish railways and bicycle home under the Mourne Mountains.

I used to bicycle down to Brede Place, the Frewens' place in Sussex (betwixt Hastings and Rye), leaving the Marble Arch at seven and getting into bed before one in the morning. This was a pleasant and exciting finale to the Eton and Harrow match. It left an impression of white country lanes packed with white dust lying in the moonlight. The whole way is unrecognisable in the present network of roads and about as much fun to bicycle as a railway track. Bicycle trips never remained memorable like hikes across country. The monotony of the pedalling subdues the interest of the scenery.

The motor meant the arrival of a new dimension in human life. The majority of human beings whom I knew in early life died without experiencing the motor. At most it was an unpleasant luxury. It has since become a rather pleasant necessity in spite of its gigantic death-roll. Roads were then untarred but not dangerous. They were continually swept by storms of fine dust. It was best to travel on a showery day. Without a doubt the greatest change that has been effected in ordinary life has been effected by the motor. More than flying, wireless, movies, incendiary bombs or other wonderful improvements in human existence, the motor has raised the values of life and heightened the possibilities of death. The change caused has been as great as the change which the centuries make when they make an amphibious animal a denizen of sea or land.

Memory recalls the first motor I saw in action in Paris in 1895. It was a joke, a menace, an outrage. Horsemen threw their noses and horses their heels into the air.

I drove for the first time in a motor driven by Mr. von André, a City broker, during Long leave in the summer of 1901. The Surrey lanes were half an inch deep in dust. We sat on high seats projected above the roof without any protection or glass, which was looked upon as dangerous. The ladies had swathed their heads and hats with veils which deprived them of shape. But they came to exhibit their courage not their beauty. It was not unlike the switchback railway at Earl's Court except that we went only half as fast. Too fast we went for the police, who used to lie in ambush behind hedges. They stopped us and proved by undeniable evidence that we had exceeded twelve miles an hour !

My uncle Murray Guthrie had one of the first cars in London in the Nineties. On a famous occasion it stopped dead and held up the traffic in Sloane Street. A supply of language was as necessary to a driver as petrol.

In 1905 there were only three undergraduates with cars at Cambridge : Walter Dunckels, Lord Caledon and a Japanese called Okura in his country, but " Ping-pong " in ours.

Caledon was the first to make the journey from London in two hours and a half and the feat was spoken of for several days. The first motor-cycle was ridden by Lord Glerawly. The horse-traffic seemed in undisputed sway of the Cambridge streets. We used a slow fly to the station or the horse-drawn tram. There were a few smart hansoms which had no doubt seen their smartest days on Piccadilly. But the curious necessity of being propelled by petrol every day of one's life had not arisen. Life was happier as well as safer when progress was by hoof, or bicycles, or shoe-leather. It was still possible to make a drive across England behind horses and to find inns and stabling all the way.

I returned to Cambridge for the summer of 1908 to coach a college crew for the May races, but also to enjoy reading every book I had no time to read before. The Classical Tripos had cut me off from English literature for three years. And so often I have been asked : What good was the Classical Tripos to you ? At the time it seemed only to give the qualifications to be a cleric or a schoolmaster. It was no doubt of far more considerable value in the Victorian century. Apart from the use of the mind, it gave one a background to the study of History or the writing of languages and even to the philosophy of modern politics.

Henceforth for me all wars, racial or civil, politics in imperial and democratic aspects, the clash of colonies and the conquest of seas could all be referred to Greek and Roman prototypes. We were much stirred by the movement for women's suffrage in those days and the Classical men discovered the whole question, even in its most unpublishable asides, had been fought out in a play

of Aristophanes four centuries before the Christian era.
Since that time analogy after analogy has suggested itself.
The Gallipoli expedition was the Athenian expedition to
Syracuse. The strife of Fascism and Communism had
its classical forms : the Tyrants, the demagogues in
Greece and Rome. In Greece, as to-day, the historians
trace the inherent failure of man's most attractive political
venture—the dream of a cultured and incorrupt
democracy.

In literature, journalism and even the lower forms of
personal expression the Classical Tripos proves valuable
in giving a grip over style. The Classics raise clearer
standards than are visible in the chaos of English
literature.

A Classical scholar may have atrophied himself in the
process, but if he writes at all, he will not write ignomini-
ously. If he reads, he will not be deceived nor carried
away. And the marks of good writing he will recognise
by reference to the greatest.

Fourth year at Cambridge was the happiest I can
remember. Rifling the College library, from all examinations set free, editing the *Basileon* and riding up and down
the towpath I could gladly have lived in Cambridge for
ever. At that moment the best friend I ever knew swung
suddenly into my life. During the four years remaining
to him I knew no other. His companionship was all-
sufficing. His ways and whims were a constant wonder if
not delight.

John Stratford Collins was a rowing man with a Trials
Cap at St John's. He was the son of an Indian general
and the last of a long line living at Wythall, near Ross, in
Herefordshire. For him the living of life was a sufficient
career and an enthralling occupation. He had no belief
in progress and was content to stay as he was. He
presided over the Musical Society in his college. He was an
authority on Liturgy and could make Church vestments.
While an undergraduate he once opened a barber's shop
in St John's complete with a barber's pole. There was no

college regulation against his doing so and, before the authorities could interfere, he and an assistant had shaved all their friends. It was his ambition to open the continental type of café in Cambridge. He had suddenly become a Catholic and was living with Monsignor Barnes, chaplain to the Catholic undergraduates at Llandaff House near Downing College. He was the best-looking man I ever met of any age. Rupert Brooke looked like a nice Sixth Form boy compared to Jack Collins, who mingled the ascetic with the æsthetic to perfection. When he was a child he had been photographed, and the photograph was purloined to appear on a Christmas card as " Percy "! It was embarrassing to travel with him, as sometimes well-behaved women rose and followed him as though unable to help themselves. He was much troubled by feminine attentions and avoided them as far as possible by the unattractiveness of his dress. He wore patched flannel trousers, crumpled collars, socks seldom and a cheap tweed cap. His theory was that women look at men's clothes first and instinctively pass the poorly dressed. Unfortunately some caught a glimpse of his features and it was always fatal. We formed a club of the worst-dressed at Cambridge together.

The delightful thing about Jack Collins was that he was the reverse of a prig. He possessed a natural cleanliness of morals but no modesty amongst friends. For the first time at Cambridge I discussed every leaf and bough on the Tree of Sexual Knowledge which God originally planted, however much man has grafted thereon. By this time Collins had acquired more than a smattering of Canon law and the Moral Theology of the Church. On all rare and abstruse points he was astonishingly learned.

The woman, whom God gave all men to think over, whether to avoid or use, was becoming a problem. Like the majority of our friends we thought that it was wrong, both religiously and socially, to give the slightest countenance to what had begun to be called " The White Slave Traffic." Looking back I reflect on the goodness and decency of my contemporaries who had complete liberty and some temptations. Father Waggett came down from Cowley and preached a Retreat at St Giles. He used strong language : " One prostitute is enough to damn a universe : such a monument of man's selfishness." Men vowed never to make the least additional need for the prostitute's calling.

Collins did not wish to marry : he was anxious to become a priest. For years until he died he had hopes of being ordained. Downside Abbey and the English College in Rome may remember him in their secret annals, for he *tried* them both in every sense of the word. He joined the Benedictines at Downside and was immensely successful as a schoolmaster. The head-master, Leander Ramsay, was a convert and had made the school a leading one. Collins adored him and worked hard with the backward boys. He had a vocation for interesting the type of boy who can never pass an examination. Lord Castlerosse was one of his pupils and has never ceased to do him credit. But when Collins desired to become a Benedictine monk, the monks, much as they liked him, refused, saying : " He will want to be Abbot before he leaves the Noviciate." But they recognised his enthusiasm and fearlessness and they added : " If this man becomes a monk, either we shall be back in Westminster Abbey in five years or our whole community will be dissolved." In consequence he had left them with good wishes and tears and was living at Llandaff House, when we fell into each other's arms.

We lived, prayed, travelled, worked and schemed together regardless of the future or of our friends who pronounced us to be madmen. As I have said, Collins was not modest but he was adamant about women. He had to be, for I have seen every woman in a restaurant stop eating and follow him with her eyes until we left. There were very few country houses where we were received, chiefly I think because Collins regarded evening clothes as effeminate or heretical.

We used to implore him to marry for the sake of his family, which had lived in a black and white house since the Wars of the Roses. They had remained Catholic till the eighteenth century, but General Collins was a martinet and a stiff Protestant and heard with horror that his beautiful son proposed to hear women telling him their miseries in the Confessional. In fact they had parted and never met again. He represented two very ancient lines and bore the double crest on his notepaper (his only luxury). Marriage would have saved the ancient blood and incidentally benefited the ancient Faith. While living at Llandaff House, he went so far as to compose a matrimonial advertisement which amused me so much that I added my name and we put it into the plural as follows :

WANTED

" Two Converts of good family (single) Cambridge B.A., desire to be canonically united to consumptive wives (sisters preferred) guaranteed to die within two years in order that their Widowers may proceed to the Holy Priesthood.

References : Catholic Chaplain at Cambridge and Cox's Bank."

We did not like to mention that they were expected to bear children, but hoped that would be understood. Unfortunately the *Tablet* refused publication, and everybody, including the Catholic bishop, was shocked! I still believe that we purposed a good thing and that some sanatorium covers the dust of two sweet spinsters who might have found their short lives happier, had they had the chance of answering our well-intended advertisement.

Jack Collins was unique. Even his hobby was odd. It was dissecting and repairing church organs. He was supremely happy pulling about stops and pipes, and could produce melody from country church organs which had been husky and wheezy for years. His vocation was very upsetting. It consisted of rescue work amongst seceded priests. He had a list of all the priests in England who for better livings or worse had abandoned the errors of the Church of Rome for those of the Church of England. At unexpected moments he would buttonhole them, fascinate or controvert them and, if possible, lead them back to their startled bishops who had long wiped them off as bad debts.

" Fishing is the most absorbing game in the world," as Vassall-Phillips, a fascinating old Etonian Redemptorist, used to say. According to Collins Vassall-Phillips was so persuasive and insistent that after a controversial lunch he always used the finger-bowls for the purpose of Baptism !

There was a Society of St Thomas of Canterbury for the Reunion of Christendom which interested us much as it contained both Romans and Anglicans. No bishop, of course, would touch it on either side. Father Hugh Benson addressed the Society as an ex-parson and was generously cheered by the Anglicans present. At the next meeting the speaker was Father ——, a priest in Roman orders enjoying an Anglican living in the Fen country. The moment he rose all the Romans left the room, which was thought unfair.

This fugitive priest was a picturesque figure in the streets of Cambridge as he always wore full fig and proved a great attraction to High Churchmen, since they felt certain that his Mass (though said in English) was valid. The sequel was fantastic and perhaps amusing. To Collins it was wildly edifying ! After giving immense scandal to all the good Catholics of the diocese and enjoying four hundred a year of good Anglican money, he died, but reverted to Rome on his death-bed. We thought it one of those rare instances when one of the children of light showed himself wiser in his generation than the children of this world !

Monsignor Barnes' roof was a refuge to eccentric Catholics and converts. He himself was a model of propriety, sanity and tolerance. He was unique all the same. He was an old-fashioned gentleman as well as a Prelate. He had been at Oscar Browning's House at Eton, had proceeded to Woolwich. Incidentally he commanded the cadets who represented the "Shop" at the funeral of thcir old comrade the Prince Imperial. He left the gunners to become a parson. Very High Church, he decorated the Church of St Ives in Huntington with a Rood and Images. His Oxford friend, the present Lord Salisbury, procured him the pleasant sinecure of the hospital at Ilford where he was able to develop his antiquarian tastes and make prolonged excursions into such conundrums as the Man in the Iron Mask, the actual burial site of St Peter in Rome, and above all Anglican Orders.

He came of an old Anglo-Indian family and remembered as a boy hearing Lord Lawrence (there was once a greater than the Lawrence of Arabia) saying : " Your father saved India by holding Gwalior and the Central States loyal in the Mutiny."

When Leo XIII reluctantly decided against the validity of Anglican Orders, Barnes no less reluctantly resigned his living and went to Rome, where the old Pope received him as the first-fruits of his Pronouncement. Afterwards he became Chaplain to the Catholics at Cambridge and Oxford. On Anglican Orders he was fascinating, for he was an antiquarian not a theologian. His theory was that Archbishop Parker, Queen Elizabeth's Primate, could not have been properly consecrated because Bishop Barlow (from whom he derived) was never a bishop at all. For years Barnes had carried on a detective work amongst documents. He discovered that whenever Barlow was concerned the records, nay the very Rolls of England, had been cut ! Was it possible that Henry VIII secured his supremacy to his conscience and satisfaction by starting a race of bishops who were not bishops—at least in the old Roman Catholic sense ?

Barnes' Paper on Barlow always ended on a humorous

note. Although Bishop Barlow failed to be registered as a Father of the Church like Anselm and Augustine, he became the Father-in-law of the Church of England. Mrs Barlow's three daughters all married bishops !

Barnes' greatest triumph was locating the long-lost body of the Senior Apostle. From old maps he worked out the exact corner where it lay under St. Peter's. This roused the interest of Cardinal Merry del Val, who accompanied him in the dead of night with a single workman. At the spot which Barnes indicated the workman tapped the underground wall and lo it was hollow ! It was his conviction that behind it lay the garden steps leading down to the tomb where the Apostle lay. No one had gazed on that sacred tomb since Charlemagne had descended and laid a silver cross on the tomb. That cross must be still there. With the rebuilding of the new St Peter's the site had been lost and was now rediscovered, but Pius X, informed next morning, would not allow the wall to be broken. Supposing . . . supposing . . . well supposing ? Let us suppose the prudent Pope was right.

Merry del Val, however, made Barnes a Prelate over Cardinal Bourne's head, for the Cardinal disapproved of promotions for converts. Barnes in spite of his gifts was never given a single honour or place of influence by the Archdiocese which he adorned. He had to pour his talents into archæology and his time upon undergraduates. Under his direction we all became amateur archæologists, learning to decipher the past from the least inscription borne by a stone with the same genial ease with which Mr Pickwick once investigated the famous stone marked with strange lettering.

In the churches of the Fenland we discovered maimed pieces of Rood Screens and picked for frescoes with kitchen knives. There are frescoes behind the whitewashes of every old church in England. Meantime Barnes was busy writing his great book on the Fourth Gospel egged on by Collins and myself, for he could be incurably lazy for days and suddenly stand up as straight

as a soldier in his long red-buttoned soutane and write a
whole book off in ten days scarcely sitting down once. In
those days the cloud of so-called Modernism was over-
hanging the Church, and priests who published books did
so at their peril. Pius X in his zeal and literal-mindedness
had started a kind of terror amongst thinking priests.
Pius X shared a certain doctrine with a very strict sect in
the Isle of Wight called " Bible Christians." Methuselah
had to keep all his birthdays and Jonah had to get into
his whale. Barnes' book cut the ground from under the
Cambridge critics, but its interpretations were daring.
Wisely it was never published. To-day it would be
thought obsolete.

Sometimes the grandfather and prophet of Modernism,
Baron Friedrich von Hügel, attended Sunday evenings
at Llandaff House. He was a layman which was the only
possible reason or cause for his not being excommunicated.
Already he had pushed Father Tyrrell off the giddy edge.
It is difficult, quite impossible, logically, to explain why
he was spared and Tyrrell cut down. There was this,
perhaps, to be said : Tyrrell was a Jesuit and had turned
a Jesuit's rapier on the Pope with grinning irony. Von
Hügel was a mystic and attended Holy Communion every
morning of his life, for fear, as Father Benson remarked,
he should return to find his excommunication waiting
with *The Times* on the breakfast table.

Life was never dull at Llandaff House. Father Benson
had started his literary career under Barnes and was now
curate at the Catholic Church down the road. His
double-tomed biography (for he died in 1914) shed little
light on the point which intrigued us most : his sudden
Ordination at Rome. The conversion of a son of an
Archbishop of Canterbury had seemed astonishingly
sensational. Church papers said that his father must
have turned in his grave in the Minster. At Cambridge
the dovecotes were particularly fluttered ; for he began
work as a Catholic curate at the same time that his brother
Arthur came to Magdalene. Within the year Benson had

given an Anglican Retreat at St Giles and returned as a fully fledged Roman priest.

As a rule converts are expected to do a three years' grind before they can be priested. How was it that Benson was let off with nine months ?

According to Llandaff House, Benson and a famous Anglican priest Father " Jane " Evans had presented themselves together to Cardinal Bourne, who was far from encouraging. Although they knew their Theology and had heard Confessions for years they were offered the same treatment as Seminarians.

Father " Jane " Evans was a strong personality and (were the conversion of the Church of England a Papal concern) should have received exceptional treatment. It was the story of Newman over again. As an Anglican Evans had filled St Michael's, Shoreditch, to overflowing. Mass was said, God was served and the Bishop of London defied. When he came over to Rome, his curates and congregation followed to the tune of three hundred souls. Jack Collins had been one of the staunchest adherents of the " Ditch," as it was affectionately called.

Cardinal Bourne, no doubt, had noticed how little obedience Father Evans gave the Bishop of London. Perhaps he drew in the reins too tightly. Evans immediately crossed the river and became a useful member of the rival diocese of Southwark. Hugh Benson was humbler and proceeded to take up his studies in Rome.

The Cardinal was a great and industrious Prelate. His personal goodness was such that no convert was worthy to kiss the hem of his robe. He swayed the destiny of the Catholic Church for a quarter of a century in England. His highest gifts were spiritual rather than intellectual. He carried his policy less by enthusiasm than by a system of unquestioning obedience. Converts were welcome, if they remained laymen, but he was disposed to put obstacles in the way of their ordination. When they did get ordained, he did his best to nullify the careers of such as Fathers Barnes, Benson and Maturin. They were all deeply discouraged till they turned to other channels ; and as for promotion the Cardinal recalled the days when there were two converts on the Bishops' Bench as the Dark Ages !

Benson and Evans arrived together in Rome ; and word of their arrival reached Pius X (I am telling the story as Jack Collins used to tell it). The Pope sent for them and examined them in moral Theology. He was most interested and decided to take a hand himself in the conversion of England. He gave orders that they should be ordained within a year. They returned to their studies and towards the following Easter he inquired whether Benson was already a deacon and was informed that Cardinal Bourne had decided otherwise. Then was Papal comment briefly supplied in the form of a single question : "Who is Pope : myself or the Archbishop of Westminster ? " To this of course the theologians could find only one answer. Benson and Evans were immediately raised to the diaconate and priesthood, critics said by the backstairs, but it was by the backstairs that lead into the Vatican.

Father Evans served in the diocese of Southwark, first in a slum called Melior Street and later in Brighton. As a temperamental Welshman he came to appreciate the Irish and confessed that he had had to change his nationality as much as his religion. He complained of the coldness shown to convert-priests. He supposed somehow that the converts " spoilt the trade," and left it at that. There was an ironical, perhaps providential, result of his going to Southwark. When Cardinal Bourne decided to get Southwark added to Westminster, Evans went to Rome to fight the scheme and helped to bring it to nothing. Churches without rows or rivalries within are liable to stagnation. There was no love lost between the dioceses of Southwark and Westminster. The two Bishops said nothing ; but their coldness to each other became a scandal to the faithful and to everybody's amusement Rome

x

ordered them to shake hands or appear together in public.
It was fortunate they were not both Cardinals or they
would have been required to add a kiss in view of the faithful.   In their way each was a magnificent Bishop.   But
they lived in difficult days.   Each took a different line
on Modernism, on Father Tyrrell (who had retired into
Southwark when he left the Jesuits), on converts and on
the thorniest of all, on the Irish question, which was soon
to desolate and hamper the dioceses of England.

When Benson presented himself as a priest within nine
months, Cardinal Bourne forbade him to preach or exercise
his ministry.   He had been sent for a year to Llandaff
House to study under Barnes and, having nothing else to
do, began writing historical novels which carried his name
farther than his preaching.   Every day he said Mass
privately in the Chapel of Llandaff House and spent the
rest of the day creating characters in the attics.   When he
was allowed to preach, he was an instantaneous success.
Only once did he try a theological sermon and on his
Rector's advice abandoned that line in future.   His
clever, emotional sermons were a success chiefly because
he knew no theology.   A preacher who is always calculat-
ing theology in his mind is like a great orator who is
thinking out mathematics instead of letting himself go.
In spite of a noticeable stammer he made a meteoric flash
in his little day.   No preacher acquired so much of the
broadcast of notoriety with so slender a transmitting set
as Robert Hugh Benson, Priest of the Archdiocese of
Westminster, on whose soul be peace !

Before he left Cambridge, Benson could not help
sketching his friends in his novels.   Jack Collins was the
hero of *None other Gods*, and *The Conventionalists* enshrined
a strange apparition from our midst : Ronald Firbank,
who was an undergraduate at Trinity Hall.   By birth
Firbank should have been a railway manager or con-
tractor.   He was a delicate and precious romanticist.
He was utterly extreme in all his aspects and amusingly
perverse.   In a rowing college like the Hall he resembled

a goldfish at the common fishmonger's. His rooms were beautifully furnished and always redolent of flowers. His slim figure and exquisite mannerisms made him a creature apart. Catholicism was not enough for him, but he must needs be an ecstatic. Benson persuaded him or imposed as a penance sitting in a rowing eight. The iciness of the weather and the heat of the coaches combined nearly to kill him. But he showed pluck and endurance and later chose an unusual profession by joining the Papal Guard. It was amusing to think of Trinity Hall as the training school for a janissary of the Vatican. He wrote a number of orchidaceous books, whose style and texture grew more and more like himself. He was a harmless and pathetic being, and died like a lily which had always been trying to break its window-box.

Another of Benson's pets was the semi-sinister figure of Frederick Rolfe, who had induced publishers and readers to recognise him as Baron Corvo. Few have ever heard of Corvo, but there is an amusing biography by A. J. Symons, which incidentally is the only book that has ever been dedicated to me.

Rolfe hung on the Cambridge horizon thanks to Benson, who took him to his artistic heart.

Rolfe wrote a number of works scarifying to the British *bourgeois*. He believed he was a Borgia reborn, and he wrote the first satisfying whitewash of Alexander the Sixth. He wrote some amusing Italian folk-tales, *In His Own Image*, which Collins lovingly called his " Fifth Gospel." It was as disturbing to the pious Catholic as to the strait-laced Protestant. It was already rare and copies had to be borrowed or stolen. It was, of course, slightly vitiated caviare for the general public, but we revelled in every page.

Rolfe was one of the few evil creatures of his generation. No one ever met him who did not suffer for it. He corrupted and he repented not. He quarrelled and he forgave not. He borrowed and he cursed the lender. He exchanged violent and vivid letters with every friend who ever tried to help him, every publisher who tried to publish him, and every priest trying to save his soul. He was a wandering spirit and he fastened on Benson like a weasel upon a fascinated rabbit. They agreed to write a book on St Thomas of Canterbury together. To Rolfe this meant social as well as financial salvation. The scheme was stopped by Benson's alarmed friends, for Rolfe's repute was lurid. Monsignor Barnes and Arthur Benson effected a rescue in conjunction. But Rolfe never forgot nor forgave. An obscene post card reached Benson morning after morning until Rolfe died pitiably in Venice, as we believed by his own hand. During his researches into the Renaissance he claimed to have rediscovered the secret of the Borgia poison which kills without leaving the suspicion of a trace.

I was as deeply influenced as Hugh Benson by this man's books. Benson went so far as to adopt his beautiful handwriting. Collins and myself endeavoured to copy his style. Anybody who has read with a fresh mind for the first time Rolfe's *Chronicles of the Borgia* or his splendid pontifical novel *Hadrian the Seventh* will know how deep Rolfe's literary influence could go. A great many people still believe that Rolfe was non-existent : a literary myth like " John Inglesant " or "Fiona Macleod."

Poor Monsignor Barnes was overwhelmed by odd company and used to murmur " all converts are mad, hopelessly mad." Jack Collins ran the chaplaincy for him, ordered meals, served Mass and arranged interviews. He quoted equally from Canon Law and from Oscar Wilde's *Philosophy for the Use of the Young*. He loved helping lame dogs or discussing life with tramps. He was as fond of upsetting a Catholic as a Protestant. At this time he decided to launch a new Order of Cranks, who since they could not live with their families or friends might be induced to live with each other, write books, edit a journal and sing the liturgy in common !

Collins then decided to demonstrate to Cambridge how

real theologians proved the Existence of God. The small Guildhall was taken, Masters of colleges were invited to the platform and an able Jesuit, Father Rickaby, was brought down from London. The success of a public meeting depends on the treatment of the hecklers, and in this case we arranged for some startling questions to be asked which Father Rickaby answered with brilliant composure. I sat in the body of the hall with other conspirators who were ordered to look as like to indignant atheists as possible. The growing wonder on the faces of the good Masters, as Father Rickaby wiped out our confident queries, caused us much mirth afterwards. It was a most enjoyable evening.

Though English of the English, Jack Collins adored Continental life and religion. Another scheme was to make the Catholic Church at Cambridge more picturesque and pleasing to God by hiring an old Italian orange-woman to sit on the steps on Sundays selling her fruit under a huge coloured umbrella such as bookies hoist at race meetings.

Like Father Benson he lived life feverishly. Both of them seemed to know that their days on earth were numbered. He was summoned to India where his father had died suddenly of the cholera. While he was in the East he attended native churches. Dusky congregations, who had never worshipped with a white man before, used to rise and bow when he passed down the aisle. He was a curious mixture of democrat and aristocrat. He used to make the words : " Blood will pay," a guiding formula to life. He simply hated the middle class and made himself intimate with paupers. He could not abide policemen because he insisted they had one way with the poor, another with the rich. He pretended to be horrified by Jesuits, whether it was their Baroque style of church building or their theatrical music which offended him. When Father Bernard Vaughan wrote a book called *The Sins of Society* Collins began to compose one called *The Sins of the Society* !

He left Cambridge in order to organise the teaching in a boys' school under the Benedictines in Ireland. At his urgent call I arrived for a week-end and stayed for the rest of the term. Provided he was allowed to follow his bent he could be both industrious and inspiring. I found the school under a great character, Father Francis Sweetman, a pioneer of Sinn Fein, whose ambition was to grow Irish tobacco. While he managed the estates, Collins ran the school He delighted in the Irish boys as they did in him. He taught the entire music and mathematics himself. The English and Classics he passed to my superintendence. His spare time was spent in building a Sacristy, painting images and teaching the upper boys how to make vestments of the real Roman colours. His rubrical sense was continually shocked in Irish churches.

The upper boys were allowed to smoke and play roulette. This was Collins' patent educational system. They soon became tired of both pursuits, which are usually forbidden in schools. There were as few restrictions as possible. Collins never punished a boy, but if one annoyed him overmuch he opened the window, picked the boy up by the collar and dropped him gently on the grass. There were no bounds, and boys who could manage a mount went hunting. They became Irish country gentlemen with a love for the land and a touch of culture. They regarded us as amusing lunatics, but they were obedient and honourable, simply because the orders given were few and they were always placed on their honour. It was an experiment, and though the school did not survive the troubles, it came nearer to producing the *mens sana in corpore sano* than any school I ever came across.

It was the happiest and most successful period in Collins' life. He had spent a year of constraint in the English College at Rome. He was too original to move with the Seminarian swim. His photograph in his Roman cassock rather resembled some beautiful demon. He had come to the unfortunate conclusion that the conversion of England could only be forwarded by the application of gunpowder to all existing Seminaries, which rather distressed the authorities. To this period belongs his invention of a new parlour game for ecclesiastics called " Dioceses," for which I still think a patent would be profitable.

Restless and reckless, he passed from one country to another, trying his vocation and never finding it. He was about to offer himself to the London Oratory when death found him among the Swiss mountains. For those who had known him, the delight and bewilderment of his acquaintanceship, the amusing intimacy of his friendship, the mixture of courage and curiosity with which he winged his life were traits which could never pass from memory. He was one of the three men I met young whose promise seemed to me the most interesting to follow in after life. What would have happened to Jack Collins, Rupert Brooke or Ernest Edghill, had they been spared by the shearing fates, I often stop to wonder. They were the three most original men I met at Cambridge and whom I should most enjoy meeting again.

The East End

*

THE EAST END FILLED A GREATER PLACE IN OUR
thought than in the mind of the present generation.
Slums are now in process of abolition. The hopelessly
impoverished and the bloodily sweated have ceased to
exist. Not so much because Socialists have secured
government as that governments have become Socialist.

At Cambridge there was a school which placed lowly
works and high ritual in the same groove. High Church
clergy were often Christian Socialists. There was no
powerful Labour Party, and the first Socialists were only
just beginning to reach the Houses of Parliament.

Every college at Cambridge except King's maintained
some form of mission in East or Southern London.
The missioners were old college men and made visitors
welcome who came to study the temporal conditions of
the poor or to improve their own spiritual welfare. I
spent an Easter vacation at Cambridge House, a settlement in the Camberwell Road, when it was under Archdeacon Conybeare. During a short visit to Oxford House
in Bethnal Green I met the youthful Dick Sheppard,
afterwards Dean of Canterbury. He was not yet ordained
and was running a boys' club with very little thought of
becoming a national figure. The East End was full of
struggling reformers, self-sacrificing clergy and humble
helpers who devoted their lives or at least their leisure
hours to work in squalid parishes and amongst rather
ungrateful people. The Club work must have borne its
own reward, but the organisers can have enjoyed nothing
except expenditure of time and money and patience.

I believe that it was due to these unknown toilers, mostly in High Church parishes, that there was so little friction between the East and West Ends. Although I lived on and off for two years in slum areas I never heard of class warfare. Socialism seemed an impossible dream and Communism was not heard of. Working-men's constituencies were quite content to return Liberals. My uncle, Murray Guthrie, used to win elections in Bow and Bromley as a Conservative, defeating such a strong popular candidate as George Lansbury. But they were always good friends, and Lansbury once said very kindly to his Tory antagonist : " If there were more like you, there would be less like me." Lansbury had come under the influence of Father Dolling, who had ended his brave days at St Saviour's, Poplar.

In those days any Labour sympathy was fraught with Christianity. The High Church clergy were often practising Socialists. It was not a question of voting, but of living their principles. There seemed a fair chance of a general Christian Front in those far-off days. A great many parishes were enriched by Irish settlements which meant a considerable vote in favour of Catholic and Church schools. Anglican priests like Robert Dolling or Arthur Stanton or Father Wainwright of the London Docks could have always led ten thousand men, so deeply were they loved. To acquire the confidence and love which these priests had won under the most adverse circumstances seemed to us worthy not only of hero-worship, but of our life's devotion.

Perhaps the most important tendency of our time for the social historians to unravel will be to show how the whole Labour movement has passed into secular hands towards Communism, in spite of the many Christian sources by which it was fed in this country. Perhaps it was due to lack of leadership from the Universities and the Public Schools. A Labour Party led by Anglican and Catholic leaders might have fulfilled some of Disraeli's early dreams as revealed in his prophetical books.

After leaving Cambridge I plunged deeply into the human morass. I passed from clergy house to clergy house in the East End between the Tower and Limehouse, and as far as Canning Town. I investigated much of the life which is described in Charles Booth's wonderful survey of London's labour and poverty. I knew Canon Barnett at Toynbee Hall.

I lived awhile in remote Plaistow with the Brethren of the Divine Compassion : a restoration of Franciscan life within the Church of England. Here priests and brothers preserved a severe rule. They wore dark habits and cowls and lived under the poorest circumstances. These were days of real poverty : before the dole, before Old Age Pensions, before all kinds of socialistic relief. The brothers marched with a Crucifix at the head of a great procession of unemployed to the House of Commons. When they slipped over the Bridge to Lambeth, the Archbishop was too nervous to see them ; at least he preferred to send a flunkey. We were not sure which alarmed him more the Crucifix or the Red Flag in the streets. Deans and dignitaries of the Church of England may go red or pink in these days, but the time to have done so was when Labour was as a sheep looking for a shepherd.

The Fathers of the Divine Compassion were the dearest of men, mostly from Oxford : Father Henry, the untidiest of the community, with cowl and bootlaces flying, and Father Andrew, a superb preacher who could really appeal to the men. When I returned from Russia with a message from Tolstoy, we held a meeting ᵥ hich I felt was making East End history. It was the only time I felt an English audience rise to me in the manner of an Irish crowd like a throbbing wave of the sea. It is difficult to say what Tolstoy meant to readers, writers and reformers. He had become the supreme European.

I do not know whether the Church of England produces such types and characters now as then. There were real labourers in the vineyard bidding for the English working men, who seem now far from any church or Christ influence—beyond even the gentle counsels of Tolstoy or even of the Divine Compassion. No Church can recover the working men until the Gospel of St Mark has been substituted for the gospel of Marx.

The Church of England was full of free-lances, who for lack of biography have fallen into oblivion. Father Dolling has survived, thanks to the best ecclesiastical biography written in our day.

There was Father Charles Marson, one of the few parsons of whom Jack Collins continued to approve. Who recalls that delectable character except as Cecil Sharp's fellow-collector of folk-song in Somerset ? Souls also he collected after his manner, which was by saying Mass and " the monkish hours," and performing many acts of startling mercy. Once he found an old gipsy woman dying in a ditch. He took her home to die a few weeks later under his own roof. That somewhat impressed the Protestant labourers of Somerset. Marson had a delicious sense of satire. When he was sent an official application form as issued by the Charity Organisation Society on behalf of some distressed person, he filled it up with the details and circumstances of Our Lord. This Marson was the man whom the Bishop of Hereford once inhibited by telegram !

There was one disquieting problem which met all investigators in great cities. Boys' clubs and men's socials were not sufficient to satisfy the ardour of all. I was much moved by the great number of women who were then living on the London streets. To-day their numbers, their bullies and their miseries are very much less in evidence than they were. Moral problems seem to have shifted in the world. The War smoothed, and certainly altered, many of the relationships between men and women. In many ways the racial good has been improved.

Eugenics, however, is one thing and spiritual issues another. It should not be impossible to reconcile what is best naturally for the race and what is best for the supernatural in the individual. Reformers seldom learn, for it is part of a reformer's constitution to wish to reform anything except himself. Inebriety and prostitution seemed the two evils which were lowering the sum of health and happiness. But they are neither to be abolished " in the absolute," as witness the chaos following the American experiment of Prohibition. One learns that relief from drunkenness does not entirely save the world, and that the abolition of prostitution would not save Society. These things reformers learn gradually. As things stand in this world, a man has some right to conceal his sorrows under conditions of cheerful sub-consciousness. And a woman has a certain right to dispose of her most personal belonging in the oldest open market in the world.

Were women to be pulled off the street whether they wished it or not ? Were men to be made models of sobriety by careful legislation ? If prostitution is to be changed, channeled and eventually abolished, the structure of Society will have to be altered. Modern conditions have changed the background of the profession, but Society still requires that men shall have other outlets besides matrimony. State and Church have compromised with sex by admitting a legalised or sacramental solution of the mutual passions. But for those who cannot keep chaste or afford a bride it seems unfair and unsocial that they should be deprived of that relief for which the huge majority of male creation will always groan. Hence the State, every State, admits prostitution with various salutary checks or concealing hypocrisies.

The individual is sacrificed to the good of the whole. The State might boil over should it be deprived of such an outlet. St Augustine said : " *Aufer meretrices* : take away the harlots and the State will collapse into confusion." Individual reformers will always work for the sake of individuals. But escape for the woman from the streets is not easy. The best that can be achieved is to make it possible for every prostitute to enter a home or asylum if she wills. It is rare, very rare, that a prostitute can close her career in marriage or Magdalenhood. The majority of them do not wish, and, even if they wish, they cannot change a profession different from every other profession in that the adepts begin without climbing at the top and slowly proceed by descending to the depths.

For sentimentalists to interfere is not wrong, but it will lead to loss of time and money. There is really no general wish nor public encouragement to put an end to prostitution. The man-power of the cities is against it. The Churches are sheepish about it and take the line of " What ye sow that shall ye reap." A minute number of women are herded into institutions where some at least find themselves " white slaves " for the first time. A few very devoted, very perfect women have been able to lift their penitents back to womanhood. That is the most that can be expected in countries where supply is free to meet the demand. Only a disciplined and absolutist State could ever deal with prostitution. The whole situation in England was certainly a discouraging quagmire. The discipline of the War introduced some laws of sanitation. The evolution of morals in the upper and middle classes, assisted since by cheap motor transit and a knowledge of birth control, has relieved the pressure on the poorer or shop-girl class. Moralists must judge whether this is an improvement. Certainly it is a change. " White slaves " have been replaced by social volunteers.

Prostitution is no longer so flagrant as it was. During the Victorian era it always struck and drew the attention of men desirous of building up a better State. How many public men have once tried to act privately before they recognised that they were struggling against a " hydra-headed wrong." Lord Llandaff told us that as a young man he had done his utmost to rescue women who were on the Euston Road, a famous beat only secondary to Regent Street and Piccadilly, all of which thoroughfares may be traversed by ladies at night without fear of molestation to-day. But I remember the Victorian play-goers picking up their skirts and passing with horror through the bedizened crowd. Both the devout and the cynical agree that Heaven will be full of prostitutes.

My uncle, Edward Hope, gave me an interesting light on the Grand Old Man which would explain a controverted side to his character. Mr Gladstone took a great and laudable interest in " fallen " women. (Father Paul Bull of Mirfield used to ask why we never hear about " fallen " men.) No doubt Mr Gladstone often worried his detectives and encouraged blackmailers. He told his friend Hope-Scott that on leaving Oxford he made a social vow that he would always offer help to any woman who happened to solicit him. This vow he kept through thick and thin, with the help of Mrs Gladstone. So Hope-Scott told my uncle.

Edward Hope survived to be Disraeli's last appointment in the Civil Service. He had two interesting connections with Catholicism. His uncle, Hope-Scott, was received into the Church side by side with Archdeacon Manning. This parted him for life from Gladstone who had been his best friend. When Hope-Scott lay dying in Surrey House (where the Regal Cinema now stands) Gladstone visited him and they talked so long and privately that Hope-Scott inquired afterwards if anyone had been secreted behind the screen. Edward Hope, whose brother became a priest and joined the Oblates of St Charles, had a share in arranging Hope-Scott's funeral at Farm Street. It was the last occasion that Cardinals Newman and Manning met. It was kept quiet that Newman would deliver the eulogy. Lord Rosebery never forgave my uncle for not giving him a hint whereby he might have heard Newman's voice.

Mention of Gladstone's rescue work was made in his " Life " and it explained an attack which was subsequently made on his morals in print and which was repelled in the courts. No Englishman is ashamed of his wild oats, but he would die rather than confess any inclination to rescue the perishing. Yet I have known many who have held out a hand of pity and charity to the woman which is in our streets.

We certainly followed the terms of Mr Gladstone's vow and questioned those who spoke first. Would they like to

go to their homes ? Would a railway ticket be serviceable ? A certain number whom I questioned proved to
be Irish and Catholic, and these could always be safely
passed to the nuns. But trying to keep a whitewashed
harlot is like keeping a white elephant. The attempt to
turn them into domestic servants is disastrous. Jack
Collins had tried doing so to his mother's despair. As
soon as their past leaked out, every other servant promptly
left the house !

We ran foolish risks and sometimes courted the most
ludicrous situations. A young lady once confessed to me
under inebriation that she was Irish and had a sailor
husband in Dublin. I arranged she should stay in a
convent under a Reverend Mother. Unfortunately,
during a long and difficult journey in a four-wheeler, she
became hysterical and I had to join the cabby on the
box. The cabby was Irish and we both said the Rosary
till we landed our pretty little fish. How amused the
Reverend Mother was !

I remember once strolling down Regent Street, as it
was in the old days, with a rowing friend who sported the
Light Blue ribbon round his hat. No doubt we looked an
easy prey and had some difficulty in getting down the
street. We were accosted by a party of girls who included
a perfect type of " England, home and beauty." We took
her aside and learnt that this was the first evening she
had ever dared amuse herself on the street. We fastened
her arm-in-arm and marched her off. We took her to her
home where we left her half in tears and half in smiles.
We gave her some gold and a severe warning. I never
saw or heard of her again. I hope she is now a respectable
grandmother. She is possibly the wife of a Member of
Parliament by now. I think she was lucky to meet us.

As soon as one's intentions were discovered to be
honourable, blackmail was inevitable from the lady's
friends. Presence of mind was sometimes necessary.
During the scare caused by " Jack the Ripper," whose
attentions were entirely devoted to ladies of the street,
the streets were naturally rather empty. A gentleman

was accosted in Berkeley Square by a lady who threatened to inform the police that he was " Jack the Ripper " if he did not furnish cash. " But I am ' Jack the Ripper,' " he answered in a flash and she fled squealing for her life.

There is always an effective riposte in the tight corners of life if one can think of it in time. A friend of mine, a famous American playwright, was crossing Paris as a young man. A seedy pimp showed him the photograph of a bedizened frump and asked in polite French : " Do you require a virgin, sir ? " My friend drew himself up and proudly answered, " I am one, sir." The Frenchman was too astonished to continue the interview. It was certainly a neat way out.

My happiest memories with the East End are associated with a settlement of Cambridge men at the pierhead in the Isle of Wapping.

Wapping lies a mile beyond the Tower of London and is cut off by three swing bridges and enormous docks from the mainland. It is circled by St George's in the East, the once infamous Ratcliff Highway and Stepney. It is bordered by ghettoes and alien colonies. Wapping was inhabited by an Irish villageful and the parishioners of St. Peter's London Docks : the field of labour of Father Lowder and Father Wainwright. It was famous as the first invasion by the High Church into the slums, and the word " Puseyite " was curiously enough still used there as a living word of reproach.

I had been living for a year in the Irish colony when Rothay and Leslie Reynolds joined me in a house jutting from pierhead over the river. Here we set up company together with Torben de Bille, son of the Danish Minister. It was a well-built house with stone flag approaches and a frontage to the ever-lively river. It adjoined the Wapping Old Stairs where sea-pirates used to be hanged, and the public-house called " The Town of Ramsgate."

From this agreeable river resort we managed boys' clubs on both sides of the river : Leslie Reynolds was the backbone of the Fisher Club at Bermondsey, and Rothay Reynolds the guardian of St Patrick's. We were pioneers,

and the youth of both parishes rose to us.   In a picturesque
and quiet old house we lived with the utmost content.
So far from inhabiting a slum we were always within a
breeze and in sight of the ever-living river.   Tower
Bridge towered up-stream like the Gates of Hercules.
Lights, ships and steamers made the evenings fascinating.
Sometimes a full-rigged ship for the Orient passed within
a biscuit's throw of our bedroom windows after emerging
from the docks behind.

The Settlement spread like wildfire and the house rapidly
was filled.   Bertrand Devas, son of the eminent economist,
arrived and became a leading spirit.   His character combined charity, manliness and a certain piquancy.   He
filled us with admiration for the Jesuit education, if
indeed he was their type and not a special flower.

There came Mr Aston, a Fellow of Downing College,
who had been received into the Church in the presence
of his Presbyterian minister, such was the tolerance of
thought at Cambridge.

There came the most amusing of our characters, Woulfe
Flanagan, known as " the Admiral," if for no other reason
than that he floated a barge upon the Thames.   He used to
proceed by water from his lodgings at Wapping to the
steps at Cleopatra's Needle in order to read the papers
at the Reform Club.   The barge was rowed by ten boys,
and " the Admiral " used to cause a sensation in his
club when the porter used to announce in a loud voice :
" Your barge is waiting for you at Cleopatra's steps, sir ! "

There was a constant coming and going.   University
men came for week-ends and stayed for months.   Ralph
Wigram used to come.   He had a brilliant career at the
Foreign Office until his death in 1936.   Before we knew
what had happened we had become an institution and a
real Catholic settlement was a reality.   This did not prevent other churches adding valued friends and members.
In the summer life became peculiarly delightful.   Sunset
was like a daily Turner canvas displayed upon the reaches
of the river.

Bertrand Devas and myself were drawn into the

Y

Catholic Boys' Brigade at Bermondsey. This Brigade
was due to the untiring perseverance of Father Segesser
and Brigadier Bradish and made a big feature of the
Southwark diocese. Every summer a big military camp
was staged for the boys near Effingham, thanks to the
generosity of George Pauling, a retired and devout con-
tractor with a fund of amusing stories from South Africa.
We had our difficulties as there was a strong feeling
amongst the Irish against any militarism or encouragement to recruit. We could not prevent many of our boys
from passing into the Old Army and astonishing the ser-
geants by their knowledge of drill. Boys' camps on our
scale could not be run without military order and gentlemen officers. The Mess was composed of chaplains and
young professional men interested in social work. We wore
uniform and marched behind drums and fifes through the
Surrey hills. It was a healthy holiday, and we obtained a
strong influence over scores of fine boys who would have
had little else to hold them to Church and discipline.
At the end of the week we were inspected by a fine old
Crimean veteran, old Sir Luke O'Connor, who had
actually been in the first batch to win the Victoria Cross.
The War, of course, made great rents in our ranks and the
Brigade itself has ceased to exist. Thirty years have
passed, but I look back upon our marches, camps, meals
and tent-life as part of the pre-War dream.

Few survive from those days. Father Segesser and
Brigadier Bradish rest in peace. Scores of our dear boys
lie in France. Aston, Devas and Gunnis were killed with
them. Leslie Reynolds went to Rome to study for the
priesthood and died all too young at the Beda.

Torben de Bille was recently killed in a motor accident.
Although he had been partially blinded as a boy he
always insisted on taking a full share in our life. He lived
in Wapping. He kept up his study and reading through
secretaries. He attended diplomatic receptions in Mayfair
when not engaged in the East End. It is true that he
once went to Lansdowne House and inadvertently sat
down on the hostess whom he had mistaken for a sofa !

But he was full of pluck and charity and courage. He could be seen feeling his way across the most dangerous crossings in London. He resented being assisted while walking, and it was only possible to take his arm by pretending to enforce some argument, for he was ready for discussion at any time and in any place. With his tall aristocratic bearing and short-sightedness he seemed the most unsuitable person to work in an East End club. But the boys took a tremendous fancy to him, and I can see him sitting at the receipt of custom on a Saturday evening. Though he could barely see, much less count their pennies, the boys were scrupulous in their honesty, and money was safer on the club table than in many a patrician hall. The club was run on trust. The boys paid their subscriptions and we paid the rent and rates and gas. In this way they came to consider the club their own and made the best of it. Living in the East End we had all reached sensible views about the so-called rich and poor. We were delighted with any visitor provided he had not come down " to do good." This we considered a hateful and Pharisaic phrase. It seemed unnecessary for people to descend upon the slums either to discover how the poor lived or to show them how the rich managed to exist ! There was something quaint and shrewd in the comment of a genuine slum-dweller : " I know the rich have their troubles : they trouble about the poor ! "

Jack Collins was not interested in the East End. He was still in search of his vocation, but he never found his abiding spiritual home. I accompanied him on a visit to Father Kenelm Vaughan, who had founded the newest and most austere Order in the Church, the Order of the Divine Expiation.

The public has heard of Cardinal Vaughan and Father Bernard Vaughan, but the name of their saintly brother Kenelm is unknown. He was a tremendous character such as only Collins would find amid the green hills of Hertfordshire. But Kenelm had had a life of astonishing adventures. He had travelled through South America distributing Spanish New Testaments to the poor and collecting money from the rich for Westminster Cathedral. Some of his stories were blood-curdling. Others were frankly miraculous. For instance, he had been present at a multiplication of the Host amongst a devout community of Indians. He had landed on an island where a desecrated chapel had proved too haunted and too possessed for service to be possible.

With his cloaked figure and glittering eyes he was like some ancient mariner. His pathetic simplicity disarmed every critic. He had founded this work of Expiation, which had received the blessings of popes and cardinals, but very few disciples. His ideas were too fantastic, certainly for the English climate, and the most eager novices seldom stayed longer than a week. He seemed to have drifted out of the Middle Ages. He was a mixture of a Troubadour of Our Lady, George Borrow and the Prophet Jeremiah. In the end the authorities sent him as parish priest to Hatfield where Collins and myself stayed as long as enthusiasm could overcome starvation. But we were deeply edified and wildly amused.

He lived in ecclesiastical squalor and ecstatic poverty in a cheap villa at Hatfield. His dwelling I could not describe with hopes of being believed, but unexpectedly I once lighted on a perfect description of " Anathoth " as it was called in a book called *A Papal Chamberlain*, by an American named MacNutt.

He wrote : " Another day I went to Anathoth. Upon entering that house, had I come across it unprepared, in Tibet or Patagonia, I should have instantly known that it was Father Kenelm's dwelling-place : it could have been created and inhabited by none other. Over the door was the symbolic TAU of carved wood and a text from the Prophet Jeremiah. I recognised a number of the well-known religious paintings of the Latin-American school. The same litter and confusion amidst which my old friend habitually lived was everywhere visible. The walls of Father Kenelm's room were painted black and over the coffin, in which he slept, stood a statue of Jeremiah weeping over Jerusalem, the only other furniture being a crucifix above a prie-dieu, an immense deal table and two austere chairs."

We had no papers nor literature save " the words of Jeremiah, the son of Hilkiah, of the priests that were in Anathoth in the land of Benjamin."

There was a third and famous chair, in which nobody was allowed to sit, for it had belonged to a saint, the Curé d'Ars. The whole house was a blend of Spanish sacristy and old curiosity shop. Over the stairs was a life-size crucifix from which hung long black human hair : some penitent woman's offering. In the chapel was an altar composed entirely of chips and fragments from all the ruined abbeys and desecrated cathedrals of England. Most of the stones had been easy to collect, but he must have had difficulty in prising off fragments from Westminster Abbey and York Minister without interference from the vergers. While I was residing at " Anathoth " he learnt that Lord Salisbury's stables formed part of a desecrated building, and we sallied forth to Hatfield to steal a chip. The coachman turned out to be Irish and we had no difficulty in extracting a relic. One of Father Kenelm's theories was that all the families which had grown up on the spoils of the monasteries would lose their heritage before the second millennium. He used to take us to see Queen Elizabeth's oak in Hatfield Park, which fine old stump he used to curse solemnly every time he passed. This was strange in so gentle a man and he added triumphantly : " And there's not a leaf left on it this year ! "

He kept a beautiful plant from South America, the night-flowering cactus (*Cereus grandiflorus*), in which he found a symbol of his life and of the penitentiary work he was striving to found. His devotions were hard and were based on Scripture. For instance, the Prophet Jeremiah had sat and wailed in a pit. This could only be imitated very incongruously in a suburban garden. The garden itself was kept in a state of deplorable ruin in order to symbolise the spiritual desolation of England. One of the rules of his Order was the performance of a daily good

deed of Expiation. One night we found he had said the
whole Office of the day a second time on behalf of priests
who had said it carelessly that day ! The dish at meals
was served with fragments of several preceding meals in
a heap. One Sunday we were served with eggs as a
treat. " For my day's penance I give you my egg,"
said Father Kenelm to me, and I can only add that I
for my penance ate it ! The famous " Curate's egg "
must have possessed a fragrant freshness in comparison !
Poor old Kenelm—the authorities were as puzzled as
ever what to do with a man who acted as though all values
in the world were reversed. He was the only Englishman
who ever obtained a reputation for sanctity in the utter-
most parts of Latin-America. No doubt he was worthy to
kneel at the tomb of St Rose of Lima. His life in England
seemed wasted and rather ludicrous, but he foretold many
sorrows and disasters to Society unless expiation and
penance were performed by the elect. He died before
the outbreak of the War, but I often think that, like Pius
the Tenth, he apprehended something that was coming.

A very different priest I met through Lord Halifax
in Father Forster, the Chaplain to the Irish Guards and
priest-in-charge of St Edward's, Westminster. He was
a gentleman of the old school, hating cant and advertisement. Lord Roberts had a deep friendship for him.
Courageous, old-fashioned and transparently honest he
said what he thought. For instance, he thought Anglican
Orders valid. The public never heard his name, but as
the Royal residences lay in his parish, he had become a
friend of King Edward VII, whom, it was supposed, he
had received at the last into the Catholic fold. How he
laughed when we charged him, but he admitted that in
old days whenever King Edward had Catholic guests at
Marlborough House he was invited to bring them the
Sacrament. On such occasions the Prince and Princess
of Wales, as they were, always met him at the door and
conducted him upstairs with lighted tapers to the bedside
of their orthodox guest. The Sacrament administered,
they led him back again without a word.

Ireland

*

LIVING IN IRELAND, ONE MUST FACE SOONER OR LATER the Irish Sphinx. Her riddle can never be answered : the why and wherefore of Ireland. The vague beauty of "the gentle maiden Eire" has launched a thousand ballads, shattered many illusions and broken the careers of all who have been lured into her strife. Failure in her cause was always worth more than success beyond seas.

The ablest and the wisest have steadily left the country for the last two hundred and fifty years. As Standish O'Grady used to say : they have passed into the aristocracies of Europe and achieved the democracies of America.

At home the politics of the past and the prejudices of the dead remain like the dregs of the tide. I was born and came into political apprehension (which in Ireland is a sort of fifth sense) during the era of Parnell. By the time I was a schoolboy he was dead, leaving Ireland like Gaul "*in tres partes divisa.*" There were Parnellites and anti-Parnellites and the Ulster Unionists.

Parnell has been forgotten or at least decently embalmed in phrases in Ireland, but the world has been deeply awakened to his romantic possibilities. Stage and screen have carried him down the present age. His predecessors, O'Connell and Isaac Butt, his successors, Justin McCarthy and John Redmond, are not remembered by as much as a ballad to-day. A man who sacrifices his pleasures to duty has done nobly, but is not memorable. The few men in history who have sacrificed their position and their country for a woman are part of the romantic heritage of

343

mankind. There was Antony and there was Parnell, and who else ? The Party which betrayed Parnell could never hoist full sail again, and when they went on the rocks they sank amid bitter wrath from their own country. Meantime, there was a decade of quiet confusion and fratricidal reproach. Ulster rested on her immovable righteousness.

With the new century I learnt to love the South. My uncle Moreton had inherited the beautiful estate of Innishannon in County Cork, and I spent the Easter of 1900 and 1901 in a relaxing sub-tropical country compared to our cold and dour North. Moreton's father had acquired the Adderley property on unpaid loans. He had been Member for Athlone without stepping foot in Ireland, and had left Innishannon to his son Richard, an intrepid explorer in South Africa and North America who unluckily left no diaries or records of his exploits. Moreton as his heir had sold the reversion of the estate for a trifling thousand. Fortunately it was picked up by his American mother-in-law, and when Richard was drowned at sea it came back to the original heir. Richard was one of the many explorers who have been supposed to have earned their fate from tampering with mummies. Certainly he had unwound an Egyptian Princess at endless length of wrapping. As a result of the mummy's curse he had been swept away by the waters, and the place of his body had never been found. So we believed. My aunt found the house at Innishannon full of mummy-heads which she had interred with Christian burial. We unburied them later and presented the less decayed specimens to the Eton Museum. But the curse by fire and water worked out and the house was burnt in the later troubles.

Meantime, Innishannon became my second Irish home. We tore away from Eton to catch the Fishguard boat to Cork. There was a light railway running down the Bandon valley. We generally missed the connection and drove on a jaunting car the sixteen miles. At the head of the village was a small house with tree-ferns growing in the conservatory. Under the high wooded banks flowed the Bandon River on its way to the Old Head of Kinsale. There was a beautiful six-arched stone bridge, hanging with ivy, under which the dipper built his nest, while great salmon proceeded through foaming shallows to the pools upstream.

Uncle Moreton was a man of many roles and dreams. In Sussex he was a squire, in Washington a currency expert, in India a financier, in Australia a mine-owner, but everywhere a naturalist. His splendid optimism persuaded him and his friends that Ireland only needed a magic key to open the door to prosperity. His bunch of keys was a big one. At one time he played with a machine for turning Irish bogs into the essence of fuel. At another he was anxious to fill Ireland's waters, stagnant and running, with the stock of Europe's fish supply. He began by introducing the rainbow trout into the Bandon River. He built fish hatcheries below the bridge, and the trout attained large proportions on an expensive diet of minced liver. Expeditions were made to the Old Head of Kinsale to reduce Ireland's population of cormorants. Moreton could pull himself to the top of a beech tree with his walking stick to dislodge a fish-mongering heron from its nest. Sometimes the county roads were full of water-carts carrying young fish to stock the neighbouring ponds and rivers. Unfortunately the rainbow trout turned out to be the only fish which commits suicide : at least they went to sea or to mud or to the vermin. We sent ten thousand of them swimming into Lough Derg in Donegal, but never was one seen again. The rainbow may be a game fish, but he hardly plays the game after all the trouble devoted to his culture.

The opposite hill-side was devoted to rearing a new game bird for Ireland : the Virginian quail. Hampers of this pretty bird arrived cheeping from America and were entrusted to Stenning, the invaluable keeper. No doubt they would have survived had they been protected in aviaries, but the Irish hawks proved relentless. I can see Moreton and Stenning anxiously watching, with guns in hand, while on the bridge stood the two most beautiful girls in the South of Ireland, Clare Frewen (Sheridan) and Gladys Payne (now Mrs Gordon). I am sure nothing more lovely has crossed the bridge since.

The County was known to us from Blarney Stone to Bandon Bridge : scores of houses which have perished since in the flames. With Lord Bandon in the chair, Moreton lectured the gentry of Cork on the finances of their country. He proved the over-taxation of Ireland to the hilt. He was convinced of the economic justice of Home Rule. In his sanguine manner he could persuade doubting landlords that they would be the first to be returned to a National Parliament by their grateful tenantries. It was already a time of transition, and with Lord Dunraven and William O'Brien for company, Moreton plunged into a new Party. Then came the dazzling moment of the election of 1909, when he was returned as Member of North-east Cork to the House of Commons.

William O'Brien was the first Irish patriot that I met. He was a genial and bearded prophet, an Irish politician without guile. His opponents called him the " Mad Mullah," but I preferred to think of him as a Quixote. At different times he gave up everything for Ireland, for Parnell and for his own private Party.

There was a growing feeling in the South towards a handshake, and already landlords, thanks to George Wyndham's noble legislation, were welcome in the Nationalist ranks. All this waving of the olive branch was cruelly reversed during the Great War, thanks to the fatuous and fatal policy of the English Government. But Cork was a happy and glorious corner of Ireland. Who remembers the Cork Park Races at Easter in 1900, when Uncle Moreton explained to us children the ethics of horse-racing ? Needless to say that at Melton Mowbray he had been a great rider and possessed the second best hands in England. There was a buoyancy about Cork

which made the Irish future seem simple. Uncle Moreton
only asked the voters to follow his ideas and the landlords
to follow William O'Brien. There were to be rainbow
trout in every river and paper money based on a silver
currency in every bank. Electric energy and fuel were
to rise out of the bogs, while poverty and sorrow were to
flee away.

I lost sight of William O'Brien after those days. The
poor old man lived to see Cork and his beloved Mallow
burnt out by the soldiery. As for Innishannon, the house
is a blackened ruin. My aunt's rose gardens offer herbage
to the donkey, and my uncle's fish hatcheries are a dwelling
for the frog and the water-hen. Stenning the Keeper lies
in the graveyard, shot by some poacher, no doubt, for he
believed, poor fellow, that my uncle's politics made him
immune from the Sinn Fein. Bandon Castle, the scene of
much hospitality, was burnt and the Cork County Club
must be thronged with shadows of an evening. The
rainbow which cheated those far-off days passed into a
mist of fire and blood. Nevertheless, those who saw
provincial Ireland in that time glimpsed the life of the
eighteenth century.

The only house still standing is that of the Paynes of
Garryhanky. They were related to the Sheares brothers
who had been executed as patriots in 1798, and their
descendants were spared in consequence a century later.
James Payne was Moreton's agent. As children we ragged
him, but now that he is dead, his ghost has been reported
as a constant revisitant to his home. The happy and
contented life can lead to haunting as much as an event
of tragedy and Irish ghosts spring from both.

Passing through Dublin on my way from Cambridge
I used to stay with some of the intellectual growths of
that eighteenth-century city : with Professor Mahaffy
at Howth or Standish O'Grady in Sandymount. Mahaffy
gave me a tome of Euripides with his comments, while
O'Grady introduced me to Elizabethan Ireland, a period

he knew as though he had lived in it. He used to describe the umbrella as " an unheroic weapon," and evening clothes as the dress of a " Hanoverian waiter." I promptly discarded both. But his Irish Saga awoke every writing man in Ireland. It was O'Grady who put Deirdre and Cuchulain back on the map. He edited the *New Ireland Review* single-handed, paying the expenses by colloguing advertisements out of Dublin tradesmen. He answered private correspondence by simply publishing it in his columns. He had an agrarian gospel which he called the war between *Bos* and *Homo :* in other words, Ireland was being smothered under the green grass of grazing. Men could only be supported by tillage. It has taken a revolution to prove that he was right.

Standish O'Grady looked the aristocratic squire to perfection in his Irish frieze and his highly accented views. Rugged of humour and insistent in his ideals he was loved and tolerated in Dublin, but he had no following. During a bitter political age he had believed that Ireland had a heroic past, when gods and supermen contended amongst her hills and upon her plains as once in the land of Troy. He combined the knowledge of geography and legend which is such an attractive means of learning either. He taught me to take the sea-road right round Ireland as the realisation of all Irish history. I think he was the best and biggest-souled Irishman I ever met. The last time I saw him I left my travelling rug under his hospitable roof. He wrote me one of his epical letters to say that he was keeping it as a hostage for my return. As it happened I never returned, and I heard that after the troubles the dear old man retired to die broken-hearted in the Isle of Wight.

The prophets and poets were sounding like voices in the wind. I met most of them, but the Home Rule controversy hushed whatever of beauty or philosophy they had to say. I suddenly realised the sweetness and pathos of Irish literature when I met with Douglas Hyde's *Love Songs of Connaught.* The Gaelic speech was perishing with all its wealth of folklore. When it seemed

at its last gasp the tide was checked and has been made
to run since in the other direction. The children of Eire
are now bi-lingual. Whether Irish will become the
language of the forum and the market none can prophesy.
At present a little Irish and less English is the characteristic of the new culture. On the other hand anybody
possessing two languages has the mental advantages of
using a two-barrelled gun. If the philology has proved
difficult, the sense that there was and is an Irish language
has supplied a tonic of pride. Irish has warmed the
children's wits better than any dead Latin or feeble
French or guttural German. Gaelic facility seemed lost
to the political generation. Once an Irish statesman was
called upon abroad for an Irish speech. He rapidly recited
the Lord's Prayer three times in succession. The sacred
syllables formed his entire knowledge of the language.

Dublin was full of men working out their dreams.
Douglas Hyde alone has lived to see his dream raised to
triumph. I can recall him on platforms of the Gaelic
League driving into delighted but bewildered audiences the
first sounds they had ever heard of their ancestral speech,
while magnificent in the background stood Lord
Ashbourne, " the Gilly-Bride," in his saffron kilts, refusing
to speak a syllable of English and pouring forth his
enthusiasm in French or Irish. In these days Charles
Gatty founded the Irish Art Companions and opened a
shop which sold only Irish wares. As a joke an Irish notice
was posted to say that English was spoken! The Irish
revival was even patronised by George Moore.

I used to breakfast with George Moore in Ely Place
after landing from the steamer. That house of pagan
pilgrimage and its slightly Olympian occupant have been
described by many pens. He was kind enough when I
called, turning from his manuscript in his shirt-sleeves to
belaud or vilify other writers. It was always a brilliant
outpouring, but he found my views reactionary, and when
he offered to influence me and teach me something of his
impeccable English style, I foolishly turned aside, and

more than twenty years passed before we met again. He had been a friend of the family in old Paris days and used to send my mother proof-sheets which she dropped in the waste-paper basket.

He came once to Glaslough, where he aroused mild indignation amongst the pheasant-shooters by appearing in a billycock hat. He showed a talkative interest in the day's sport, and inquired the name of a rather curious bird which he had seen skulking under the laurels. It turned out to have been a fine specimen of the hen pheasant.

He took me severely to task on the wearisome Catholic controversy. He maintained that Protestantism was the background of literature, and that the Council of Trent was destructive of style. I only ventured to correct him once with a suggestion. He was telling his oft-told story of hiding behind the screen while his father was talking confidentially with Archbishop MacHale. The Archbishop was saying : " Depend upon it, if it had not been for Paul we should not have anything to-day . . . " when approaching steps cut short this frank discussion on early Christianity. In other words it was St Paul who founded the Christian religion. Moore seemed genuinely annoyed when I suggested that they were discussing the University question, and that MacHale was referring to Paul Cullen, Archbishop of Dublin.

In later years I wrote some foolish epigram about Moore which my publisher refused to print unless it was referred to Moore himself. His reply was typical : " I don't care what you call me as long as you don't call me a Catholic." That was presumably the only insult he could not swallow.

There was a really strange story about Moore on a shooting party. He once remarked casually : " We know more than we know and I know young B—— will shoot me." His word proved true, for when he left his place among the guns and wandered into the woods he was peppered by B—— aforesaid.

His father had been one of Ireland's finest amateur riders, and Moore felt that as his father's son he should show courage in the hunting-field. Charles Hunter mounted him, and though he was badly kicked over the knee, he continued to follow the hunt. On his return his boot was found full of blood, but he never winced.

Everybody in Dublin told stories about him, but he told them best of all. I remember a ridiculous one he told of hearing of the death of Robbie Ross and mistaking the name for Gosse. Now Gosse was a flattering critic, and Moore walked up and down bewailing his loss and showing every sign of literary grief. At the end of the performance he was informed that it was Ross, not Gosse, and he was mourning the wrong man. He promptly said : " No— I can't go through it all again for Ross," and returned to his work.

Gosse paid Glaslough a visit. I was interested to find from his conversation that Swinburne and Cuchulain had the same three colours in their hair : golden, reddish gold and red. To Gosse I owe the delightful afternoon of a Derby Day spent on the terrace of the House of Lords to meet Andrew Lang and Austin Dobson.

It is strange how literary values chop and change. Who would have believed in 1900 that George Moore would be blithely afloat forty years later while George Meredith would have sunk under the weight of his own bullion ? In Dublin Moore had been spitefully classed with the " Old Moore " who wrote almanacs, but he returned to become the literary rage of Ebury Street. His gifts were powerful : the industrious choice of the right word and the agreeable swaying of his sentences. He was born without style or heart (a writer's two necessities). He found himself a style in the cafés of Paris, whence he used to write letters which would have marked an illiterate housemaid. A heart he never grew, not even to replace the conscience he had dismissed so angrily. He wished to become a British Zola, but he became an Irish Goncourt. Without heart or conscience he could catch the raw details of life. He attended the funeral of a child unknown to him simply to observe the mother's grief, as his hostess angrily discovered. He was more anxious to tell than to kiss. The kisses of his adolescence seem to have been mythical. Naturally he hated having so little to his moral discredit, but he was lacking in what Irish moralists call the " stuff of sin." At most he was a fiery sheep, but he never really troubled a ewe.

He protested against the prudery in Irish libraries and against every form of Irish celibacy from the ox to the priest. But his rage on that point was subconsciously directed against himself. Smooth and industrious, he was fated to go down the literary furrow like an ox himself. He never begot a character, but he respun the characters he met in life or the tales he had read in the past until his tapestry was reckoned the best in his time. Not in vain were the laborious years he spent correcting the punctuation of his youth. He began his writing with a slug's track, but he passed out upon the song of a swan. No doubt he suffered the last infirmity of great writers and imitated himself endlessly. Perhaps rising young writers need not do better. If he is remembered by 1950 it will be by his style alone.

I never met a Victorian writer of the first class. Uncle Moreton afforded us a mild approach to Kipling who had admired him immensely in India. Perhaps I may quote a letter Kipling wrote to me about Moreton :

" He lived in every sense except what is called common sense, very richly and widely, to his own extreme content. If he had ever reached the golden crock of his dreams, he would have perished. Later on when you have explained how wrong his Bimetallism was, you may see wisdom justified of her amazing child in this particular. Also, which does not count for much now, of course he was wholly a Sahib."

Henry James was another neighbour of Uncle Moreton's

in Sussex. I might have met Meredith or peeped at
Swinburne, but I must be content with what I did see
and hear of great authors : Henry James abusing George
Moore and George Moore abusing Hardy. Moore again
and again called Hardy " the abortion of George Eliot."
Henry James, having met George Moore, gave as his
considered opinion : " I found him consecutively,
consistently and unimportantly foolish."

He was not always as foolish as that. I never heard him
talk without interesting the company. The last time that
we met we talked on ghosts. Utterly he disbelieved in all
the spirit world. He required a sign : nothing less than
the appearance of his father. That he admitted would
change the world for him and the next.

George Moore cast off his country and his religion,
betrayed friends and Faith, but to his art he remained
serenely true, and for that he may be forgiven. When an
Irishman ceases to believe in ghosts it is a sign that he has
put his Irishry from him.

No chapter about Ireland should be unhaunted by some
ghostly memory. I have always loved ghosts and ghost
stories as a distraction, an escape ; even as a side key to
the enigma of life.

I heard several ghost stories from old Dr Campbell Hall,
the best of the old Irish county doctors. His predecessor,
Surgeon Andy Young, had dreamt in Dublin that he saw
a man called Garland murdered at the gates of Bessmount
two miles out of Monaghan. He returned by coach,
and when told of the murder, replied : " I know all
about it." He knew where the body lay, and on his
private hint the police arrested the murderer.

Dr Hall had a strange story about Ballinode Rectory.
A previous rector had killed himself after an unlucky
love-affair. A lady in Dublin had accepted him on
condition that he rebuilt his Rectory, which he had
faithfully accomplished. She then refused him and he
committed suicide, leaving the Rectory cursed. Dr Hall
attended the wife of Mr Weir, the new rector. After he

z

had successfully delivered the child, he heard the woman
at the lodge mutter : " That will be no good, for when
there's a birth at the Rectory there'll be a death in the
year." This was the curse, and had always been fulfilled.
Very anxiously Mr and Mrs Weir counted the days until
the year was out. On the last night when they seemed
clear of danger, the Weirs gave a feast. At ten o'clock
the same night Dr Hall was summoned and found
Mr Weir had fallen down some stone stairs and broken his
neck. The curse had beaten the clock by a few hours.

The most vivid of his stories concerned a dour farmer
who lived with a hatchet-faced sister near Castleshane.
A very pretty girl in the neighbourhood had been sold
into marriage with him to the distress of all the young
men courting her. The young wife was reduced to slavery
by the avaricious couple. The same day that she had a
child she was forced to get up and work. An issue of
blood followed and, naturally, the poor girl died. There
was great local indignation, and the husband had to be
placed under police protection. The girl's mother, who
had been responsible for the marriage, solemnly cursed
the man : and Dr Hall was duly summoned to attend
him. He was thrown from a pony one evening, with the
result that he broke his neck, but retained enough life to
die a slow and agonising death. Dr Hall knew nothing
about the man, but when he returned to the Monaghan
Hospital that night the nurse, who had happened to
attend the dead girl, questioned him : " Was there a
woman there with a hatchet-face ? "

" There was."

" Then it must have been the same man whom the
mother cursed, promising him a horrible death within the
twelve month." And so saying, the nurse fainted right
away.

THE BALLAD OF JOHN GILLILAND

It was the strong John Gilliland
Who farmed at Edenbrone :
And hard he was to man and beast.
He wrought them to the bone.

John Gilliland went marketing
Fairdays at Castleshane :
And there he met a farmer's girl
As ripe as summer grain.

He went into her father's house
And showed his share of gold :
The price of all that he had reared
And all that he had sold.

John Gilliland poured out the coin
Like butter from a dish :
" Then take my daughter " said the man
" And put her to your wish."

John Gilliland took home his bride
To be his sister's slave :
His sister had a hatchet face,
Her eyes were like the grave.

" Now fetch the cattle in the morn
And drive them from the byre :
And get thee down upon thy knees
To sift away the fire."

And on the day she bore his child
John Gilliland watched stern :
" Now leave the babe upon thy bed
And go to twist the churn."

" John Gilliland," she cried that night,
" I'm dying in my pain :
I fear there's blood upon the pat,
Your churn will keep a stain."

John Gilliland rose up to see :
He made so little reck.
" My churn is sweet and clean to-night
My butter has no speck."

She died before the dim of dawn,
Before the hills were grey :
Her limbs were cold to all the warmth
The sun poured down that day.

John Gilliland would give no wake,
No neighbours came to mourn :
He only cursed a woman died
And cursed a mouth was born.

They told the mother of the girl.
It sickened her to bed :
She cursed him while she was alive
She cursed him from the dead.

She never told a soul her curse
Nor said her secret word :
But only muttered what would be
When her black prayer was heard.

" John Gilliland within a year
Shall fall upon his neck :
What though his churn be sweet and clean,
His butter keep no speck ! "

It was the strong John Gilliland
Who farmed at Edenbrone :
Who went to drive his cattle in
And rode upon his roan.

Whate'er it was his pony saw
She threw him on his head :
Some say it was the girl he met
And some the mother dead."

My ballad was written years later and read to the nurse
in the case. She commented : " How did Mr Leslie know
the man's pony was roan ? " I didn't know. I put it in
to make a good rhyme, but it was correct.

Dr Hall was our family doctor, and three generations
rose up to call him blessed. He had doctored the county
for half a century and could sometimes give better advice
than specialists. He could amputate at the hip with one
assistant only or take out a kidney in days when it was
regarded as a spectacular operation. In leisure moments
he bred champion roses which won gold medals under
various county family names : Lady Dartrey, Lady Leslie,
etc. Rich and poor, Catholic and Protestant had immense
faith in him, and he was followed to the grave by the
bishops of the two Churches.

Ireland was so much a land of sport that games
appeared less on the horizon. There is a curious distinction in life between those who pursue game and those who
pursue games. I suppose that blood is the difference
between the two pursuits. I remember the appearance
of golf in the County Monaghan and the mild scorn of
the natives. Cricket, of course, has never suited the Irish
climate or temperament. But transplanted to Australia,

the Irish race has produced the greatest of cricketers :
O'Reilly or McCabe.

We introduced a cricket club at Glaslough and played
at least one match against Caledon over the Armagh
border. A diminutive brother of Lord Caledon made
most of the runs. A few years later he nearly saved
Harrow towards the end of " Fowler's Match," when
Eton won the most astonishing game in history. At
Glaslough we always received unexpected help from the
gamekeeper who acted as umpire and would never allow
one of the family to be run out, standing his ground with
the unshakable decision : " Home ! "

Football was introduced and became so rough that the
game had to be confined to one religion. Horace Plunkett
told the story of a match he once watched near Dublin.
The game was proceeding merrily in one corner while the
ball lay forgotten in another part of the field. As a rule
Protestants played hockey and Catholics hurley. In
Belfast football leagues the rival religions sometimes met,
and after the defeat of a predominantly Catholic team a
supporter of the victors could be heard to mutter :
" There'll be heavy hearts in the Vati-can to-night."

The beautiful Irish dancing was entirely a Catholic
accomplishment. The Protestants thought dancing
wrong. Catholic bishops have since scotched modern
dances, but the graceful steps we used to learn from
country dancers around Glaslough were danced without
touching, much less clutching, between sexes. An Irish
proverb calls for the dancers to " show death in their
faces and lightning in their heels," a wonderful contrast in
emotions.

Morality is too secure in Ireland to be endangered by
modern gyrations. Priests and parsons kept a watchful-
ness upon their parishes and married off couples before
they finished courting. Illegitimate births at home
occurred at very rare intervals : two or three in a decade.
But disasters sometimes befell the innocent. One of our
girls returned in family difficulties from Aughnacloy

Fair. In vain she was asked to reveal the name of the man. " She blamed it on the sweets " was all we were told.

I heard of a priest who arranged the removal of an official, whom he suspected in a telling phrase of " lowering the virginity of the parish ! " In war or peace the morality of Irish women has remained the strictest in Europe. There used to be a good sale for hat-pins in the west which the girls purchased not to fasten their hats, for they wore the lovelier shawl over their long black hair, but to protect themselves while being courted !

How far the blood of the gentry and the peasantry mingled in the old days cannot be accurately decided. There are few old families which have not more than foster-relations in the mountains. Until the barrier of religion arrived, the Irish women absorbed the sons of the invaders, and out of their marriage arose the mediæval Irish nation with Celtic blood and Anglo-Norman names. The penal laws made the intermarriage of Catholic and Protestant a felony and social degradation. All romance and interbreeding became secret. In the eighteenth century the illegitimates (they were called by-blows !) hung around the big house, and it was considered bad taste for a visitor to ask the name of any young man about the place.

In one famous instance a landlord, who was singularly deformed, drove his future English wife into the mountains surrounding his Irish home so that she could see for herself that his natural children were as good as any !

The *droit du seigneur* no doubt existed in the Irish social system, though under another name. When the old age pensions were first awarded I remember a handsome old crone like Lady Macbeth demanding her pittance with pathetic indignation. " If I had my rights I would be better than any of you." The lawyer whispered to me that she came from Lord Roden's stock and indeed her big-boned nose and silvery hair would have done credit to any earldom.

Folk shared with us a belief not only that my grandfather could do no wrong, but that he could get anything
done that he chose. Traces of the old feudal power
existed. In the Fifties the railway had been diverted to
Glaslough and farm-houses swept out of its course
although the straight line lay two miles south through
Middletown. When the Famine came, miles of high wall
had been built to give work, and enormous drains opened
like water-courses down the hill-side. Every Irish
demesne has a colossal wall dating from that time. An
old lady of the past century assured me that the six-mile
wall round her demesne had been built to keep the
starving peasants from ransacking her gardens ! Strangest
of all, our curling river (called Mountain Water or Fairy
River) had been straightened and the whole course shifted.
As a result a big ash tree had not only changed its banks
but the name of its townland. My grandfather's most
considerable exercise of power had lifted the dead when
he built a chancel to the old church. A number of graves
had to be moved to make room. I do not know how this
was achieved, for the family to whom they belonged
not only protested, but lay down upon their father's
grave and swore they would lie there till the Day of
Judgment. When the chancel was finally built and such
of our ancestors as could be discovered moved into the
new vault, a Maltese Cross was spotted by the shocked
vestry. There are some things no Irish landlord could do,
and to erect the Sign of the Cross over a Protestant
church is one. It was brought tumbling down. The
tradition was strongly Protestant, though my grandfather
divided the lodge gates strictly between the churches.
Murdock, the agent a century past, had boasted that he
left no Catholic within sight of the road between Glaslough
and Caledon. The people believed he had been dismissed
and had afterwards met some of the old tenants in
America. These had caught him, tied him to a tree and
left him to starve to death, " the fresh loaves rotting under
his nose." His successor, Cunningham, reared a famous

horse on our hill called Downpatrick, which was second
in the Grand National. He built a distant row of cottages
into which he exiled all who displeased him. This new
row of dwellings was divided by a fire into two blocks,
and to our surprise the inhabitants decided to call one
Sodom and the other Gomorrah.

Whatever are the Celtic traits, there is an apparent
gulf in character and temperament between English and
Irish even when their bloods run into the same veins.

There used to be an amusing manner in vogue in Paris
for distinguishing different peoples in detail. " One
Englishman makes a club, two a golf match and three a
new colony." One Irishman was said to make a political
party, two a fight and three entailed High Mass ! The
formula for Poland was simpler : one Pole means the
Polish Question, two Poles the Polish Question, three
Poles the Polish Question !

I became subject to the vague undetermined movement
called the Celtic Movement, of which the Gaelic revival
was its Irish manifestation. Welsh nationalism, the
Scotch clan-spirit, Breton pardons, and the Cornish
Jack the giant-killer are others.

He who ventures upon the Celtic side of life, literature
and history enters upon a quaking bog, but what a fascinating quagmire !

European culture has been built up entirely from the
Greek and Roman. It was the controversy over Ossian
in the eighteenth century which started the dream, the
suspicion, the hallucination that Europe had other
ingredients, and that out of the barbarians proceeded the
Celts, whose blood and imagery still haunt Western
Europe. A lost race, a disappearing language, a suppressed
religion : how fascinating ! To go Celtic is no doubt a
waste of time, but then Time was made to be wasted by the
Celts. Nobody in the three kingdoms knows for sure how
much Celtic blood he has inherited with its touches of
second-sight, its susceptibility to ghost-lore and its vague
belief in magics and wonders. But there it is. It carries

a memory of the old musics and languages and inspires people to become surpliced Bards at Eisteddfod or to wear the coloured kilts of the clans or to steep themselves in the Irish Saga.

Few readers have ploughed the *Silva Gadelica* of Standish Hayes O'Grady. Bulky and expensive, this rare and glorious volume came to me even as the translated Homer of Chapman dawned on Keats. What with fantastic lives of Irish saints, the real Fenian tale, and fairy stories as grotesque as gargoyles, a new world swam under my ken. I read that dishevelled mass of phantasy therein called " the Colloquy of the Ancients," where the sublime and the humorous jostle madly. Can it be said that most of Homer is tame in comparison ? I felt my mind transfigured while poring over the *Silva Gadelica :* one of the ten books which have influenced me. I feel sorry for those who have never wandered into a wild wood so different from the sacred grove of the Academy.

The *Silva Gadelica* answered Mahaffy's bitter sneer that the old Irish literature contained only " the silly or indecent." Here was the refutation with the exception of one story (a very good one about the King of Greece's daughter) which the translator preferred to put into Latin. But how many passages in the Old Testament had much better been retained under the same cloak of chastity ? Mahaffy was an enigma in his way. He refused to think there had ever been any culture save Latin and Greek. As for the Celtic, he tempered his scorn for the old Irish book-men by his pity for the young students of Gaelic, so many of whom died young. As he said, they were under a curse, but I wonder what he would have said had he lived to see Douglas Hyde installed in the Vice-regal, sacred to the Ascendancy, unless to utter his most famous aphorism that Ireland is a country where the certainty never happens and the unexpected always takes place.

How angry Mahaffy was when I met him at a railway station wearing an Irish kilt. He waved indignantly and

explained to the wondering porters how wrong I was
archæologically. But he admitted next day that it was
a convenient vesture in which to pursue the snipe over
flooded bogs.

The only Fellow of Trinity from whom I heard a good
word for Irish was Professor Jack Bury. He told me how
much he regretted not knowing it when he was writing his
Life of St. Patrick. Jack Bury had what Chicago gunmen
call a " baby face." So youthful did he appear that when
the new Professor of History went into a restaurant at
Cambridge the waiters asked Mrs Bury if the young gentleman would take a glass of milk. He was the only man in
the Empire who could be found to pick up the weight of
Acton's learning.

A Fellow of Trinity has since magnificently edited the
" Book of Armagh." This famous manuscript is called
in Irish the " Canon of St Patrick," just as its fellow in the
Library at Trinity, the " Book of Kells," is really the
" Gospel of Columcille." Perhaps these two books have
done more than any others to inspire beholders with the
strangeness and wonder of Ireland's past. Mahaffy used
to vaunt that the British Museum would give all its
illuminated manuscripts for the " Book of Kells." For
a thousand years it was believed to have been written
and designed by angels. With that comment let it rest
unapproached and unsurpassable in a class by itself :
the Queen of all the Books of the Western World.

The " Book of Armagh " had been a neighbour of ours,
for, when this priceless heirloom of the nation came into
the market, it was Dr Reeves, the poor Rector of Tynan
two miles away, who purchased it, though he expected
to live on skilly for a year to make up the price of £300.
The Primate, Lord John Beresford, came generously
to the rescue, paid the money and made Reeves the
custodian. In this manner the book returned to Armagh
where it should have remained for ever. Its story has
been very tragic. It had been the title-deed held by the
Archbishops of Armagh during the Middle Ages. Primate

after Primate exhibited the book as the token of Primacy until Archbishop Oliver Plunkett, who was executed at Tyburn. One of the witnesses against him was the hereditary Keeper of the Book, which he pawned to pay his journey to London to swear away an innocent life.

Lord John deposited it in Trinity, Dublin. While scholars were examining it, the Primate died and the "Book of Armagh" was never returned to Armagh. Primate Alexander was anxious to recover the volume, but Trinity were obdurate. When he decided to go to law it was represented to him that the scandal of the lawsuit would be more than the Church of Ireland could stand. This was the story I had at first hand. But what is the result in the whirligig of time? The "Book of Armagh" finds itself to-day under Irish rule instead of the jurisdiction of Belfast.

There are few left who remember Archbishop Alexander well. He was a remarkable link with the past, for he was the last Irish Bishop appointed by an English government in the far-off days before the Disestablishment. He used to say with a humorous sparkle that he had been a bad enough character to be turned out of the House of Lords. He had sat for Derry on the Bench in the unimaginable Sixties when Irish Primates drove to Westminster in a coach.

He was a High Churchman and had heard Newman preaching at Oxford. I used as a boy to listen with wonder to his description of those more spacious days. He had known and loved the Oxford which bred a Newman and a Gladstone. They had been his heroes until Newman passed to Rome and Gladstone disestablished him! He had been through all the battles following Disestablishment and the later Home Rule struggles. He sent his blessing, as Primate, to the dying Gladstone.

When Gladstone disestablished the Church of Ireland, the High Churchmen were fiercely attacked. Dr Alexander was stoned in the streets of Dublin by the Protestant rabble. The Athanasian Creed, the Emblem of the Cross and the faintest ritual were assailed. A prohibition was added to the Prayer Book against the use of incense or any substitute for incense, whatever that might be ! It was pointed out that incense was used in the Bible. The angry answer was that the Papists must have placed it there !

Ireland was no place for High Churchmen who found themselves between the devil and the deep sea. A Dublin clergyman finding himself forbidden to place a cross on or before his altar, suspended it from behind ! Their opponents boasted that a carriage umbrella would cover them all. In the Clogher diocese we had Canon Young, the son of Surgeon Andy, who upheld High Church principles at Ballybay. It was not easy, and the Cross would have been thrown down on his wife's grave had he not threatened to put the damages on the Rates. But he outlived all his opponents including his Bishop, whom he much embarrassed when he knelt and kissed his lordship's wedding ring !

The Dean of Clogher was Dr Ovenden, an artist, scientist and carpenter, always a welcome guest at Glaslough. He made a carved screen for the church in Enniskillen with his own hands and with his own hands the Bishop forced him to take it down. My grandmother used to tell the story with tears. Such were the sorrows of High Churchmen in Ireland. The famous Dr Magee had also had trouble with the good Orangemen when he was Rector of Enniskillen, but the English had a better opinion of him and made him Archbishop of York.

Time soothes all controversies to sleep even in Ireland ! even on religious matters ! The Church of Ireland, Protestant as she is, forms a valued and welcome part in the new Ireland. She affords a social leaven in the South and a civilising influence in the North, without which the country would suffer real loss. She has contributed too many great names to be disregarded as an Irish community. Antiquities, industries, politics and literature owe her a debt. Tolerance and security form the least gratitude which can be meted to a Church which gave Ireland Emmet, Lord Edward Fitzgerald, Smith O'Brien, Parnell, Reeves, the Standish O'Gradys and Douglas Hyde.

With the death of Queen Victoria the old era of ascendancy really passed. She had disliked Ireland and feared the Irish. For close on forty years she omitted to visit her other island. Both English and Scotsmen took shots at her, but no Irishman ever drew a trigger on her. It would be almost fair to say that she never gave the Irish a chance. Certainly it would be fair to say that she boycotted Ireland. She had several reasons for dislike. She was a true Protestant, and she found the Pope in spiritual possession of the fairest island in her dominions. A rather blood-thirsty passage escaped into her published letters. During the Irish Rising of 1848 she wrote to King Leopold : " I think it now is very likely to go off without any contest which people and (I think with right) rather regret. The Irish should receive a good lesson or they will begin again." (This is now omitted).

Later she was aggrieved when Dublin refused a site for a statue of the Prince Consort. She was foolish not to encourage a Royal residence in Ireland. It was once proposed to make a Sandringham at Killarney for the Prince. But the Queen was jealous of his taking the place of the Prince Consort anywhere—even to wearing the Garter. There were interesting letters from Disraeli to Lord Mayo on this, which I read at Palmerstown before they perished in the flames.

When she came in 1900 she received a delirious welcome from a feudal people. The Irish troops in the Transvaal had made her realise that Ireland deserved a kind word. Queen Elizabeth had met Shane O'Neill, but there was no great Irish leader to settle things with Queen Victoria. She met the shrewd and simple Cardinal Logue at tea. With unintentional irony he asked if she were making a long stay !

The address of Edward VII to the Irish people showed

a new spirit : " For a country so attractive and a people so gifted . . . a brighter day is dawning. . . . Its realisation will depend largely upon the steady development of self-reliance and co-operation." It was almost a benediction of the coming Sinn Fein. But was 1903 too late ?

Without being loyal to the Crown in principle, the Irish can be Royalist on occasions. They fought for the House of Stuart with pathetic courage. Were the Stuarts not the rightful sovereigns of both realms ? And who were the Republicans under Charles I ? Not the Catholic Irish. Sir Phelim O'Neill, the leader of the Rebellion of 1641, could have saved his life, had he consented to give evidence against the King. The Scotch, who stayed Jacobite, have been endlessly praised by the romantic English. The Irish Jacobites were summed as only bloody rebels !

What a reception the Irish gave George IV !

What a reception they gave Edward VII !

This was largely due to the personality and policy of George Wyndham. He was the last romantic figure in the House of Commons. I cherish every glimpse and memory of him. I first saw him at Eton visiting his boy Percy. What hopes and happiness lay before father and son ! Old Percy, the grandfather, had been a visitor to Glaslough and was touched when I offered to dedicate to him a small Natural History I was writing. Within twenty years I had seen the three generations pass away with Percy's death in the field.

In Cambridge days I stayed at Saighton where George Wyndham lived with Sibell Grosvenor. Saighton Grange (in spite of its name, which is pronounced Satan) had been the country residence of the Abbots of Chester. The Virgin's statue survived on the outer wall and the highest ritual of the High Church brightened the chapel. George Wyndham kneeling in his riding clothes while the vested priest prayed and Lady Grosvenor swung the censer was like a scene out of the " Idylls of the King." In the late evenings he read aloud in his library from the Elizabethans. And fresh from his glowing chivalry, I would catch the Irish mail at Chester and reach Dublin in the morning. George Wyndham achieved the Land Act which brought a close to the war between landlords and tenants. Thus far triumphant, he staged King Edward's reception in Dublin. It roused deeper welcome than that accorded to Queen Victoria. Here was the King who wished to see Ireland governed according to Irish ideas. As a good European he had often sensed the reproach of Ireland abroad. He pressed George Wyndham and Sir Anthony MacDonnell to give him an Irish solution. The Orange North, acting on the Tories, refused it in any shape and under any consideration.

George Wyndham's laurels were green, and he should have passed happily to another office, but the King commanded him to stay and settle the Irish Question. It is history how the Irish Question settled poor George Wyndham. He resigned in an agony of grief. He had done so much, but he was not allowed to do more. The gods kindly let him die before the Great War. The Irish Question, as he left it, became the bane of both the great Parties in turn and finally wrecked the Irish Party itself.

The Irish Question was insidious, seductive and sometimes overwhelming to those who fell under its appeal. It was the only form in which politics ever appealed or presented themselves to me. At Eton I was reading John Redmond's speeches carefully. Before I went up to Cambridge I spent an afternoon at the Commons with Mr Haldane (later the first Socialist Lord Chancellor). He proved most informing, philosophical and affable. For an hour we walked up and down the historic Hall of Westminster. Like all Liberals of the time he talked and argued as though Ireland was the most important axis to English policy. He was certain Home Rule was coming and advised me to enter Parliament.

Many years passed before I met him again. By that time he had been twice Lord Chancellor. He had been as cynically thrown over in politics as Wyndham or Parnell, but he had a philosophy which floated him over the waves. He was neither realist like Parnell, nor idealist. Reviled and repudiated because of his friendship for Germany he survived to be acknowledged by the Army chiefs as the greatest of War Secretaries. His great metaphysical soul is now with the Hegel and the Schopenhauer and the Kant whom he admired. I hope that he has found a " spiritual home " at last.

To-day Ireland is a rather forgotten island beyond the Isle of Man, from which proceed depressions in the weather, horses and jockeys and sweepstake tickets. Irish politics seem something between an ancestral dream and a distant muddle. That they can ever upset British statesmen and British governments again seems impossible. For a generation no election could be fought in England without the Irish issue arising in some form. In London society people could not meet each other on account of conflicting Irish views. There had been no such social fissures since the days of the Reform Bill. At least as an obstruction to England the Irish Question is gone.

Forty years ago I used to attend the House of Commons. Winston had been recently elected for Oldham on his return from the Boer War. He took me down to the House as a schoolboy and placed me in the gallery. He then intruded very fiercely into debate with one eye on the Speaker and one on me. I was very nervous whether he would be allowed to complete his say, for the old men looked very disapproving. I heard some legendary characters speak : old Labby looking like a dropsical wasp, and Sir William Harcourt like a Jumbo whose trunk had been amputated.

The Irish were massed in the Opposition benches. Redmond delivered his best Ciceronian, while John Dillon

was content to look daggers. There was always a new
Irish story passing through the lobbies, just as there
is always a new improper story to be gleaned from the
Stock Exchange. I met Swift MacNeill and John Clancy.
Clancy had delivered one of the most cherished of Parliamentary Bulls : " Whether it is a Calamy or not, it is
untrue ! " I heard poor old Edward Blake speaking.
He was a colonial statesman who had thrown up a good
career in Canada to become an Irish ranker.

Tay Pay O'Connor, the champion professional Irishman,
was much in evidence : " The great he-rogue with a
wonderful brogue." Before he died this son of sedition
had mellowed into a respected " Father of the House."
Like most of the older Nationalists he best talked about
Parnell, whose betrayed memory rankled at the back of
their souls, whatever line they had taken, for or against
their creator.

The most eccentric member of Parnell's original legion
that I met was Frank or " Crank " Hugh O'Donnell.
He came straight out of a Charles Lever novel. He had
helped to make and then to excoriate Parnell. He was
a Nationalist and a Cosmopolitan. He was a Catholic
and an anti-clerical. He was a henchman of Cardinal
Manning, but delivered himself of a satirical poem
(" The Message of the Masters ") against the late Cardinal
O'Donnell, who once read me passages aloud amid bursts
of uncontrollable laughter.

Dr O'Donnell was then Bishop of Raphoe and a trustee
of the Irish Party. He made an attractive picture in his
Donegal Palace, with his handsome features, noble stature
and waving white hair. He was an Irish speaker, and at
his evening prayers I first heard the Rosary recited in
melodious Irish. We drove twenty miles over the mountains to some Gaelic festival on an Irish jaunting-car.
All the road he entertained us with amusing stories of the
old days. He described how the first church organ came
to Donegal and how the old Bishop had entrusted it to
his musical sister Ellen. She was sent away to take lessons

2 A

in the art of playing this unknown instrument, but did not feel sufficient to face the opening ceremony. A professional organist was called in and with such effect did he play that the simple congregation, who had never heard an organ before, swung round and continued their devotions in the direction of the sound. The Bishop found the entire congregation with their backs to him and the altar. He stopped the service in order to recall them and to explain that the organ was made by human hands and was not an expression of supernatural music as they supposed. And seeing the wonderful success of the organist, he could not help adding (so the diocese always believed), " Wait till Ellen comes ! " And the phrase became a proverb in the diocese. Whenever the good Bishop purposed or proposed anything there was a whisper amongst his diocesans : " Wait till Ellen comes ! "

It was in the telling of the story that the Bishop excelled with his soft intonations and his beautiful face lighting up like an Irish rushlight flickering in an alabaster lamp. He had come through the whole Parnellite split without scars. In his passionate devotion to Ireland he was like some Polish patriot prelate. In his old age he succeeded to the Primacy and received the Red Hat.

In those days the memory of Parnell still pervaded Irish life, and his passing was remembered like a great and terrible storm. His story has been told many times and the least details have been scooped by biographers. Here are a few odds and ends, should a final " Life " be ever attempted. His sister, Mrs. Dickenson, once published an amazing story of his disgrace and rustication at Cambridge, and how a girl, whom he seduced, committed suicide in the Cam. This fantasy was repeated by reputable historians. In my time at Cambridge efforts were made by Irishmen to clear the name of the dead leader. John Redmond devoted a considerable sum to searching the records of inquests. There was never the slightest trace or proof that anything of the kind ever happened. In fact it was a madwoman's dream which she sold to a publisher to make a sensation.

The real tradition about Parnell was verifiable in my time, as old Professor Newton (who wrote the Bird Dictionary) was still alive at Magdalene. According to him Parnell was sent down for a provoked assault. One evening Parnell was waiting by the side of Station Road (the exact spot was shown me) when it was still a rural road between banks and hedges. A townsman the worse for liquor passed twice and each time insulted him. Parnell, tradition said, was brooding on the sorrows of Ireland. Whatever were his thoughts, his action was brief and simple. He knocked the townee down. Action was brought in the courts and as Parnell was faulted he was rusticated for the rest of the term. He preferred never to return.

Towards the end of the Parnellite split, when Irishmen were bitterly divided over the merits of Mrs O'Shea, a young relation of hers heard her insulted at a dinner-party and launched out with his fist. The insulter, who had no idea of the other's close connection with the lady, rose and received a blow in the face, fell and killed himself against a marble fire-place. Murray Guthrie had been present and used his influence for the accident to be hushed up. He gave the young man a large sum to leave the country for the time. I believe that death was the only casualty during that particular Irish war.

Murray Guthrie was one of my many uncles in Parliament. His good looks made him prominent even in a well-dressed House. In the opinion of *La Belle Otero* he was the best-looking man she had ever seen. Though he could catch the eye of any woman, he had, he told me, the greatest difficulty in catching that of the Speaker. His early death was a tragedy, for although only forty he had qualified as an Alderman to become Lord Mayor of London, the great ambition of his life.

John Dillon was the most interesting to hear talking about Parnell. The Redmond brothers remembered him

as adoring henchmen. Tim Healy could not help being
bitter, perhaps because he had admired him most. But
John Dillon estimated him with a historian's poise.
Dillon, a most practical and level-headed Parliamentarian,
had an extraordinary ghost story about Parnell. Years
after his death Dillon was attending a performance of
opera in Munich when he saw, as he believed, the identical
figure of Parnell standing in conversation. Naturally he
drew near and to his amazement recognized the voice
and even the familiar phrase of Parnell. When he made
himself known, the stranger knew him not. Dillon was
left wondering where he stood.

It was possible that Parnell's tremendous personal
identity had so impressed itself on his followers that
under certain emotions the memory produced hallucina-
tions. Curiously enough another Irish member had a
similar experience in Australia, and John Howard Parnell
has recorded in his book about his brother a very vivid
reappearance of Parnell's at Avondale, the family home.

Parnell laid down the Irish field of battle on which
statesmen and politicians fought during the subsequent
generation. I always regret that I never saw him nor
heard Gladstone. Children should have free access to
the House of Commons, and nurses should be allowed to
wheel their perambulators on the Terrace. Children
could thus have a chance of taking a memory of the great
down the corridor of life.

Joe Chamberlain I saw once, but quite accidentally.
The first important party I attended in London I stumbled
upon the great man. As I turned a corner I almost
tripped over the chair on which he was sitting and talking
to Violet Granby. It was shortly after his return from
South Africa. He looked exactly like his caricatures
save for a haggard look in his eye. He enjoyed being ' the
best hated man in England," a compliment which he has
bequeathed to Neville. It was a thrilling moment trying
to overhear what he said to Violet Granby, though it

was an extinguished statesman talking to a faded beauty.
Still I would rather have heard him than any of the rising
men in the room, and I would rather have paid compliments to her than to any of the younger women present.
I forgot all else at that party, even the name of the hostess
or where it was, but I can visualise those two who were
stars in their different worlds.

What associations could be conjured up with Joe!
Here was the swordsman who had survived his duels with
Randolph and Dilke and Parnell. Even Gladstone had
not blunted his steel.

He had been blackballed at the Reform Club : one of
those famous and honourable blackballings which occur
in the best-regulated clubs and only to be compared with
Birrell's blackballing at Brooks's, Locker-Lampson's at
the Garrick and Professor Mivart's at the Athenæum.
Locker-Lampson was the Bibliophile and Mivart the
critic of Darwin. The history of the Blackball in English
life has not yet been written. What more satisfactory
motto can a man carry into middle life as he looks back
on the past than : " Sometimes Blackballed but never
Blackmailed ? "

I only know one better and it fell from Kipling during
one of the visits to Brede : " It is better to *do* wrong than
to *be* right." It was impressed on me because Kipling
wished that he had written the words.

It will remain a pointer for my old age that I should
have fought a Parliamentary Election in the reign of
Edward VII. Had I been successful I should have been
a Member of Parliament before Baldwin reached the
House.

I was still living at Wapping when I was introduced
to John Redmond at the height of his struggle for Home
Rule. It seemed assured to him by the great Liberal
majority at his back. Progress, Labour, Education,
Ireland—the whole Empire were then in the hands of the
Liberals, and the Liberals were supposed to be only
subject to the Nonconformist Conscience. Only iron

events could have abolished the Liberal Party in England and snuffed out all forms of conscience in the world.

I became acquainted with the Irish Party at the House and very benevolent and hopeful they seemed compared to Parnell's desperate legion in the Eighties. They included one Socialist in " Wee Joe " Devlin and a Rural Anarchist in Lawrence Ginnell. There were county gentlemen like John Redmond and Sir Thomas Esmonde, a remnant of the Parnellites and a few University men like Hugh Law and Stephen Gwynn. They formed a constitutional party playing the Party game within the Empire and demanding a very reasonable scheme of local government called Home Rule. The Tory Party, greatly to their discredit, had accepted Ireland as a convenient field from which to fight their way back to power.

John Redmond spoke like a classical orator and looked like a Roman Emperor. He looked upon Home Rule as a foregone conclusion. He expected that old families, who had been represented in old days on College Green, would return to Dublin. I aspired to the hope of sitting one day in that magnificent building, which is still dedicated to the Bank of Ireland, and gave my name as a Nationalist candidate for the approaching election. I understood that I would succeed to the first vacancy in the County of Monaghan.

Redmond was sincere and impressive. Like his brother he had never betrayed Parnell. He was far from revolutionary though he spoke to me of the wickedness of Lord Clanricarde, a miserly character who not only evicted wretched tenants, but when they clung to the roadside spent considerable sums in obliterating the traces of their poor little homes.

This roused me to white heat and I asked : " Why was Clanricarde not shot instead of better men than he ? " To this there was no reply. Redmond believed the Irish troubles could be settled without shedding a drop of blood. He was an old-fashioned squire without guile and with few suspicions. He judged Belfast by the genial Protestants of the South, and he had never heard the Irish proverb bidding Irishmen fear the English smile like the heels of a horse.

A few weeks later I was startled to receive a telegram at Wapping to say that I had been chosen Nationalist candidate for Derry City. I consulted the papers, which I seldom read, and learnt that a General Election was imminent. Never was a candidate less prepared. It was the Christmas of 1909, which seemed spoiled when Asquith appealed to the electors for a renewal of his power to face the Irish situation. The horizon was darkened by the veto of the Lords and Lloyd George's Budget. There was indeed a German menace, but Haldane was expected to smooth it out by a visit to Berlin. The real and only question in people's minds was Ireland !

I arrived at the Dublin North Wall without an election address or luggage. After a talk with Redmond at the old Gresham I picked up Stephen Gwynn and we set out for the constituency. There I found that canvassing was unnecessary. Not a soul knew me by sight. It was not even necessary to leave my hotel, as every voter would vote strictly according to the side his ancestors had taken at the Battle of the Boyne. Derry elections were always the most exciting in Ireland. Nationalists and Unionists were narrowly divided. The seat had once been held by Justin McCarthy by one vote. A turnover of twenty-five votes could settle the election. There was no heckling at meetings. It was a question of polling 98 or 99 per cent on both sides. Voters returned without being fetched from London or Glasgow. Voters as far as Canada had already started on their journey home. On the day of the polls the sick and even the dying were taken on stretchers and allowed to make pathetic signs of their political convictions at the entrance of the booths.

The Unionists naturally voted to a man for my opponent, the present Duke of Abercorn and Governor of Northern Ireland. Amid tense scenes I was defeated by

fifty-seven votes. It needed two more elections and a
Protestant-Liberal candidate before the city could be
won for Home Rule. There was another election in 1910,
and my second defeat did not justify me in proceeding to
a third contest in 1913, which was won by Mr Hogge,
my principal Protestant supporter. So ended the most
desperate and hard-fought series of elections during the
century. They were the last stand-up struggles fought
on the old historical grounds in Ireland. I think the
election of 1910 was worth fighting. Had it not been
fought, the Nationalists would never have had the heart
to fight again.

One of the unexpected and rather delightful features of
the elections was Uncle Moreton's return for a Cork
constituency. William O'Brien nominated him by the
sheer power of his prestige. " We would elect your old
hat " was all the voters remarked when Moreton was
proposed. There was no opposition, and Moreton, exhilar-
ated on finding himself an M.P., tried to carry O'Brien's
flag into Kerry. He borrowed Arthur Vincent's car
from Muckross, but returned it in a very battered condition. William O'Brien's name did not extend out of
Cork. Seated in Parliament Moreton would only speak
about India and silver rupees and bimetallic currency.
Once O'Brien excused his vagaries by saying his heart
was of gold. In a flash Tim Healy answered : " Not
entirely gold—Moreton's heart must be bimetallic.
He has discussed the Silver Question too often ! "

There were excitements between my elections. King
Edward died and my brother had to fight a duel in the
same week. There is no reason why an affair of honour
should not be told after a quarter of a century.

He had been posted with the Rifle Brigade in Egypt and
as A.D.C. to the General Commanding had occasion to
meet Egyptian royalty. He exchanged letters with a
relative of the Court married to a distinguished Pasha.
There could be no doubt of the lady's virtue, but an

intercepted letter gave her husband occasion to send a challenge. The Pasha was famous both as a polo-player and a swordsman.

In consequence my brother had to leave Egypt at twenty-four hours' notice, while a small but select committee consisting of Charlie Beresford and Lord Cromer decided unofficially that the challenge should be accepted. The War Office were approached and agreed that he need not send in his Commission unless the affair reached the papers.

The swordsmanship of the British Army was not as good as their pheasant shooting, and several weeks were required for practice. Fortunately both my brother and father had fenced for the Army. He was able to acquire an iron guard and with a fine French fencer as his second put up a stiff defence. In fact it was half an hour before the Pasha could break through with a thrust which cut muscles in my brother's fingers. Under the terms of the duel he could withdraw with honour. He had offered all possible satisfaction in the old-fashioned way. There can be very few modern wives who have raised such serious consideration between a husband and an admirer. I have heard of a husband challenging a lover who had left his wife in the lurch and refused to return.

For those who would care to see the written *procès* of a duel for future reference—the following is the document that lies before me :

" —— *Pacha si considérant gravement offensé par Monsieur Norman Leslie a chargé messieurs W. de Blest Yane et Miguel Yturbé de lui demander une reparation par les armes. Monsieur Norman Leslie a prié le Commandant Bardet et Genefes Breittmayer de le representer. Les quatre témoins ont reconnu qu'une rencontre était nécessaire, les deux adversaires ayant antérieurement admis le principe. L'arme choisi est l'épée de combat.*

Trois minutes de combat.
Deux minutes de repos.
Le combat cessera sur le consentement du blessé.
Fait en double à Paris le 13 Mai 1910."

The lady, for whom my brother risked his life and his commission, was unable to retain her discretion. She had dispatched a secret representative to Paris who telegraphed her the result. She immediately telegraphed back to my brother.

Naturally he was never allowed to see her again.

The first difficulty after the duel was to muzzle the Press. This was achieved by my brother's second, who immediately left his card on every London correspondent in Paris promising a challenge, should their London office print a word on the subject.

The same evening my brother returned safely to London with two much-dented duelling swords under his arm. The nuns at Tyburn, who had carried on an intercession during the duel, received a bouquet tied up in the regimental colours. All fear of mention in the Press disappeared at the sudden death of King Edward with Halley's comet still in the skies. The incredibly historical reign of George V had begun.

The Irish Question continued. There were more elections. I much enjoyed a brief campaign in Tyrone where Tom Kettle was returned by a small majority. I found myself speaking from a wagon-brake with Kettle, Joe Devlin and Archer, John Redmond's son. Kettle became a professor in the new University in Dublin and was killed in France. " Wee Joe " was left high and dry as a Belfast member at Westminster in a House which knew not Joseph. All three died without seeing their Irish hopes fulfilled.

The campaign was one of youthful oratory, and I think we gave the crowds full value for their torchlights and bonfires. In days before the wireless an election with speeches and crowds was a cherished amusement. " Wee Joe " was called a " duodecimo Demosthenes," and could touch tears and laughter from any audience in Ulster. In private he once blew out his lungs for us, and they were harder and stronger than any bellows I have ever blown in a forge. I have a memory of him speaking out of an open window in Omagh into a rainy and pitch-black night. Only by the tremors and murmurs did we know that a great crowd stretched down the street on whom Joe was playing like a harmonium. He was the most emotional speaker I have ever heard. His funeral caused a wonderful outburst in Belfast where the Orangemen adored him as one of themselves, a boy who had risen from scouring pots to Parliament by sheer grit and gab. As he walked through the streets his political opponents would call out : " Wee Joe : Wee Joe ! Up with Wee Joe," and then recalling his religion would add : " Hell to your soul all the same ! "

Tom Kettle was the hope and promise of the Irish Party. I can hear him making his last peroration to the electors after this wise : " To-morrow is polling day, but should by some unexpected chance to-morrow also turn out to be the Day of Judgment, no elector of East Tyrone will forget to perform his last duty on earth. He will record his vote first and then proceed to judgment ! The Tyrone elector who has duly voted for Ireland will not fear to meet the final scrutiny of souls," and so on : and how the electors cheered and wailed with that curious cry which could only be heard at Irish wakes or football matches.

Tyrone went wild under electioneering. Every village flushed orange or green under the sedate grey of everyday life. The countryside blazed with bitter humour and paraffin torches. No doubt that has all gone, and willy-nilly Tyrone has become a member of the Northern Government. Tyrone must be a milder, perhaps even a melancholy, place without those closely contested elections.

The funniest situations were always arising. One gentleman was most anxious to be the Nationalist candidate, but Redmond would not endorse him in spite of his pleadings. Thereupon he forged and postered the most enthusiastic letter possible in his own favour and had it signed in enormous letters " JOHN REDMOND." He was, of course, elected, but Redmond was seriously annoyed and refused to have him in the Party till " Wee Joe," who saw the joke, insisted that any man who was capable of such eloquence was worthy of membership in the Irish Party. But it was an eloquence he never quite touched again.

After Kettle's victory we rushed round the constituency. We found a small market town, which I had never seen before nor have visited since, divided into two hysterical groups. The Nationalists were trying to light a bonfire, while a thin line of police were striving to prevent the Unionists from trampling it out. The wailing of the defeated from down a side-street was as the sound of many exasperated banshees.

There was a place called Tullyhoge which we reached later and found ominously quiet. We stopped, and from a passing inhabitant learnt that it was entirely Orange, and that no Papish dared live within fowling distance. Fortunately the community had retired to bed and we could pass before the alarm was given.

On another occasion we received our deserts and were pickled from a hedge. It was raining, and the discharge was received by our umbrellas, but what adventures we wove round those proofs that we had been under fire !

Tom Kettle ! may he too rest in peace ! Somewhere near Guillemont in France lies the first Professor of Economics at the National University.

Looking back at those days I feel that only Disraeli had the subtlety and imagination really to understand Ireland when he said : " Irish treason is a fairy-tale and Irish sedition a child talking in its sleep."

During those few years that remained before the out-

break of the War perhaps all the nations were talking in
their sleep. All were following their courses: fated,
fateful and fatal.

In Ireland the factions moved no less blindly. The
Ulstermen armed themselves with conviction and determination. They won admiration and eventually imitation
from the South. They were stirring and great-hearted days
for Ireland. In every Ulster parish men of true-blue
qualities were drilling their best, while often on the
next hill-side the Irish Volunteers were repeating their
manœuvres. On certain occasions they borrowed the
rifles of their opponents!

It was pleasant in those day of internecine strife to
visit Plunkett House in Dublin where dreams and
creameries were assorted by Sir Horace Plunkett and his
friends. With undying optimism Sir Horace traced the
lines whereby Ireland could become self-sustaining. All
his papers were burnt in an incendiary fire so that his
story will never be told. Quiet, ferrety-eyed, sub-acidly
humorous, obstinate in his knowledge, smilingly contemptuous, sub-consciously critical of Ireland—he gave
her all, his wealth, his name, his career, his brain and his
love.

At Plunkett House I met the mystical A.E., George
Russell, perhaps the only genius to come into Ireland
during the twentieth century. Poets and farmers could
appeal to A.E. with equal certainty. His rich elemental
mind was equal to any question about phosphates or
theosophy. He was one of the few people I ever met who
could see fairies.

Moreover, he could paint them tripping along or
blowing horns out of flowers.

I have written down evidence for fairies in cabins in the
Donegal mountains, but the most remarkable I secured
through Dr Hall from an honest practical Protestant
farmer living near Castleshane demesne in Monaghan.
There was nothing to say when he calmly described the
fairies' procession and how he stood aside to let them

pass. They might have been so many sheep going through a gate !

I am convinced that people can have a second sight and a sixth sense of which we wot little. On the Ulster borders I knew a wise old painter of academical standards who had retired from Dublin and lived alone in a haunted house. He was convinced that the fairies had touched up a landscape he was painting on the borders of a small fairy lake in our woods. He would only sign it with mention of " help from others." And so it was exhibited in Dublin. What scrupulous honesty !

Sir Horace kept open house at Foxrock. He had built what the old Irish would have called a *grianan*, or sun-house, fashioned to catch as much sunlight as is granted to an Irish day. Here schemers and dreamers met in the clear-cut atmosphere. Sir Horace had the same panoramic brain as my Uncle Moreton. He could visualise the most distant schemes and count even more distant figures in profit. They were both wonderful talkers and each was surrounded by friends who backed them. Sir Horace's schemes did at least lay the foundations of all modern agriculture in Ireland. Moreton's partook too much of the rainbow. Both had fantastic projects for Ireland, and I never knew why they seemed to ignore each other. Between them they had the charm to bring the old Ascendancy into touch with the new Ireland, but at mention of each other's name there was a silence of a rather unpleasant kind as when a corpse comes to the surface of a drinking well, and it might be a calf and may be only a cat !

The puzzle was solved when both happened to be staying together at Glaslough and to everybody's dismay not only refused to speak, but ignored each other's existence in the same room. Moreton had come to survey the possibilities for rainbow trout in Lough Emy. Sir Horace had completed arrangements for starting a new industry with an advance of £10,000 made by my American brother-in-law. Neither project was successful. The

doom which awaits rainbow trout in Irish lakes has already
been mentioned. Sir Horace used the American bounty
to open a timber-mill for sawing lumber in Sligo, the
county where my brother-in-law had seen birth. He had
quite forgotten that the local forests had disappeared
two centuries previously.

It was sad that Moreton and Sir Horace would not
speak, but it appeared that they had once managed rival
ranches in the wild and woolly West of America in the
Eighties. Moreton's had been a failure and Sir Horace's
a success. In the end Moreton's Committee in London
had asked Sir Horace to supersede Moreton. Twenty
years had passed, but speech between them was impossible. Yet I cannot imagine anything more brilliant and
amusing than to have heard them discussing Ireland in
spite of the transatlantic strain.

The most vivid conversation piece I ever heard was at a
dinner party which was entranced, confounded and
fascinated listening to Willie Yeats and George Moore
when they were not on speaking terms with each other.
Each ignored the other, but set about catching an audience
who were only too delighted to turn from the brilliance of
one to the counter-brilliance of the other.

Sir Horace is the only modern Irishman who has
merited a public statue in Dublin. We often talked
intimately as the sun went down upon the Wicklow
mountains behind his house. If he had had a political
party I would have joined it. He could not join the Irish
Party because of the pledge which was exacted from the
members. His pride would not allow him to sign obedience to John Dillon, whom he regarded as the dark angel
of Irish politics. Both political Parties distrusted and
pretended to dislike him : the Unionists because he was
indifferent to the Union and the Nationalists from envy
that his ability was not enrolled under their banner. It
would have done Ireland enormous good if he had become
a Nationalist M.P. Perhaps his sarcasm was too delicate
for the House.

It was the same on the religious question. He had brought wild criticism on himself by criticising the uneconomical excess of church-building in Ireland. He was divided in his spiritual beliefs, but he told me that only the doctrine of eternal damnation prevented him from becoming a Catholic. He had not heard Cardinal Manning's definition of hell as a place of eternal torment eternally untenanted. He bore his invalid life with austere courage. I could never believe he ranched with the roughest and shared in the life of the mining camps. He told yarns of the wild days in the West that have passed : of dancing halls which the miners rushed, carrying away the girls in the manner of the rape of the Sabine women. It was the memory of pioneer days which gave him his streak of courage. He was the first man to drive a motor-car in Ireland, and in his last years in England, he learnt to fly. I never knew him braver than facing an operation in a lone Chicago hospital. I hung about the place all day in order that an Irishman might be near him, should he die. But he survived to see Ireland through her last pack of troubles. The time came when he left the ruins of his burning home to retire to England where he died still full of plans but hardly of hope.

Another grand figure in Irish life was Francis Joseph Biggar of Ardrigh, who under the trammels of a Belfast solicitor kept the soul of one of the United Irishmen of 1798. Learned and sentimental, he kept open house for all who were stirring the Irish broth. In theory he remained a Presbyterian, but in practice he was all Franciscan. He sought and preserved the relics of the dead patriots with the loving tenderness of an " Old Mortality " himself.

For me it was good fortune to steer into his orbit. He had the glowing faith in everything and everybody Irish which Horace Plunkett reserved for his own schemes and supporters. Biggar resembled Plunkett in his lack of bitterness, then a scarce virtue in Ireland. His extreme views did not prevent him being a favourite with every creed and class. He was a great antiquarian. He passed through Ulster saving the fragments of the High Crosses. He imbued the Orangemen with a respect if not an enthusiasm for Irish antiquities. He restored the old castle at Ardglass. He kept pipers and launched poets. In his dreams he was " the O'Neill " returned from a past remote from the politics which clashed around him.

The sad and goaded figure of Roger Casement was in and out of Ardrigh in those days. By day he would sit talking rebellion to Bridget, Biggar's dear old cook, and the night-time he would disappear, walking Belfast or the Antrim hills. His work for natives had unhinged his mind. He had wrestled against corruption.

I accompanied Biggar to the Celtic Congress which was held in Brussels during the Exhibition of 1911. Ireland was immersed in the Home Rule struggle, and there was little interest in the Celtic movement. Every brain in Ireland was set for or against the passing of a measure for which no one would care the feathers on a wren's rump to-day. But Biggar was determined to show the Irish flag abroad. With the Red Hand of Ulster floating from a flagstaff, kilted pipers and a procession of friends and schoolboys, we passed through the Belgian streets. The procession included the great archæologist, Count Plunkett, and the widow of the historian Green who exhibited some obsolete instruments of Irish music from a horse-drawn cab. The Belgians were entirely mystified by the gesture.

Later in the week two teams of hurley players arrived from the south of Ireland. They had received no nourishment on the way and played a correspondingly fierce game on their arrival. The ground selected for their exhibition of the national game was Cardinal Mercier's garden at Malines.

Thanks to a letter from Wilfrid Ward, I was able to meet the great and patriotic Cardinal in days before his name had reached world-wide fame. He was good enough to ask me to lunch alone and we discussed Anglo-

2 B

Catholicism and Modernism, Lord Halifax and Father Tyrrell to our hearts' content. He was passionately interested in both. There were many points concerning the oddities of English religion on which I could give him information. It was delightful to meet a Roman Cardinal who took the Church of England seriously and hoped for reunion with the Pope on possible terms. I always remember asking him why he was so hard on Father Tyrrell, who had been one of our heroes in Cambridge days. The conflict between them had arisen out of the very closeness of their approach. I learnt that when Father Tyrrell was cast from the Jesuits there were only two archbishops in the world who offered to be responsible for him : the Archbishop of Belgium and the Archbishop of San Francisco. But there was no place for the seething originality of Father Tyrrell in the Church of Pius X.

Tyrrell was Irish enough not only by name but by temperament. He had a malicious love of irritating his superiors or flicking grave Cardinals with his very accurate peashooter. Unclaimed by the Church of his origin or his adoption Father Tyrrell belongs to the legion of Irish free-lances who have played their parts in every country but their own.

There was no religious writer whom we read with more enthusiasm at Cambridge as Anglicans and High Churchmen. He had the same charm that Cardinal Newman's writings exerted on our fathers. It is incredible that Tyrrell's are forgotten to-day. The beauty of his English, the mystery of his thought and his amazing power of pouring the old wine into new bottles were certainly as great as Newman's. But he utterly lacked Newman's sweetness and pathos. He was without the genius or personality which made Newman an evening star, albeit a misty one, for his generation. Tyrrell posed for a time as a morning star in the theological skies, but he fell like a bolt which has missed fire. Tyrrell seemed to possess the same battery of gifts and talents, but they broke off short. Something was lacking, theologians would say charity, without which all can be but a tinkling cymbal. To-day we should say he lacked personality, the curious mixture between the charm and uniqueness of the starlike soul that certain individuals share with none other. In spite of an angel's pen, which he could dip in blood or tears, Father Tyrrell was arid and bitter, almost crude and cruel, and he thrust himself into darkness. When he was excommunicated, he received an address of sympathy from the young men at Cambridge, whose souls he had touched with fire. I think the present Dean of Winchester and the Master of Corpus were among them. As to his writings I shall feel to the end of my days what Cardinal Mercier confessed to me his own feelings had been. He gave us to think of Newman . . . Abélard . . . Lamennais !

I know no sadder finish for an Irishman than John Redmond's. Tyrrell had wrought and dreed his own weird. But Redmond was the victim of strong circumstances that came about him like waves of the sea and sank him under a tide he could not master.

During those days before the War Redmond was sanguine but spineless. He did not know how to deal with the outbreak of Ulster Volunteers under Carson or later with the rise of Volunteers in his own camp. He stood as a Constitutionalist between two armed forces.

The whole Irish Question had resolved itself into its last stage when a phantom boundary was being judged and readjusted and shifted between certain Irish counties : Tyrone and Fermanagh, Cavan and Monaghan. If Ulster had been Unionist and Protestant throughout, there would have been no difficulty. Partition of the whole province would have been simple.

The difficulty was that some counties were closely divided politically and the question was where exactly to lay the line of partition. It was as delicate a measure as trying to blow soap bubbles in the midst of a Rugby scrum. Both leaders realised that partition was inevitable : partition of Ireland and partition of Ulster. In 1913 Redmond, out of pure tactics, offered to accept partition of Ulster, but Ulster was confident that she could hold herself together as a whole. In the following year both leaders became hard pressed, and the King's growing anxiety forced a conference in Buckingham Palace. Carson then offered a clean cut of all Ulster. Redmond's refusal was the turn in history. No doubt both were playing tactics, each always offering what he felt the other was bound by his own promises to refuse. Nevertheless had Redmond accepted the clean cut of Ulster as a whole, time has shown that she would have voted herself into the Free State. As Tim Healy once said : " Irish weapons have two edges and no handle."

About this time Sir Horace was running round with a scheme for keeping Ulster under Home Rule for ten years with the right to vote herself out at the end. As he said : " Temporary inclusion is better than total exclusion." When he suggested it to Asquith, the Prime Minister had to confess that he had already offered Carson better.

The secrecy of those days was incredible. Both sides had hidden arms and secret codes. Nobody trusted the mails or his neighbour. The extraordinary thing was that both sides kept each other's secrets from the English Government, which became more and more bewildered. I remember a deputation of Protestant Home Rulers who came over to see Asquith in disguise. They set up their particular views in type with their own hands, not trusting Catholic or Protestant workmen. All copies were eventually burnt except two which were left in Downing Street. Carson, having organised his own army, provided his followers with their own post and ciphers.

Both sides indulged in gun-runnings which have become historical. After the Nationalists had purchased arms in Belgium there was some difficulty in transporting them to Ireland. They were brought to Howth in a private yacht steered by an English officer, Gordon Shephard, who afterwards perished in France at the top of the air-service. In Eton days we had messed together, shared excitements and fagging. I had lost sight of him, but he had become a pioneer of Army flying and an intrepid yachtsman. He had sailed his small ship all the way to Kronstad and on the way home taken sketches and photographs of German fortifications, which had caused equal embarrassment to the Foreign Office and satisfaction to the Admiralty.

We called him the "Sheep" on account of the curiously ovine expression he could assume at times. This was particularly useful when the Germans arrested him as a spy! When the War broke out, he was offered the choice of one of the few flying machines in commission or of a torpedo-boat in the North Sea. His brief entry into Irish waters remains historical, for it enabled the Irish Volunteers to arm in response to Ulster and provided Dublin with the wherewithal for the rising two years later.

Meantime the poets were busy. Kipling leaped into the fray with a wild ballad for Ulster. Tom Kettle replied with some stirring lines as though "a bucketful of Boyne would put our glorious sunburst out." Kipling ought to have known the Irish better. Many years ago he scribbled to an aunt of mine : "It is very pleasant to hear you like Kim. Of course he was Irish. He had to be. The Irish (southern) are the Orientals of the West."

In the midst of the arming and counter-arming the Home Rule Bill was passed in the Commons. It was a Derby day and the winner carried green colours, which seemed an omen, but the same week befell a sign more sinister : the *Empress of Ireland* sank in the Gulf of St Lawrence. For me it was an omen that Ireland's domestic empery would sink no less.

Edward Carson was the great and deciding figure of those days in Ireland : the idol of Ulster and the inspiration of Sinn Fein. I should feel honoured that he should have stopped on his campaign in 1909 to deliver a speech against my electoral prospects. Some months before his death I ventured to ask him some questions of historic interest. What was his final offer to Redmond at Buckingham Palace in 1914 ? He told me he had offered the clean cut—Ulster to remain a unity intact, but Redmond in his blindness had declined the offer.

Redmond could not afford nor dare to face his northern supporters if he left them on the other side of the hedge ; but had he accepted ? Home Rule would have been in force over the three provinces at the outbreak of war with very different prospects for the luckless Redmond. And Ulster ? She would have voted herself easily into unity with the rest of Ireland. The simple key (though it turned both ways) was and is that Ulster has a Nationalist majority taken as a whole, but the six counties (the present northern citadel) can hold themselves together by a fairly safe Unionist majority. Once again the fate of Ireland turned on a move as subtle as a move at blindfold chess.

Redmond could not dare nor bear to throw over his friends in Ulster as a whole nor relinquish them to their political enemy. That this was the true tactics was shown ten years later when the Belfast Junta cleverly saved themselves from the Treaty by throwing over the poor Unionists who had trusted them in Cavan, Donegal and Monaghan.

A quarter of a century of Irish History has passed and to have stood on the same platforms as John Redmond, Tom Kettle and Joe Devlin is already a historical memory.

A curious link with the past befell me at the Derry Election of 1910. A very old man voted for me who had voted in an election in the days of O'Connell. Later I met old Dr Emmet in New York aged over ninety. He was a great nephew of Robert Emmet. When I suggested that the photographs of his grandchildren little resembled the pictures of Robert Emmet he replied that Dr Madden, the historian of the United Irishmen, had told him that the pictures of Emmet did not resemble the hero. It was interesting that this old man had spoken to Dr Madden who had known many of the United Irishmen personally.

An entire generation of Unionists and Nationalists has passed away. All that they had fought for or against was obliterated after the rising of 1916. They died bewildered and saddened on both sides of the fence.

It was remarkable how many died of that romantic but Irish complaint : the broken heart, and how many crept away in the coming years and died out of the land to which they had given their enthusiasm.

John Redmond died in London shattered by his own shattered hopes. John Dillon was too proud to utter lament and sank in silence. Standish O'Grady went away to the Isle of Wight and died forgotten save by the writers he had touched with his wand. How many Irish mountains shine in a heroical light thanks to his writings.

There was a great dispersion of the literary men. Some were shot and some became " wild geese." George Russell (A. E.) was the last to leave, but he died outside Ireland. He was a master of Theosophy and went his way seeking rebirth amongst another people. Perhaps he was one of the great Initiates, and certainly he will be one of the few Irishmen to be remembered in a hundred of years.

The graves of the illustrious Irish of the time are scattered. Of them Denis Macarthy could have written when he wrote lamenting the foreign graves of Moore and Goldsmith, lines not well enough known :

> " There's a grave that rises on thy sward, Devizes,
> Where Moore lies sleeping from his land afar :
> And a white stone flashes o'er Goldsmith's ashes
> In the quiet cloisters of Temple Bar."

Ireland had no Valhalla, no Westminster Abbey.

It was pathetic to see how the old generation took their politics on both sides. Old Lord Londonderry, whose whole life had been an impassioned though illogical protest against Home Rule, died, according to those who knew him best, of a broken heart. When Home Rule was placed on the Statute Book, he simply said no more.

And I think Edward Carson was noble enough to die with his heart broken as well. He made the best bargain he could over the Treaty, but he was not strong enough to hold out against his own people for the clean cut of Ulster. He allowed the grandees and shop-keepers of Belfast to throw out the three counties of Cavan and Monaghan and Donegal. But he was too great a gentleman and fighter not to have felt the abandonment of his friends too bitterly for words. His last visit to Belfast was for the astonishing purpose of unveiling his own memorial statue which he had thoroughly deserved. There was no statue for Redmond or Casement or Horace Plunkett.

Patrick Pearse, the first President of the Irish Republic, has been commemorated by a fine bronze in the Dail. His part was unexpected, but decisive in Irish history. He carried out the eight days' rebellion which signified to the Irish race that the Parliamentary movement no longer even promised Irish freedom.

I used to see him at his School, which gave a joyous hope to Gaelic Ireland and a new departure to Irish education. Here he was in his element, talking with bilingual vivacity or nourishing silent hopes of a rebellion. Full of dream and courage he cut the Gordian knot over which Gladstone had failed and Redmond fumbled.

The Volunteer movement absorbed Pearse and his devoted friends. When they volunteered they were ready to rise and when they were captured they were ready to die. From that moment Ireland was assured of her place as a nation.

Ghosts

*

G HOSTS HAVE PLAYED THAT SECONDARY BUT COM-
forting part in my life that the detective of fiction plays in
busier lives of the day.

The ghost story has always fascinated me in the manner
that it fascinated Augustus Hare, Father Hugh Benson
and the late Lord Halifax.

As ghosts we shall make our final escape from this
existence. Meantime the ghost story offers one of those
escapes which neutralise the tedium or sometimes the
worry of life.

I have always had a sound respect if not an entire
belief in ghosts. Stories about ghosts seemed an exciting
variant to the fairy story. They make a contradiction
to the materialism of our times. There remains a great
deal in life which cannot be explained. And this adds a
relief and even a relaxation to life.

It is remarkable how all belief in ghosts is being lost
amongst peasants and country folk. On the other hand
the belief has increased amongst upper classes. It is
possible that in another generation ghosts will only
appeal to a limited and educated number.

For those who are interested in ghosts there are three
methods of approach or contact.

Firstly : to seek them in the quarters they are reputed
to haunt.

Secondly : to raise them in " the Cave of Endor," by
means of mediums and prophetic persons.

Thirdly : to allow them to pass into one's own experience without research or invocation.

It is very rarely, perhaps once or twice in a lifetime,

that one partakes in a ghostly experience. If it is but once in a lifetime one should be content. Any inexplicable happening should be recorded as scientifically as an experiment in Science itself. The time will come when Science will put together the data of all supernatural happenings and deduce an unsuspected law of Nature therefrom. As Provost James used to say : " There appears to be a good deal behind it all, but we don't know how."

In Ireland ghosts walked in the background rather more than less. They were to be expected. But it was always strange when the supernatural made itself felt in England. England is not particularly a Celtic country nor inhabited by superstitious people. It is mainly inhabited by realists, practical dealers, materialists tempered by ideals of tradition or decency or honour rather than by any belief in the invisible and intangible.

In my experience of English life there have always been ghosts round the corner.

When we came to live at 10 Great Cumberland Place, we found ourselves two doors from a famous ghost. At least ten different tenants attempted to live there in our time. The story was that a butler had once committed suicide there and was wont to forget himself at times and to answer the bell ! This was sufficiently alarming.

Countess Hoyos told us that while she occupied the house she had a terrifying experience. While she was writing one day, she noticed that someone (her own butler she supposed) had entered the room to tidy-up. She summoned him to her desk and handed him some letters which to her amazement fell to the floor and the apparition (for apparition it was) disappeared. She rang the bell and the footman answered the bell. She asked where the butler had gone after leaving the room and learnt that he had been out the entire afternoon. It was someone else in the room. But who ?

On another occasion in the same house a lady noticed

that someone had entered where she was writing and was standing by the fire. Without looking up she ordered him to return in ten minutes to post her letters. The figure disappeared. Soon afterwards the butler entered and she said she had told him to wait for ten minutes before he returned. He protested that he had not been in her room that afternoon.

Another occupant of the house was once expecting her brother (I think they were Delaskis) and a room had been prepared for him. When she went down to dinner, she noticed that the room was occupied. It was lit up and there was a figure crouching before the fire. She waited below for her brother, as she supposed, to descend. When she sent to hurry his descent, she was told that he had not yet arrived at the house.

With a series of similar rumours at our door, it was impossible not to believe in the uncanny. The reputed ghosts in Mayfair would outnumber the ghosts in any equal area of the Celtic borderlands. I can think of veridic ghost stories from Connaught Place, Upper Brook Street, Berkeley Square and Ebury Street. The old houses with their associations with the ghostly and the historical in their dossier are being swept away. People pass into flats which have not been stained or coloured by the invisible ink of the past. In a few more generations there will be a percentage of haunted flats. No doubt, all the old ghosts and historical hauntings will have perished under the devastations of " Sir Robert MacAlpine Limited." People living never think that they may possibly be included in the supply of new ghosts.

At Cambridge I became deeply interested in the investigation of ghosts. Cambridge was the home of Psychical Research. The names of Myers, Sidgwick and Gurney were still bruited amongst those who had known them. At King's we sat in solemn séance with note-books or we made excursions to haunted homes.

Until the Provost pointed it out to us, we entirely overlooked that there was a haunted set of rooms under our own nose in Gibbs' Building which might have offered a preliminary field of investigation. A man called Brocklebank had died there in great trouble thirty years before. Though he made no appearance, he was earthbound to a certain extent and his voice was sometimes heard in a scream over the washstand. It had been heard by Mr Luxmoore, the Eton master, who was in tune with the supernatural world. And at night the sounds of dropping water could be clearly distinguished.

The most famous ghost at Cambridge was known as the " Corpus Ghost." It was believed that Dr Henry Butts, Vice-Chancellor of the University, had hanged himself in his garters at Corpus Christi College after preaching the University sermon one Sunday afternoon. This was as far back as the eighteenth century. The rooms had not been inhabited for years, but in Victorian days Mr Moule, a tutor of the college, had been allowed to occupy them. Tradition said that he had found himself compelled to crawl out of the rooms on his hands and knees in daylight. He would never tell his story, but he insisted that the rooms must be closed to human habitation. In my first year they were allocated to an unfortunate Freshman, whose nervous state became such that his friends appealed to the members of the Psychical Research at King's for advice and assistance. A few of us visited Corpus and solemnly read the Exorcism Service with disturbing results, of which an inaccurate and rather lurid account appeared in the *Occult Review* (January 1905).

There were many accounts bandied about the University during an excited ten days, but no version was set down by those who were present. The late Cyril Foley published an account in the *Sunday Express* (December 5, 1926), which was referred to me as a surviving witness. I could only say that though much had passed from my memory of the details, the impression given to me appeared correct.

Here it is and let it remain the *locus classicus* of the Corpus Ghost :

" There was at that time a Cambridge Psychical Research Society, and it happened on this particular evening of October 1904 that three members of that society were gathered together in the room of a Kingsman.

" I shall refer to him in the story as the Kingsman, but I am permitted to say that he was a young man of temperate habits, a very distinguished King's scholar, and about to take up Holy Orders.

" The other two were Mr. Shane Leslie and Mr. Wade, also an Ordinand.

" They had been discussing, among other things, these very rooms when, at about ten minutes to ten an excited undergraduate from Corpus burst in upon them and implored them to go to the assistance of the occupier of the rooms, who was, he said, in great distress.

" He told them that the poor man was reduced to such a state of nerves that he could do no work. A face had been seen at his window from the Old Court, after the door had been ' sported ' and the room left empty.

" Footsteps were heard in one room while the occupant slept in the other. It was a case requiring definite action. Something more than an appeal to the tutor or a consultation with the college porter.

" The Kingsman leapt to his feet.

" ' This is an Evil Spirit which must be exorcised,' he said, ' and I am going to take it by the throat. Will you two stand by me ? '

" They agreed to do so. He then opened a cupboard, disclosing a temporary altar, from the tabernacle of which he drew a phial of holy water, and the four then set off for Corpus.

" As they passed through the Great Court of King's the college clock struck ten, and it was only by doing ' level time ' that they got down the King's Parade and through the Gate of Corpus on the last stroke of the hour.

" Their guide directed them to the ill-omened and

ivy-clad rooms in a corner of the Old Court, where they were met by the pale occupant, who told them that it was impossible to stay in the rooms under prevailing conditions.

" The Kingsman said, ' In these cases we can only use exorcism, which Christ bequeathed to His Holy Church.'

" They entered the room, and the Corpus man, a young ordinand of singular piety, produced a large Crucifix from the folds of his gown.

" This the Kingsman took, and without preamble raised it above his head, and began to chant the terrible words of the Exorcism Service in which the fiend is personally addressed and defied.

" The Corpus man had shut the door, and there was no light in the room except that given by a tiny twinkling fire.

" At the termination of the Exorcism the three men remained silent.

"Nothing occurred, and Leslie was about to speak when the Kingsman suddenly cried, ' The Thing is here! '

" With nerves on edge they peered into the gloom.

" ' The Thing is watching me,' he said. ' Push me slowly forward, hold up my arms, but do not get in front of the Crucifix as you value your lives.'

" His companions upheld his elbows, as Aaron and Hur once supported the aching Moses.

" Leslie, who had hold of one of his arms, felt it suddenly stiffen, and at the same moment the Kingsman cried out, ' The Thing is pulling me, hold me tight or I shall lose the Crucifix.'

" Like some powerful magnet, the Evil Thing was actually drawing him out of the grasp of his companion. It was a veritable ' pull devil pull baker ' situation.

" It was also a terrifying one. The atmosphere of the room had become surcharged with an intangible yet all absorbing Evil, which sapped the strength and numbed the senses. It had become a definite tussle, a combination of a tug-of-war and a Rugby scrum.

" All the human competitors were bathed in a cold perspiration of fear and effort. The affair became intolerable. Fortunately the Kingsman kept his head.

" There was only one thing to be done. ' Push me right into the Foul Fiend,' he said, and crying out ' Limb of Satan avaunt in the name of the All Holy,' the whole party crashed into the ancient panelling of the room.

" In a state more easily imagined than described, they picked themselves up, gathered round the fire, and poked it into being.

" ' The Thing is gone,' said the Kingsman.

" None of the other three dared speak.

" He then took the flask of holy water from his pocket and began to sprinkle the room. Some drops fell in the fireplace with a Demoniacal hiss, and the Kingsman, swinging round, pointed to the open doorway of the bedroom, and said : ' The Thing is in there.'

" Without hesitation or assistance, and minus the crucifix, he sprang through the doorway of the bedroom. It was a courageous but unsuccessful manœuvre, for with the speed of thought he was hurled back through the doorway, and fell in a heap at their feet.

" The situation was as follows : The Kingsman was crawling about on the floor, searching for the half empty flask of holy water which he had dropped in his fall. Wade was in a corner of the room holding the crucifix over the cowering Corpus man, while Leslie, on his knees near the fire, devoid of initiative, and having, as he admits, given up all hope, was praying pitifully.

" They were a beaten side—beaten by an innings and a hundred runs—by ten goals to nothing—devoid of cohesion and volition, prisoners of war, captured by Satan, vanquished and manacled by the powers of evil, and doomed to death.

" They could only stare vacantly into the blackness of the bedroom, out of which the evil Thing was slowly advancing. Their tongues clove to the roof of their mouths. They could not cry for help.

" And then, framed in the square-cut darkness of the doorway, the Thing appeared.

" It bore a human shape, and was menacing, but beyond that, no one could afterwards visualise its exact aspect. But upon one point they were all agreed. It was cut off at the knees !

" Crash ! Crash ! Crash !—something was happening outside their mentality. Crash ! again, and the door was burst open and floods of light and excited undergraduates poured into the room. Their listening impatience had mastered their fear of the occult.

" The situation was temporarily saved. It is easy to imagine the remarks of the uninstructed rescue party. ' Where is the ghost ? Does it bite ? ' etc. etc., but it was significant how quickly their attitude changed from gay to grave, a change not altogether due to the obvious distress of the principal actors, but rather to the inexplicable and uncanny atmosphere of the room itself.

" ' The thing has ascended into the room above, and we must follow it,' said the plucky Kingsman.

" The three-principals, leading a mass of supporters, started up a tiny flight of stairs, and entered the room of a medical student who was reading, unconscious of the terrors of the room below.

" Now it so happened that he was a pronounced atheist and had been ragged in consequence some little time before. He naturally thought that this invasion was a repetition, and being of a stubborn disposition, got off his anti-spiritual views first.

" ' This is just the room where the Thing is sure to have gone,' said the Kingsman, and the undergraduates, crowding the doorway, grinned approval, while the occupant of the room proclaimed the nullity of the spirit world.

" The Kingsman advanced with uplifted crucifix towards the corner of the room, and the medical student darted daringly in front of him.

" The Kingsman warned him not to do so, but he

persisted, and to the horror of every one fell in a heap on the floor, murmuring, ' I am cold, I am cold, I am icy cold.'

" For the first time the unconvinced spectators were awed, for here was proof indeed—the scoffer, turned into a humble and dejected heap of clothes, huddled up in a corner and complaining that he was ' icy cold.'

" The Kingsman, protecting him with the crucifix, soothed him back to sanity. Every spectator was struck dumb with fear and amazement. Nothing further of psychical interest occurred beyond the rather natural collapse of all three, who were conducted back to their rooms. The only wonder was that the Kingsman had borne the strain so long and so courageously.

" By this time the undergraduates were thoroughly roused, and, pouring down the stairs, rushed into the haunted rooms below, and completely demolished them.

" Led by some brawny oarsmen, they broke up all the cupboards and tore down the ancient oak pannelling.

" There was the devil of a row the next morning. The Corpus authorities forbade any Kingsmen to enter their college—an order which, had I been a Kingsman, I should most certainly have obeyed—and did their best to hush up the whole affair, in which latter objective they were joined by the University authorities.

" The principals agreed among themselves never to divulge what they had seen and experienced while they remained undergraduates, and the whole affair died a natural death.

" The rooms, or what remained of them, were closed. But, all said and done, though it goes much against the grain, as an old Cantab, to do it, I personally give the devil that fight, on points."

After thirty-five years it is interesting to test the debris which Time leaves in the memory with what must now pass as history. Several of the lurid details have entirely escaped my mind. On the other hand several

2 C

others remain as vividly as on the night of the exorcism. I remember the curious sensation of feeling my hair rise with a prickling sensation from my scalp. This is a sensation I have only felt actually once since. I remember for about ten days having the unpleasant sensation that something was following me. Only with plenty of hard rowing and hours of hard reading did every effect of the " Corpus Ghost " quit my impressionable, slightly credulous, but actively observant mind.

Another Cambridge ghost story I owe to Lord Haldane. It is worth remembering because the evidence proceeds from two legal minds.

As a young man Haldane attended a house-party in the country. Much fun was being made by the guests of Spiritualism. But one of the guests, the late Lord Justice Rigby, looked grave and remained so silent that Lord Haldane said to him afterwards : " From your face I think you have had some experience which kept you silent."

Rigby answered that when he was an undergraduate at Cambridge, he woke early once on a summer's morning and noticed a shadow across his bed. He looked again and saw between himself and the rays of the sun the head and shoulders of an old man in an ancient dress. His face was benign and his hands were in the act of blessing.

Within a few days of this manifestation Leonard Courtney, who was also at Cambridge at the time, awoke to see a man of malignant appearance in mediæval dress gazing at him from the foot of the bed.

Haldane afterwards asked Courtney what he remembered about the manifestations. Courtney confirmed all that Rigby had said. He added that neither he nor Rigby had ever been able to make up their minds what it meant.

The evidence for ghosts seems to be clear and abundant even in spite of many instances which it is not difficult to disprove. The " Corpus Ghost " reads like a phantasmagoria exerted on the minds of over-religious undergraduates, but there is no gainsaying the testified memories of such clear minds as Rigby and Courtney when recorded by so legal a brain as the late Lord Haldane's.

Charlie Beresford never hesitated to tell his ghost story. He had been serving on H.M.S. *Raccoon* in the Mediterranean when his father died in Kensington. He went on deck and saw his father lying in his coffin (May 4, 1864).

Looking round the circle of marriage connections I could point to a number of connections with the uncanny. Two of my uncles occupied famous haunted houses in the country : Levens Hall in Westmorland and Brede Place in Sussex. Haunted houses are like volcanoes. They are extinct, dormant, or periodically active. Brede was dormant but Levens was undeniably active.

Levens had had a tragic history. Owing to a familiar type of curse it had never passed from father to son, but always zig-zagged up and down the family line. Two families including the Bellinghams had been swept out. It had reached the late Sir Josceline Bagot who married Dosia Leslie. He omitted to mention the story of the curse and took her to Levens for her honeymoon. The first afternoon she spent at Levens she saw an old woman pass through the yew hedges and then disappear. She followed fruitlessly and reported what had happened to her husband who told her the story. A woman had died on the bridge with her child after being refused access to the Hall. She had cursed the place saying that no heir would succeed until the River Kent, which flowed through the park, had ceased to flow, and a white deer had been dropped in the park.

My aunt had three delightful girls but no son.

During the hard winter of 1894–5 the Kent was frozen and the agent telegraphed to her in London : " Kent frozen solid : now is your chance." In the next week she had a boy who at least came of age and inherited before his early death. He was succeeded by his uncle, Dick Bagot the novelist, who succumbed within the year. There were no more of the name to inherit.

My own experiences of sleeping at Levens were per-fectly peaceful, but my mother, riding over the bridge on an early bicycle, saw an old woman in her road and repeatedly rang her bell in vain. In the end she toppled through the figure which she described as a sensation like an icy wind.

Another uncle of mine took Levens for a winter and brought his old housekeeper with him. She, poor soul, was so frightened by meeting a figure on the stair that she died on the spot.

I always kept track with happenings at Levens, although there were some occurring before Josceline Bagot's tenancy which were too painful for words. They were told me in confidence by a neighbour. After the death of the last male heir of the Bagot name the place was let for many years to an eminent industrial family who were Catholic and could bring the spiritual resources of the Church to bear upon the building. The spectral woman had last been seen by a clergyman at Desmond Bagot's funeral crossing the road in front of the procession. This might well have been the last appearance, but some years later a young lady at the Hall saw a woman moving over the flooded park. Suddenly she realised that there was no splash or ripple following the figure ! Levens is not now inhabited, but the beautiful furniture remains and the whole Hall can be visited as a show by tourists passing on the northern road near Kendal.

The other haunted house which I have known so well that I feel likely to haunt it myself one day, is Brede Place near Hastings, in Sussex. Brede is a Manor perhaps as well preserved as any in the country. Until recently there had been no serious repairs since the reign of Queen Elizabeth. It possessed a mews for hawks and a chapel with a galleried screen and beautiful carved stone window. There were many staircases and a roof full of snoring owls. It possessed a name in popular folk-lore : " The Giant's House," and this sinister memory made it avoided after nightfall. Certainly no gipsy or poacher or trespasser came near after dark, nor was it possible to get anything delivered from the village.

It had been for two centuries on the Frewen estate : Sometimes used by gamekeepers and sometimes let to the adventurous. Stephen Crane, the American novelist, lived his last months as an author here. My aunt Clara bought it from her brother-in-law for a thousand pounds. The roof was patched up and the underground passages bricked and boarded. In the winter it was an ice-chest, but in summer it was delightfully cool. Behind the solid stone walls it was a rambling, creaking, ghost-shotten house. In any night of moon it looked gaunt and eerie and like nothing on earth.

We used to come to Brede for school leave. As children we were kept wildly busy all day and mildly frightened all night. A journey into a remote part of Sussex forty years ago was quite an expedition. We took a slow train to Rye on a railway then called " The London, Chatham and Dover." From Rye we drove behind an old horse attached to a buggy the seven miles of road to Brede. The drive was generally preceded by tea with Henry James at Lamb House. James was then the only " foreigner " in the little native sanctuary of Rye. It has since become the stamping ground of the tourist and the tripper. But in old days the grass grew between the cobbles in the street.

We found Henry James very voluble. He was deploring that people no longer read his books. To us children it seemed wonderful that they ever had. He had found himself a divine corner in the county which has been more rudely invaded than any other county. He sat behind a high-walled garden within sight of Winchelsea and the far distant retreating sea. He would walk slowly under the towering aisles of Rye Church to which he was fond of playing amateur sacristan. Then he would deplore the ruined beauty of Rye and point out the stones of the old Land Gate which an economical age had used to build a warehouse. And there were other outrages against

antiquity, such as Tudor houses torn down to make a
bank.   Any interference with the tradition or beauty of
Old England was purgatory to his fine Bostonian soul.
He accepted all English life except the ancient game of
cricket ; and there is a memory of Henry James attending
a match at Rye seated with his back to the players and
pouring forth a succession of delicately poised sentences
to an admiring group of ladies.

Life is a bridge, says the Chinese proverb, and there
is no time to build houses thereon.   But there are certain houses which one passes through during a lifetime.
Unconsciously they become landmarks of the soul.
Reminiscence and refreshment will always return between
their walls.   Hence the sentiment which the French express
by the song " *la vieille maison grise.*"   Men return to
their old homes of childhood or to their old schools in
hope of finding their own ghosts.

There are certain houses which become frequented by
the spirits or emanations or perhaps only the memories
made visible of those who have passed that way.   Under
some kind of astral chemistry the atmosphere of such
houses becomes open to their appearance.   Old roofs, old
corners, old roads often become a trysting-place for
what the Irish call " souls in need of settlement."   Some
places become almost manufactories of ghosts.   One
ghost seems to attract another.   Under certain circumstances that we certainly do not understand they become
developed like the old family photographs which come to
light after they have lain in a drawer for years.

Apart from what the middle ages have bequeathed to
Brede there was a strange instance of a modern spirit
becoming attached to the building.   Some twenty-five
years ago a girl staying in the house was seized with
one of those griefs which are too great for youth to bear.
She attached a shoe-lace to Uncle Moreton's old shooting
gun and scattered her brains all of a lovely summer's day.
The room in which the tragedy took place was never

used again until Hugh brought a native servant home from Nigeria. The black boy was given this room to sleep in. In the middle of the night the unfortunate native crawled out of the room and found his way to the bedside of his master whom he informed with fear and trembling that he had seen a girl in white standing over him. With difficulty he was quieted and the room was once more closed.

And I like to believe that my aunt Clara Frewen had made an appearance since her death in 1935 within the walls she loved so deeply.

For years all her love and happiness were concentrated within the stone walls of Brede. Hers was a tragic life. She needed so little to make her happy. Small things gave her unending pleasure, but financial nightmares weighed her down as long as I can remember her.

Brilliantly gifted, restlessly adventurous and continually prophetic before his day, her husband bore the nickname of " Mortal Ruin." I think it was the wittiest twist that I ever heard given to a man's name. Moreton Frewen's schemes never ceased to ruin his friends; and Clara's quarterly income was only a drop in the bucket with which he set out again and again towards the Well of Riches only to feel the Silver Cord break under him every time. Her children found her once crawling in the dark praying with all her soul that one, only one of Moreton's schemes, would come right. They bade her desist, for God does not hear prayers on behalf of speculators.

She showed infinite pluck and when the bailiffs entered her London House, she gave each of them five shillings to pretend they were footmen and open the door. The servants were never paid wages. It seemed rather a happy solution of the domestic problem which is such a trouble to modern housewives. Servants, who loved my aunt, remained in her employment as friends. Those who only served for lucre simply took up their bags and departed. The butler stayed for years. Only in moments

of desperation did he offer some article of value to the
pawnbroker. Once Clara was passing through Hastings,
when she caught sight of a lovely set of Worcester china,
which she thought would exactly fit with hers at home.
Her surmise was correct for they were her own set which
she bought unwittingly and brought back to Brede.

It seemed sad to see her dying in a little Home at St
Leonard's. Yet she had had her day. She had been one
of the prettiest girls in Paris at the close of the Empire.
She had danced her first quadrille with Marshal Bazaine,
who surrendered Metz to the Germans a few months later.
She had danced with the Prince Imperial and been invited
to stay at Compiègne with the Empress. She used to
dance with the Prince in the evenings until his mentor
arrived and with a low bow informed His Imperial High-
ness it was bedtime.

She could have married into a leading Protestant
family in France which had applied for her hand. But
fate drew her to Moreton Frewen, a honeymoon in the
Rockies and a life divided between the social diversions
of Victorian London and financial rack and ruin. It was
no wonder that she turned to Brede for a little peace and
repose. And no wonder that she was seen to come
smilingly forward . . . some months after her death.

Uncle Moreton had no time for ghosts between his
unceasing schemes and ventures. He used to sit in the
old chapel day after day typing like mad. All over the
world floated his wonderful correspondence and his letters
could be as thrilling as his yarns.

He had the true version of Lord Poulett's dream about
his famous Grand National horse the Lamb. It was rather
thus: Poulett's horses were ridden by a gentleman rider, Mr
George Ede, who rode as " Mr Edwards " and was due to
ride the Lamb at Aintree for the great event in 1871. The
Lamb was also carrying the family fortunes and Poulett was
in a highly nervous state. He had a dream that he saw the
Lamb win the Grand National all right, but to his surprise
a Mr Pickernell whose racing name was " Mr Thomas "

carried the Poulett colours, cerise and blue. Poulett accepted the warning and asked Mr Ede to stand down, which he did on condition that the true reason was given. Mr Pickernell was given the mount and it was just as well, for Mr Ede was killed in the Sefton Steeplechase on the day before the Grand National was won. Had Mr Pickernell not been already engaged it would have been impossible to pick up a chance jockey the previous night.

Curiously enough Uncle Moreton, who died in 1925, was one of the few of the dead whose apparition I have seen.

There is a type of apparition which is visible to a sleeper in the first moments succeeding sleep. It has nothing to do with the previous dreaming nor has it any particular reason for appearance. It has occurred to me three times and each time so vividly as to be overwhelming. For several hours after each appearance I could not collect myself sufficiently to continue with ordinary life. My senses told me I had seen figures from the other world. This has only occurred to me after waking and while feeling perfectly assured that I was awake.

I awoke at Glaslough two years after Uncle Moreton's death and to my surprise I saw him standing in the room. I was completely in possession of all my senses and could see every object in the room. Uncle Moreton said very deliberately to me : " I don't mind what you have written about me, but Uncle Stee will mind very much."

I had recently written a sketch of his career which I had classed under " Sublime Failures." This message was apparently correct, for Colonel Stephen Frewen, Lord Carson's father-in-law, was much annoyed, as I learnt later.

It was all so vivid that I could not think of anything else for several hours.

On two other occasions the same thing has happened to me. In 1912, a few weeks before my marriage, I was staying at the Cedars on Long Island with a future brother-in-law. I awoke on a bright sunny morning and perceived that a woman in a dark dress was watching me intently. Who she was I never discovered. I rubbed my eyes but she took quite a long time to disappear.

On a third and more recent occasion this happened to me again while lecturing in America. The apparition was of a man whose funeral I had attended two years previously in London. I had known him intimately and shared his thoughts and anxieties. He had had a great career in the War but was always harassed in his mind by the slow and relentless approach of history. At one time I was preparing to write his apologia, but in the end he decided to leave his fame to posterity. His appearance was calm and collected, but on the great subject between us he said nothing. For several hours I was under the spell of what I had seen before I could brush it from my mind and go about my ways.

I cannot explain these appearances unless they were developed out of my psychic memory, but why and how ?

Life is perhaps too short to devote to the study of the conditions following its apparent extinction, whether they are a transfiguration or a continuation.

My old French tutor, Monsieur Counort, used to waive all religious controversy on the simple plea that Protestants and Catholics would have all Eternity in which to argue and that it was better to take life peacefully. Similarly we shall all be ghosts or have the opportunity of being ghosts one day and need not devote overmuch of our passing time and attention to a question which will be assuredly answered and finally settled.

Almost everyone has had a ghost story in the course of life. Most people prefer to secrete or forget any incident not referable to the immediate laws of time and space as we conceive them.

When the B.B.C. arranged a recent series on " Things I cannot explain," I introduced the only effective super-normal or super-natural happening in my life under the title of " Ten Minutes outside Time."

I add the script in the form in which it appeared afterwards in the *Listener* :

" The majority of people have once or twice tasted—what shall I call it ?—the uncanny or the inexplicable or more simply a ghost story. But often they prefer to say nothing about it. I know a distinguished soldier who has told me what I consider the best ghost story of this time but he usually keeps quiet because its recital might make people laugh at him. For the same reason naval officers have preferred not to report the Sea Serpent to the Admiralty.

" The last time that I enjoyed a conversation with the late Dr Montague James, Provost of Eton, we discussed ghosts apart from his own wonderful ghost books. We were discussing how perfectly normal incidents became extraordinary by happening or seeming to happen outside time. The last words Dr James ever said to me I remember always. He assured me of his entire conviction of the world of ghosts, but added : ' Depend upon it but we do not know the rules.'

" Ghostly phenomena or happenings take place outside the working of the rules such as we know them working in time or space. Our idea of time is of an ever flowing and all sweeping stream which moves steadily in one direction. It is difficult to imagine it as a kind of omnipresent flood stretching on all sides at the same time. We prefer to look at a watch and say time flies or progresses. But standing outside time is the only way in which I can describe an experience which I reckon the most vivid of my life. It is a ghost story, but with dates, facts, places and even a few surviving witnesses to my tale. Even so there is no explanation.

" It was in March, 1924, when I was working in London and received word that my wife was not well at Cannes on the Riviera, and that I should come out as soon as I could. It was a week-end when I arrived in Paris. It was Sunday, March 9, that I proposed to take the ' Rapide ' or express train south. I brought no luggage save a bag, and carried my dressing-gown over

my arm. I was in a great hurry and telegraphed to a
friend in Paris, who survives to recall the incident. He
gave me lunch and we spent the afternoon motoring.
The ' Rapide ' was due to start at 8.10 that evening,
and my friend left me at the great station of the Paris,
Lyons and Mediterranean route about an hour before
the train started. He was an American priest and is
now a Canon in Rome.

" I had not engaged a seat and it was too late to take
a sleeper. I represented my case and how necessary it
was for me to travel by that train. Whether I paid
extra or not, I was accommodated with a seat in the
restaurant, and there I laid my humble belongings.
With an hour or so to kill I decided to stretch my legs
by walking up and down the platform so well known to
the thousands who travel south every year to the
Riviera. I began walking up and down past those
endless iron pillars. Half-way down I turned and
retraced my steps. The next ten minutes are un-
accountable in time. At the spot where I turned on
each lap of my walk I became aware that the figure of
a woman was standing and looking in my direction.
I could describe her as an Italian-looking lady wearing
deep mourning. Of one thing I felt certain. She wore
a black hood over her head. Every time that I completed walking the length of the platform she was
waiting for me, and her eyes were turned full upon me
until I became quite expectant of their piercing brilliance.

" How can I describe them ? They were anything
but the glad eye. They were sad and luminous. Their
effect was not so much fascinating as hypnotic. I
think that is the only description I can give of them
after several years, thirteen years actually, since they
had such a curious and decisive effect upon me. After
I had passed her for the third or fourth time my
feelings were not as agreeable as might be the case with
a susceptible traveller ; but decidedly uncomfortable.

" Looking back after the years with my full ordinary

senses, I do not believe now that such a person as I have described was ever standing there visible to the eyes of all who passed, but that I was being subjected to a remarkable hallucination. For reasons I cannot understand and under rules that I do not know, her visual appearance was admitted to my sense of sight and at the same time I became conscious or subconscious that she was telling me in French that I must change my train. The words that formulated in my mind were, *il faut changer de train.* And they were repeated. I was in a mental condition which admitted no argument or reasoning with myself. I was in a mood partly nervous and partly adventurous. I felt no apprehensions. But I felt that something very novel and intensely personal had glided into my life of which an hour before I had not had the least knowledge. I was tired and I had had a certain amount of brain-fag before I left London. Now I had a feeling that I no longer controlled my own initiative, and that it would be a complete and welcome relief to be advised, guided, controlled and even commanded. I turned round and I obeyed. I took my belongings out of the ' Rapide ' and after a short inquiry I took my seat in a slower train which was leaving later for Marseilles from the next platform. I looked round, but I never caught sight of my strange guide again. I walked down the platform but she had utterly disappeared.

" As I say, I do not believe that she was ever visible or audible to anyone who was not at the time in a receptive state of mind or imagination. I suppose I imagined it all but I cannot regret that I did. The slow train was very crowded and I settled myself down with five others in a single compartment and prepared myself for an uncomfortable night sitting up. Horns and whistles blew to announce the departure of the ' Rapide,' and I became aware that the train in which I had first taken a seat was slowly moving out of the station. I leaped out and watched. It was then that I first experienced a feeling, a dreamy but very vivid feeling, that I was fey. That is the only word which the language supplies to describe a state of waking dream which can be so much more vivid than the processes of ordinary humdrum life. I watched in a fascinated way the train as, slowly and noiselessly, it stole away. Then again I had the feeling that time was standing still or at least that I was standing aside from time. It was eight o'clock in the evening and the departing train was brilliantly lit, but it crossed my eyesight more brightly than any train I had ever seen. My vision was like that of a man suffering from short sight who has suddenly been furnished with excellent glasses. He almost feels that he has received a new sense. Life instantly furnishes a brighter blue, a more radiant red, while blurred lines become almost mathematical.

" I watched the train. It might have been for ten seconds, but it might have been for an hour. It was so timeless. Every carriage that passed was imprinted upon my mind and memory, and for days afterwards I could recall every person I glimpsed. Two remain with me to this day : the Chef with his cap who looked almost transfigured in his white array against the night : and a face that peered for a moment on the platform and then disappeared behind a drawn blind. Others were settling down for the night and then, as when a brilliant dream comes to an end, the whole panorama suddenly ceased and I turned back into my dingy train wondering whether I could be such a fool as I thought I was.

" I slept and half-slept all night, and was heartily glad when we reached Marseilles. Thence it was a brief journey to Cannes, which I did not reach till two the next day. I did not feel very enthusiastic when I found myself at my destination. I had not telegraphed the exact hour of my coming, and this was fortunate. In any case there was nobody to meet me and I made my way to the hotel where I was expected.

" Here I was joined by a Canadian friend with a car who offered to take me for a drive. Casually she mentioned that I was lucky not to have been on the ' Rapide ' that night. I felt overwhelmed. ' But I was,' I said. ' Oh, no, that was impossible or you would not be here. The ' Rapide ' met disaster some hours after leaving Paris. There have been a dozen casualties and some well-known people from England are reported to be killed.'

" This gave me a considerable shock and I hurried round to make inquiries. It was no use saying I had been on the train for a while, as no one believed me. During my experience in Paris I had never as much as dreamed of an accident. It had not occurred to my mind that there was any danger. I had obeyed an impulsion that I could not resist, but which did not seem connected with any sinister import. I learnt to my regret that among the casualties had been an old Eton acquaintance, De Falbe. It was some time before I realised that I had only just missed being in a railway accident. My next feeling was one of relief that I had missed such an excitement, but on reflection I realised that I had passed through a much more exciting one on another plane.

" When I returned to Paris I gave an account of what had happened to me to a group of people interested in spiritualism. I was told that the accident had been the cause of several incidents in the spirit world, of which mine was but one. It was explained to me as the attempt of somebody beyond the veil trying to get into touch with some friend in the train who had not been responsive to the message. In my state of mind I must have received it and interpreted it to myself. Be that as it may, the facts remained that I had been taken to catch one train and had arrived on another. To me it remains as inexplicable as the wireless would be to my grandfathers."

Select Index

★

A

B

C

D

E